Vocational

and Career

Education:

Concepts

and Operations

Calfrey C. Calhoun
The University of Georgia

Alton V. Finch
The University of Mississippi

Wadsworth Publishing Company, Inc.
Belmont, California

Education Editor: Roger Peterson
Production Editor: Joanne Cuthbertson
Designer: Dare Porter
Copy Editor: Karen Evarts
Technical Illustrator: John Foster

ISBN 0–534–00437–7

L. C. Cat. Card No. 75–21411

Printed in the United States of America

1 2 3 4 5 6 7 8 9 10—80 79 78 77 76

Body type set in Aster 10/12

Contents

Preface **vii**

Introduction **ix**

Part 1
Conceptual Dimensions of Existing
and Emerging Career-Related Programs 1

Chapter 1
Personal-Societal Needs
and Vocational Education **3**

Introduction **3**   *Vocations and Personal Needs* **7**
Vocations and Societal Needs **12**   *Employment Trends* **20**
Summary **24**   *Activities* **26**   *References* **27**

Chapter 2
Historical Perspective of
Vocational-Technical Education **31**

Introduction **31**   *Legislation Prior to 1900* **33**
Legislation Between 1900 and 1960 **34**   *Legislation Since 1960* **42**
Summary **52**   *Activities* **53**   *References* **56**

Chapter 3
Factors Influencing Varied
Aspects of Vocational-Technical Education **59**

Introduction **59**   *Philosophical Factors* **59**
Economic Factors **69**   *Economics of Vocational Education* **75**
Sociological Factors **76**   *Summary* **81**   *Activities* **82**   *References* **84**

Chapter 4
Relationship of Vocational
Education to Other Educational Emphases **87**

Introduction **87**   *Vocational Education in Relation
to General Education* **87**
Career Development in Relation to General Education **89**
Vocational Education in Relation to Career Development **90**
*Vocational Education in Relation to Vocational
and Technical Education* **91**
Developing Role of Career Education as a Concept **92**
Content and Method of Vocational Education **95**   *Summary* **98**
Activities **99**   *References* **102**

Part 2
Career Development:
An Expanding Emphasis in Education 103

Chapter 5
Theory and Design of Career Education **105**

Introduction: The Evolving Concept of Career Education **105**
Overall Objectives and Characteristics of Career Education **110**
Principles of Career Education **120**   *Career Education Models* **123**
Federal Models for Career Education **126**
State Models for Career Education **135**
Local Career Education Programs **140**   *Summary* **142**
Activities **143**   *References* **144**

Chapter 6
Implementing Career Education:
Issues, Problems, and Needs **147**

Introduction **147**   *Through the Elementary School* **147**
Through the Middle School **148**   *Through the Secondary School* **150**
Through Higher Education **153**   *Teacher Education* **155**
An Appraisal of Career Education **162**   *Needs of Career Education* **168**
Summary **178**   *Activities* **179**   *References* **180**

Chapter 7
Career Guidance in Vocational Education **183**

Introduction **183**   *Developmental Theory and Career Guidance* **184**
Career Guidance at the Elementary Level **189**   *Career Guidance at the
Middle School Level* **192**   *Career Guidance at the High School Level* **193**
Career Guidance at the Postsecondary Level **195**
Trends in Career Guidance **199**
Evaluating Career Guidance **199**   *Summary* **200**
Activities **201**   *References* **202**

Part 3
**Operational Dimensions of Vocational Education as
a Component of Career Education 205**

Chapter 8
Institutions Providing
Vocational-Technical Education 207

Introduction **207**   *Public Educational Institutions* **208**
Other Institutions **225**
Summary **227**   *Activities* **228**   *References* **234**

Chapter 9
Organization of
Vocational and Technical Education 237

Introduction **237**   *National Efforts* **238**   *State Efforts* **246**   *Local Efforts* **253**
Summary **259**   *Activities* **260**   *References* **263**

Chapter 10
Curriculum Structure and
Strategy in Vocational Education **265**

Introduction **265**   *Approaches to Curriculum Development* **265**
Models for Curriculum Design **272**   *Curricular Needs Assessment* **281**
The Vocational Education Family **282**   *Vocational Education Enrollments* **296**
Evaluation of Vocational Curricula **300**   *Summary* **300**
Activities **302**   *References* **306**

Chapter 11
Research and Vocational-Technical Education **309**

Introduction **309**   *The Focus of Vocational Research* **310**
Types of Educational Research **311**   *Research Competencies* **311**
Translating Research into Practice **313**
Problems in Vocational-Technical Research **317**
Analysis of Research **319**   *Sources of Funding for Educational Research
and Development* **320**   *Preparation of Research Proposals* **327**
Examples of Vocational Education Research **335**
Summary **339**   *Activities* **340**
References **342**

Chapter 12
State and Federal
Support for Vocational Education **345**

Introduction **345**   *State and Local Tax Support for Schools* **347**
Federal Aid for Vocational Education **350**   *Vocational Education Acts* **353**
Research Related to Financing Vocational Education **365**

Expenditures for Vocational Education **366**
Summary **373**   *Activities* **374**
References **375**

Chapter 13
Public Relations for
Vocational-Technical Education **377**

Introduction **377**   *Public Relations in the Changing
Educational Scene* **379**   *Principles of Public Relations* **385**
Public Relations Checklist for Vocational Education **387**
Summary **397**   *Activities* **398**   *References* **399**

Chapter 14
Evaluation in
Vocational-Technical Education **401**

Introduction **401**   *Guiding Philosophy of Evaluation* **402**
Benefits of Evaluation **405**   *Evaluation Systems and Models* **409**
Program Evaluation **416**   *Measurement and Data Collection* **427**
Issues in Evaluation **433**   *Measuring Cognitive, Affective, and
Psychomotor Outcomes* **434**   *Evaluation for Accreditation* **439**
Summary **441**   *Activities* **443**   *References* **446**

Appendices **449**

Appendix A
Sample Needs Assessment Instrument **451**

Appendix B
Sample Course Evaluation Form **463**

Index **469**

Preface

This volume is based on the need to communicate the philosophical bases of vocational and career education as they relate to the nature and broad goals of American education, societal needs, and personal fulfillment. It builds on the need to understand the basis for the growth of career education as a broad emphasis in education, and to understand the crucial role that vocational education plays in the ultimate success of career development. Thus it integrates the foundations of vocational education, its history and philosophy, into the broader context of career education. In addition, the supporting functions of career counseling and guidance are shown in their important relationship to vocational and career education. While viewing vocational education as a component of career education, the authors have brought the two together in order to show their conceptual and operational relationships.

The text, intended for anyone with an interest in the learning or teaching of the fundamentals of vocational and career education, is uniquely designed for undergraduate and graduate courses in principles, history, philosophy, and foundations of vocational and career education. It is well adapted for use in in-service teacher education classes in foundations of vocational education, vocational counseling and development, history and philosophy of vocational education, and vocational career development. Vocational educators in agribusiness education, business-office education, distributive education, home economics education, health occupations education, industrial arts education, and trade and technical education will find the book appropriate for developing student knowledge of objectives, principles, and content in these vocational fields. Researchers and consultants will find that the book provides a wealth of source material covering the history and development of vocational education, including special attention to related legislation, as well as to the organization and structure of vocational education at all levels. The relationship of vocational education to emerging programs of career development will be of interest to school counselors and to counselor teacher educators. School administrators interested in the theory, organization, and design of vocational and career development programs will find the volume to be a valuable source of information.

The suggestions and assistance of many individuals have been indispensable in writing this book. The authors are most indebted to Dr. Marjorie Calhoun, whose tireless research, original ideas, and constructive criticism contributed immeasurably to the development and improvement of the manuscript. The reviewers of the draft and revised manuscript made numerous suggestions for desirable revisions. They are: Aaron J. Miller, The Ohio State University; Marlin L. Langlois, The Ohio State University; Annelle Bonner, University of Southern Mississippi; and Gloria Taylor, University of Southern Mississippi. We are also indebted to June Brady, Laura Cartwright, Dorothy Gambill, Willie F. Guy, Brenda Hare, Darlene Hussey, Opal Melvin, Carolyn Monaghan, Gladys Riley, Burma Schumpert, Julia Simmons, Carrie Strange, and Howard Frederick for activities related to Chapters 2, 4, and 8. Marilyn G. Butler contributed the sample needs assessment instrument contained in Appendix B.

We also wish to acknowledge the following administrators for furnishing information and assistance: D. B. Blanton, Houston, Mississippi Public Schools; Gene H. Meadows, Oxford, Mississippi Municipal Schools; Sam Yarbrough, Superintendent, Lafayette County, Mississippi Schools; Don W. Locke, Director, Business and Industrial Complex, Oxford, Mississippi; and James F. Goolsby, Superintendent, Valdosta, Georgia, City School System.

We acknowledge with deep appreciation the following publishers for permission to quote from copyrighted materials that have been cited in the text: Houghton Mifflin Company, Pitman Publishing Corporation, American Vocational Association, Inc., American Technical Society, Prentice-Hall, Inc., American Association of Colleges for Teacher Education, National Association of Secondary School Principals, Charles E. Merrill Publishing Company, Olympus Publishing Company, Association for Supervision and Curriculum Development, California State Department of Education, National Business Education Association, Arizona State Department of Education, American Association of Junior Colleges, Charles A. Jones Publishing Company, Clearing House, American Personnel and Guidance Association, College Entrance Examination Board, The Association of Childhood Education International, The Macmillan Company, McGraw-Hill Book Company, Phi Delta Kappa, Inc., and the International Reading Association.

Special appreciation is expressed to the publisher for support, cooperation, and encouragement throughout the development and revision of the manuscript. All who have contributed to the volume have been concerned that it contribute to better understanding about vocational education in the context of career education in contemporary American life. For the experience that made possible the writing of this book, we are indebted to our colleagues and students in the vocational and career education movement.

Appreciation is expressed to Mary Alice Simpson, who typed impeccable copies of some portions of the original manuscript.

Finally, we deeply appreciate Maria, Alan, and Marjorie, and Norma, Clair, and Leona, who gave up many family activities so that this work could be completed. To them this volume is dedicated.

Introduction

Every person involved in the process of educating Americans must have a working acquaintanceship with career education. The forces currently shaping the directions in which education is moving necessitate the involvement of educators as well as those outside the educational establishment in the formulation and operation of effective educational programs. Because of society's current insistence that every individual leaving the public school system have some type of occupational skill appropriate to earning a living, new importance is attached to vocational education as a vital component of career education. It is thus imperative that vocational teachers and teachers of traditional academic courses at all levels—elementary, middle school, high school, community college, and college, as well as supervisors, administrators, and other education officials at the local, state, and national levels—develop a working relationship with vocational and career education. The purpose of this text is to articulate the foundations of vocational and career education and to give educators a sharper perspective of their role in career education.

To accomplish this objective, the text has been divided into three major parts: Part 1, Conceptual Dimensions of Existing and Emerging Career-Related Programs; Part 2, Career Development: An Expanding Emphasis in Education; and Part 3, Operational Dimensions of Vocational Education as a Component of Career Education.

The conceptual dimensions of existing and emerging career-related programs are developed in the first four chapters. In Chapter 1, Personal-Societal Needs and Vocational Education, the student is introduced to the effects of societal and personal needs on educational programs designed to train workers for the labor market. Labor forecasts from the Bureau of Labor Statistics and other sources are interpreted so as to reflect current and emerging labor needs. The effects of change in the employment picture are examined in relation to educational opportunities and requirements. The effects on vocational education of new technology, of mobility, of the changing status of women, and of human organizational behavior are also discussed.

Chapter 2, Historical Perspective of Vocational-Technical Education, presents the impact of federal legislation on the development of vocational education in the United States. For purposes of analysis, the legislation is divided into three developmental stages: (a) legislation enacted prior to 1900, (b) legislation enacted between 1900 and 1960, and (c) legislation enacted since 1960. The thesis is developed that the failure of social, religious, and business organizations to deal with the nation's educational problems have forced the federal government to do so on an expanding basis over the years.

In Chapter 3, Factors Influencing Varied Aspects of Vocational-Technical Education, emphasis is placed on philosophical, economic, and sociological factors. The philosophical factors that are discussed focus on the question: What knowledge and/or skill is of most value to teach? The economic factors center on the effects of labor-market needs on career development. Sociological factors are examined with relation to the effects of social class and industrialization on preparation for vocations.

Chapter 4, Relationship of Vocational Education to Other Educational Emphases, provides an overview and definition of vocational education as it relates to general education, to career development, and to vocational and technical education. Definitions of the content and method of vocational education and the historical relationships between vocational and general education are drawn. The roles of both vocational education and general education in an individual's overall career development are emphasized. Attention is given to the developing role of career education as a concept in this chapter, even though it is treated as a continuing thread throughout the entire text and is treated intensively in Chapter 5 as a phenomenological development.

Part 2, Career Development: An Expanding Emphasis in Education, is treated in Chapters 5, 6, and 7. Chapter 5, Theory and Design of Career Education, focuses on a discussion of the structure of career education and its potential value as an influence pervading the curriculum at all educational levels. The characteristics and objectives of career education, at various educational levels and as seen through different programs, are examined. Different approaches to the organization and structure of career education are presented, including variations in developing models (school-based, employer-based, rural-residential-based, and home-community-based). Attention is given to the reasons for an increasing emphasis on career education as a concept and as a system of learning.

Chapter 6, Implementing Career Education: Issues, Problems, and Needs, develops the concept that career education is a lifelong educational process. An examination is made of the role and objectives of career education at the elementary, middle school, secondary, and higher education levels. The chapter also focuses on issues, problems, and needs, including leadership, finances, the role of vocational education, the role of the American Vocational Association, criticisms, fallacies and fantasies, the concept of infusion, and the federal role in career education.

Emphasis is given in Chapter 7, Career Guidance in Vocational Education, to the questions of how, why, and when individuals are channeled into particular educational routes, that is, toward particular career objectives. Attention is also given to how, why, and when individuals are guided into the various *vocational* disciplines. Emphasis is placed on the need to inform individuals of career options available to them through multiple educational routes. Attention is given to the need for knowing (a) how to make career choices, (b) the qualifications required for specific career choices, (c) job expectations for specific career choices, and (d) the financial and personal remuneration to be expected. Attention is directed to the role of the teacher, the guidance counselor, the administrator, supervisor, and other individuals concerned with the guidance process. Examples are provided illustrating (a) different methods of recruiting students into the various vocational disciplines, (b) the need for follow-up and placement of individuals when they leave the program, and (c) techniques for obtaining and various uses of follow-up data on individuals.

Because the field of education is beginning to give as much recognition to vocational education as has been traditionally given to academic education, it has become important for all professional educators to be more perceptive of the role of vocational education in career education. Part 3, Operational Dimensions of Vocational Education as a Component of Career Education, is devoted to this topic.

Chapter 8, Institutions Providing Vocational-Technical Education, describes the general and specific objectives of vocational education and career development in existing and emerging educational programs at the following levels: elementary school, middle school, high school, and postsecondary schools. Specific attention is given to the objectives of vocational education in business-office and distributive occupations, agri-business occupations, home economics occupations, trade and industrial occupations, and health-related occupations. Basic organization, objectives, principles, and types of training programs offered by agencies other than public education institutions are presented.

Chapter 9, Organization of Vocational and Technical Education, presents the structure of federally reimbursed, as well as nonreimbursed, programs of vocational education at the national, state, and local levels. The role of the Bureau of Occupational and Adult Education in the U.S. Office of Education, state boards for vocational education, and the state division of vocational education, as well as the local organization of vocational education, are treated. The use of advisory committees and the preparation of local and state plans for vocational education are also presented, as are the principles and practices of state and local supervision of vocational education.

Chapter 10, Curriculum Structure and Strategy in Vocational Education, introduces the differing philosophical concepts of curriculum structure, traditional and contemporary, and both group-oriented and individually oriented curricula in the various vocational areas.

Chapter 11, Research and Vocational-Technical Education, focuses on the status and needs of research in vocational education; the types of research being conducted; competencies needed by vocational teachers, supervisors, and teachers who conduct research; research centers responsible for conducting, coordinating, and disseminating vocational education research; procedures to be followed in developing research proposals; and examples of research being conducted in the field.

In Chapter 12, State and Federal Support for Vocational Education, the specific sources of funding for vocational education—federal, state, local, private, and public—are examined in detail. The purposes, requirements and allowances, amounts available, and eligibility criteria for funding are analyzed. Particular attention is given to teacher responsibilities associated with implementation of funded vocational programs. Some attention is given to the planning, writing, and submission of research proposals for funding; however, this topic is treated in detail in Chapter 11.

Particular attention is given in Chapter 13, Public Relations for Vocational-Technical Education, to the development of positive relationships with internal and external school publics. Principles, techniques, and media affecting school public relations are examined as they apply to the implementation of strong and viable vocational programs. Public relations is viewed as a two-way process, a cooperative effort for mutual understanding and effective teamwork between the community and the school. Emphasis is placed on the development of a continuous program of interpretation, involvement, and cooperation as the school seeks to serve the individual and vocational needs of its various publics.

Chapter 14, Evaluation in Vocational-Technical Education, applies recognized principles and processes to the measurement and evaluation of outcomes of instruction in vocational education. Systems for evaluating individual progress in the classroom and for measuring overall effectiveness of vocational courses, instruction, and programs are presented. Evaluation as a basis for improving instructional decisions is stressed.

The title of the text, VOCATIONAL AND CAREER EDUCATION: CONCEPTS AND OPERATIONS, is not meant to imply that vocational education and career education are two parallel components of education. Rather, the title underlines the close and complementary relationship of vocational education as a crucial component within an effectively functioning system of career education.

Part 1

Conceptual Dimensions

of Existing

and Emerging

Career-Related Programs

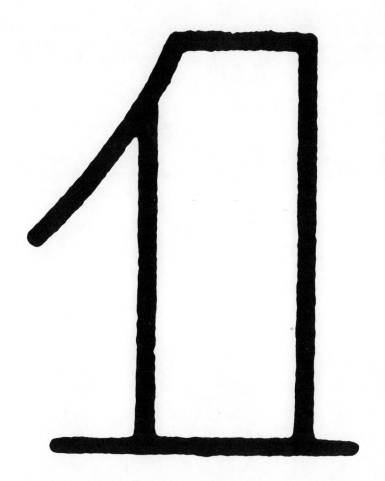

Chapter 1

Personal-Societal

Needs

and

Vocational Education

Introduction

□ *Vocational education faces a unique challenge in the years ahead—a challenge rooted in the social and economic welfare of people. In the contemporary social scene with its large city problems, the ghettos, school dropouts, and a variety of disadvantaged groups, the need for vocational education stands out clearly* (1).

Vocational education has always been shaped by the changing needs of people. Historically, vocational training was necessary to sustain the family unit. Later the concept of socially useful work as a means of improving oneself, in a moral sense, became a well-documented part of the Judaeo-Christian culture. As nations developed, trained workers became important to the realization of national goals and thus vocational education received national endorsement and financial support.

Vocational education as we know it in the United States grew out of a social need for an educated work force. As a function and responsibility of our educational system, vocational education has been responsive and adaptable to societal change. Although its overall dimensions include social, educational, and manpower considerations, its basic concern is for the people who provide the goods and services required by society. Ultimately it must provide both productive and self-satisfying job settings through which institutions and individuals can realize their goals.

What Vocational Education Means

Throughout this text, *vocational education* and *occupational education* will be used as equivalent terms, and both include technical education. Both terms are intended to mean any form of education, training, or re-training designed to prepare persons to enter or continue in paid employment in any recognized occupation. The only occupations excepted from this definition are those designated as professional or that require a baccalaureate or higher degree. Clearly this definition gives a very broad and inclusive meaning to vocational education. Yet it expresses the concept established by the Federal Vocational Education Acts, and it defines a scope of responsibility that vocational leaders accept. Such fields as agricultural education, business and office education, distributive education, trade and industrial education, health occupations education, and home economics education are specialized programs of vocational education.

Vocational education also includes the vocational guidance and counseling that precedes or parallels the preparation for employment or reemployment. Federal legislation incorporates such guidance services into vocational education and provides funds for its support. When vocational education is viewed broadly, it includes all of the above areas and services.

It should be understood by the reader, however, that the terms vocational education and occupational education carry different meanings in some parts of the United States. In some states, for example, occupational education programs are legally defined as "work-study" programs for slow learners, whereas vocational education programs are defined as federally reimbursed job training programs. Legislation currently being considered in Washington, D.C., defines vocational education as secondary school programs, whereas occupational education is proposed by the American Association of Junior Colleges to mean all postsecondary vocational education.

What Career Education Means

Conceptually, career education represents a combination of old and new emphases in education. The U.S. Office of Education in 1971 gave impetus to its growth by developing four models of career education: school-based, home-based, employer-based, and residential-based. Developmental aspects of the theory and structure of career education are treated in Chapters 5 and 6.

Basically, career education provides a core for the total educational program, using the job as a unifying force for all school disciplines. In this sense, career education represents a total system wherein all general education offerings take on new meanings relating to careers and work. Career education emphasizes student awareness and orientation to work, appreciation for the dignity of work, exploration of career opportunities and requirements, and specialized vocational preparation. As a continuous thread within a comprehensive instructional program, it facilitates the career development of students by involving them in orientation, exploration, decision-making, job-preparation, and placement experiences. It provides students with a learning environment and goals that relate their total education to the world of work.

In 1971 the state directors of vocational education, meeting in Las Vegas, Nevada, listed the characteristics that serve to clarify the content and process of career education. Career education:

1 enhances rather than supplants all educational programs; serves as a vehicle to improve the learning process

2 is an integral part of the present structure of all schools

3 involves all students and all educators

4 involves extensive orientation and exploration of occupational opportunities

5 is dependent in its implementation on the commitment to and obligation to fulfill the philosophy of career education from all levels of the community, government, and institutions of higher education

6 emphasizes individualized instruction and student involvement in career attainment

7 humanizes the educational process as it encompasses the self concept and its relation to the world

8 is a continuum that begins with preschool and extends throughout public school and employment

9 contributes to student incentives, aspirations, and expectations

10 includes specific preparation for occupations through vocational education or other appropriate educational experiences

11 develops realistic occupational choices

12 promotes positive attitudes toward all useful work including psychologically rewarding endeavors

13 permits each student to realistically assess personal attributes as a part of setting life goals

14 provides a means of articulation from grade to grade and from level to level

15 is not necessarily synonymous with vocational education, but vocational education is a major part of career education

Career education focuses on broad self-realization, social responsibility, and affective value components, whereas vocational-technical education focuses more specifically on role, skill, and competence. Thus it is useful to view vocational education as a component of the larger concept of career education.

Social Environment of Jobs*

Social scientists from a variety of disciplines and public leaders at all levels have begun to focus more attention on the motivational and orientation factors involved in occupational preparation, placement, and adjustment. Such interest has been a result of the growing recognition that our society is experiencing difficulty in adjusting the labor supply to changing individual and occupational requirements. In many cases, individuals desire a type of employment in demand by society, but they cannot obtain the necessary training. At the same time, persons who want lower-skilled jobs find fewer of them available as the processes of industrialization, mechanization, and the use of cybernetics diminish the need for such work.

Occupational education includes two related needs: the needs of society to fill required positions so that the economic system will operate efficiently, and the needs of individuals to find personally satisfying positions in the occupational structure.

A basic requirement of society is that positions necessary to its continued existence be filled by capable individuals. In addition there is a widely shared premise that we should always use human talent and skills to their limits. While we strive to avoid an energy crisis by efficient use of our natural resources, we must also make more effective use of our human abilities and talents.

To the individual, an occupation is an important source of social identity. A person's occupation has direct significance for self-fulfillment and social prestige. It consumes a major portion of one's daily life and determines to a large extent other personal facets of one's life—kinds of association with others, income security, life style, and even the life chances of one's family.

A particularly vital area of concern to career education is personal fulfillment. If someone aims at a particular occupation but does not attain it, he or she will likely feel some degree of deprivation. In our society many children are led to believe that their achievements are limited only by their desires and efforts. This belief has a tendency to produce relatively high goals that are not necessarily compatible with existing opportunities or even with individual capabilities. Individuals who do not realize their career goals can allow this deprivation to affect their evaluation of society and their relation to it. Meeting the *internalized occupational needs* of individuals is a prime objective of career education.

The process whereby individuals are trained and placed in the occupational structure of our society is complex. Factors that normally interact to determine the final outcome include the characteristics of the individual, the individual's network of social relations, the structure of society

* The term *job* is used to apply to a regular remunerative position, as opposed to a piece of work or a task. *Occupation* refers broadly to the principal business for which one is prepared. Thus an individual may hold a job inside or outside his area of specialization.

and its dynamic properties, and the individual's perception of the interrelationship of these factors.

Individual Rights vs. Societal Needs

This text focuses on both the occupational needs of individuals and the labor requirements of society. One's selection of a particular kind of work has important implications both for the individual and for the total society. Every society must somehow arrange to get people to do what has to be done to maintain a healthy environment. It must distribute its human and natural resources, both in quantity and quality, so that societal goals will be satisfied.

As Goldhammer (2), succinctly points out, our nation's position of leadership demands a strong economic base which, in turn, requires new skills and increased levels of efficiency and productivity if we are to survive in world competition. In these rigorous times of accountability and management by objectives, it is easy to forget that the individual is paramount in our free society. The problem is one of balancing the requirements of society against the essential freedom of its individuals.

Vocations and Personal Needs

To understand the role of the occupation in a person's life, we must first understand the individual and his or her needs. The old concept of economic security has proved inadequate to explain why people work as they do. It is true that a large number of workers in our nation are categorized as unskilled or semiskilled. One of the primary aims of most working people is economic security, that is, having a job available on a continuous basis so that income will not be interrupted. But if individuals worked just to make a living, as soon as food and shelter had been assured, work would stop. Studies of morale and job satisfaction in industry have shown conclusively that much more is involved in and expected of a job than a pay check.

Theories of Basic Individual Needs

Many authors have discussed the needs or drives that seem related to work in various ways. Cleeton (3) lists food, bodily well-being, activity, sharing of thoughts and feelings, dominance over people and elements, self-determination, achievement, approbation, and ideation. Vernon (4) found that drives that influence university women in selecting an occupation are social conformity, altruism, activity, independence, power, superiority, social admiration, pleasure, and ease. Hendrick (5) postulated a work principle which states that people seek and find primary pleasure in the efficient use of mind, hands, and tools to control or alter the environment.

Fraser (6) classified human needs into three general categories: 1. Material needs are those basic to body maintenance, including food, clothing, and shelter. 2. Companion needs are associated with living and interacting with other people and encompass factors such as urbanization and job specialization. 3. Ego needs include those factors that differentiate individuals from each other. This category emphasizes the worth and importance of the individual.

How do such needs affect individuals in their occupations? There is little agreement among psychologists on the structure of a basic personality theory. The work of Maslow, as it relates to occupational behavior (7), views the individual as an integrated whole, motivated by fundamental goals or needs, some of which are largely unconscious. Of particular importance for the psychology of occupations is Maslow's arrangement of needs into the following:

1 physiological needs

2 safety needs

3 need for belongingness and love

4 need for importance, respect, self-esteem, independence

5 need for information

6 need for understanding

7 need for beauty

8 need for self-actualization

The above needs are arranged in the order in which individuals strive to satisfy them. A person will first be concerned with the need for food and drink. When these are satisfied, one can think of shelter and safety, then of companionship, and so on. The most direct way to develop a life at a higher need level is through adequate gratification of the lower needs. Maslow does not make a special point of individual differences in the strength of the basic needs, but these differences surely exist and are of considerable importance. It is obvious that the higher needs, such as a need for information or beauty, are much stronger in some individuals than in others, and the strength of these needs is of direct importance for occupational choice. Such differences can occur quite apart from the degree of satisfaction of other needs.

Relationship of Basic Needs to Occupations

The application of Maslow's theory to occupational psychology is fairly obvious. In our society there is no single situation so potentially capable of satisfying basic needs at all levels as a person's occupation. With respect to the physiological needs, the usual means for satisfying hunger and thirst is through money from the job, money that can be exchanged for food and drink.

The same is true for the safety needs. This principle applies not only to the possibility of securing housing and medical care, which cut down the incidence and severity of disease, but also to safety in a long-range sense. This principle assures that these provisions will be available to a person not only during the working period but afterward in terms of pensions, savings, and so on. It has been demonstrated repeatedly that many persons will choose a job that promises security over one that pays more but cannot be counted on to last.

The need to be a member of a group, to give and receive love, is also one that can be satisfied in part by the occupation. To work with a congenial group, to be an intrinsic part of the functioning of the group, to be needed and welcomed by it, are important aspects of a satisfactory job. One of the unconscious values inherent in a job may be the opportunity it provides for the individual to win approval—of his or her immediate superior, of groups of people, or of other particularly significant persons (8).

Perhaps satisfaction of the need for esteem from self and others is a big part of the occupation. In the first place, entering an occupation is generally seen, in our culture, as a symbol of adulthood, an indication that a young man or woman has reached a stage of some independence and freedom. Having a job carries a measure of esteem. What importance it has is seen most clearly in the devastating effect on some individuals when they are out of work.

The need for self-actualization may be met by individuals through any one of several occupations, but the strength of this need may well be the key factor in differentiating those who put enormous yet easy and pleasant effort into their work from those who do not. This factor of happy effort and of the amount of personal involvement in the work is probably the single most important factor in work success. At least in many occupations it appears that those who have attained high status have put great effort into their work. Studies of eminent persons have noted that more effort than ability is needed for great achievement. Witty and Lehman (9), for example, have pointed out that works of genius have emanated from individuals of moderate capacity who had impelling drives to accomplish. In a sense, unused capacities might just as well not be present.

Persons in the lower socioeconomic levels show security needs more frequently than do people in higher socioeconomic positions, as indicated by Maslow and others. This may be true because people in higher socioeconomic levels have already satisfied this need, whereas those in lower socioeconomic levels have not. With the security need satisfied, other and higher needs take its place, and so we find people in the upper occupational strata showing desires for self-expression, esteem, leadership, and interesting experiences more often than we find such manifestations among the lower occupational groups.

When considered in relation to the needs of groups, the basic needs of individuals take on additional meaning. How do we explain the basic behavior of individuals within the employment setting? Let us examine briefly the theories of McGregor and Herzberg, each of whom has conducted extensive research into the motivation of individuals in relation to their jobs.

Human Behavior in Organizations

Douglas McGregor (10) classifies the philosophies of dealing with individuals into two broad divisions, *Theory X* and *Theory Y*. These theories are considered basic to an understanding of the two most prevalent approaches to studying human behavior in organizations. The characteristics of each approach are outlined in Table 1.1.

Table 1.1   Traditional and Current Behavioral Theories

Theory X, the traditional view	Theory Y, the current view
the average person dislikes work inherently	the average person does not inherently dislike work but, depending on conditions, may find work to be satisfying or punishing
the average person will avoid work if possible	
most people must be coerced, controlled, or threatened with punishment to get them to work toward the achievement of organizational goals	most people will exercise self-direction and self-control to achieve organizational objectives under certain conditions
the average person prefers to be directed, to avoid responsibility	the average person will seek to attain his or her firm's objectives under certain conditions
the average person has relatively little ambition and wants security above all	under proper conditions the average person will seek responsibility
	the capacity to use imagination and originality is widely found in the population, but most people do not use all their mental potential

The early view of behavior, Theory X, is based on limited experience and little or no scientific study. Theory Y outlines some critical features of human behavior and motivation that spring from controlled experiments by highly trained researchers. It points out that people have wants or needs that are never completely fulfilled.

Herzberg (11) and others who have researched the area of job motivation have argued that one must be aware of those factors that serve as motivators to the worker and those that do not. Some factors do lead to superior job satisfaction and performance. Thus, says Herzberg, possibility for growth, responsibility, achievement, advancement, and recognition are motivators. But there are other factors—termed hygiene, maintenance, or dissatisfiers—whose absence leads to dissatisfaction but whose presence does not motivate but merely prevents dissatisfaction. Good working conditions are not motivators; they can only reduce job dissatisfaction. For positive motivation one must turn to the motivators such as growth and achievement possibilities. Herzberg's theory of job enrichment has gained wide acceptance in management circles because it has tended to develop among employees a feeling of greater responsibility for their work.

Although there are many similarities in their needs, individuals do vary in the intensity of those needs and in their means of satisfying them. As indicated by Fraser (12):

☐ *The need to earn a living, to feel that one is liked and accepted in the various groupings to which one belongs, and to achieve a certain significance as an individual, these are the basic elements in everyone's motivation. Where the differences appear is in the methods of satisfaction, for in the modern pluralistic society there are all sorts of activities for which one can be paid, all sorts of different groupings each with its own way of life, and all sorts of activities which will make one important in one or other of these groupings. Each individual will have his own pattern of satisfaction, or his own range of activities which give him a financial companionship or status dividend. These will be personal and peculiar to the individual and may never accord exactly with that of another individual.*

Concepts Related to
Work and Individual Occupations

The preceding relationships between people and their work may be characterized by several basic concepts.

1 We live in a work-oriented society In our society, work and work-related activities consume the major part of an individual's waking hours. When a male reaches maturity, he is expected to obtain a job. In increasing numbers women are also encouraged, and in some cases, expected, to seek employment outside the home. The average man expects to work approximately forty years, and the average woman can expect to work at least twenty-five years although she may enter and leave the labor market several times. Despite the pressures for a shorter work week and earlier retirement, there is much evidence to suggest that the personal and social values of continuing employment tend to outweigh the disadvantages. Work is a major source of identity for the individual, especially those of the middle class or those who accept middle-class values.

2 Work provides situations for satisfying individual needs People work for many reasons other than money. Ginzberg and others (13) have identified three different types of satisfaction from work. The first, and most obvious, are the *extrinsic satisfactions,* or tangible rewards of work. These include salaries and bonuses. Second are the *intrinsic satisfactions* derived from two sources: (a) the pleasure that comes from engaging in work activity, and (b) the sense of accomplishment that is experienced from meeting social standards of success and personal realization of abilities through achievement. The third type of satisfaction includes extrinsic satisfactions associated with physical and psychological conditions of a person's work. These include clean, comfortable working conditions, fringe benefits, and congenial co-workers.

To the typical person in a middle-class occupation, working means having a purpose, gaining a sense of accomplishment, and expressing oneself. Not working, it seems, would leave one aimless and without opportunity to contribute to society. It must be remembered, however, that all workers are not middle class and so may not share such an orientation to work.

Work also serves noneconomic functions. In a national sample of 401 employed men, Morse and Weiss (14) found that work does not simply function as a means of earning a livelihood. Most of these men indicated that even if there were no economic necessity involved, they would continue to work. It is through the producing role that most individuals tie into society; it is an essential element in helping them to maintain their sense of well-being.

3 Work is directly related to an individual's social life An occupation is central to one's sense of dignity, opportunity, and a social life. The consequences of not being able to work or of being denied the opportunity to work at the level of one's competence is not merely a matter of monetary loss; equally important is the consequent loss of social status. The individual's status in the community, based on the esteem in which he or she is held, will depend largely on the type of work that is done and how well it is performed. It is quite evident that one's choice of friends and leisure-time activities, even one's residence, is conditioned to some degree by one's work and one's relationship with co-workers.

A person's occupation in American society today is his or her single most significant, status-conferring role. Whether it be high or low, a job status allows the individual to form a stable self-conception and to establish a position in the community.

Vocations and Societal Needs

Vocational education through the years has been responsive to the needs of society. Historically the apprenticeship system for training workers was sufficient to meet the demands of emerging industry. But when geographic and occupational mobility of workers accelerated, and improved technology required a higher degree of trained skills, society turned to the schools to supply its need for trained workers.

Effects of Technology

Throughout history the continuous processes of technological change have influenced human culture in that they have always affected the nature of people's efforts to earn a living. Until quite recently, however, the pace of technological change was slow, and there was much overlap from one generation to another in social, cultural, and economic patterns. Particularly in relation to occupations, the changes were not fast enough to seriously disrupt the character of most workers' performance. A useful occupation learned in youth could be counted on to produce a livelihood as long as a person was likely to work.

But today the accelerating pace of technological change is able to produce complete changes in the nature of an occupation within a few years. Although automation is usually associated with this process, it is but one aspect of a broader movement consisting of many interacting and powerful technologies. Technological advances cause present jobs to disappear and also result in the emergence of previously unknown occupations. Often the persons who performed the old jobs are not capable of undertaking the new ones because they require further education and retraining.

Occupations created by new technology seem to have several characteristics that differ from occupations that tend to be phased out: 1. They usually involve fewer manual skills and more cognitive understandings. 2. They often call for skills of a higher order and for the use of more technical knowledge. 3. Their performance usually requires a more complete, functional general education than the jobs they replaced. 4. In many cases the worker needs more maturity in order to fill the job successfully. As a result of these characteristics of newer occupations, versatility may be more valuable than a high degree of specialization.

Modern technology is creating an increasing number of occupations that provide services rather than goods. Sometimes these occupations call for combinations of traditional skills. In the area of agri-business, for example, occupations related to the sale and servicing of agricultural machinery demand a combination of skills. In addition, these new occupations often demand different kinds of skills, which may be described as interpersonal or social, in addition to technical knowledge. The retail clerk, for example, must be knowledgeable about the merchandise and must relate effectively to the customer in an interpersonal sense.

Although technology eliminates some unskilled and low-skilled occupations, it also tends to upgrade skill and training requirements in the more highly specialized jobs. It is beginning to affect middle-management and higher levels of the occupational structure so that retraining is becoming a continuing aspect of employment. Technology has had profound effects on agricultural occupations where increases in the average size of farms, rapid mechanization, and improved fertilizers, feeds, and pesticides have led to much increased output with sharply decreased employment.

Nevertheless, the effect of technology on occupations is quite variable.

It should not be assumed that all older occupations have become obsolete or that they should be excluded from vocational education programs. The rate of change in different occupations varies widely, although in all occupations the rate of change tends to increase. It is not expected that this trend will be reversed.

The vocational educator needs to be well informed about the progress and current developments in technological change, so that he or she may respond wisely and so that programs which are planned and operated will remain continually relevant. One should not be surprised if changes which presently seem remote occur much sooner than expected, so flexibility and the ability to anticipate need will be essential. If the program of public vocational education cannot exhibit this flexibility, other public and private agencies will be created, often on an ad hoc basis, to meet the needs.

Implications of Technology for
Vocational and Career Education

A career, in the sense of a stable pursuit of a single occupation throughout the work life of the individual, is becoming increasingly unattainable in our industrialized society for a large portion of the work force, and serial careers are becoming a reality. Thus an individual may expect to hold several different occupations during a lifetime. Also, with the passing of craftsmanship in industry and with the changes resulting from more advanced technology, an increased percentage of the working population is no longer able to follow occupations that offer the kind of identity historically available in work.

Because the portion of the day that must be devoted to the business of earning a living is decreasing, the search for a meaningful use of leisure is becoming more intense. It is an open question whether leisure activities can supply the individual with a needed source of identity and meaning. In many instances the individual will choose to spend some of this time in continuing education and retraining for vocational or avocational purposes.

The practices and policies of vocational education have always been determined by the existing state of technology and its attendant social and economic realities. Before the rate of technological change had reached its present level, these practices did not often require reexamination or revision. The assumptions on which they were based remained valid for long periods of time. Because of social changes induced by technology, however, this is no longer true. Some of the practices and policies of the past are no longer appropriate, whereas others are still useful or need only minor modification. Still other policies may continue to be viable for the foreseeable future. Vocational educators must learn to continually reexamine their positions and to respect traditions only so long as they are compatible with the real needs of people.

In the past there has been a tendency for most pre-employment vocational education to be planned as terminal education. Provision has always been made for the periodic updating of workers through extension forms of vocational education, but this updating has usually meant only intermittent training for those engaged in stable, lifetime occupations. It is now clear that no form of education, vocational or nonvocational, can become terminal but must be planned as open-ended and continuous. It must provide workers with complete retraining for new jobs, as well as for continuity in present jobs. A major responsibility of vocational education will be to develop a readiness and capacity for a lifetime of learning and relearning.

Need for extended scope Vocational education has traditionally emphasized preparation for the highly skilled and technical occupations in agriculture, the skilled trades, office and distributive occupations, and home economics. This emphasis has meant that its services have largely been directed toward those who could qualify for such occupations. But current technological change requires that vocational education extend its services to all possible categories of occupational life, excluding the professions that are served by the professional schools. This extended scope will include education for persons at various social and economic levels regardless of age or sex. In short, vocational education will need to offer preparation for any form of work for which workers are needed and for which individuals can possibly be helped to qualify.

Occupational change and career choice Vocational educators will need to be informed continually about broad occupational changes and their implications. This means more than discovering what new tools, materials, or processes are coming into use in particular trades or jobs. It involves current knowledge of major social and economic trends and a wide perspective of the social, political, and economic forces that shape the occupational life of the nation. To keep abreast of such trends requires more than periodic studies or surveys of local conditions; it will be necessary to tap many sources of information, including agencies of government, business, industry, and education. In addition there will be a greater need for vocational counseling to assist those who are making career choices. The vocational educator and the trained counselor will need to work hand-in-hand, with each respecting the role of the other.

The importance of general education Technological advances raised the basic educational requirements for most jobs. As a result the skills acquired through general education—reading, writing, speaking, and calculating—are becoming an even more essential foundation for work. Their importance is being felt in at least three ways. First, more and more jobs require a higher level of general education as a prerequisite for learning their specialized aspects. Second, the skills and understandings developed by general education—especially those of a verbal, scientific, and mathematical nature—turn out to be the actual, on-the-job skills of more and more occupations (the paramedical occupations are an example). Third, a substantial amount of general education is needed to provide the future worker with the intellectual tools needed for continued learning, in fact, for a lifetime of learning a living.

There are important training implications to this demand for workers with skills related both to technical content and to general education. As technology accelerates, there is a greater need for the development of skills composed of both intellectual and manipulative components. More jobs will take on the characteristics of technical occupations, but many of these jobs will not be related to the physical sciences. Instead, they will reflect the growing shift to occupations oriented toward the social and personal services such as law enforcement and health care. Ultimately, most of this training will take place in programs that include part or all of the thirteenth and fourteenth years of school.

The results of technology In planning for new programs of vocational education or for the improvement of existing programs, management and labor must understand the influence of swift technological change. The kinds of work for which individuals prepare will continue to undergo changes, both in nature and in content. For many workers, continuity in work life will be interrupted, requiring fresh preparation for new tasks. No education can be considered terminal. Generally, jobs will tend to disappear in inverse order to the amount of education and skills they require; those jobs that make the fewest educational demands will always be the most vulnerable. The relative need for manual and craft-type skills will likely decrease, even as the overall need for skilled workers increases. The new skills for the new jobs will tend to be of a different order. Technical knowledge and conceptual skills will become major ingredients of many occupations while technical knowledge combined with social skills will be required by many others. For most workers a more complete general education will be a necessary foundation for further training. Career choice will become more complex and will call for more assistance from professionally trained people who keep up to date on the changing occupational opportunities and requirements. Career decision making will tend to be prolonged and, together with an extended period of general education, will somewhat advance the age at which serious vocational preparation will be begun. Future career programs must achieve greater flexibility in order to satisfy more diverse needs; the opportunity to contract for services that are not normally available in the standard school setting should increase this flexibility.

Effects of Mobility

Mobility is a characteristic of American society. A person moves from one coast to the other to accept a better position. Education helps the children of artisans and laborers to climb social and economic ladders. Our whole population shows substantial mobility, and most mobile of all are members of the specialized professions. Movement from one region to another, from one type of work to another, serves the wishes and ambitions of the individual as well as the good of society.

From the standpoint of analyzing the labor market, it is useful to think of several kinds of mobility. Mobility may be classified as moving from one place to another, from one function to another (such as from teaching to business management), from one type of employer to another, or from one specialty to another. All of these types of mobility are interrelated, and they are all related to education and ability.

Occupational mobility By being mobile, men and women are able to take advantage of new and better job opportunities. This is the first advantage of mobility: the greater opportunity it provides individuals to move into the work they find most interesting or rewarding. If people could not move from one job to another, they would be stuck for life in the kind of work or in the company they had chosen—or that had chosen them—at the beginning of their career (15).

According to Taylor (16), participants in the American labor force change jobs, on the average, every three to five years. Most upward occupational mobility occurs between the ages of 25 and 45. By age 50, most workers have reached the high point on the occupational ladder, and during the last 15 to 20 years of the work cycle, little occupational mobility occurs.

Occupational mobility is good for the individual and for society. Society benefits when workers are interested in their jobs and when workers have the freedom to move to new areas, new positions, and new kinds of work. In fact, labor mobility is one of our most effective means of keeping the supply of talent in reasonable balance with the work society wants done.

Of course, there are means other than job mobility to keep supply and demand in balance. When labor is in short supply, people come out of the labor reserve, for they are attracted by the salaries or by the kinds of work available.

Geographic mobility At the present rate, each year approximately 20 percent of all Americans one year of age or over change residence, and about 6.5 percent migrate across county or state lines.

Geographic mobility is most pronounced in specific segments of society, for the following reasons. First, disadvantaged workers, both rural and urban, move in hopes of bettering themselves. Second, professional and technical workers move for occupational reasons and as a means of upward social mobility. Third, many thousands of military families are moved periodically both within the United States and to other countries. Fourth, skilled workers, such as construction workers, move seasonally to follow demands for their services. Finally, thousands of college students attend school both in- and out-of-state and are significant participants in the increased mobility that is characteristic of our country (17).

A special aspect of mobility in recent years is the surge into the suburbs and both into and out of the inner cities. This movement is not only a shift of living locale for a considerable portion of the population, but it also involves a definite change in ethnic composition (18).

Mobility and education The level of education completed by a worker affects both the type of job for which he or she can qualify and the amount of mobility necessary for continued growth and advancement (19). The occupational categories that are currently expanding require more education than those that are not. Because of the average increase in the educational level of United States workers, the typical labor force entrant now has at least a high school education, and the workers who do not graduate from high school tend to be screened out of better jobs. These educational patterns lead to mobility patterns as the undereducated often *must* move after a long and fruitless search for work locally, and the educated move *voluntarily* as an outgrowth of the expanding market for their services. People are either pushed into leaving an area by adverse conditions or they are pulled into an area by favorable conditions.

One should not assume, however, that because the labor market is composed of more highly trained workers, occupational mobility is essentially vertical rather than lateral. Just the opposite is true. It is difficult for individuals to begin on the bottom rung of a career ladder and with some additional training work their way up to the top. In fact, there is a limited amount of vertical mobility with much lateral mobility. For example, people who are trained as electronic technicians may move laterally in and out of a variety of jobs that require similar training. But seldom does an electronic technician move vertically to the position of engineer or research scientist. The same is true of paramedical technicians who seldom become physicians. Certification and state licensing requirements contribute to this limited vertical mobility.

Challenge of Retirement

Modern society, with its higher standards of living, its public health controls, and its advances in medical treatment, has succeeded in establishing a higher life expectancy for its workers. Most individuals spend about one-third of their lives preparing to enter the labor force, another third in the labor force, and a final third in retirement. Yet while increasing numbers of workers live longer and have many more years of potential productive work activity, society's accepted ages for required or voluntary retirement have not changed appreciably. Many workers who can and want to continue working must leave their jobs at a specific retirement age. It is also expected that they will be happy with their retirement status, whether or not they agree.

The retired individual is expected to "settle down" to the one remaining work-environment reinforcer (often one with reinforcement value reduced to almost an imperceptible level)—a continuing retirement check. Concurrently, there seem to be many individuals who see retirement as their reward for years of hard work, who prepare for it as an ultimate goal, and who want to retire as soon as the system will permit.

In either case, whether the worker is required to retire or whether he or she wishes to retire, it is likely that relatively few individuals have truly planned a satisfying retirement. Many of them have probably viewed retirement only in a rather abstract way as an expected, but desirable, state of affairs. For example, a view that is frequently encountered is that the life style of retired people is characterized by increased recreational activity. Now that they have the time, they can golf, camp, boat, dance, play chess, paint, and the like. They are able to do these things because they are now "free to do them," whether or not they have ever learned to do or to prefer them. It is often assumed that when people retire they will not only be able to but they will also want to change their life styles to include more recreational activities. A related attitude is that retired people should be encouraged to relax and do nothing. Naturally such an abrupt change can have unsettling effects on many individuals.

Society's retirement problem is not simply one of the increase in numbers of older persons; it is a problem that requires planning and individualizing of retirement. It is a problem that might focus less on expected changes in mature people and more on what these people bring to retirement (20). The opportunity for continuing education for vocational, avocational, or aesthetic purposes can make the lives of older people more productive and satisfying to themselves and to society. One of the encouraging signs on the educational horizon is the fact that an increasing number of universities are developing programs in gerontology, the study of problems of the aged.

Changing Status of Women

In 1972 over 40 percent of married women with children under 18 years of age were in the labor force—an increase of almost 50 percent over 1960 (21). As this figure suggests, women are becoming an increasingly potent factor in the labor force. A number of developments have served to bring women as workers to new prominence, including (a) the relaxation of restrictions against entry into occupations traditionally viewed as masculine strongholds; (b) vast changes in the occupational structure that have seen the displacement of many unskilled jobs requiring sheer physical labor by others demanding general education and special skills; (c) the spread of part-time employment and the equalization of job opportunities for single and married women; (d) the changing attitudes toward family roles; and (e) the establishment of day-care centers.

Part of the change in the role of women stems from current patterns of family size and spacing of children. More women are completing their childbearing in the early years of marriage. This fact, when coupled with a tendency to marry at an earlier age, has produced a dramatic change in the career patterns of married women. For increasing thousands of young women, the choice is no longer between career and family but toward alternatives that combine marriage and family responsibilities with very real, if interrupted, commitments to career opportunities outside the home (22). Also linked to woman's increased participation is the divorce rate; that is, more women must work to support themselves and their families.

Federal antidiscrimination laws and statutes have, more recently, resulted in the redesignation of job titles previously restricted to male or female workers. For example, the job title "foreman" has been changed to "blue-collar supervisor" in the standardized job nomenclature. Another evidence of the equalization of job opportunities for women has been the increased recruitment by business and industry of qualified females for executive level positions.

Federal laws have acted to some extent to mitigate the effects of age and sex discrimination in employment. In 1963, the Equal Pay Act, an amendment to the Fair Labor Standards Act, provided that no employer may discriminate solely on the basis of sex in determining the wage rates of men and women who are doing equal work under similar conditions. In the following year, a national policy of fair employment practices was set forth in the Civil Rights Act. Title VII, Equal Employment Opportunity, provides that in their hiring and training practices, employers, employment agencies, and unions may not discriminate on the basis of race, color, religion, national origin, or sex. The Age Discrimination in Employment Act of 1967 prohibits age discrimination by employers, employment agencies, and labor unions against individuals between the ages of 40 and 65. The purpose of this act is to promote the employment of older persons based on their ability rather than on their age, to prohibit arbitrary age discrimination in employment, and to help employers and workers find ways of meeting problems arising from the impact of age on employment. Title IX of the Vocational Education Amendments of 1972 prohibits discrimination on the basis of sex in federally funded vocational programs.

Employment Trends

Employment patterns have shifted considerably over the years and are expected to continue to do so. During the 1970s eight out of every ten jobs will not require a college degree, a fact that emphasizes the importance of vocational-technical education. The following section provides an overview of employment prospects for the principal occupational groups as they are expected to occur between 1972 and 1985, as projected by the Bureau of Labor Statistics of the U.S. Department of Labor (23).

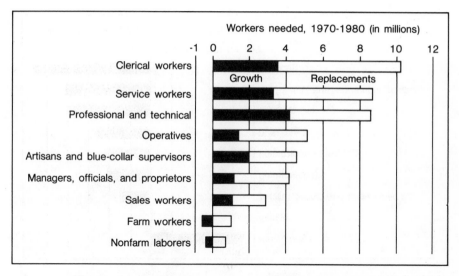

Figure 1.1 Replacement and growth needs. Source: Bureau of Labor Statistics.

Replacement/Growth Needs

Although growth is a key indicator of future job outlook, as indicated in the following section, more jobs will be created between 1970 and 1980 from death, retirement, and other labor-force separations than from employment growth, as indicated in Figure 1.1.

Replacement needs will be particularly significant in occupations that have a large proportion of older workers and women. For example, clerical workers—second largest among the occupational groups—ranks first in replacement/growth needs. Although the amount of paper work in offices continues to proliferate, much of it is handled by part-time workers or by workers with ambitions to move into higher-paying management positions.

Furthermore, large occupations that experience little growth may offer more job openings than fast-growing small ones. An examination of Figure 1.1 indicates that among the major occupational groups, openings for operatives (semiskilled workers such as truck, bus, and taxi drivers, or factory workers) resulting from growth and replacement combined will be greater than openings for artisans and blue collar supervisors (carpenters, tool and die makers, machinists), although the rate of growth of artisans will be almost twice as rapid as that for operatives.

Growth Within Industries

The majority of our nation's workers are employed by those sectors of the economy that provide services—trade, government, finance, public

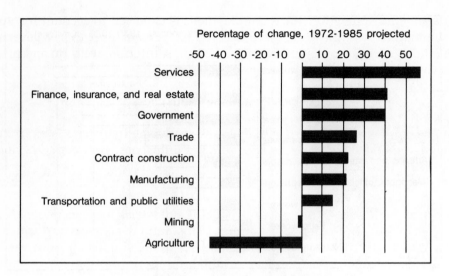

Figure 1.2 Tomorrow's jobs. Through the mid 1980s, employment growth will vary widely, by industry. Source: Bureau of Labor Statistics.

utilities, personal and business services. According to the U.S. Department of Labor, by 1985 approximately 58.8 million workers will be needed in the service-producing industries. This number represents an increase of 38 percent over the 1972 level. Such growth is a reflection of changes in personal and societal needs and organization. For example, the shift from a rural to an urban society has resulted in a demand for more city services such as garbage pickup and street maintenance, police and fire protection, public health departments, and better schools and educational personnel. Rising personal incomes and living standards have brought accompanying demands for improved urban and suburban services. And the increase in population has resulted in the necessity for *more* services.

While the growth rate is expected to be faster in the service-producing area than in goods-producing industries, the growth pattern will vary within both sectors as reflected in Figure 1.2.

Service-Producing Industries

Although trade is the largest division within the service-producing industries (19.8 million workers projected by 1980), the largest increase in growth between 1972 and 1985 will be in services, finance, and government employment. Manpower requirements in health services and business services such as accounting, data processing, and maintenance specifically contribute to the approximately 38 percent projected increase in services.

Finance is the smallest of the service-producing divisions, but it is experiencing rapid growth. By 1985 job employment is expected to have expanded 42 percent over the 1972 level.

Local and state government employment is expected to account for approximately two-thirds of the projected 42 percent growth, as governmental agencies providing education, health, sanitation, welfare, and protective services continue to increase.

Goods-Producing Industries

The employment growth rate in goods-producing industries is approximately one-third that of service-producing industries. Between 1972 and 1985, the increase is projected to be 13 percent (30 million workers) in goods-producing industries as compared to 38 percent in service-producing industries.

Since the late 1940s the goods-producing industries have accounted for less than half the nation's work force. This employment pattern can be attributed primarily to automation and technology and improved work skills of the labor force that have resulted in increased productivity without increased employment. Concurrently, a rising standard of living and a demand by our society for more services has contributed to the increase in numbers of service workers.

Manufacturing accounts for more than two-thirds of the goods-producing workers (22.1 million by 1985) and is expected to increase about 23 percent between 1972 and 1985 along with contract construction. Contingent on reduced inflation and a stable economy, one would project more industrial plants, commercial buildings, schools, houses, apartments, and government agencies to contribute to this growth.

Labor needs continue to decline in mining and agriculture because of labor-saving technological changes, with employment reduced by 2 percent in mining and 45 percent in agriculture by 1985, as compared to 1972.

These widely different employment patterns and changes have occurred and will continue among the goods-producing industries. Inflation and a tight-money market could slow the rate of growth even more in all goods-producing industries.

White-Collar vs. Blue-Collar Employment

Given a stable economy, total employment is expected to increase by 24 percent between 1972 and 1985. However, the demand for white-collar workers will be more than double that for blue-collar workers—37 percent as compared to 15 percent. The slower than average growth of blue-collar and farm workers reflects the expanded use of labor-saving machinery.

As American industry continues to become larger, more complex, and more mechanized, its occupational structure reflects these changes. Perhaps most significant has been the trend to fewer blue-collar and more white-collar workers. Since 1956 the number of white-collar workers has exceeded the number of blue-collar workers. Because the demand of our society for more services is likely to continue, we can expect a continuation of the rapid growth of the white-collar occupations (professional, managerial, clerical, and sales workers) through the 1980s.

Blue-collar workers—artisans, operatives, and laborers—can expect a slower than average growth; service workers will experience a faster than average growth. Farm workers can anticipate a further decline in employment, although widespread food shortages may stimulate this sector. Again, the effects of technology and automation will tend to stabilize employment in blue-collar occupations.

Outlook and Education

Employers are seeking people with higher levels of education because occupations are more complex and require greater skill. Furthermore, employment growth in the future will generally be fastest in those occupations requiring the most education and training.

High school education has become standard for American workers. However, many occupations are becoming increasingly complex and technical, requiring specific occupational training above the secondary level, such as that obtained in postsecondary vocational-technical schools and in community colleges.

Potential workers who do not receive good preparation for work will find competition for jobs more difficult in the years ahead. On the other hand, people who have acquired skills or good basic education will have a better chance for interesting work, good wages, and steady employment.

The intrinsic value of vocational education lies in its relationship to the social and economic development of the nation (24): "Vocational education is a social process concerned primarily with people and their part in doing the work society needs done; it is concerned with preparing people for work and with improving the work potential of the labor force." We have learned, also, that simply providing a person with job skills is not enough (25): "We must accept the belief that it is a responsibility of education to help young people find a meaningful role in society in which they can make interesting contributions and accept increasing responsibilities."

Summary

Vocational education is concerned with preparing people for work and with improving the training potential of the labor force. It covers any form of education, training, or retraining designed to prepare people to enter or to continue in paid employment in a recognized occupation. Career education, as a concept, represents a total system for the infusion of general education offerings so that they take on new meaning about careers and work. Career education rests on broad self-realization, social responsibility, and affective (value) components, whereas vocational education focuses more specifically on role, skill, and competence. Thus vocational education may be viewed as a component of the broader concept of career education.

Vocational preparation must always be viewed against the backdrop of the needs of society and the needs of the individual. While meeting the demands of the economy, the abilities of individuals must be used to the fullest. Individuals establish social identity and status through the occupational role. Meeting the internalized job needs of individuals is a crucial objective of vocational and career education.

Studies of human needs and job satisfaction among employees have given us insights into the psychology of occupational adjustment. Fraser classified these as material needs, companion needs, and ego needs. Maslow arranged individual needs into a hierarchy, ranging from the purely physiological needs to the need for self-actualization. He saw the occupation as a potential means of giving satisfaction to one's basic needs at all levels. McGregor developed a theory that contrasted a traditional and a current view of worker behavior. Herzberg identified "satisfiers" and "dissatisfiers" in the job environment and developed a theory that maximizes the need for job enrichment.

Vocational education has been affected by social problems such as automation, mobility, retirement, and the changing status of women. A changing technology emphasizes the need for an expanded scope of career education choices. The portion of the day devoted to earning a living is decreasing, and an individual may expect to experience several careers in a lifetime. Vocational curricula should facilitate occupational mobility as a means of keeping our supply of human resources in reasonable balance with society's requirements. The problem of retirement focuses on the need for planning and proper individualization to meet one's objectives. The equalization of job opportunities for women and changing attitudes toward family roles have resulted in career patterns for approximately one-half of all women.

Employment prospects maximize opportunities in the service-oriented industries as contrasted with the goods-producing sector of the economy. The fact that eight out of ten jobs do not require a college degree emphasizes the importance of vocational-technical education. Occupational forecasts project a continuation of the rapid growth of white-collar occupations. Replacement needs are particularly significant in occupations that have a large proportion of part-time workers or women. For example, the category of clerical workers—second largest among the occupational groups in size—ranks first in replacement-growth needs.

Employers are seeking people who have higher levels of education because jobs are more complex and require greater skill. In the long run, employment growth will be fastest in those occupations requiring the most education and training. For example, professional occupations will show the fastest growth throughout the 1970s and beyond. These facts contain significant implications for all phases of public education. The career education movement may be a means of effecting an optimal integration of what has commonly been thought of as the academic and vocational components of the curriculum.

Activities

For review

1 What is the relationship of vocational education to career education?

2 What are some of the basic or personal needs which motivate people? How do these needs affect one's choice of a vocation?

3 Contrast McGregor's *Theory X* and *Theory Y* as basic philosophies of worker behavior.

4 What is the essence of Herzberg's theory of job satisfaction?

5 Discuss the effects of automation and changing life styles on occupations.

6 What implications do the effects of automation and changing life styles hold for vocational and career education?

7 What are the beneficial effects of mobility on individuals and society? How does the level of one's education affect his or her mobility?

8 Explain why the increase in manpower needs has shifted from blue-collar to white-collar workers.

9 Why would an occupation with a large percentage of growth not necessarily be a better career choice than one with a smaller percentage of growth?

10 Discuss the effects of technology on (a) goods-producing industries, (b) service-oriented industries, (c) blue-collar workers, (d) white-collar workers.

11 Discuss the relationship between education and unemployment and youth and unemployment.

12 Compare Maslow's and Fraser's classifications of human needs. How are they alike? How are they different?

For discussion

1 Do you think that occupations and program training for occupations are becoming standardized nationwide? If not, should they be?

2 Can and should there be greater uniformity in vocational education programs as an aid to successful migration? How could this be achieved?

3 Why is it becoming increasingly difficult for individuals to find their identity through an occupation?

4 What three activities in your life do you think will give you the most satisfaction?

5 Defend or refute a mandatory retirement age for workers in business, industry, and education.

6 What role should labor trends and forecasts play in vocational education curricula at the secondary and postsecondary levels?

For exploration

1 Administer an instrument such as the Minnesota Job Satisfaction questionnaire to yourself or the class. Ask your instructor to assist you in interpreting the results.

2 Research the meaning of the Protestant work ethic. Then debate the following: "Resolved, that every able adult should experience some type of prolonged paid employment."

3 Identify three to five specific societal concerns in your community. How does each affect vocational education?

4 Review a research study in the area of job satisfaction and prepare a summary report for the class.

5 Select a job title and review it in the current *Occupational Outlook Handbook* and in an older edition. What changes, if any, are there in description of duties, educational requirements, and demand? How has technology influenced the job?

6 Prepare a report on federal legislation that has affected the role of women in the labor force.

References

1 Advisory Council on Vocational Education, *Vocational Education: The Bridge Between Man and His Work,* U.S. Department of Health, Education and Welfare, Office of Education (Washington, D.C.: Government Printing Office, 1968), p. v.

2 Keith Goldhammer and Robert E. Taylor, *Career Education—Perspective and Promise* (Columbus: Charles E. Merrill Publishing Company, 1972), p. 4.

3 G. A. Cleeton, *Making Work Human* (Yellow Springs, Ohio: Antioch Press, 1949).

4 M. D. Vernon, "The Drives Which Determine Choice of a Career," in *British Journal of Educational Psychology,* Vol. 8, 1938, pp. 1–15.

5 I. Hendrick, "Work and the Pleasure Principle," *Psychoanalytic Quarterly,* Vol. 12, 1943, pp. 311–29.

6 John M. Fraser, *Psychology: General-Industrial-Social*, Third Edition (London: Pitman Publishing Company, 1971), pp. 72–73. (Reproduced by permission)

7 A. H. Maslow, *Motivation and Personality* (Boston: Harper and Row, 1954).

8 Henry Borow, ed., *Man in a World of Work* (Boston: Houghton Mifflin Company, 1964), p. xv.

9 P. A. Witty and H. C. Lehman, "Drive—A Neglected Trait in the Study of the Gifted," in *Psychological Review*, Vol. 34, 1926, pp. 364–76.

10 Douglas McGregor, *The Human Side of Enterprise* (New York: McGraw-Hill Book Company, Inc., 1960), pp. 33–57.

11 Fred Herzberg, *Work and the Nature of Man* (Cleveland: World Publishing Company, 1966).

12 John M. Fraser. See Ref. 6, p. 83.

13 E. Ginzberg et al, *Occupational Choice* (New York: Columbia University Press, 1951), p. 217.

14 Nancy Morse and Robert Weiss, "Function and Meaning of Work and the Job," in *Vocational Behavior: Readings in Theory and Research*, ed. Donald G. Zytowski (New York: Holt, Rinehart and Winston, 1968), pp. 7–16.

15 Dael Wolfle, *The Uses of Talent* (Princeton, N.J.: Princeton University Press, 1968), p. 80.

16 Lee Taylor, *Occupational Sociology* (New York: Oxford University Press, 1968), p. 80.

17 Alvin Toffler, *Future Shock* (New York: Bantam Books, Inc., 1971), p. 83.

18 Carrol H. Miller, "Historical and Recent Perspectives on Work and Vocational Guidance," in *Career Guidance for a New Age*, ed. Henry Borow (Boston: Houghton Mifflin Company, 1973), pp. 23–24. (Reproduced by permission)

19 Davis Kingsley, "Urbanization—Changing Patterns of Living," in *The Changing American Population*, ed. Hoke S. Simpson (New York: Institute of Life Insurance, 1962), p. 19.

20 Lloyd H. Lofquist and Rene V. Davis, *Adjustment to Work—A Psychological View of Man's Problems in a Work-Oriented Society* (New York: Appleton-Century Crofts, 1969), p. 80.

21 Carrol H. Miller. See Ref. 18, pp. 33–34. (Paraphrased and reproduced by permission)

22 Donald H. Blocker, "Social Change and the Future of Vocational Guidance," in *Career Guidance for a New Age,* ed. Henry Borow (Boston: Houghton Mifflin Company, 1973), p. 52.

23 U.S. Department of Labor, Bureau of Labor Statistics, Bulletin 1700, *Occupational Outlook Handbook* (Washington, D.C.: U.S. Government Printing Office, 1974–75 Edition), pp. 15–22.

24 Melvin L. Barlow, "Changing Goals," in *Vocational Education: Today and Tomorrow,* ed. Gerald G. Somers and J. Kenneth Little (University of Wisconsin: Center for Studies in Vocational and Technical Education, 1971), p. 11.

25 Grant Venn, *Man, Education and Manpower* (Washington, D.C.: American Association of School Administrators, 1970), p. 16.

Chapter 2

Historical Perspective

of

Vocational-Technical

Education

Introduction

Many factors have influenced the development of education in our nation, not the least of which is the heritage of America's early settlers. In spite of their widely divergent backgrounds, these early immigrants were strongly united on two beliefs. First, they believed in the worth of the individual and placed the dignity of the individual above the dignity of the masses. The belief "that government is best that governs least" has permeated the character of our government. The same is true with respect to government's role toward education. For many years the responsibility was left to local communities, states, and private groups to provide for the education of citizens. Even in the later decades of the twentieth century, local communities are continuing to strive to maintain control of their schools.

The second strong belief shared by the early settlers was the notion that individuals should be free to earn their livelihoods in whatever way proved most profitable. This belief formed the backbone of the free enterprise system, with profit as the primary motivating force. An important notion of this system was that the role of government in such areas as business, religion, the home, and education should be limited. But as the population increased and with it the complexity of life, government became more and more powerful in its efforts to protect the freedom of individuals. The quest for profit and the necessity for competition in business and industry had limited the extent to which these institutions could cope with problems of the poor. As a result the national government assumed more and more responsibility for regulating the lives of the nation's citizens in the attempt to provide equal opportunity for all.

As the nation changed from a predominantly agrarian to a highly industrialized economy, vast social, educational, religious, and cultural changes were taking place. All of these changes were reflected in the national legislation relating to education. For this reason, it seems appropriate for us to look at the historical development of the role of the federal government vis à vis the education of its citizens.

The social, religious, and business institutions that might have dealt successfully with many of the nation's problems neglected to do so. In effect, the failure of these institutions to deal successfully with these problems forced the federal government to fill the vacuum. As Commager (1) vividly illustrates:

□ . . . for a century and a half almost every major reform in our political and social system has come about through the agency of the national government and over the opposition of powerful vested interests, states, and local communities. . . . It is the national government that freed the slaves . . . gave blacks the vote, guaranteed them political and civil rights . . . gave the suffrage to women . . . extended the suffrage to those over 18 . . . composed a one-man, one-vote rule on reluctant states . . . provided labor with a Bill of Rights, wiped out child labor, regulated hours and set minimum wages . . . launched the campaign to conserve the national resources . . . provided Social Security . . . brought about medicaid and medicare . . . imposed "due process of law" on local police authorities . . . set standards for education at all levels.

Commager also points out that the national government has been able to take all of these actions because the problems involved are national, not local, in scope. When the people felt the need for national direction and unity with respect to educational problems, they turned to the national government for leadership.

Federal legislation in the field of education can be classified into three developmental stages. The first stage, comprising those legislative enactments prior to 1900, may be called a period of little or no federal legislative involvement. The second stage, 1900–1960, was a period of rapid economic and industrial development and can be characterized as a period of conflict in the beliefs of the American people—conflict between the belief that the government that governs least is best and the belief that it is necessary for the national government to assure the best kind of education for all individuals. The belief was developing during this period that it is the responsibility of the national government to see that people are trained to operate the complex machinery necessary to provide the material and service needs of the nation's people. As a result there were a number of education acts passed by the national government, legislation that was characterized by an increasing yet still limited role of the national government in the field of education.

The third developmental stage began in 1960 when the federal government appeared to be entering fully into the educational processes in partnership with the states, local governments, and private institutions. For the first time the government seemed to be intentionally influencing, regulating, and controlling in an attempt to assure that individuals acquire the knowledge, skills, and attitudes needed to develop and maintain careers.

In the pages that follow we will examine in turn the legislation of each of these stages.

Legislation Prior to 1900

In limiting the powers of the federal government to those powers specifically provided in the United States Constitution, the Tenth Amendment—in effect since 1791—assured that each state would have the responsibility for educating its citizens. Even so, the federal government realized that the security and welfare of the nation as a whole lay in the ability of an educated citizenry to govern itself. It tried to make some provision for the education of citizens so that they would be competent to govern themselves.

Land Ordinance of 1785
and Northwest Ordinance of 1787

The federal government's first participation in education came indirectly in the form of laws governing the settlement of new territories in the West. In the passage of the Ordinance of 1785, Congress required that certain Western lands be divided into six-mile-square townships, which were then to be subdivided into thirty-six sections, with the sixteenth section set aside for the support of education (2). In the passage of the Ordinance of 1787, Congress specified (3): "Religion, morality, and knowledge being necessary to good government and the happiness of mankind, schools and the means of education shall be forever encouraged." By the time that Ohio, the first state in these new Western territories, was admitted to the Union, the practice of setting aside the sixteenth section of each township to support education was firmly established. Without entering directly into the education of the various states, the federal government through these two acts expressed an interest in the education of the nation's citizens.

Morrill Acts and the Hatch Act

During the nation's first century of growth, its industrial and agricultural development depended primarily on the practical, trial-and-error methods of men carrying on these activities and on their intellectual capacity to be more often right than wrong. Because the purposes of higher education were primarily to prepare men to enter the ministry and law, the pressing needs of the country to apply scientific procedures to the use and development of its natural resources for industry and agriculture were generally ignored, except for attempts on a very small scale in some states. The purposes of grade-school education were primarily to teach reading, writing, arithmetic, and religion and to prepare pupils to enter college in preparation for entering the ministry or law.

In the first half of the nineteenth century a few institutions were established that gave indirect opportunities for students to prepare for other more practical occupations, but these institutions were slow in developing and could not meet the expanding needs of the nation. As it became more evident with the passage of time that the nation's natural resources were being used at a rapid rate and that the need was pressing to prepare individuals for industrial and agricultural careers, the government acted. The Morrill Act of 1862 was the first legislation passed by the national government to support vocational education (4). Proposed by Congressman Justin Smith Morrill of Vermont, the act granted 30,000 acres of land to each state for each senator and representative it had in Congress. Income from the sale of such lands by the states would be used to create and maintain agricultural and mechanical arts colleges. With the passage of this act, the federal government made it possible for many private citizens who could not otherwise do so to prepare themselves for practical careers in agriculture and industry while at the same time acquiring the cultural and intellectual attributes associated with a general education. Institutions of higher education receiving support under the Morrill Act of 1862 came to be known as land-grant colleges because their financial support for vocational programs came primarily from the sale of land provided in the act. This legislation is referred to by Commager (5) as ". . . the most important piece of legislation on behalf of education ever passed."

Additional support for these institutions was later provided through the Second Morrill Act of 1890. This Act provided each land-grant institution with an additional $15,000 annually. The work of these institutions in preparing individuals for careers in agriculture and industry was further supported by the passage of the Hatch Act in 1887. This Act provided $15,000 annually to each state to establish agricultural experiment stations. Such stations worked closely with land-grant institutions to provide help to farmers and to upgrade the nation's agricultural methods.

The Morrill Acts of 1862 and 1890 and the Hatch Act of 1887 advanced the cause of agricultural and industrial education and research in the several states. New agricultural and mechanical arts colleges were established, and some established colleges expanded their curricula to include more practical studies in agriculture and industry. In addition those acts set a precedent for future involvement of the federal government in education. Through various amendments and additions these Acts continue their influence.

Legislation Between 1900 and 1960

The federal government was much more reluctant to interfere with the rights of states and local communities to provide education at the elementary and secondary levels than it was at the college level. Prior to 1900 the Ordinances of 1785 and 1787 were the only federal acts that affected education at the elementary and secondary levels. However, to show its interest in the education of American citizens in general, the federal government established the United States Office of Education in 1867. The Office of Education was established essentially as a collecting and disseminating agency for educational information. Although its role in education has been greatly expanded, it continues to provide a means of evaluating the effectiveness of educational activities. Although several other attempts were made to pass legislation affecting vocational education below the college level prior to 1900, it was not until the second decade of the twentieth century that such legislation was enacted. The principle of states' rights was too firmly established; the states and local communities were afraid that federal legislation would mean federal control. It was felt that federal control would mean the loss to the states and local communities of the right to determine who should go to school and what should be taught.

By 1900 the nation was beginning to feel that the multiplicity of educational standards, objectives, and beliefs that resulted from the relative federal inaction was having serious effects on the welfare of the nation. Under academic oriented curricula, the nation's schools were not meeting the needs of many school-age individuals. Drop outs were excessive. Industry was finding it costly to train its own workers. The ability of industry to mass-produce goods was effecting a decline in the classic apprenticeship system as the primary method of developing highly skilled artisans. By assigning workers to perform only one small part of a job, industry could increase production with fewer skilled workers. Under these conditions, the nation was creating a highly uneducated, highly unmotivated class of citizens who, as they reached adulthood, became more and more of a burden to the nation rather than productive, contributing citizens.

The nation's leaders began to see the need for a better educated citizenry to cope with the myriad of twentieth-century problems related to population, industrialization, urbanization, automation, and the need for more skilled workers. The clamor began for public educational institutions to perform this training. Noting the lack of attention to these problems on the part of states, local governments, and private institutions, Congress enacted a series of acts that vastly expanded the concept of federal assistance. We will discuss the more important of these acts as they relate to vocational education.

Smith-Hughes Act

The first federal enactment designed to ease the nation's dilemma was Public Law 64–347, known as the Smith-Hughes Act of 1917 (6). The Act was sponsored by Senator Hoke Smith and Representative Dudley Hughes, both from Georgia. Passage of this law followed several years of concerted efforts by professional agricultural and industrial organizations, by congressmen and senators from several states introducing numerous bills and resolutions, and by study commissions to evaluate the state of the art in vocational education. The work of the Commission on Industrial and Technical Education (Douglas Commission of Massachusetts) and the National Society for the Promotion of Industrial Education were highly influential in providing leadership and guidelines for development (7). The Smith-Hughes Act provided funds for three areas of vocational education at the secondary level—agriculture, trade and industry, and home economics. Funds were also provided for the training of teachers in these fields, and provisions were made for the study of the need for commercial education.

This example of the federal government's concern for the preparation of the nation's young people for productive adulthood established another precedent for future generations to follow. Although the provisions were narrow and specific, they were forward-reaching and considered appropriate in 1917.

To pay salaries of teachers, supervisors, or directors of agricultural subjects for fiscal year ending June 30, the Act made the following appropriations:

Years	Funds (in millions)
1918	$ .5
1919	.75
1920	1
1921	1.25
1922	1.5
1923	1.75
1924	2
1925	2.5
1926	3 (and for each year thereafter)

These funds were allotted to the various states on the basis of the proportion of the state's rural population to the total rural population of the nation. The Act also allotted to each state a minimum of $5000 through 1923 and a minimum of $10,000 thereafter.

Identical amounts were provided to pay salaries of teachers, supervisors, or directors of trade, home economics, and industrial subjects. These funds were allotted to the various states on the basis of the proportion of the state's urban population to the total urban population in the nation. A minimum of $5000 through 1923 (after 1923, $10,000) was allotted to each state to carry out the provisions of this section of the Act regardless of a state's urban population. Not more than 20 percent of these funds could be used to pay salaries of teachers of home economics.

To pay for the preparation of teachers, supervisors, and directors of agricultural subjects and teachers of trade and industrial and home economics subjects for the year ending June 30:

Years	Funds (in millions)
1918	$ .5
1919	.7
1920	.9
1921	1 (and for each year thereafter)

These funds were allotted to each state on the basis of the proportion of the state's population to total population of the nation. A minimum of $5000 was allotted to each state through 1919 and a minimum of $10,000 to each state after 1919, regardless of a state's population.

Please note that funds were appropriated in the Smith-Hughes Act to carry out the provisions in the Act. These funds were to be perpetual in nature. In most subsequent federal-aid-to-vocational-education legislation the funding has not been appropriated but rather has been authorized to be appropriated. Appropriations for funding have thus required separate legislative acts, and most often the appropriations to carry out the provisions do not equal the authorizations made in the acts.

The Smith-Hughes Act provided controls over the use and administration of these funds. To share in the funds, each state had to designate or to create a state board with power to administer the funds in cooperation with the federal board that was also created by the Act. The Act designated that the Federal Board of Vocational Education would be composed of the Secretaries of Agriculture, Commerce, Labor, the United States Commissioner of Education, and three citizens to be appointed by the President and approved by the Senate. One of these persons was to represent manufacturing and commercial interests, one agriculture, and one labor. Members were to receive the sum of $5000 annually. Their duties were to make studies pertaining to the establishment of vocational schools and to the instruction in agriculture, trades and industries, commerce and commercial pursuits, and home economics. An annual appropriation of $200,000 was made for these studies and to administer the Act.

The Smith-Hughes Act also required each state board to prepare plans showing how it expected to use its allotment of funds, the kinds of schools and equipment in use, courses of study, methods of instruction, qualifications of teachers, qualifications of agricultural supervisors and directors, plans for training teachers, and plans for supervising agricultural education. Further, each state was required to submit an annual report of the work done, showing receipts and expenditures. The Act provided that funds allotted for salaries of teachers and for the training of teachers must be matched by the state.

Education for trade, home economics, and industrial education must be provided in schools or classes under public supervision or control. The purpose of such education was to fit students for employment. The education had to be of less than college level for persons over fourteen years of age. It provided for cooperative programs for those students not employed and provided that one-third of the funds to pay salaries must be applied to the salaries of teachers of part-time students already employed. The Act further provided that the Federal Board of Vocational Education make an annual report to Congress on the administration of the Act.

George-Reed Act

The George-Reed Act of 1929 (Public Law 70–702) authorized funds for home economics education and agricultural education (8). The Act authorized appropriations to supplement funds provided under the Smith-Hughes Act. These appropriations were to be divided equally between home economics and agriculture, for a five-year period to be awarded on June 30 of each year as follows:

Years	Funds (in millions)
1930	$ .5
1931	1
1932	1.5
1933	2
1934	2.5

The authorization did not extend beyond fiscal year 1934. The way of allotting funds under the George-Reed Act was different from the way funds were awarded under the Smith-Hughes Act. Agricultural education funds were allotted on the basis of farm population rather than rural population; home economics education funds were allotted on the basis of rural population rather than urban population.

George-Ellzey Act

The George-Ellzey Act of 1934 (Public Law 73–245) replaced the expiring George-Reed Act (9). It authorized funds as provided in the George-Reed Act through fiscal years 1935, 1936, and 1937, except for an annual authorization of $3 million. Whereas funds authorized by the George-Reed Act were to be divided equally between home economics and agriculture, funds authorized by the George-Ellzey Act were to be divided equally among agriculture, trade and industry, and home economics education. Funds for agriculture and home economics were allotted on the same basis as in the George-Reed Act. Funds for trade and industrial education were allotted on the basis of the proportion of the state's nonfarm population to the total United States nonfarm population, rather than on the basis of the proportion of the state's urban population to the total United States urban population, as provided in the Smith-Hughes Act. The funds in this act were authorized in addition to the continuing funds appropriated in the Smith-Hughes Act.

George-Deen Act

The George-Deen Act of 1936 (Public Law 74–673) replaced the expiring George-Ellzey Act with a continuing authorization of more than $14 million annually, beginning with the 1938 fiscal year (10). For the first time, distributive education was authorized as an appropriation—in the amount of $1.2 million annually. An authorization of appropriations of $12 million annually was made to be divided equally among agricultural education, home economics, and trade and industry. Funds were allotted as in the George-Ellzey Act. Funds for distributive education were allotted to each state on the basis of the proportion of the state's population to the total United States population and territories. This is the first act in which federal funds for vocational education were provided for the education of people in territories held by the United States. Authorization was also made to provide an additional $1 million for teacher training (above that provided in the Smith-Hughes Act). Through this act the role of the federal government in vocational education was increased substantially.

George-Barden Act

The George-Barden Act of 1946 (Public Law 79–586) expanded the role of the federal government in vocational education by an even greater amount than did the George-Deen Act (11). One of the major factors contributing to this legislation was the need to provide a means for thousands of returning World War II veterans to acquire employable skills in a rapidly expanding economy. The George-Barden Act amended the George-Deen Act to include additional authorized appropriations of $10 million annually for agriculture, $8 million for home economics, $8 million for trade and industry, and $2.5 million for distributive education. From a beginning appropriation in 1917 under the Smith-Hughes Act of $1.5 million for salaries and training of vocational teachers, supervisors, and directors, the federal government had expanded its annual appropriations to over $28 million. Minimum annual allotments to individual states to carry out provisions of vocational education were increased from $10,000 to $40,000 in agricultural education, home economics edu-

Table 2.1   Federal Appropriations to Vocational Education (in millions)*

Acts	Agriculture	Trade industry	Home economics	Distributive education	Total
Smith-Hughes Act (by 1926)	$ 3	$3	—	—	$ 6
for teacher training, etc, in all areas					1
George-Reed Act (by 1934)	1.25		$1.25	—	2.5
George-Ellzey Act (by 1937)	1	1	1	—	3
George-Deen Act (by 1938)	4	4	4	$1.2	13.2
for teacher training, etc, in all areas					1
George-Barden Act (by 1946)	10	8	8	2.5	28.5

* The amounts for Smith-Hughes are annual appropriations; all other amounts are annual authorizations. The amounts for each act after Smith-Hughes are supplements to Smith-Hughes, and each supplemental Act replaced its predecessor. The year following each Act indicates when the maximum funding shown was reached.

cation, and trade and industrial education, with an additional annual minimum of $15,000 for distributive education.

Greater flexibility was provided as to the use of these funds. States could use funds for salaries and expenses of state directors of vocational education and vocational counselors, for work experience programs, for youth group activities, and for equipment and supplies. Significant amendments were made to the George-Barden Act in 1956. Practical nursing was added to the federally supported vocational program with an an-

Table 2.2   Methods of Allotment of Federal Funds to States*

Acts	Agriculture	Trade industry	Home economics	Distributive education
Smith-Hughes Act	rural	urban	urban	—
George-Reed Act	farm	urban	rural	—
George-Ellzey Act	farm	nonfarm	rural	—
George-Deen Act	farm	nonfarm	rural	total
George-Barden Act	farm	nonfarm	rural	total

* Allotments were made to states according to the ratio a state's population (either rural, urban, farm, nonfarm, or total) held to the nation's population (in the same categories). Allotments for teacher training funds under the Smith-Hughes and George-Deen Acts were determined according to the state's total population to the national population.

nual authorization of $5 million to 1961. Area vocational programs were provided an annual authorization of $15 million to 1962.

These legislative acts illustrate an intermediate stage of legislation as the federal government moved toward a total commitment to assisting the states in the development of vocational education. Data in Table 2.1 show the pattern of funding in these acts, and data in Table 2.2 show the methods of allotting these funds.

Other Legislation

During the period of rapid industrial, technological, and economic growth and development following World War II, the federal government assumed more and more responsibility and authority toward all aspects of society. In addition to the vocational education acts that have been reviewed here, many other acts were passed between 1900 and 1960 that were aimed primarily toward general education but that had some effect on vocational education. Some of these acts should be briefly reviewed.

The Fess-Kenyon Act was passed in 1920. Known as the Industrial Rehabilitation Act, it provided federal aid for the vocational rehabilitation of industry-disabled persons. This Act was preceded by legislation in 1918 that had provided for the rehabilitation of disabled World War I veterans. Although the legislation covered only four years, it was the beginning of a series of supplemental acts. The first appropriation for fiscal year ending June 30, 1921, for $.75 million, had grown to an annual appropriation of $3.5 million in 1939. The provisions for administration of the Vocational Rehabilitation Acts and for the participation in them by states (and eventually territories when allotments were made to them) were similar to the provisions for vocational education under Smith-Hughes and subsequent acts. Subsequent amendments included the LaFollette-Barden Act of 1943, which provided for the rehabilitation of war-disabled civilians. The Vocational Rehabilitation Amendments of 1954 authorized new funds and new ways of allotting these funds. By 1957, authorization was made for an annual appropriation of $65 million for vocational rehabilitation.

Another legislative act that affected the direction and development of vocational education was the Servicemen's Readjustment Act of 1944. Known as the GI Bill of Rights, the purpose of this act was to assist World War II veterans to readjust to civilian life. The Act subsidized the cost of education and included subsistence for thousands of veterans. Few requirements were placed on the veterans; they simply were to select the kind of training and/or education they wanted, apply for admission to a recognized training program, and maintain the academic standards necessary to continue in the program. The veteran was allowed time for participation in accordance with the time he had been in service. Subsequent legislation passed along these benefits to veterans of the Korean War and the Vietnam War.

The National Defense Education Act of 1958 was passed following the Soviet Union's placement of the first man-made earth satellite into space, Sputnik I, in 1957. The nation felt that this breakthrough indicated that the United States was behind in the sciences, and Congress acted quickly to correct the situation. Vocational education benefited in that the act provided for the training of highly skilled defense technicians in vocational education programs not of college level, and it provided for counseling and guidance programs to identify and encourage able students.

Other federal activities between 1900 and 1960 that have assisted the development of vocational education in the United States include the National Youth Administration, founded in 1935 to provide job training and part-time work for unemployed youths; the Civilian Conservation Corps, founded in 1933 to help unemployed young men obtain work; and the National Science Foundation, created to support research and education primarily in the mathematical, physical, engineering, biological, and medical sciences.

Legislation Since 1960

The 1960s were years characterized by turmoil—the Vietnam War, internal conflict from social and religious strife, and the frustrating pace of life in a highly complex society. Out of this turmoil grew a social consciousness regarding society's problems. There was a growing consensus that the federal government should act to solve problems of unemployment, of the rising cost of living, and of the desperate need for qualified skilled workers in business and industry. Whereas the nation was beginning to feel the pinch of having too few trained technicians, it was also beginning to see that it had oversold the necessity of a college education. In spite of the steadily increasing involvement of the federal government and the states in more and more expensive programs for vocational education, the problems of unemployment and underemployment continued to grow. There was a growing concern that the nation's educational system was not meeting the needs of the people. The dominant learning activities in the nation's public schools continued to center around preparation for a college education. With the thrust of educational efforts continuing in this direction, the nation's drop-out problems multiplied; welfare problems mounted as people developed the attitude that "the government will care for me." Growing numbers of people who had no skills, no self-respect, and no values plagued the nation's inner cities and countryside.

One of the first efforts in the 1960s to correct these ills through vocational education was the Manpower Development and Training Act of 1962. This Act was designed to train unemployed workers for available jobs and to retrain underemployed workers for jobs with greater responsibilities. A new thrust was being made toward correcting the country's problems with the provision requiring the Secretary of Labor to make studies of the needs, uses, and development of the nation's manpower.

By the early 1960s the country was ready for massive assaults by the federal government on the problems of unemployment and underemployment. The nation was demanding a reorientation of education to provide for vocational education as well as for college preparation. A panel of consultants on vocational education was appointed at the request of President John F. Kennedy in 1961 to review and reevaluate federal legislation for the purpose of improving vocational education. Much of what was recommended by this panel became a part of the Vocational Education Act of 1963 (12).

Vocational Education Act of 1963

The Vocational Education Act of 1963 (Public Law 88–210) represented the beginning of the federal government's total commitment to vocational education (13). It was the purpose of this Act to maintain, extend, and improve existing vocational education programs; to develop new vocational programs; and to provide part-time employment necessary for youths to continue their vocational training on a full-time basis. This legislation was designed to provide all persons with ready access to vocational training or retraining in areas for which they were suited and for which there would be employment opportunities. For the first time the needs of people were emphasized rather than the labor needs of the nation.

The nature of the federal government's commitment to vocational education is exemplified by the fact that authorized appropriations in the Vocational Education Act of 1963 were more than double the authorizations of the George-Barden Act of 1946 and more than eight times the appropriations made under the Smith-Hughes Act in 1926. Appropriations for the fiscal years ending June 30 were authorized as follows:

Years	Funds (in millions)
1964	$ 60
1965	118.5
1966	177.5
1967	225

Fifty years after the first appropriations of $1.5 million for vocational education under the Smith-Hughes Act, the federal government authorized appropriations that were nearly 150 times greater. Ninety percent of the authorized funds were to be allotted to the states on the basis of formulas designed to consider the number of persons in various age groups needing vocational education and the per capita income in each state. The formula that was used required that 50 percent of the allotted funds be used for the 15–19 age group, 20 percent for the 20–25 age group, 15 percent for the 25–65 age group, and 5 percent for all groups regardless of age. A minimum allotment of $10,000 was stipulated for each state.

The funds were to be used, under an approved state plan, for the following purposes:

1 vocational education for high school students

2 vocational education for persons who had completed or left high school and who were available for full-time study in preparation for entering the labor market

3 vocational education for persons who had already entered the labor market and needed training or retraining to achieve stability or advancement, except those persons who were receiving training allowances under the Manpower Development and Training Act of 1962, the Area Redevelopment Act, or the Trade Expansion Act of 1962

4 vocational education for persons with academic, socioeconomic, or other handicaps that prevented them from succeeding in the regular vocational education program

5 construction of area vocational education school facilities

6 ancillary services and activities to assure quality in all vocational education programs, such as teacher training and supervision; program evaluation; special demonstration and experimental programs; development of instructional materials; and state administration, leadership, and evaluation

At least one-third of a state's allotment for the first five years was to be used for construction of area vocational school facilities for training persons who had completed or left high school and were available for training to enter the labor market. Three percent of the funds were to be used for ancillary services unless a state convinced the Commissioner of Education that it could meet its purposes on less. Ten percent of the funds appropriated were to be used by the commissioner to support research and training programs.

The Act specified that each participating state should have a state plan for vocational education, and state matching funds were required. The Act defined vocational education as (14):

☐ . . . *vocational or technical training or retraining which is given in schools or classes (including field or laboratory work incidental thereto) under public supervision and control or under contract with a State board or local educational agency, and is conducted as part of a program designed to fit individuals for gainful employment as semiskilled or skilled workers or technicians in recognized occupations (including any program designed to fit individuals for gainful employment in business and office occupations, and any program designed to fit individuals for gainful employment which may be assisted by Federal funds under the Vocational Education Act of 1946 and supplementary vocational education Acts, but excluding any program to fit individuals for employment in occupations which the Commissioner determines, and specifies in regulations, to be generally considered professional or as requiring a baccalaureate or higher degree). Such term includes vocational guidance and counseling in connection with such training, instruction related to the occupation for which the student is being trained or necessary for him to benefit from such training, the training of persons engaged as, or preparing to become vocational education teachers, teacher-trainees, supervisors, and directors for such training, travel of students and vocational education personnel, and the acquisition and maintenance and repair of instructional supplies, teaching aids and equipment, but does not include the construction or initial equipment of buildings or the acquisition or rental of land.*

The Act required that an advisory committee on vocational education be established in the United States Office of Education. The responsibility of this committee was to advise the Commissioner of Education on the preparation of general regulations, on policy matters relating to administration of the Act, and on procedures governing approval of state plans. The Act also amended the George-Barden Act and the Smith-Hughes Act so that there was more flexibility as to the use of funds. For example, funds allotted for agricultural education might be used for vocational education in any occupation involving knowledge and skills in agricultural subjects. It did not require that such occupation involve work on the farm or in the farm home, and such education could be provided without supervised or directed practice on the farm. This flexibility reflected new trends in agri-business activities. By defining programs designed to fit individuals for gainful employment in business and office occupations programs as vocational education, the Act gave direct federal support for the first time to business and office education. The Act also made permanent allotments to states for extension of practical nurse training. In addition to the advisory committee, the Act required the Secretary of Health, Education, and Welfare to appoint a 12-member advisory council on vocational education in 1966 to review the administration of programs. The council was to cease to exist after January 1, 1968, by which time it was to have reported its findings and recommendations. Such a council was to be appointed periodically thereafter.

The Vocational Education Act of 1963 spelled out in detail the provisions for approving work-study programs for persons aged 15 to 20. Funds were to be allotted on the basis of the proportion of each state's population in this group as compared to the total population of this age group in the United States. A state was required to submit a supplementary plan for administration of such a program. The Act authorized appropriations for work-study programs as follows, for each fiscal year ending June 30:

Years	Funds (in millions)
1965	$30
1966	50
1967	35
1968	35

These funds were not required to be matched for the first two years. Later, each state was required to contribute 25 percent of the funds necessary for the program. Students were limited to working 15 hours each school week and to earning $45 per month during school, except under special conditions.

The Act also provided that no department, agency, officer, or employee of the United States should exercise any direction, supervision, or control over the curriculum, program of instruction, administration, or personnel of any educational institution or school system.

Vocational Education Amendments of 1968

The 1968 Amendments to the Vocational Education Act of 1963 (Public Law 90–576) firmly entrenched the federal government's commitment to vocational education (15). In effect, this Act virtually cancelled all previous vocational education legislation except for the Smith-Hughes Act, which was retained for sentimental reasons as the first legislation passed by the federal government for secondary vocational education. Passage of this act appeared to illustrate a degree of national frustration, as the nation sought frantically for solutions to its growing ills. In spite of all the monies that had been channeled into activities designed to alleviate the problems of unemployment and underemployment, the problems continued to grow. New solutions would center around a reorientation of educational objectives, with equal emphasis placed on the preparation for work as well as on the preparation for higher education. It was felt that solutions should center on changing people's attitudes about work, helping people to see, to feel, and to think "dignity" in work, not just dignity in the professions. This Act authorized the appropriation of millions of additional dollars for vocational education in the attempt to find solutions to the nation's problems.

The Vocational Education Amendments are divided into three titles. Title I, Amendments to the Vocational Education Act of 1963; Title II, Vocational Education Leadership and Professional Development Amendment of the Higher Education Act of 1965; and Title III, Miscellaneous Provisions. The Act is summarized here so that the extent to which the federal government assumed responsibility for promoting vocational preparedness might be examined.

Title I is divided into nine parts—Part A, General Provisions; Part B, State Vocational Education Programs; Part C, Research and Training in Vocational Education; Part D, Exemplary Programs and Projects; Part E, Residential Vocational Education; Part F, Consumer and Homemaking Education; Part G, Cooperative Vocational Education Programs; Part H, Work-Study Programs for Vocational Education Students; and Part I, Curriculum Development in Vocational and Technical Education.

Data presented in Table 2.3 (comparing the authorizations of the 1968 Amendments and the Vocational Education Act of 1963) reveal the extensiveness of the increased involvement by the federal government in vocational education. Ninety percent of these funds were to be allocated to State Vocational Education Programs and 10 percent to Research and Training in Vocational Education. Allotments of these funds were to continue as provided in 1963.

The Amendments provided that the National Advisory Council be increased from 12 to 21 members to be appointed by the President, rather than by the Secretary of Health, Education and Welfare for three-year terms. The council became a permanent part of the federal government's control over the use of the funds to serve the nation's needs. Several reports have been issued by the National Advisory Council on Vocational Education. These reports have dealt individually with (a) the national attitude toward vocational education as a system designed for someone else's child; (b) the approach of federal funding to reduce the flow of untrained manpower into the pool of unemployment; (c) employment as an integral part of education; (d) the problems involved in local support, state plans, the lack of federal initiative, and the need for effective national planning for vocational education; (e) those forces that appeared to prevent the adoption of some of the recommendations of the first four reports; (f) counseling and guidance and what must be done to provide sound counseling systems; (g) vocational student organizations and their role in vocational and career education; and (h) a national policy on career education. Reports of the National Advisory Council have constituted a significant influence on vocational education legislation.

Similarities and differences of the possible uses of funds under the Vocational Education Act of 1963 and under the Amendments of 1968 are shown in Table 2.4. The extensiveness of the increased authorizations in general and the specifications of amounts to specific programs indicates the total commitment of the federal government to vocational education.

The Amendments of 1968 require much more detailed state plans and thus lead to considerably more control over local programs. For example, the plan must be prepared in consultation with the State Advisory Council. It must be based on several criteria: periodic evaluations of programs, services, and activities in terms of manpower needs and job opportunities; determination of needs of population groups by geographical locations; and ability of local communities to pay for education. Opportunity must also be given for persons to participate in a public hearing with respect to the state plan.

Table 2.3 Authorized Appropriations of the Vocational Education Act of 1963 and the Amendments of 1968 (in millions)*

1963 Act	1968 Amendments
for maintaining, improving, and extending existing programs and for developing new programs:	for state vocational education programs and for research and training:
$ 60 1964	$355 1969
118.5 1965	565 1970
177.5 1966	675 1971
225 each year thereafter	675 1972
	565 each year thereafter
for work-study and residential schools:	for the handicapped who cannot succeed in the regular vocational program:
$30 1965	$40 1969 and 1970
50 1966	for exemplary programs and projects:
35 1967	$15 1969
35 1968	57.5 1970
	75 1971
	75 1972
	for residential schools:
	$40 1969
	45 1970
	35 1971
	35 1972
	for consumer and homemaking education:
	$25 1970
	35 1971
	50 1972
	for cooperative vocational education programs:
	$20 1969
	35 1970
	50 1971
	75 1972
	for work-study programs:
	$35 1969
	35 1970
	for curriculum development:
	$ 7 1969
	10 1970
	for vocational education leadership and development:
	$25 1969
	35 1970

* Funds indicated are for fiscal year ending June 30.

Table 2.4   Use of Funds—Vocational Education Act of 1963 and Amendments of 1968

1963 Act	1968 Amendments
for vocational education programs for high school	for vocational education programs for high school students including programs designed to prepare them for advanced or highly skilled postsecondary vocational and technical education
for those who have completed or left high school	same
for those who have entered the labor market and who need training for stability*	same
vocational education for those who have academic, socioeconomic, or other handicaps	same
for construction of area vocational education school facilities	same
for ancillary services: teacher training and supervision, program evaluation, experimental programs, and development of instructional materials	same
(emphasis given to providing for the training of those who have completed or left high school and for construction of area vocational school facilities)	for vocational guidance and counseling for vocational training through arrangements with private vocational training institutions
ten percent annually used by Commissioner to make grants to colleges or other nonprofit agencies for research and training programs	ten percent annually used by commissioner and state board on an equal basis for research and training at least 10 percent of the allotment shall be for the handicapped who cannot succeed in a regular program

* Except for persons receiving training allowances under the Manpower Development and Training Act of 1962, the Area Redevelopment Act, or the Trade Expansion Act of 1962.

Under Part D of Title I, Exemplary Programs and Projects, provision is made to reduce the high level of youth unemployment—particularly those youth with academic, socioeconomic, or other handicaps—by providing occupational orientation and guidance. It is the purpose of this provision to stimulate new ways to create a bridge between school and earning a living. Section 143 (a)(2)(A) emphasizes the need to establish, operate, and evaluate exemplary programs designed to familiarize elementary and secondary school students with a broad range of occupations and the special skills that they required. The need to upgrade people in economically depressed areas and in areas of high unemployment in terms of their abilities to be intelligent consumers is emphasized in Part F, Consumer and Homemaking Education.

The 1968 Amendments made provision for the complexity of curriculum development caused by the diversity of occupational objectives, by variations due to geography, by differences in educational levels and types of programs, and by the wide range of occupations—agriculture, food processing and preparation, trade and industry, distribution and marketing, technical, public service, health services, business and office occupations. It was the purpose of Part I, Curriculum Development in Vocational and Technical Education, to assist states in developing curricula for new and changing positions and to coordinate improvements in and dissemination of existing curriculum materials.

Title II, Vocational Education Leadership and Professional Development Amendment of Higher Education Act of 1965, provided a way for experienced vocational educators to spend full time in advanced study for a period not to exceed three years. It provided opportunities to update occupational competencies of vocational education teachers through exchanges of personnel between vocational education programs and commercial, industrial, or other private or public employment and to provide programs of inservice teacher education and short-term institutes for vocational education personnel.

Title III dealt primarily with amendments to the Elementary and Secondary Education Act of 1965 and the Amendments of 1967 and the Adult Education Act of 1966. It required that the Commissioner of Education study the feasibility of consolidating all education programs funded by the federal government.

Other Legislation

During the 1960s the federal government became totally committed to the development of "our nation's most priceless resource"—education. Other acts that were not directly aimed at vocational education nevertheless contributed financially and in other ways to vocational efforts. Many vocational programs directly benefited from such legislation as the Elementary and Secondary Education Act of 1965 and its subsequent amendments (16). The purposes of this act were to bring better education to millions of educationally disadvantaged youth; put the best educational equipment, ideas, and innovations within reach of all students; advance the technology of teaching and the training of teachers; and provide incentive to those who wished to learn. In addition the act recognized the relationship between low achievers and poverty; the correspondence between quality teachers and instructional resources and effective teaching and learning; and the gap between current educational research and existing practices.

Other federal programs passed in the 1960s that supported education include:

Section 12 of the National Foundation on the Arts and the Humanities Act of 1965

Economic Opportunity Act of 1964

Educational Television Facilities Program of 1962

Higher Education Facilities Act of 1963

Higher Education Act of 1965, Education Professions Development Act

The Education Amendments of 1972 (Public Law 92–318) amended the Higher Education Act of 1965, the Vocational Education Act of 1963, the General Education Provisions Act, the Elementary and Secondary Education Act of 1965, and other Acts, in addition to making other provisions. One of the provisions of the 1972 Amendments, Section 1056 (b)(1)(D) of Title X, calls for the (17):

☐ . . . *development of a long-range strategy for infusing occupational education (including general orientation, counseling and guidance, and placement either in a job or in postsecondary occupational programs) into elementary and secondary schools on an equal footing with traditional academic education, to the end that every child who leaves secondary school is prepared either to enter productive employment or to undertake additional education at the postsecondary level, but without being forced prematurely to make an irrevocable commitment to a particular educational or occupational choice; . . .*

The Amendments define postsecondary occupational education as (18):

☐ . . . *education, training, or retraining (and including guidance, counseling, and placement services) for persons sixteen years of age or older who have graduated from or left elementary or secondary school, conducted by an institution legally authorized to provide postsecondary education within a State, which is designed to prepare individuals for gainful employment as semi-skilled or skilled workers or technicians or subprofessionals in recognized occupations (including new and emerging occupations), or to prepare individuals for enrollment in advanced technical education programs, but excluding any program to prepare individuals for employment in occupations which the Commissioner determines, and specifies by regulations, to be generally considered professional or which requires a baccalaureate or advanced degree.*

In addition the Amendments provided for the establishment of a Bureau of Occupational and Adult Education in the United States Office of Education. Title II incorporated industrial arts education into the definition of vocational education where it contributed to the purposes of vocational education. It also included volunteer firemen. The provisions of vocational education were extended through the year 1975. Consumer education, the lack of it and the need for it, received further attention in the Amendments of 1972. The Act encouraged and supported development of new improved curricula to prepare consumers for participation in the marketplace. It created the position of Director of Consumer Education in the Office of Education. The Amendments also dealt with assignment and transportation of students to school and with sex discrimination.

The most recent legislation, the Education Amendments of 1974 (Public Law 93–380), provided firm support to career education (19). In this Act Congress expressed the need for every person completing secondary school to be prepared for gainful or maximum employment according to ability. Congress also provided that each state and local educational agency should carry out a program in career education. The importance Congress attached to career education was further emphasized in the Act with the establishment of the Office of Career Education in the United States Office of Education. In addition, the National Advisory Council on Career Education was established to advise the Commissioner of Education on matters relating to the development, implementation, and evaluation of career education throughout the United States and to determine the need for future legislation.

Summary

This chapter has focused on the influence of federal legislation on the development of vocational-technical education. For purposes of study, the legislation was arbitrarily divided into three stages: (a) legislation passed prior to 1900, (b) legislation passed between 1900 and 1960, and (c) legislation passed since 1960.

Five major acts passed during the decades prior to 1900 that affected the development of federal legislation are presented in this chapter. The Land Ordinance of 1785 and the Northwest Ordinance of 1787 established the federal government's interest in the education of United States citizens. The Land Ordinance of 1785 required that newly developing territories set aside land for the support of education, and the Northwest Ordinance of 1787 encouraged the establishment of schools and the means of education. The Morrill Acts of 1862 and 1890 provided support to establish and maintain agricultural and mechanical arts colleges. The Hatch Act of 1887 provided funds for the establishment of agricultural experiment stations. These acts reflected the need for a more scientific approach to the development of agriculture and industry.

The period between 1900 and 1960 was characterized by rapid development of the technology necessary to support an expanding industry, and by social, civil, and economic strife. During this period two world wars took place, a major depression occurred, and the desegregation movement was started. Public educational institutions were more concerned with the intellectual development of individuals than they were in preparing individuals for work. During this period there was an increasing need for skilled workers, and the nation looked primarily to the federal government to provide a means for training skilled workers. The Smith-Hughes Act of 1917 was the first of a series of acts designed with this purpose in mind. The Act provided support for vocational education at the secondary level. It included support for agriculture, trade and industry, and home economics. Other acts passed during this period supporting vocational education included the George-Reed Act of 1929, George-Ellzey Act of 1934, George-Deen Act of 1936, George-Barden Act of 1946, Fess-Kenyon Act of 1920, LaFollette-Barden Act of 1943, Servicemen's Readjustment Act of 1944, and the National Defense Education Act of 1958. All of these acts were directed toward improving the education of individuals through vocational education, increasing the availability of skilled manpower, and hopefully attacking some of the social, civic, and economic ailments of the nation.

The third stage, the period since 1960, has been characterized by a total commitment of the federal government to vocational education—in partnership with the states, local governments, and private institutions, yet intentionally influencing, regulating, and controlling education. The federal government has been attempting, in its legislation, to assure that all individuals acquire the knowledge, skills, and attitudes needed to develop and to maintain careers. The legislation that has grown out of this total commitment includes the Manpower Development and Training Act of 1962, Vocational Education Act of 1963, Vocational Education Amendments of 1968, Elementary and Secondary Education Act of 1965, the Education Amendments of 1972, and the Education Act of 1974. The Vocational Education Act of 1963 brought most of the legislation passed prior to that time, except for the Smith-Hughes Act, into its provisions. With the legislation passed since 1960, the federal government has made a dedicated attempt to redirect the public education processes so that career development and preparation of individuals for work becomes as much a part of the goals, objectives, and activities of education as are intellectual development and the preparation of individuals for college.

Activities

For review

1 Identify two strong beliefs of early settlers of the United States that affected the role of government in education.

2 Why were states and local communities afraid of legislation by the federal government?

3 What belief is considered to be the backbone of the free enterprise system? *a person should be able to earn a living as he likes*

4 Why did Commager think it necessary for the federal government to become involved with educational problems?

5 Name legislative ordinances and acts prior to 1900 that proved significant to vocational education.

6 Why was the United States Office of Education established?

7 What was the first major legislation appropriating money for vocational education for secondary schools? *Smith-Hughes*

8 Who made up the Federal Board of Vocational Education as designated by the Smith-Hughes Act? *commerce, labor & agriculture*

9 What type of vocational education was provided by the (a) Smith-Hughes Act, (b) George-Reed Act, and (c) George-Ellzey Act?
H.E, T&I, Ag.   H.E. AG.   H.E, T&I & Ag
10 Under what act was distributive education first appropriated?
George-Dean
11 On what basis were funds for distributive education allotted to each state?

12 What was the common name of the Serviceman's Readjustment Act of 1944?

13 State the purpose for the Manpower Development and Training Act of 1962.

14 When did the federal government make a total commitment to vocational education? *after 1960*

15 State the purpose of the Vocational Education Act of 1963.

16 What was the responsibility of the Advisory Committee on Vocational Education established in the United States Office of Education?

For discussion

1 Contrast the social and economic conditions of people during the three developmental stages of federal legislation for vocational education as discussed in this chapter: (a) prior to 1900, (b) 1900–1960, and (c) 1960-present. Include specific legislation enacted during each period.

2 The idea is presented in this chapter that individuals who are governing and being governed are greater than the government itself. Would we have the same type of vocational education in the United States today if our system of government were such that the government was considered more important than the worth and dignity of the individual citizen?

3 Contrast the provisions of the George-Reed Act with the provisions of the Smith-Hughes Act.

4 Relate the following statement to the Manpower Development and Training Act of 1962: The climate was right to reorient people toward the dignity of work.

5 What are the similarities between the Vocational Education Act of 1963 and the 1968 Amendments? How are they different?

6 Discuss occupational education as provided by the Education Amendments of 1972.

For exploration

1 Investigate sixteenth-section land as provided in the Land Ordinance of 1785:

(a) Does it exist in your county or parish?

(b) Is income derived from it? If so, how is it obtained and used?

(c) If no sixteenth section land exists, how was it disposed of?

2 Determine through interviews with education officials and legislators and through published research the methods used to allocate funds for vocational education on the local, state, and national levels.

3 Prepare brief biographical sketches of the following people, including milestones in their lives that led them to support vocational education:

(a) Hoke Smith

(b) Dudley Hughes

(c) Carl Perkins

(d) Henry Steele Commager

(e) Justin Smith Morrill

4 Compare the responsibilities of the Advisory Committee on Vocational Education in the U.S. Office of Education as authorized by the Vocational Education Act of 1963 to the responsibility of a local advisory committee for vocational education.

5 Read and critique one article on federal legislation pertaining to vocational education.

6 Debate the following topics:

(a) Resolved that vocational education is designed only for the economically, socially, and culturally deprived.

(b) Resolved that the Smith-Hughes Act is the most significant federal legislation passed affecting the development of vocational education.

7 Consult with educational, manpower, governmental, and/or labor officials to determine the types and sources of funds being derived from federal sources to finance vocational education programs in your locality. Identify specific acts under which funds are being received.

8 Research state and federal activities for the five years preceding the passage of the Smith-Hughes Act.

9 Investigate the most recent federal legislation not discussed in this chapter that has become law. How is it similar to the legislation discussed? How different? How does it affect vocational education in your community? In your state? Invite a knowledgeable official to discuss this legislation with your class.

10 Investigate the work of the Douglas Commission, appointed in 1905 to examine manual training programs in Massachusetts. What influence did the commission have on vocational education in the United States?

References

1 Henry Steele Commager, "Only the National Government . . ." *Today's Education*, Vol. 62, No. 6, September–October 1973, pp. 47–48.

2 John C. Fitzpatrick, ed., *Journals of the Continental Congress*, 1774–1789, Vol. 28 (Washington: Government Printing Office, 1933), pp. 375–386.

3 Francis N. Thorpe, ed., *The Federal and State Constitutions, Colonial Charters, and Other Organic Laws*, Vol. 2 (Washington: Government Printing Office, 1909), p. 961.

4 George P. Sanger, ed., *The Statutes at Large, Treaties, and Proclamations of the United States of America*, from December 5, 1859 to March 3, 1863, Vol. 12 (Boston: Little, Brown, and Company, 1863), pp. 503–505.

5 Henry Steele Commager, ed., *Documents of American History*, Fourth Edition, Vol. I (New York: Appleton-Century-Crofts, Inc., 1948), p. 412.

6 Public Law 64–347, *The Statutes at Large* . . . from December 1915 to March 1917, Vol. 39, Part I (Washington: Government Printing Office, 1917), pp. 929–936.

7 John A. McCarthy, *Vocational Education: America's Greatest Resource* (Chicago: American Technical Society, 1950), pp. 15–39.

8 Public Law 70–702, *The Statutes at Large* . . . from December 1927 to March 1929, Vol. 45, Part I (Washington: Government Printing Office, 1929), p. 1151.

9 Public Law 73–245, *The Statutes at Large* . . . from March 1933 to June 1934, Vol. 48, Part I (Washington: Government Printing Office, 1934), pp. 792–793.

10 Public Law 74–673, *The Statutes at Large* . . . from January 1935 to June 1936, Vol. 49, Part I (Washington: Government Printing Office, 1936), pp. 1488–1490.

11 "Vocational Education Act of 1946," Public Law 79–586, *United States Statutes at Large*, 1946, Vol. 60, Part I (Washington: Government Printing Office, 1947), pp. 775–778.

12 Panel of Consultants on Vocational Education, *Education for a Changing World of Work* (Washington: Government Printing Office, 1963).

13 "Vocational Education Act of 1963," Public Law 88–210, *United States Statutes at Large*, 1963, Vol. 77 (Washington: Government Printing Office, 1964), pp. 403–419.

14 Ibid, p. 408.

15 "Vocational Education Amendments of 1968," Public Law 90–576, *United States Statutes at Large*, 1968, Vol. 82 (Washington: Government Printing Office, 1969), pp. 1064–1098.

16 "Elementary and Secondary Education Act of 1965," Public Law 89–10, *United States Statutes at Large*, 1965, Vol. 79 (Washington: Government Printing Office, 1966), pp. 27–58.

17 "Education Amendments of 1972," Public Law 92–318, *United States Statutes at Large*, 1972, Vol. 86 (Washington: Government Printing Office, 1973), p. 319.

18 Ibid, p. 322.

19 "Education Amendments of 1974," Public Law 93–380, *United States Statutes at Large*, 1974, Vol. 88 (Washington: Government Printing Office, 1975).

Chapter 3

Factors Influencing

Varied Aspects of

Vocational-Technical

Education

Introduction

In this chapter we will look at the philosophical construct for vocational education. Emphasis will be placed on the effects of three foundational factors on the evolving philosophy of vocational education: 1. philosophical factors—What knowledge and/or skill is of most value to teach? 2. economic factors—How do labor-market needs affect career development? and 3. sociological factors—What are the effects of social class and industrialization on preparation for vocations?

Philosophical Factors

Vocational educators recognize that two questions are fundamental to the development of a sound vocational program: What should be taught? and How should it be taught? Answers to these questions involve the establishment of priorities. Over the years there have evolved some fundamental assumptions and principles that tend to give unity and direction to vocational education planning. Our beliefs about the individual and his or her role in a democratic society and about the role of education in the transmission of socially approved standards are the source of these fundamental principles.

With the development of a democratic philosophy of education in the United States, universal schooling became part of the national ideology. Maximizing each individual's chances for life-long learning and attainment of the "good life" became the ultimate goal of our educational system. Because it was necessary for most Americans to work in order to eat, the vocational objective became an important link in the educational chain.

There is, naturally, disagreement as to what the goals of vocational education should be. But current beliefs and practices are rather firmly rooted in the historical development of the field. The Morrill Act of 1862 placed the national government and the states in support of publicly financed education designed to train youth in two kinds of occupations that predominated at that time—agriculture and industry. Consequently, the development of vocational education was, from that point, tied closely to specific federal legislation. The philosophy and objectives of vocational education leaders were reflected in the provisions of controlling legislation.

Many of those who led the fight for the introduction of vocational education into the school curriculum did so because of a strong philosophical commitment to equality of educational opportunity. They believed that the high school of that time was concerned only with the needs of youth who were preparing for college. Because education beyond the high school was pursued by only a very small minority of college-age youth, the college-preparation emphasis was held to be undemocratic and unfair to the great majority of young people, most of whom never finished high school.

Changing School Population

At the time when the famous representative committees of the National Education Association (NEA) began their work around 1893, there were only about 700,000 students in the high schools. The purposes of American secondary schools were narrow and incoherent until the Committees of the NEA began to study the broad goals of the secondary school in our country. For example, the Committee of Ten in 1893 gave direction to schools and helped to standardize the curriculum of the high schools. The Committee on College Relations in 1897 helped to standardize college entrance requirements. The Commission on the Purposes of Secondary Education proposed the Seven Cardinal Principles of Education in 1918. The work of these and later committees clarified the goals and problems of secondary education and established the principle that the schools' purposes were preparation for life rather than for further education.

At the end of the nineteenth century, the secondary school population was still relatively homogeneous, coming from about the same family backgrounds and preparing to enter occupations favored by the higher echelons of society. In contrast, the high schools of today harbor young people with widely varying aptitudes and abilities. Half of the students leave school after the tenth grade, and many who remain participate much more passively than actively in their own education. They may be potentially good citizens, but their interests lie outside, not inside, the school. It is unrealistic to believe that these young people can be attracted by the kind of exercises in abstract thinking that characterize much of the high school curriculum.

Socialization of Education

Whether we like it or not, the American high school is not merely a scholastic institution; it is also a social institution. From the beginning, sociological and humanistic reasons have been used to justify the need for vocational education. From one point of view there may also be a socio-economic component, for it can be argued that those who are trained for a job, and so become wage earners, will more likely turn out to be contributing citizens who will be assets to society. By performing its primary function of preparation for useful employment, vocational education is likely to contribute indirectly to many other social benefits.

It is characteristic of the socialization of the high school that the only committee report of the NEA that had an effect similar to that of the Committee of Ten, namely the Report on the *Cardinal Principles of Secondary Education* in 1918, defines the goal of education in a democracy in the following terms (1):

□ *The purpose of democracy is so to organize society that each member may develop his personality primarily through activities designed for the well-being of his fellow members and of society as a whole. . . .*

Consequently, education in a democracy, both within and without the school, should develop in each individual the knowledge, interests, ideals, habits, and powers whereby he will find his place and use that place to shape both himself and society toward ever nobler ends.

That was obviously a commendable goal. But a comparison of the emphasis on subject matter in the work of the Committee of Ten with the main ideas of the report on cardinal principles reveals a change from subject-centeredness, however diluted, to a social concept of education. The committee's seven cardinal principles of secondary education identified the goals for survival and social adjustment that would provide the common core of study for all: health, command of the fundamental processes, worthy home membership, vocation, citizenship, worthy use of leisure, and ethical character. To understand the change, it is worthwhile to remember that the report on the cardinal principles was written at the end of World War I, a war that had had a calamitous effect on the stability of education. A period of intense analysis and a reformation of American education was underway.

Influence of Pragmatism

In the first quarter of the twentieth century, there occurred not only an enormous shift in school population but also a profound philosophical rethinking of the nature of education. Men such as William James and John Dewey were propounding a new philosophy—known as pragmatism, instrumentalism, or experimentalism—which, for many teachers, was quickly replacing the German-influenced idealism and the religious interpretation of education. Historically, pragmatism entered a vacuum that had already been opened by the disintegration of transcendentalism. The new philosophy offered the prospect of a more valid or "scientific" method, which the new "Science of Education," as well as the other "social sciences"—still uncertain of themselves—were most anxious to acquire. Pragmatism emphasized the concrete over the more abstract problems of life; it showed the significance of social institutions and the evolutionary character of societies and their ideologies. In fostering "progressive" education, it also gave the professionally interested teacher new hope that through the introduction of these experimental methods there might be an increasing chance to develop student initiative, rather than merely to convey year after year the same subject matter, irrespective of the interests of the students.

The pragmatic revolt, which was climaxed by James (2), Bode (3), Dewey (4), and Kilpatrick (5), had an enormous effect on American education. Within less than a hundred years American education changed profoundly, partially because of the influence of these thinkers, who believed that education, like science, ought to be emancipated from traditionalism and ought to be based on scientific methodology and scientific assumptions. The educator should turn to the problem-solving method, which involved a felt need, analysis of the problem, experimentation with various solutions, tentative theories, verification, and the forming of a conclusion that could be concretely applied. Like the scientists, educators should be hypothetical in their approach to life, and they should be more concerned with methodology than with ultimate standards.

John Dewey was a strong proponent of vocational education. Traditional liberal education had created a snobbish spirit; it had led to a worship of the classics and had created a disdain for manual activity. Vocational education would bridge the gulf between knowledge and action and would develop a more cooperative spirit through learning by doing. The distinction between the fine arts and the industrial arts was to be minimized. *Talk* about art was regarded as being inferior to *experience* in art. Dewey contended that traditional liberal education did not provide the skills and attitudes necessary for living in an age of science.

Vocational vs. General Education

Early spokesmen for vocational education defined the general education offerings of the high schools and colleges as liberal education. They considered these liberal studies to be education for an aristocratic elite, a type of education that was contrary to the spirit of American democracy. Vocational education was needed, they felt, as a form of practical education for the masses to counterbalance the emphasis on liberal education for the elite. This distrust of liberal education by vocational educators has never been fully overcome, and attitudes ranging from suspicion to near hostility toward liberal education can still be found among some vocational educators.

Educational and social thinking has become increasingly opposed to the whole concept of separating vocational and general education. Just as educational separatism on racial grounds has become unacceptable, so any form of educational segregation based on the occupational future of young people is being rejected. Such segregation leads to undesirable status distinctions between individuals because of their occupational choices and to false superiority-inferiority attitudes toward equally essential aspects of education. The report of the 1967 Advisory Council on Vocational Education concluded that vocational education is not a separate discipline within education; rather, it is a basic objective of all education and must be a basic element of each person's education (6).

Principles of Vocational Education

The movement toward a planned system of vocational education was a gradual process. In the late 1800s and early 1900s the growing industrialization of the nation demanded more trained workers. Because vocational education was so closely related to the economic development of the nation, the need for national planning became imperative.

Public discussion and interest in the educational needs of the labor force were stimulated by the report of the Douglas Commission, which recommended a system of vocational education for the state of Massachusetts. In 1906 the National Society for the Promotion of Industrial Education brought its study of occupational needs to public attention. Subsequently this organization and its successor, the National Society for Vocational Education, served as a sounding board for early discussions related to the rationale and emerging principles of vocational education. Charles A. Prosser, executive secretary of the National Society for Vocational Education, played a major role in laying the groundwork for favorable public opinion and extensive federal support of vocational education. During the 1940s he generated a series of theories that attempted to reconcile vocational education practices to the modern psychology of learning. These theories, which have made a substantial contribution to the administration and instruction of vocational education, are identified as follows (7):

Theory 1 Vocational education will be efficient in proportion as the environment in which the learner is trained is a replica of the environment in which he must subsequently work.

Theory 2 Effective vocational training can only be given where the training jobs are carried on in the same way with the same operations, the same tools and the same machines as in the occupation itself.

Theory 3 Vocational education will be effective in proportion as it trains the individual directly and specifically in the thinking habits and the manipulative habits required in the occupation itself.

Theory 4 Vocational education will be effective in proportion as it enables each individual to capitalize his or her interests, aptitudes and intrinsic intelligence to the highest possible degree.

Theory 5 Effective vocational education for any profession, calling, grade, occupation or job can only be given to the selected group of individuals who need it, want it, and are able to profit by it.

Theory 6 Vocational training will be effective in proportion as the specific training experiences for forming right habits of doing and thinking are repeated to the point that the habits developed are those of the finished skills necessary for gainful employment.

Theory 7 Vocational education will be effective in proportion as the instructor has had successful experience in the application of skills and knowledge to the operations and processes he undertakes to teach.

Theory 8 For every occupation there is a minimum of productive ability which an individual must possess in order to secure or retain employment in that occupation. If vocational education is not carried to that point with that individual, it is neither personally nor socially effective.

Theory 9 Vocational education must recognize conditions as they are and must train individuals to meet the demands of the "market" even though it may be true that more efficient ways of conducting the occupation may be known and that better working conditions are highly desirable.

Theory 10 The effective establishment of process habits in any learner will be secured in proportion as the training is given on actual jobs and not on exercises or pseudo jobs.

Theory 11 The only reliable source of content for specific training in an occupation is in the experience of masters of that occupation.

Theory 12 For every occupation there is a body of content which is peculiar to that occupation and which practically has no functioning value in any other occupation.

Theory 13 Vocational education will render efficient social service in proportion as it meets the specific training needs of any group at the time that they need it and in such a way that they can most effectively profit by the instruction.

Theory 14 Vocational education will be socially efficient in proportion as in its methods of instruction and its personal relations with learners it takes into consideration the particular characteristics of any particular group which it serves.

Theory 15 The administration of vocational education will be efficient in proportion as it is elastic and fluid rather than rigid and standardized.

Theory 16 While every reasonable effort should be made to reduce per capita cost, there is a minimum below which effective vocational education cannot be given, and if the course does not permit of this minimum of per capita cost, vocational education should not be attempted.

Barlow (8) identified the following as principles growing out of the foundation years that had culminated in the passage of the Smith-Hughes Act of 1917. He feels that these principles have not changed even though their implementation has brought about new approaches.

1 Vocational education is a national concern Labor, education, business, industry, agriculture, and the public supported the economic need for a national framework of vocational education.

2 Vocational education provides for the common defense and promotes the general welfare The effectiveness of vocational education in improving the economic welfare of individuals and families, and in providing the base of skills for defense of the nation, has been consistently demonstrated during periods of war and peace.

3 Vocational preparation of youth and adults is a public school responsibility The democratization of public education brought with it a favorable consensus on the need for vocational education in the public school system.

4 Vocational education requires a sound basic education The technological age has consistently placed a premium on a sound basic education for *all* students. The design of vocational education has always reinforced this assumption.

5 Vocational education is planned and conducted in close cooperation with business and industry The concept of an advisory committee as a means of keeping programs attuned to the needs of business and industry illustrates the cooperative dimension of program planning.

6 Vocational education provides the skills and knowledges valuable in the labor market Program content is based upon analysis of the needs of the labor market. Placement and followup studies test the degree to which the product of the program (the student) adjusts and makes progress in the job.

7 Vocational education provides continuing education for youth and adults The outreach of vocational education through the trade extension and other adult vocational programs has contributed significantly to the "industrial intelligence" of the labor force. The problem of retraining and life-long learning is a foundation element in the structure of vocational education.

Barlow's principles, which describe the rationale on which vocational education was based in its foundational years, may be compared with the assumptions made in 1968 by the National Advisory Council on Vocational Education (9):

1 Vocational education is the right of everyone who desires and can profit by it, and it is the responsibility of the schools to provide for it within the curriculum *This assumption precludes program limitations as they now exist in many instances, and establishes the need for a broader and more inclusive vocational program based upon individual needs and work opportunities. Such planning establishes the base for the schools to become responsible for the student in transition to the next level of education or to work.*

2 Vocational education is a continuous process from early childhood throughout life *The process can be roughly divided into four phases which prescribe themselves to general levels of education. The types of programs which are appropriate and can be planned for each level are (a) informational and orientational, (b) orientational and exploratory, (c) exploratory and preparational, and (d) upgrading and retraining.*

3 Vocational education, like general education, is a responsibility of the total school and cannot be limited to a single discipline or department.

4 Vocational education programs can be developed which serve as non-blocking career ladders, and they can be planned to be consonant with the goals of both general and vocational functions of education.

Such statements of principle act as basic rules both for evaluating present programs and for guiding future actions.

Assumptions of
Vocational Education

Underlying the principles of vocational education are a number of assumptions that enjoy wide acceptance and that provide consistency and direction to overall efforts in the field. They have a democratic orientation toward the fundamental worth of the individual and toward the responsibility of society to help people develop their capabilities to the fullest extent possible.

Thompson (10) identifies the following basic assumptions:

1 *Vocational education can develop a marketable man by developing his ability to perform skills that extend his utility as a tool of production.*

2 *Vocational education is the means of acquiring the basic skills essential for equal competition in the marketplace.*

3 *There need not be a dualism between vocational and general education.*

4 *Vocational education is economic education as it is geared to the needs of the job market and thus contributes to national economic strength.*

5 *Vocational education is education for production to serve the ends of the economic system and is said to have social utility.*

6 *Vocational education at the secondary level is concerned with preparation of the individual for initial entry employment.*

7 *Vocational education should be oriented to the manpower needs of the community.*

8 *Vocational education should be evaluated on the basis of economic efficiency. Vocational education is economically efficient when (a) it prepares students for specific jobs in the community on the basis of manpower needs, (b) it insures an adequate labor supply for an occupational area, and (c) the student gets the job for which he was trained.*

For those engaged in vocational education, it is evident that a body of philosophical assumptions and principles has evolved that gives direction to the field. Such assumptions and principles are rooted in the changing needs of students and of industry, and they contain elements of theory and practice that have frequently been incorporated into law.

Philosophical Effects
of Federal Legislation

Unlike most other educational fields, vocational education and federal legislation are so closely interwoven that it is not surprising that the latter reflects the principles and practices of the former. Vocational education after the Smith-Hughes Act was oriented toward preparing students for specific occupations. Similarly, the vocational objectives of the 1960s and 1970s illustrate changes of a social, economic, and political nature as reflected in the Vocational Education Act of 1963 and the Vocational Education Amendments of 1968.

■ The 1963 Act declared that vocational education cannot be limited to the skills necessary for a particular occupation.

Mangum (11) pointed out that this change had deeper significance than was at first apparent:

□ *By implication, the test of appropriateness of training was no longer to be, "Was the skill in high and growing demand?" but "Did the individual get the job of his choice and prosper in it?" Not that training for obsolete skills was contemplated. The difference was a matter of emphasis, with training for successful employment the primary goal and meeting skill requirements a means to that end.*

■ The 1963 Act and the 1968 Amendments further changed the objectives and principles of vocational education by redefining the field.

The new emphasis was not only on training for certain occupations but also "new and emerging ones," and not just skills training but remedial or related academic and technical instruction as well as preparation for enrollment in advanced technical education.

■ Special attention was to be paid to the needs of disadvantaged and handicapped for whom special techniques and supportive services would be necessary to enable them to achieve satisfactory employment.

■ The 1963 Act defined the objectives of vocational education as the development of the individual rather than the specific needs of the labor market.

■ The Acts of the Sixties specified that education should no longer be compartmentalized into general, academic, and vocational components.

Beaumont (12) sums up the new philosophy of vocational education contained in the Vocational Education Amendments of 1968 by citing a number of statements that were given "serious consideration" by the House Committee on Education and Labor Report No. 1647:

☐ *Any dichotomy between academic and vocational education is outmoded.*

☐ *Developing attitudes, basic education skills and habits appropriate for the world of work is as important as skill training.*

☐ *Pre-vocational orientation is necessary to introduce pupils to the world of work and provide motivation.*

☐ *Vocational programs should be developmental, not terminal, providing maximum options for students to go to college, pursue postsecondary vocational and technical training or find employment.*

☐ *Occupational education should be based on a spiral curriculum which treats concepts at higher and higher levels of complexity as the student moves through the program.*

☐ *Vocational preparation should be used to make academic education concrete and understandable, and academic education should point up the vocational implications of all education.*

☐ *Within the context of these statements, vocational education should be able to serve the demands of a technological society and the needs of man for a liberalizing experience in his educational development.*

With the possible exception of the first statement in the preceding series, it could be pointed out that there was little that was new in these ideas. All too frequently in the education field, ideas and issues seem to arise *ex nihilo;* each additional generation is left to rediscover the persistent and perplexing problems that characterize the field. At the same time, however, even if these ideas have been around for a while, their discovery and review by lawmakers is a reflection of the concerns of the electorate and should be viewed as a sign of progress.

Vocational Education Method

There have been frequent suggestions that vocational education, with its strong emphasis on the doing types of activities, could offer an alternative path to learning for those with a low aptitude for verbal learning. The value of vocational education as a teaching-learning method may be greater for some students than its substantive value as skill training. The 1968 report of the Advisory Council on Vocational Education strongly recommends this alternate emphasis, especially in view of follow-up studies that reveal a relatively low proportion of high school students making occupational use of specific vocational skills learned in school. There is evidence that occupational education can often re-motivate the student who has lost interest in school. When combined with well-coordinated work experiences in actual employment—experiences that are carefully coordinated with in-school studies—the general education outcomes for the student can often be excellent (13).

Economic Factors

At this point let us explore two major aspects related to the economics of vocational education: vocational education as a contributor to society's economic mainstream and the economics of vocational education itself.

Labor is a basic component of our economic system. About two-thirds of the national income goes to those who work for wages and salaries. Wages—including fees, commissions, and salaries—represent prices paid for labor that is expended in the production of economic goods and services. Real wages—the amount of goods and services that money wages will purchase—must be earned before they can be paid. Marginal productivity limits the amount that can be paid to workers, but it does not always determine the amount that employers actually pay.

The Role of Labor

One explanation that has been advanced to explain wages and wage rates is the theory of demand and supply. The demand for labor means the amount of labor of a certain kind that will be used in production at various wage rates. The demand for labor is derived from the demand for what labor produces. The supply of labor is derived from the amount of labor that will be offered for use in production at different wage rates. Like demand, the supply of labor is always specific. Labor is perishable; it cannot be separated from the person; its supply does not change quickly; and it is not highly mobile. Standards of living affect the supply of labor, and certain laws for the control of wages and the regulation of labor may also affect its supply. We may say that wages and wage rates depend on the demand for and supply of labor. At the same time, certain other factors usually affect wage rates, such as custom, public authority, monopoly, and bargaining by employers and employees.

The movement toward the adoption of guaranteed wage plans and supplementary unemployment benefits is gaining momentum in large segments of business and industry. We do not know just how far the movement will go or what its effects on the different kinds of workers will be.

Economic Bases of Vocational Education

Historically, the development and availability of vocational education, as a source of labor supply, has paralleled economic growth. Under the heavy labor demands at the end of the eighteenth century, the nation faced a serious shortage of skilled labor. The country had come to depend on European immigrants, who had brought with them a background in skilled trades. But now the immigrant stream was diminishing, and the nation lacked an adequate apprenticeship system for training workers. Trained laborers were needed to operate the rapidly growing number of farms and factories.

Faced with a labor shortage, industry and agriculture, the two largest segments of the economy, called for programs of vocational training in the public high schools. The idea that vocational education should be designed to supply the labor needs of particular segments of the economy became embedded in the law with the passage of the Smith-Hughes Act, and it persisted in vocational legislation until 1963. In the early 1960s it became obvious that the concept of vocational education, if it hoped to meet the nation's needs, must be redesigned to serve people of all employable age groups and categories rather than particular segments of the economy. As Leighbody stated (14):

□ *The Vocational Education Act of 1963 did not reject the goal of meeting the nation's economic needs, but it turned the emphasis of the program toward meeting the needs of people. . . . This would, of course, satisfy the need for trained workers, but the change in emphasis is nevertheless significant. It reoriented vocational education to more sociological and humanitarian goals.*

Technological Factors

As technology has advanced, it has left in its wake a high average unemployment among unskilled workers. The view that automation, in the long run, creates more jobs than it displaces has been widespread, but it is being challenged today. The immediate effects of technological unemployment fall heaviest on those least able to withstand its effects—the untrained and undereducated, especially the 16- to 20-year-old group.

Until recently economists generally believed that in order to solve our unemployment problems we must attain a sufficient increase in the rate of our national economic growth. The consensus now, however, seems to be that in simple terms of increased production and consumption, the kind of growth rate that we need cannot be fully attained. In the future the rate of economic growth will increasingly depend on the rate of technological development—which, in turn, will depend on the availability of technically trained personnel. The shortage of fuel and other natural resources may also serve as a major impediment to technological progress.

Federal legislation of the past quarter century has done much to alleviate the problem. There is a feeling among many, however, that merely improving education will not eliminate or even substantially reduce unemployment, that to gain ground we must accelerate the pace at which we improve education. Thus education becomes the intermediary between technology on the one hand and labor on the other.

Vocational Education
and the General Welfare

Freedom of occupational choice is both an American ideal and a national concern. Federal legislation has sought to facilitate occupational choice by providing funds to the states for the development of vocational education programs. The justifications for such funding are based on the right of each individual to a total education, the responsibility of society (through the public schools) to provide such instruction, and the effect of vocational education on the economic strength of the nation. A central tenet of vocational education has often been expressed by the phrase, "to fit for useful employment." Useful employment leads to economic improvement, which leads to a better standard of living for the individual, and this gain, in turn, becomes a gain for society. Vocational education, therefore, has been thought of as a wise business investment both for the individual and for the nation.

According to the 1974–75 *Occupational Outlook Handbook*, men who had college degrees could expect to earn more than $600,000 in their lifetime, or nearly three times the $214,000 likely to be earned by workers who had less than eight years of schooling, nearly twice that earned by workers who had one to three years of high school, and nearly one and two-thirds as much as high school graduates. Clearly the completion of

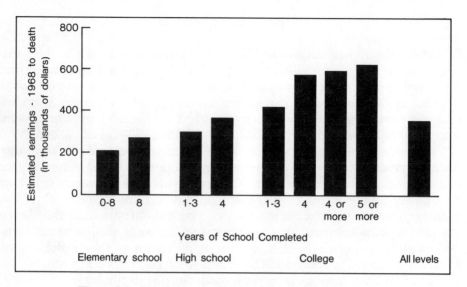

Figure 3.1 Lifetime earnings for men by level of schooling. Source: *Occupational Outlook Handbook*, Bulletin
1785. (Washington, D.C., U.S. Department of Labor, Bureau of Labor Statistics, 1974–75 Edition), p. 22.

high school pays a dividend. A worker who had only one to three years of
high school could expect to earn only about $31,000 more than workers
who had an elementary school education, but a high school graduate
could look forward to a $94,000 lifetime income advantage over an indi-
vidual completing elementary school, as indicated in Figure 3.1.

Changes in the Economic Structure

The nature and amount of formal education offered through the public
school system reflects the social and economic demands of the times, as
is evident in the philosophical changes in education over three distinctly
different periods in our history.

Agrarian period In its early years America was predominantly an agricultural nation. Education served two primary functions: facilitation of
the basic literacy assumed necessary for meaningful participation in the
democratic process and "acculturation of the masses of immigrants of
many languages and backgrounds who flooded into the new melting pot."
(15) It was a fact of American society in those days that adult roles in the
economy were accessible with a minimum of formal education. In addition the growing economy had ample uses for those without formal educational preparation.

Industrial period From an agricultural society emerged a complex
industrialized economy, which reached its peak during World War II.

"With half a world to feed and arm and with the cream of its own labor force committed to military combat, the United States economy was forced in the early 1940s to multiply its output almost overnight." (16) A large part of the required manpower was inexperienced and, as Evans (17) has stated,

□ . . . *school shops and laboratories were re-equipped, instructors were recruited, and 24-hour-a-day vocational instruction began, oriented to skills in national as well as local demand. Before the war's end, the public schools had trained 7.5 million people for industrial contributions to the war.*

Employers were now able to choose well-prepared persons who had been trained under programs such as the G. I. Bill. In addition, a technology was designed to use these already-trained persons rather than their poorly trained competitors. During the industrial era, vocational education was guided by the Smith-Hughes Act and its prevailing philosophy of training in specific occupational categories to meet the needs of the labor market.

Technological period Although vocational education made major progress during the industrial years, the impact of automation and technological advance pointed up two central failures of prevailing philosophy: its lack of sensitivity to changes in the labor market and its lack of sensitivity to the needs of various segments of the population. By concentrating on the job requirements of industry and restricting its efforts to secondary school age students, the Smith-Hughes Act failed to give priority to the vocational needs of all groups in the community and to the demands of a fast-changing society (18).

The rapid rate at which technological changes are occurring creates a need for vocational education programs that are flexible enough to adapt to an ever-changing economy. Leighbody (19) lists the areas in which technological breakthrough is occurring:

1 The energy breakthrough *When the means for releasing the energy of the atom were achieved, man gained access to a new source of energy which is theoretically unlimited. The possibilities for using this new energy are just beginning to be understood.*

2 The health breakthrough *The combined knowledge from a number of technologies which has improved health and lengthened life has also brought new social and political demands for universal health care, and one result is the appearance of several new health related occupations and a greatly increased need for workers in all the fields of health.*

3 The production breakthrough *New applications of several technologies, in combinations which are often referred to as automation, have brought a whole new dimension to the capacity of the economy to produce goods*

and services. A production explosion has occurred in agriculture and in manufacturing.

4 The knowledge breakthrough *The introduction and continuous refinement of the computer has brought about a revolution in our capacity to manage and process information and data for testing observed experimental data for relationships and meaning. This has made it possible to telescope into a few years the recording, classifying, and storing of amounts of new knowledge which would formerly have required several decades to acquire. Since a major part of business and scientific research consists of recording and processing data, an enormous expansion in these areas has been possible, with a relatively small increase in manpower.*

5 The communications breakthrough *One of the most dramatic effects of the electronic age has occurred in the field of communication. Whole new galaxies of occupations have emerged with this development, in which intercontinental telecasts of good quality, via satellite, are now commonplace, and very successful telecasts from the moon have been demonstrated.*

6 The breakthrough in space *The tremendous achievements in space exploration, including the moon landings, have been made possible by the employment of very advanced and exotic technical accomplishments. Some of these have already found their way into use for other purposes which promise great benefits to mankind, and the transfer of knowledge from space technology to other useful applications has begun.*

Leighbody (20) summarizes the characteristics of our economy that have implications for vocational education programs:

1 *More goods are produced for more consumers, but with a smaller portion of the work force required to produce them. However, those who are thus employed must be better educated and must possess more sophisticated skills and knowledge than their predecessors.*

2 *More food and fiber is produced and more people are better fed and clothed by fewer and fewer farmers . . . but those who remain and those who will be needed in the future require much greater knowledge of scientific agriculture, coupled with business skills and training.*

3 *Nearly all jobs call for a higher level of education for entry than they formerly did, and a longer period of general education prior to occupational specialization. Today a high school education is hardly sufficient for a decent job, and a very large number of people are continuing their education beyond it.*

4 *The need for manual skills in most jobs is decreasing, while cognitive, social, and interpersonal skills are more and more in demand.*

5 *Already more people are employed in providing services for other people than in producing goods and food for them. Two-thirds of the work force is now engaged in what may be broadly classified as service occupations. This is a remarkable reversal of the distribution of occupations from the time when the first programs of vocational education were established.*

6 *In addition to the shift in the distribution of jobs, as technology advances it creates wholly new jobs and categories of jobs, and these too tend to demand better educated and better trained workers. Computer programmers, air traffic controllers, environmental control specialists are a few among the great many new occupations which were either non-existent or rarely found a quarter century ago. In drafting the Vocational Education Amendments Act of 1968, the Congress showed its awareness that many new and unusual occupations were emerging in the economy, by providing that some of the funds for vocational curriculum development should be used to prepare for them.*

Economics of Vocational Education

In this section we will look at the economic aspects of vocational education itself, including the matching feature of vocational legislation and the efforts toward accountability.

Matching Feature
of Vocational Funds

Federal funds for vocational education have been distributed among the states on the basis of formulas determined by population and per capita income. Matching provisions of earlier laws required that the states put up an equal amount of state dollars for federal dollars allocated.

This matching feature of vocational education funds has in the past prevented many states from receiving their share of federal assistance. Because the matching of federal funds was accomplished primarily by local expenditures, local school districts with a low financial base were particularly hard hit. In practice, the wealthier school district received proportionately more and the poorer school district received less than its fair share of funds. The Vocational Education Amendments of 1968 established the limit of the matching requirement when it specified that no local district shall be denied access to federal vocational funds due to lack of matching funds.

Reimbursement on
Excess-Cost Principle

Local schools and states are obligated to provide general education for all students and an equivalent expenditure for those enrolled in vocational education programs. Many states have established uniform rates of 50 percent vocational reimbursement to local schools for selected items, the largest of which is teachers' salaries. An emerging practice is that reimbursement should be based on only the *differential costs* between providing general education or college preparatory, and vocational or occupationally oriented education. In this way, the federal government reimburses the local school district for the extra cost required to provide vocational programs.

Consistent with the above principle is the assumption of reimbursement, or support based on services rendered. As Tomlinson (21) has observed,

☐ *Major changes in the amount of money accruing to a local school district will result when these principles are applied. The numbers of students served, amount of services rendered, quality of service and cost of services rendered will be used as a guide for support rather than the teacher's salary, regardless of quality, need, or number of students enrolled.*

The Principle of Accountability

The needs of education always seem to outweigh the available resources. Educational costs at all levels are escalating, and in most states a larger and larger portion of the total budget is earmarked for educational purposes annually. As the tax burden has increased, the public has increasingly looked for evidence that resources have been well spent and that quality and efficiency have been realized in accomplishing educational goals.

Measures of accountability have been difficult to apply to vocational programs because of the lack of valid data on which to base an evaluation. Even the National Advisory Council on Vocational Education has been hampered in its investigations by a lack of concrete information regarding economic effectiveness. However, improved systems of educational planning and computerized recordkeeping and evaluation now make it possible to identify cost and achievement relationships.

It is not unreasonable to expect that in the relatively near future each vocational education department will be expected to specify its course objectives in measurable achievement terms. These objectives will then have to be justified in terms of the allocated resources and the actual results achieved. In this way, performance standards and cost effectiveness will become a basic component of vocational education.

Sociological Factors

As society has changed, so has the nature of work. As Barlow (22) so aptly phrased it:

□ *A century ago the primary ingredients needed by people who wanted to enter the labor force were a willingness to work, a strong back, and a modicum of education. But with the passage of time, society has changed. We have moved from the farm into the factory, we have become better fed, and the result of our productive labor has produced an affluence among people in general which is without precedence in any other society.*

Vocational Education and Social Welfare

An examination of federal legislation reveals that Congress has recognized the social values of vocational education, with programs open to all regardless of sex, race, creed, or national origin. Section I of the Vocational Education Amendments of 1968 stipulates that persons of all ages in all communities will have ready access to vocational training or retraining that is suited to their needs, interests, and ability to benefit from such training. Much of the emphasis of federal law in the educational arena has been toward the equating of social and economic opportunities.

The vocational education movement has from its beginning reflected concern over social and economic conditions. There has always been an element of philanthropy in the thinking of those who have been interested in vocational education, a feeling that the general uplifting of the masses through training for work was an attainable goal. This idea is still reflected in the large variety of federally funded job training programs that are directed toward improving the lot of the disadvantaged members of society.

Congress has recognized the relationship of education and work in such pieces of legislation as the Manpower Development and Training Act of 1962, which provided training and retraining for the unemployed; the Area Redevelopment Act, which provided training or retraining for unemployed and underemployed persons in specified redevelopment areas; the Economic Opportunity Act, a multi-level program to aid the impoverished through such activities as work experience, community action, and the Neighborhood Youth Corps; and the more recent Comprehensive Education and Training Act of 1973, which consolidated previous manpower legislation.

The social and economic values of vocational education have been elaborated by Shoemaker (23), who points out the expanding role of education for work:

□ *Most jobs today and in the future will require formal training, and preparation for initial job entry is a basic responsibility of public education.*

We must choose between increased welfare or an expanded program of preparing for work. At the same time, we see that job preparation and remedial education programs for adults are too expensive to serve as a continuing solution to current social and economic problems. Instead, a complete re-evaluation and reformation of our public educational system represents the only hope to solving our economic and social problems. An expanded and improved system of vocational education and guidance must be a major part of the change in our educational system.

Educational innovation requires increased categorical financial aid for specific programs as well as general aid for overall development. This aid must come from federal, state and local sources.

The education and supportive services needed for our modern society will require a broad student base and broad tax base.

The purpose of education is to perpetuate and improve the society in which it exists. Our technological society requires that everyone receive the opportunity to earn an adequate living. It further requires that young women be prepared for the dual responsibilities of home management and wage earning.

To survive, public education must accept greater responsibility. Services must be expanded and improved. Education must be prepared to account for both successes and failures.

Social Forces
Affecting Vocational Education

During the 1960s and early 1970s, vocational education received widespread attention and critical scrutiny. A number of forces have influenced its direction and growth.

1 The national program of vocational education has been studied by citizens' commissions In 1961 President Kennedy charged the Panel of Consultants on Vocational Education with the responsibility for considering the then-current vocational education legislation in relation to changing social conditions. Its report, *Education for a Changing World of Work*, was to serve as a basis for modernizing and improving job training, and it set the stage for the passage of the Vocational Education Act of 1963.

The national Advisory Council on Vocational Education, appointed in 1967 by President Johnson in accordance with requirements of the 1963 act, produced a report, *The Bridge Between Man and His Work*, which resulted in substantial changes in the law in the form of the Vocational Education Amendments Act of 1968. Under this Act, a continuing national Advisory Council on Vocational Education was created; it submitted its first annual report of findings and recommendations to President Nixon in 1969. The national Advisory Council on Vocational Education, as well as each state advisory council, is charged with the regular review of vocational education as a basis for systematic updating.

2 Job training is viewed by many as a partial solution to current social problems Many persons look to vocational education for at least a partial solution to the social problems attendent upon America's unemployment. The 1969 report, as well as subsequent reports, of the national Advisory Council on Vocational Education have placed equal faith in the capacity of vocational education to "solve the major social problems of our time." Such faith is based on the grounds that more vocational education would reduce the violence, distrust of society by the young, campus and inner-city revolt, and minority group unrest that has plagued our nation throughout the 1960s and early 1970s.

3 Cooperative planning through advisory committees reflects the interests and priorities of employers, schools, and communities The cooperative planning involved in developing vocational programs—ranging from the identification of needs through the discussion of alternative systems to the attainment of consensus required to put a program into operation—is basically a social process that reflects the principle of freedom of choice. Advisory committees, an innovation in vocational education, assist school boards in planning programs of vocational education at the local, state, and national levels. These committees, which largely reflect the interests and priorities of employers, schools, and communities, make their decision based on the changing social, economic, and political conditions as they perceive them.

4 Automation has broadened the scope of vocational education The recommendations of the Panel of Consultants on Vocational Education, which resulted in the Vocational Education Act of 1963, were made during a period when the effects of automation were causing large-scale unemployment. As a result the panel recommended a broadening of the scope of vocational education. In order to make training available to more people, new and emerging occupations were recognized. The Vocational Education Amendments of 1968 went even further in that they specified that all occupations were to be included in the realm of vocational education except those classified as professional and that required a baccalaureate or higher degree. It has been estimated that this definition of vocational education covered 90 percent of the nation's occupations.

Concept of Social Class

The American college was originally thought of as the training ground for society's leaders, whereas the high school came to be considered as the school that offered terminal education for the masses. If in the high schools vocational education were to become the alternative to college preparatory studies, two kinds of education—one for leaders and one for workers—would become a reality. Many thoughtful educators sensed a danger in this approach, the danger of an educational dualism based on social class which, if widely accepted, might strengthen social stratification. The possibility that a caste system might be created in American society through a dualistic educational process was debated during the

Table 3.1   Occupations Classified by Interest and Level of Responsibility* (26)

Interest field	Level of responsibility			
	Levels 1–2	Level 3	Level 4	Levels 5–6
service, personal- social	counselor, social worker	YMCA official, detective	barber, cook	taxi driver, watchman
business, contact	broker, stocks, sales man- ager	auto salesman, retailer	auctioneer, poll inter- viewer	peddler, bootblack
business, organization	banker, union official	accountant, employment manager	cashier, credit clerk	file clerk, messenger boy
physical science, technology	professional engineer, chemist	contractor, radio operator	electrician, mechanic	truck driver, machine operator
biological science	physician, pathologist	medical tech- nologist, chiropractor	dental hygienist, X-ray tech- nician	agricultural aide, laboratory tester
outdoor, physical	district ranger, manager, (large farm)	county agri- cultural agent, game warden	miner, diver	gardner, lumber jack
general, cultural	editor, teacher	radio announcer, reporter	law clerk, court reporter	copy boy, library page
arts, entertain- ment	designer, music arranger	advertising writer, showman, entertainer	photogra- pher, window decorator	stagehand, showcard writer

Levels 1–2: professional and managerial; Level 3: semiprofessional and small business; Level 4: skilled; Levels 5–6: semiskilled and unskilled.

Source: Max F. Baer and Edward C. Roeber, Occupational Information (*Chicago: Science Research Associates, 1964*).

discussions that led to the passage of the Smith-Hughes Act, and some clearly viewed vocational education as the appropriate form of education for the lower classes. The first report of the National Advisory Council on Vocational Education stated that the majority of Americans felt that vocational education was designed for somebody else's children. It further accused the nation of intellectual snobbery where vocational education was concerned. "Clearly, in the minds of some," Leighbody (24) has stated, "the goal of vocational education is to meet the needs of those who are less fortunate economically, socially, and intellectually."

Problem of Occupational Status

In most cultures, less social prestige is accorded to those who perform society's more routine tasks than to those who do the intellectual work. But from the beginning of the American experience, there has been a strong tradition of egalitarianism, which has helped sustain the ideal of the classless society. Yet every thoughtful American knows that a hierarchy of social class exists in this country and that it is closely related to occupations. What has been accomplished in the United States is a degree of economic and social mobility, which is greater than that to be found in almost any other country. Nevertheless, every occupation possesses a varying degree of prestige, which is not entirely related to the financial rewards it carries.

At levels above the underprivileged, social stratification in the United States is less sharp and more fluid than in almost any other western country, but nevertheless it exists. Studies (25) indicate that there is general consensus among Americans as to the prestige value of various kinds of occupations and that four factors seem to enter equally into the public's prestige ranking: (a) the economic returns of the occupation, (b) its social contribution, (c) the amount of education and training it requires, and (d) the extent to which it deals with intellectual matters. It is clear, too, that one of the factors, the amount of education and training needed, exerts an influence on each of the other factors. It would be a mistake, however, to assume that the benefits of additional education and training are automatic, because these, in turn, are affected by factors such as economic conditions, demand and supply of labor, and the effects of government regulation.

Other criteria of occupational status include the degree of responsibility required by the work (see Table 3.1); types of symbols, tools, and materials used by the worker; degree of authority given to workers; degree of intrinsic interest in the work; and the degree of initiative required in the work.

Summary

The philosophy of vocational education has been affected by philosophical, economic, and sociological factors. It is grounded in our democratic belief in the optimal development of each individual citizen in accordance with his or her interests and needs. Objectives, principles, and practices in the field have closely reflected the social and economic changes in our nation's history as well as the pragmatic educational philosophy of John Dewey, with its strong emphasis on experience-centered learning. The assumptions of vocational education, as expressed by its leaders and echoed in the Federal Vocational Education Acts, have increasingly reflected the belief that vocational education should be a basic element in every individual's education. There is also widespread consensus that it should be offered by all public school systems on a continuing basis, that it is inseparable from sound general education, and that it should serve the humanistic needs of all students as well as the demands of a technological society. There is an increasing recognition of the value of vocational education as a teaching-learning method for general education.

The availability of vocational education, as a source of labor supply, affects the economic welfare of the nation. Vocational education is sensitive to the needs of a fast-changing society, and the effects of automation have accentuated the importance of the field as an intermediary between technology and labor. There is continuing evidence of the economic value of education to individuals as reflected in increased lifetime earnings for higher levels of education and training. Current demands are being made by taxpayers for accountability for achievement in line with the costs of education. Vocational education programs and courses are being examined as a basis for the establishment of priorities and specification of measurable objectives essential to the demonstration of cost effectiveness.

Much of the emphasis of federal vocational education acts has been toward equating social and economic opportunities for all Americans. Our democratic society endorses, as a basic right of the individual, freedom in the selection of an occupation. Job training has been viewed as a partial solution to social problems of the day on the grounds that more vocational education would promote national economic security and reduce social unrest. There is still some problem with the concept of vocational education as an appropriate form of education for the lower social classes only. Despite the American ideal of a classless society, a hierarchy of social class exists that is clearly related to occupations. It is known that occupations possess varying degrees of prestige or status related to such factors as their economic returns, amount of education required, social contribution, and intellectual content. Social stratification in the United States is more fluid than in other western countries, with the amount of education and training a strong influence on the social mobility of the individual.

Activities

For review

1 Explain the major philosophical differences underlying the Smith-Hughes Act and the Vocational Education Acts of the 1960s.

2 Compare the educational needs of our citizens during the agricultural, industrial, and technological periods. Relate these needs to vocational education.

3 What were the basic shortcomings of the Smith-Hughes Act? How were these corrected in the 1963 act and the 1968 amendments?

4 Leighbody listed six areas in which the breakthrough of technology has occurred. Rank these areas according to their importance for vocational education. Justify your choices.

5 What influence does a person's occupation have on his or her social status?

6 What is the philosophy underlying the distribution of vocational education funds as defined in the Vocational Education Amendments of 1968? What philosophy is implied by the "matching" characteristics of such legislation? What changes were made in the matching feature under the 1968 amendments?

7 Charles A. Prosser, a leader in the Life Adjustment movement of the 1940s, proposed sixteen theories for vocational education. For each of these theories, indicate whether it is or is not still valid and why.

For discussion

1 Some educators and legislators have viewed vocational education as a solution to the social ills of the times. Others have expressed doubts as to the extent to which job training can alleviate the plight of the disadvantaged. Select one point of view and defend it.

2 How has our changing school population influenced the philosophy of vocational education?

3 How might vocational education minimize the problem of social stratification?

4 Why is it important for a teacher, a department, and a school to have a philosophy of education?

5 How is vocational education related to social mobility?

6 What type of vocational education is automatically included in principles of taxation that apply to the support of *general* education? What type of vocational education requires additional justification if it is to be tax supported?

For exploration

1 Using a reference such as Wirth's *Education in the Technological Society*, summarize the contributions of David Snedden and Charles Prosser to vocational education.

2 Compare the positions of Snedden and Prosser with John Dewey with regard to the role of vocational education.

3 Select one course that you have taught or that you plan to teach, and develop a statement of philosophy for it.

4 Interview two vocational educators and two non-vocational educators regarding their philosophy of vocational education. How are they alike? How are they different?

5 Interview a teacher and summarize the method of learning that he or she uses as a basis for instruction. Then observe a classroom situation under the teacher's direction and summarize the learning principles you saw in action.

6 How is vocational education related to each of the following? (a) general education, (b) specialized education, (c) liberal education, (d) liberal arts, (e) cultural education, (f) career education, (g) professional education.

7 Develop your own table of occupations, using one or more of the criteria for occupational status or prestige described in this chapter.

References

1 *Cardinal Principles of Secondary Education*, A Report of the Commission on the Reorganization of Secondary Education, appointed by the National Education Association, Bulletin 1918, Vol. 35 (Washington, D.C.: Department of the Interior, Bureau of Education, 1918).

2 William James, *Pragmatism: A New Name for Some Old Ways of Thinking* (New York: Longmans, Green and Company, 1907).

3 Boyd H. Bode, *How We Learn* (Boston: D. C. Heath and Company, 1940).

4 John Dewey, *Democracy and Education* (New York: The Macmillan Company, 1928).

5 William H. Kilpatrick, *Philosophy of Education from the Experimentalist Outlook*, Forty-First Yearbook of the National Society for the Study of Education (Chicago: The University of Chicago Press, 1942).

6 Gerald B. Leighbody, *Vocational Education in America's Schools: Major Issues of the 1970s* (Chicago: American Technical Society, 1972), pp. 29–30. (Reproduced by permission)

7 Charles A. Prosser and Thomas A. Quigley, *Vocational Education in a Democracy* (Chicago: American Technical Society, 1949), pp. 217–232. (Reproduced by permission)

8 Melvin L. Barlow, "Foundations of Vocational Education," in *American Vocational Journal*, Vol. 42, No. 3, March 1967, pp. 17–19. (Reproduced by permission)

9 *Vocational Education—The Bridge Between Man and His Work*, General Report of the Advisory Council on Vocational Education (Washington, D.C.: U.S. Department of Health, Education and Welfare, November 1968), p. 192.

10 John F. Thompson, *Foundations of Vocational Education* (Englewood Cliffs, N.J.: Prentice-Hall, Inc., 1973), pp. 91–102. (Reproduced by permission)

11 Garth L. Mangum, "Curriculum Response to Occupational Trends," in *Vocational Education: Today and Tomorrow*, eds. Gerald G. Somers and J. Kenneth Little (Madison: University of Wisconsin, Center for Studies in Vocational and Technical Education, 1971), p. 36.

12 John Beaumont, "Philosophical Implications of the Vocational Education Amendments of 1968," in *Contemporary Concepts in Vocational Education*, ed. Gordon F. Law (Washington, D.C.: American Vocational Association, 1971), p. 13.

13 Gerald B. Leighbody. See Ref. 6, pp. 73–74. (Reproduced by permission)

14 Ibid, p. 7. (Reproduced by permission)

15 Rupert N. Evans, Garth L. Mangum, and Otto Pragan, *Education for Employment* (Ann Arbor: University of Michigan, Institute of Labor and Industrial Relations; Wayne State University; and National Manpower Policy Task Force, 1969), p. 3.

16 Ibid, p. 4.

17 Ibid, pp. 5–6.

18 Arthur G. Wirth, *Education in the Technological Society* (Scranton: International Textbook Company, 1971), p. 166.

19 Gerald B. Leighbody. See Ref. 6, pp. 56–57. (Reproduced by permission)

20 Ibid, pp. 58–59. (Reproduced by permission)

21 Robert M. Tomlinson, "Implications and Reflections: The Vocational Education Amendments of 1968," ed. Gordon F. Law, in *Contemporary Concepts in Vocational Education* (Washington, D.C.: American Vocational Association, 1971), p. 31.

22 Melvin L. Barlow, "Changing Goals," in *Vocational Education: Today and Tomorrow*, eds. Gerald G. Somers and J. Kenneth Little (Madison: University of Wisconsin, Center for Studies in Vocational and Technical Education, 1971), p. 11. (Reproduced by permission)

23 Byrl R. Shoemaker, "People, Jobs and Society: Toward Relevance in Education," in *Contemporary Concepts in Vocational Education*, ed. Gordon F. Law (Washington, D.C.: American Vocational Association, 1971), pp. 20–21. (Reproduced by permission)

24 Gerald B. Leighbody. See Ref. 6, p. 9. (Reproduced by permission)

25 Ibid, pp. 124–125. (Reproduced by permission)

26 Max F. Baer and Edward C. Roeber, *Occupational Information* (Chicago: Science Research Associates, 1964). (Reproduced by permission)

Chapter 4

Relationship of

Vocational Education

to Other

Educational Emphases

Introduction

What is general education? What is the relationship of vocational education to general education and to career education? It is the purpose of this chapter to examine the relationships of vocational education to general education, to career education, to career development, to vocational and technical education, and to look at the content and method of vocational education with respect to the developing roles of each concept.

Vocational Education in
Relation to General Education

It has already been established that the purpose of vocational education is to prepare persons for an occupation or to retrain those who need additional skills. Such work should provide personal satisfaction and social usefulness as well as the means for earning a living. It should not be considered professional and should not require a baccalaureate degree. To define general education, to determine its overall purposes, and to see its relationship to vocational education, we need to take a look at the development of the objectives of education.

Historically, the major objective of public education in America has been to prepare individuals for living, not to prepare individuals to make a living. The belief has persisted that a person who has developed his or her mind, body, and character through formal exercises in cultural and intellectual disciplines would automatically be in a better position to enter an occupation than an individual who has not so benefited. Traditionally, Americans have held a Platonic view of education, which emphasizes that the only education worthy of being called education is that which prepares individuals to be perfect citizens. Although Plato (1) recognized the importance of training for work, he considered it debasing and only worthy of those who would be "workers"—not worthy of those who would be "rulers." According to Goldhammer and Taylor (2), the American people have looked upon cultural and intellectual development as the most desirable educational goal for all individuals, and they have viewed the attainment of this goal as a continuing educational process, from the elementary grades through college.

In view of this attitude, the most desirable route students could follow in high school was the academic route, which prepared them for college. The least desirable route through high school became the vocational route, which prepared the individual for work following high school. People who chose to follow this route, when it was available, were "looked down upon."

Between these two routes in most high schools has been a "general" curriculum, which has been designed as an alternate curriculum for those students who do not want to prepare for college or to follow the vocational curriculum. In many schools, however, there has been no vocational curriculum designed to prepare students to enter an occupation immediately following graduation from high school. Students not preparing to enter college have thus been forced to follow the general curriculum because there has been no other choice available. Many students who could have benefited more from a vocational curriculum have chosen to follow the general or academic, simply because there was no other choice or because of the stigma attached to the vocational route (3).

Traditionally, the highest goal that parents might have for their children has been to provide them with a college education. As a result of this ideal, many students who might have experienced success in some other curriculum, choose to drop out of an educational system in which they have experienced failure much more readily than they have experienced success. They are not "academically" inclined, and they feel they get nothing from school that will be of lasting value.

But in spite of the high drop-out rate through the years, preparation for college has continued to be the major aim of public school education. Because most colleges have emphasized the so-called general education courses—English, social studies, the sciences, and mathematics—public schools have continued to provide a preparatory academic curriculum. Colleges have not generally recognized courses in the vocational education programs—business, agriculture, health, home economics, trade and industry, and distributive education—as adequate preparation for entry. Only very recently has there appeared to be a trend among colleges toward the acceptance of a broader-based high school education that includes vocational courses.

A form of social-class distinction has developed around the three public school curricula. At the top of the social and economic scale are the college-bound students (the smallest percentage of the total school-age population), for whom the high school program is primarily designed. At the bottom of the social and economic scale are the work-bound students, also a small percent of the total school-age population. Between these two levels on the social and economic scale are found the great majority of the students who are being "terminally" prepared "for life," whatever that means. These students, when they are graduated or when they drop out, will not go on to college and will have acquired few skills with which they can earn a living (3). They fear becoming those people in our society who perform the unskilled, semiskilled, or skilled work tasks that require little intellectual ability and creativity, who are "looked down" upon by most of our society, including those who actually perform such tasks. They will enter the labor market poorly prepared and will more likely become burdens to society rather than contributing members.

Career Development in Relation to General Education

Our definition of general education implies that the purpose of education is to prepare the individual for living and that this preparation is best obtained through formal education designed to develop the individual culturally and intellectually. Our definition of career education implies that the development of the individual culturally and intellectually is a "worthwhile" goal, but it is a goal that should be achieved through the utilitarian approach of career awareness, orientation to work, and appreciation for the dignity of work. Career education thus contributes to the general education of each individual. According to the American Vocational Association Task Force (4), it is the responsibility of career education to help individuals to develop:

1 *favorable attitudes toward the personal, psychological, social, and economic significance of work*

2 *appreciation for the worth of all types and levels of work*

3 *decision-making skills necessary for choosing career options and for changing career directions*

4 *capability of making considered choices of career goals, based on development of self in relation to the range of career options*

5 *capability of charting a course for realization of self-established career goals in keeping with individual desires, needs, and opportunities*

6 *knowledge, skill, and attitudes necessary for entry and success in a career*

Helping students to develop these accomplishments should be accepted as the responsibility of all levels of educational preparation. It is generally accepted that the responsibility of the elementary school would be to make the individual aware of the world of work, of different careers, and of the respect and dignity of all work and careers. Students should gain this awareness through all their educational activities (5).

Career exploration should be a major responsibility of the junior high school or middle school. The individual is given an opportunity to become familiar with different occupations and professions and the kinds of skills, attitudes, and knowledge generally considered necessary to be successful in such careers. Frequently, career-exploration activities occupy a separate time slot in the school schedule so they can be scheduled concurrently with the student's other subjects. The emphasis is still on general education at this level, but career exploration and orientation should permeate all subject matter.

The beginnings of occupational preparation are found at about the ninth-grade level. Students may be given an opportunity for some practical hands-on experience in several work skills, or they may develop some special skills designed to help them enter the work world. Such practical career exploration may be viewed as preparation of the individual for entry into the world of work or it may be viewed as a necessary basis for wise career judgments (6).

For most academic students at the high school level, career education is more general and exploratory; these students plan to go to college and so are delaying preparation for work until their college years. For these students, career development goals, congruent with the first five responsibilities identified by the AVA Task Force, should be emphasized in all academic subjects. The high school should assume the responsibility for encouraging each individual to acquire some type of job entry level skills, regardless of the curriculum being pursued (7).

The purposes of career education are increasingly becoming synonymous with those of general education. As a concept career education is placing as much importance on the objective of American education, which is to prepare the individual to make a living, as it is to that traditional objective, which is to prepare the individual for life. Increasingly, preparing the individual to make a living is preparing him for life.

Vocational Education in
Relation to Career Development

Elementary School

At the elementary school level, the purpose of career development in relation to vocational education is to make the individual aware of the world of work through the types of careers that can be pursued, those that are considered professional and require a college degree and those that are not. At this level vocational education activities are undertaken as a part of general education. A student becomes acquainted with some work tools and might acquire a cursory use of them. These activities are undertaken to give the individual job entry level skills that can be put to immediate use should he or she withdraw from school (8).

Middle School

The purpose of career development in relation to vocational education at the middle school level is to provide the individual with the opportunities to explore work attitudes, skill requirements, and knowledge required for those clusters of occupations that do not require a baccalaureate degree. The individual might at the same time explore clusters of occupations that require advanced training beyond the secondary level. During these years the best kind of guidance and counseling should be available to assure that students have adequate information and understandings about job requirements, life styles, personal interests, and abilities. One major objective is that all students acquire an appreciation for the dignity of work and a respect for all workers, regardless of the kinds of work they do (9).

High School

The purpose of career development in relation to vocational education at the high school level is to provide the individual with job entry level skills for a cluster of occupations. This cluster of occupations might require the pursuit of skills, knowledge, and attitudes in a particular area of vocational education, such as agricultural education, business and office education, home economics education, health education, distributive education, industrial and technical education. Career development at this level implies a relationship between vocational activities and general education activities, with all learning experiences made personally relevant to the individual. For example, students should see that good English is necessary to good communication with peers, subordinates, and superiors in a work environment. Students should see themselves as contributing citizens, as more effective workers, and therefore as happier persons if they acquire the skills, knowledge, and attitudes afforded by vocational education experiences (10).

Vocational Education in Relation to
Vocational and Technical Education

Though we have stated that technical education is considered a part of vocational education, it is well to examine the terms with respect to their relationships. Vocational education is that education (training) necessary to perform work tasks that require varying levels of skill to perform but that do not require complex-to-highly-complex cognitive understandings. Technical education, on the other hand, refers to that education (training and education) necessary to perform work tasks of varying levels of skill but that also require complex-to-highly-complex cognitive understandings.

In addition, vocational education at the secondary level is responsible for providing the knowledge, skills, and attitudes necessary for job entry level skills in a particular occupational area. It can also provide the basics necessary for advanced study at the postsecondary level. Technical education at the secondary level, however, does not provide for job entry level skills, but rather it provides preparation for advanced study at the postsecondary level to acquire job entry level competencies (11).

Since World War II, with the increasing need for individuals trained to perform highly technical tasks, increasing emphasis has been given to technical education. There is an increasing need in business, industry, and government for people who can perform specialized tasks that require complex cognitive and psychomotor learnings. It is not essential that individuals have baccalaureate degrees to perform these tasks, although some do have such degrees. However, those persons performing technical skills acquired in an undergraduate degree program are more likely to have jobs that are considered professional. Usually, technical education is considered to be more closely allied with vocational education than it is with academic education. Although it requires an academically oriented intellect, it has a work-oriented objective. The term "trade" is commonly associated with vocational skills; the term "technician" is commonly associated with technical skills. "Tools" are usually thought of as being used by workers in a particular *trade;* "instruments" are usually thought of as being used by technicians (12).

A person following a technical education in a postsecondary program will most likely follow a curriculum well grounded in science and/or mathematics. On completion of the program, the person in all probability could expect to become a technician and serve as a paraprofessional to an individual who has received one or more college degrees. For example, an individual who has trained to be a dental technician in a program requiring less than a baccalaureate degree will most likely work as a paraprofessional for a dentist who has earned more than one college degree.

A person following a vocational education in a postsecondary program will most likely follow a curriculum that is not well grounded in science and/or mathematics. On completion of the program, the person in all probability could expect to work in a trade with his or her peers. For example, an individual who has trained to be an auto mechanic in a postsecondary vocational school will probably work with other auto mechanics who have had about the same training he or she has had.

Developing Role of
Career Education as a Concept

Career education, vocational education, general education: What are the relationships? In the preceding paragraphs the relationships have been discussed with respect to formal public education from kindergarten through high school. But it is generally agreed that the responsibility for education begins in the home and that the community itself must assume a major responsibility both for in-school learning and for out-of-school learning. In addition the concept of career education goes far beyond the secondary level. Continuing education is growing in popularity, providing a means through which drop outs and graduates of secondary and postsecondary school programs can acquire vocational training and retraining. Career education is giving impetus to the long-standing notion that education continues throughout life or at least throughout the working career. Changing technology is requiring that workers be retrained over and over again. Career education can be primarily vocational education at the postsecondary level when the purpose of such education is to train or retrain for employability or promotion in a job where a college degree is not involved. But even at the postsecondary level it is the responsibility of the training program to provide general education that is relevant to the vocational training and that will tend to make the individual a better citizen.

Career preparation is generally recognized as a legitimate purpose for pursuing an education leading to a college degree, although there is a great deal of debate, which we will not review in detail here, as to the educational content that best prepares a college student for a profession. It is not our intention to examine the various career routes that are available at the college level. Because we are primarily interested in career education at less than the baccalaureate level, we simply want to establish here that career education does exist at the college level and that it is a part of all degree-granting programs.

All of these thoughts lead to the notion that career education is a new way of looking at the total scheme of education. It is our intention to develop the idea that career education is not just vocational education or general education. Rather, it is vocational education, it is general education, and it is academic education. As a concept, career education gives new emphases to the total education of individuals. As much importance is being given to vocational education, which prepares individuals for "life" by preparing them to make a "living," as has been traditionally given to academic education, which prepares individuals for "life" by preparing them for college. The public school, through pressures of the community, is beginning to restructure its programs so as to provide learning activities that will have holding power on individuals who might otherwise drop out of the traditional, academically oriented curriculum. Career education is providing a "thread" that runs throughout the academic and vocational programs, giving relevance to each and making it possible for individuals to identify themselves and their roles in society. Career education is providing opportunities for individuals to view all aspects of work and contribution that all kinds of work make toward the welfare of humankind.

Career education makes learning activities designed to prepare a person to become a carpenter, a typist, or a cook just as important and worthwhile in the school curriculum as learning activities designed to prepare a person to become a doctor, lawyer, or scientist. Career educa-

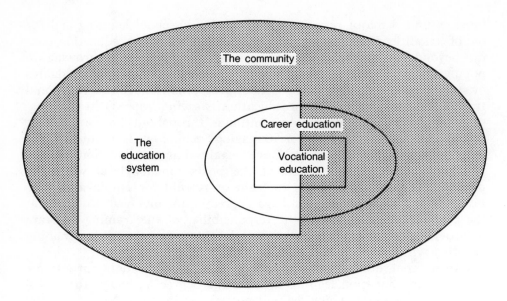

Figure 4.1 Career education's place in education (13).

tion seeks to integrate the curriculum in such a way that literature, American history, and biology are seen to be as relevant to the student preparing to be a carpenter, a typist, or a cook, as to the student planning to be a doctor, lawyer, or scientist.

One image of the place of career education in the total educational scheme is reproduced in Figure 4.1. In this Figure, Hoyt et al (13) make the point that there is no reason to establish priorities among careers, culture, citizenship, family life, and self-awareness as education objectives. They feel that none of these priorities is mutually exclusive and that each objective contributes to each of the other objectives. They make the point that careers, other than professional, have never been a significant objective of education in this country. This model exemplifies the authors' statement (13):

☐ *Conceptually, it [career education] is as if a variety of monitors were installed within the education system. One representing the career objective would comb the entire education experience to identify those segments which could usefully contribute to career success. Other monitors would have the same assignment for citizenship, culture, family life, self-awareness, and other education objectives. None would compete, all would cooperate, and each objective would be strengthened by pursuit and achievement of the others.*

We agree with this concept of career education as a variety of monitors combing the entire educational system, but we view the visual image differently. Our view, shown in Figure 4.2, ascribes to career education

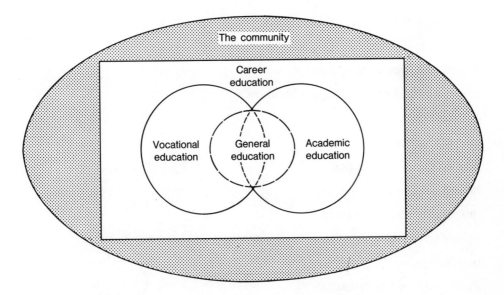

Figure 4.2   An alternate view: Career education's place in education.

a more centralized position in that it serves as the focal point for the total educational system. Vocational education and academic education have equal roles in the system; they overlap, so individuals following a vocational curriculum acquire some academic preparation and individuals following an academic curriculum acquire some vocational preparation. General education is equally important to both curricula.

Content and Method
of Vocational Education

The content and method of vocational education varies with the school, with the level of education, and with the philosophy of the school administrators. Schools that are traditional in nature, which place emphasis on preparation for life through a college-oriented curriculum, will provide less content in vocational preparation, and the method of instruction will be more theoretical than practical. Schools that are more modern in nature will place as much emphasis on preparation for life through preparation for work as they do on preparation for life through preparation for college. These schools will give equal emphasis to college preparation and to vocational preparation, and the method of instruction will be practical as well as theoretical. To structure objectives, activities, and materials, these schools will use the fifteen career clusters identified by the United States Office of Education:

agri-business and natural resources

business and office

communications and media

consumer and homemaking education

construction

environmental control

fine arts and humanities

health

hospitality and recreation

manufacturing

marine science

marketing and distribution

personal services

public services

transportation

Many guidelines that have been developed by national, state, and local agencies, such as those prepared by the Division of Vocational and Technical Education of the Mississippi State Department of Education (14), provide excellent resources for developing objectives, activities, materials, and evaluation procedures for these career clusters.

Elementary School

At the elementary school level, where the emphasis is on career awareness, career education will be integrated into the subject matter areas. The teachers should plan units of instruction developed around career awareness, whether the major objective of each unit is to develop reading skills, writing skills, or arithmetic skills. Activities should be designed so that individuals at this level are made aware of career clusters in a systematic way rather than in the traditional way of acquainting them with some types of work-careers in a hit-or-miss fashion. In too many instances such exposure has been inadequate both with respect to materials and methods used and teacher receptiveness. Teachers should systematically plan activities such as field trips, resource speakers, and role-playing experiences in addition to traditional classroom activities that use individualized instructional materials. Where possible, closed-circuit television programs should be used as well as film strips, teaching machines, slides, cassettes, and films. Students might be given some hands-on experiences with tools designed to acquaint them with certain vocations, but the objective would not be to provide any job entry level skills at this level.

Middle School

At the middle school level, where emphasis is on career exploration, career education should continue as an integrated part of other subject matter areas. Teachers working in committees, with the help of resource specialists and guidance counselors, should plan units of instruction in the subject matter areas developed around the fifteen occupational clusters identified by the U.S. Office of Education. Students should begin to receive help in the decision-making process of self-analysis to determine strengths, interests, and abilities toward certain careers. Certainly by the ninth grade students should have some hands-on experiences in selected occupational activities. Those who definitely show lack of abilities to follow academic programs and who show inclinations of dropping out should be guided into activities designed to give them vocational competencies as quickly as possible; some of these students might even begin cooperative work experience activities if it can be demonstrated that they would profit most from such activities. In these years students should definitely begin to develop well-informed concepts of careers toward which they might begin preparation and some idea of what the future holds for people who follow certain careers.

High School

At the high school level, the emphasis is on occupational implementation. Even so, career education must continue to be integrated into subject matter areas. During these years students should be guided into making decisions as to career choices they will follow. Those who select a career that requires advanced study toward a college degree should be certain that their program prepares them for admission to the college of their choice. Those who select a career that does not require college level study should be guided into either the academic or vocational curriculum, depending on the individual's personal situation. Individuals should be made aware of the consequences of their decisions and of changing their career objectives. The freedom of career choice should be a continuing characteristic of career education. An individual might follow the academic curriculum with no intention of going to college, or the reverse would be a choice: to follow the vocational curriculum with every intent of going to college. It should always be possible for an individual to follow the vocational education curriculum to acquire entry level skills so that he or she can be prepared to go to work immediately following graduation from high school, but at the same time take those courses required for admission to most colleges. In any event, even the individual who follows the rigid academic curriculum should acquire some type of vocational skill while he or she is in high school.

The methods at the high school level for individuals following the academic curriculum should be similar to the methods of the middle school programs, although more individualization of instruction should be provided. Individuals should be able to move along at their own rates; they should be evaluated in terms of their performance in meeting terminal objectives rather than in terms of their having met certain subject requirements and having earned so many Carnegie units of credit. Intensive training laboratories and cooperative work experiences should be provided as capstone activities for those individuals planning to enter an occupation immediately upon graduation from high school. The method should be highly oriented toward hands-on activities.

Postsecondary School

At the postsecondary level, career education should continue as a vocational curriculum for entry level skills or for more advanced vocational or technical training or retraining. Adult education has been primarily designed for drop outs, for individuals who want to train for a different career, or for individuals who want to upgrade their present skills for job advancement. At the postsecondary vocational-technical level of education the emphasis should be almost totally hands-on training, unless the individual is having to learn and acquire basic skills and knowledge necessary to begin such activities.

Summary

This chapter has examined the conceptual relationships of vocational education to general education, to career education, to career development, and to vocational and technical education. Content and method of vocational education has been conceptually presented with respect to these relationships.

Traditionally, people have viewed the academic curriculum, which has been oriented toward college preparation, as the most prestigious secondary program and consequently the most desirable route to follow at the secondary level. The vocational curriculum, oriented toward preparation for work, has been viewed by some as the least prestigious and consequently the least desirable route. The general curriculum, oriented toward no specific goal other than graduation, has been followed by most students because it does not require the rigorous intellectual concentration of the academic program and does not carry the stigma of preparing the individual for work.

Career education as a concept is designed to change people's attitudes with respect to these three traditional secondary programs; it is expected to fuse the three routes so that all education is career oriented. All curricula would then emphasize dignity in all work. All students, regardless of career objectives, would be expected to have some type of vocational skill by the time they graduate from high school.

Technical education is considered a part of vocational education and might be started at the secondary level or the postsecondary level. At the secondary level, it usually requires more study at the postsecondary level to acquire job competency skills. It is most frequently distinguished from strictly vocational education by the need for a more scientific/mathematics-oriented curriculum and by the relationship that the worker has with professionals in his or her field who hold jobs requiring college degrees.

At the awareness level content and method of vocational education are integrated into general education objectives and activities, so that individuals are made aware of work through career clusters in a systematic way. Individuals are then given opportunities to explore their abilities and interests with respect to several of the career clusters. Where needs are identified, appropriate vocational skills might be started; otherwise, career activities are integrated into traditional subjects. Career education at the preparation level is primarily vocational education (secondary and postsecondary), when the purpose of such education is to train or retrain for employability or promotion in a job where a college degree is not involved. General education provided at this level is made relevant to the vocational training and is intended to make the individual a better citizen.

At all levels, career education encompasses vocational education, general education, and academic education. Although it is not all of education, it gives new emphases to all education and provides a thread that runs throughout the academic and vocational programs, giving relevance to each and making it possible for individuals to identify their roles in society.

Activities

For review

1 Describe the three traditional curriculum routes a high school freshman might choose to follow through high school.

2 Why do a majority of parents want their children to graduate from college?

3 Why has there been such a high drop out rate in the secondary schools?

4 What is career education and why is it important?

5 What are the primary functions of career education?

6 How is career education coordinating vocational and academic curricula in public schools?

7 What are the responsibilities of the elementary school, middle school, and high school regarding career development in relation to vocational education?

8 Distinguish between vocational and technical education.

9 Describe the content and method of vocational education at the elementary school, middle school, high school, and postsecondary school levels.

10 What are the responsibilities of the elementary, middle, and high schools regarding career development in relation to general education?

11 Assuming that career education incorporates the entire educational spectrum, how can adults fit into this spectrum?

For discussion

1 According to the American Vocational Association Task Force, career education has various responsibilities in career development. Discuss these responsibilities and the level of educational preparation at which they are applicable.

2 Discuss how vocational education relates to vocational and technical education.

3 What are the relationships in your locale between general education and vocational-technical education? If you could make any change in these relationships, what change would you make? Why?

4 Compare the philosophy of career education held by Hoyt et al with your own philosophy.

5 Relate this statement to career education: "Preparing individuals to make a living is preparing them for life."

6 Discuss three courses of study available to students in most high schools and the prevailing attitudes generally held about each. Have attitudes changed? If so, how?

7 Trace the changes in the attitudes toward vocational education since World War II.

For exploration

1 Make a survey of last year's high school graduates in your community to determine what percentage is attending college, what percentage is employed, what percentage received vocational training while in high school, and what percentage of those who received vocational training are employed in related areas or are enrolled in related areas in college. Be prepared to present your findings to the class and to discuss the effectiveness with which the school is meeting its objectives.

2 Conduct a survey of career education in either your local elementary, middle, or high schools. Prepare a summarization sheet telling what is being done, how it is being done, and what needs to be done. Determine the scope and intensity of career education programs in your community, state, and nation. Be prepared to present your findings to the class.

3 Use the *Dictionary of Occupational Titles* to determine the kinds of jobs available in one or more of the occupational clusters.

4 Survey people in your community to determine how they feel about vocational education. Suggested groups are teachers, academic students, vocational students, factory workers, farmers, business people, and other professional people. Be prepared to present your findings to the class. Do attitudes vary among groups?

5 Make a study of students who have dropped out of school for the past five years to determine why they dropped out of school.

6 Make a survey of your local school system to determine what curricula are available. Are curricula designed to meet the needs of every individual?

7 Read and critique one article on career education. How do the writer's ideas relate to the ideas expressed in this chapter?

8 Write a position paper on one of the following statements or be prepared to debate it in class. Your information should be documented carefully.

(a) Career education is more important than vocational education.

(b) A college education is the desired goal for persons entering the public school system.

(c) The most desirable route an individual can follow in high school is the academic route.

(d) Forcing students to follow the general curriculum causes drop outs.

(e) Each high school student, whether college bound or not, should have at least one salable skill when he or she leaves high school.

(f) Only those students who have a high IQ should take college preparatory courses; those students who do not have high IQs should take vocational courses.

(g) Too many students are enrolled in college-preparatory programs; too few are enrolled in vocational programs.

9 Invite the following persons to participate in a panel discussion on how education can best benefit *all* the people.

(a) a public high school counselor

(b) a vocational-technical school director

(c) a college dean or professor

(d) a businessman

10 Ask two individuals to speak to the class on the advantages and disadvantages of following an academic high school program and a vocational program. ·

References

1 B. Jowett, translator, *The Dialogues of Plato*, Volume Two (New York: Random House, 1920), p. 424.

2 Keith Goldhammer and Robert E. Taylor, *Career Education: Perspective and Promise* (Columbus, Ohio: Charles E. Merrill Publishing Company, 1972), pp. 18–20.

3 Rupert N. Evans, *Foundations of Vocational Education* (Columbus, Ohio: Charles E. Merrill Publishing Company, 1971), p. 29.

4 "Task Force Report on Career Education," in *American Vocational Journal*, Vol. 47, No. 1, January 1972, p. 12.

5 J. Harold McMinn and Reese Ishee, *Introduction to Career Awareness, Career-Centered Curriculum for Vocational Complexes in Mississippi*, Exemplary Project #0–361–0067 in Vocational Education Conducted Under Part D Public Law 90–576 (Jackson, Mississippi: Division of Vocational and Technical Education, Mississippi State Department of Education).

6 J. Harold McMinn and Reese Ishee, *Career Exploration, Level I and Level II, Career-Centered Curriculum for Vocational Complexes in Mississippi*, Exemplary Project #0–361–0067 in Vocational Education Conducted Under Part D Public Law 90–576 (Jackson, Mississippi: Division of Vocational and Technical Education, Mississippi State Department of Education).

7 John B. Stevenson, *An Introduction to Career Education* (Worthington, Ohio: Charles A. Jones Publishing Company, 1973), pp. 159–162.

8 J. Harold McMinn and Reese Ishee. See Ref. 5.

9 J. Harold McMinn and Reese Ishee. See Ref. 6.

10 John B. Stevenson. See Ref. 7.

11 Rupert N. Evans. See Ref. 3, p. 183.

12 Roy W. Roberts, *Vocational and Practical Arts Education*, Third Edition (New York: Harper & Row Publishers, 1971), pp. 288–311.

13 Kenneth B. Hoyt, Rupert N. Evans, Edward F. Mackin, and Garth L. Mangum, *Career Education: What It Is and How to Do It*, Second Edition (Salt Lake City: Olympus Publishing Company, 1974), pp. 34–35.

14 J. Harold McMinn and Reese Ishee. See Ref. 6.

Part 2

Career Development:

An Expanding

Emphasis in

Education

Chapter 5

Theory

and Design

of

Career Education

Introduction: The Evolving
Concept of Career Education

The American public school system has always been the focus of much attention and debate. Does the system provide the type of experience needed by today's young people and adults, many of whom will live out much of their lives in the twenty-first century? Frequently the critics have been much more vocal than those who have sought to defend public education, and the system has undergone sharp changes in direction from time to time, as in the post-Sputnik era. It has been pointed out in previous chapters that our system of education is a reflection of our society and of the personal and social needs of its citizens. The continuous and accelerated nature of change in our lives has made it necessary that education, as the chief vehicle for life preparation, be appraised more frequently and intensively than in the past.

Some have said that our system of education stifles initiative, demands conformity with the system, lacks relevance to the real world, is too content-centered, denies equal educational opportunities to all, disregards the needs of learners, and is too costly. Increasingly such discontent, coupled with a shortage of economic resources, has raised some fundamental doubts about the validity of traditional aims and procedures now prevailing in public schools. A well-documented case could be presented for the effectiveness of public education in this country, for the evidence of its success is all around us. However, the demands for alternatives to the present educational system are growing, and policymakers at national, state, and local levels are under pressure to find better ways to develop more relevance, quality, and equality of educational opportunities for students throughout America.

Solutions to the problems of learning are being introduced through competency-based teacher education, community schools, nongraded schools, open schools, computer-assisted instruction, flexible scheduling, systems-oriented curricula, humanized learning, and a plethora of technologically sophisticated approaches for individualizing learning. Proposed prescriptions are numerous and, while there is agreement as to the need for change in the schools, there is no consensus as to how it is best brought about. Nevertheless, there are indications that the need for change is beginning to result in recognized movements that may bring about sweeping changes in our system of public education. One such movement is career education. In early 1971, Dr. Sidney P. Marland, U.S. Commissioner of Education, provided the initial federal thrust toward career education for all students. Since that time, under the leadership of Commissioner T. H. Bell, career education has become a major goal of the Office of Education and a primary concern of educators throughout the nation.

Career education is an evolving concept and has both advocates and critics. The range of meanings and the implications of career education are treated in this chapter. Past and present conceptualizations of career education are presented, and the reader is challenged to think creatively about the dimensions of career education. The principles, objectives, and characteristics of career education are treated, and examples of national, state, and local models are reviewed.

Roots of Career Education

As an educational emphasis of the seventies, career education revives some educational measures of earlier eras, and it contains some elements that are new. The struggle to introduce vocational education into all educational curricula was identified with the careers of David Snedden, an educational administrator; Charles Prosser, a lawyer; and John Dewey, a philosopher, among others. Snedden was an advocate of integrating occupational education into the general curriculum. Prosser argued for social efficiency and the need for all students to prepare for useful employment. Dewey saw vocational education as a means of liberalizing education (1).

The historical, philosophical, psychological, sociological, and economic antecedents of vocational and career education have been presented in previous chapters. In summarizing the historical, philosophical, and conceptual bases of career education, Herr (2) identified five points relative to the emergent visibility of career education:

1 *Virtually every concept which is presently embodied in career education has been advocated at some point in American education.*

2 *Both vocational education and vocational guidance were direct responses to the . . . industrial character of the U.S. in the late 1880s and 90s as well as the first two decades of the twentieth century.*

3 *Advocacy of vocational education and vocational guidance has largely been precipitated by economic and industrial needs . . . in the last decade, this situation has largely reversed, with individual needs being considered the major base from which educational programming must begin.*

4 *Until approximately 1960, . . . the categories of vocational training were defined by occupational or industrial needs or, in some cases, inertia. Since 1960, however, increased attention has been focused on the needs of special groups of persons—i.e., the disadvantaged, the handicapped, the academically retarded . . .*

5 *. . . these elements have constituted support for articulating, from the kindergarten through post-secondary education, a series of increasingly complex educational experiences which would be available to all students, to out-of-school youth and to adults. Further these experiences are seen as requiring not only vocational preparation in a continuum from job entry to highly complex technical skills but also vocational guidance in a continuum oriented to pre-vocational and educational awareness, attitudinal development, awareness of personal strengths and potentialities as well as the development of decision-making abilities.*

Marland's Proposal
on Career Education

The concept of career education is undoubtedly one of the more potentially far-reaching influences affecting education in this century. A great deal of publicity, discussion, and federal funds have been devoted to efforts to restructure public education around the idea of career education. What does career education include? To answer this question, it is necessary to examine the circumstances under which it has developed.

In an address to the Convention of the National Association of Secondary School Principals at Houston, Texas, in January 1971, Dr. Sidney P. Marland, Jr., then U.S. Commissioner of Education, deplored the tendency toward dividing public education into *academic* and *vocational* components. He proposed an emphasis on *career education*, which would effectively redirect all public education so that persons completing school programs at grade 12 would be ready to enter higher education or to enter useful and rewarding employment. Commissioner Marland deplored the inadequacy of traditional curricula and practices that result in irrelevant general education for over half our high school students who, being prepared for neither jobs nor college-level work, tend to leave school at the earliest legal moment. Marland called for a replacement of the term "vocational education" with "career education" and a new educational unity of academic preparation with career programs. He envisaged the blending of the academic and vocational programs into a "totally new system" and placed a high priority on its implementation (3):

☐ *True and complete reform of the high school, viewed as a major element of overall preparation for life, cannot be achieved until general education is completely done away with in favor of contemporary career development in a comprehensive secondary education environment. This is our ultimate goal, and we realize that so sweeping a change cannot be accomplished overnight, involving as it does approximately 30 million students and billions of dollars in public funds.*

Although Marland did not attempt to provide a specific definition of the scope of career education, he left little doubt that the full support of his office would be given to fostering changes and programs designed to implement the new system. He proposed a four-fold plan (4) for career development:

1 *major improvements and updating of occupational education emphasizing newer vocational fields and a sound educational base underlying all specific skills training*

2 *more flexible options for high school graduates to continue on to higher education or to enter the world of work*

3 *a closer liaison of vocational education and people from business, industry, and organized labor with more work experience opportunities for students*

4 *a new commitment at all levels—federal, state, and local—toward developing leadership and commitment to the concept of career education*

Commissioner Marland's challenge to the educational community for further discussion and clarification of the concept of career education evoked wide reaction and varying definitions. Some embraced the term to include all of education, whereas others used it to describe "the new vocational education." An individual's view of career education seemed to be much affected by his or her own particular vantage point in the educational spectrum.

At this point, let us examine the positions taken by two organized professional groups that were vitally affected by the trend toward career education.

Views of State
Directors of Vocational Education

In 1971 the National Association of State Directors of Vocational Education met at Las Vegas and proposed the following assumptions as inherent and essential aspects of career education (5). They suggested that career education

1 *is not synonymous with vocational education, but vocational education is a major part of career education*

2 *enhances rather than supplants public school educational programs*

3 *is an integral part of the total public education enterprise*

4 *involves extensive orientation and exploration of occupational opportunities*

5 *involves all students and all educators*

6 *emphasizes individual instruction and student determination*

7 *is a continuum that begins at kindergarten and extends throughout employment*

8 *contributes to student incentives and aspirations*

9 *includes specific preparation for occupations*

10 *assures realistic occupational choices*

11 *promotes wholesome attitudes toward all useful work*

12 *permits each student to realistically assess personal attributes as a part of setting life goals*

13 *provides a means of articulation from grade to grade and level to level*

The state directors further elaborated the goals toward which they proposed to work (5):

1 *the retention of vocational education as a significant and identifiable component of career education*

2 *the development of curriculum, beginning at the kindergarten level, that provides to the student an increasing value and appreciation of the dignity of work, the knowledge of the world of work, and the need for and satisfaction of acquiring a saleable skill*

3 *necessary changes in teacher education which will provide competent career educators as well as vocational educators*

4 *additional funding for all components of career education including but not limited to additional funding for the Vocational Education Acts in order to carry out the vocational role in a system of career education*

5 *the redirection of present general education funds into the implementation of career education programs*

6 *the establishment of effective coordination so that articulation is provided between all levels of education*

7 *the acceptance of the characteristics of career education as stated*

American
Vocational Association Position

In 1971, an American Vocational Association Task Force on Career Education, composed of 100 national vocational education leaders, formulated a position paper (6) titled "A Concept of Career Education." These vocational educators viewed career education as

---

■ . . . a people-oriented concept which is responsive to public demand for both relevance and accountability. It is a life-long process. . . . All types of occupations and all levels of occupational endeavor are contained within its parameters.

■ . . . providing for the focus of the educational system upon career development, thereby expanding options for individuals and helping them achieve self-determined objectives.

■ . . . providing a unifying core for the total educational enterprise, with intensive occupational preparation as a significant aspect.

■ . . . comprehensive in the sense that it is broadly based; dynamic with respect to its capacity to change; programmatic because it is purposeful, planned, and experience-centered; and integrative because it draws together many aspects of the total educational program.

■ . . . accommodating individual differences through a continuous experience-centered and evaluative process which facilitates development of awareness, orientation, exploration, decision-making, and preparation.

■ . . . helping individuals develop favorable attitudes toward the personal, psychological, social and economic significance of work.

■ . . . placing all participants on the next educational or occupational step and assuring that all school-leavers are prepared for work.

Whereas the positions taken by such groups generally supported the emerging trend toward career education, the opinions of individuals were perhaps more effective in elaborating its potential. In the following section, we will examine the views of several eminent educators in terms of the objectives and characteristics they envision for career education.

Overall Objectives and
Characteristics of Career Education

A generally accepted definition of career education has not yet been made. However, consensus appears to be developing in relation to its overall parameters, objectives, and goals.

Some Key Concepts
of Career Education

Goldhammer and Taylor (7) indicate that career education is designed to capacitate individuals for their several life roles: economic, community, home, avocational, religious, and aesthetic. Designed for all students, career education should be viewed as lifelong and pervasive, permeating the entire school program and even extending beyond it. As Goldhammer and Taylor put it (7):

□ *Career education is a systematic attempt to increase the career options available to individuals and to facilitate more rational and valid career planning and preparation. Through a wide range of school and community resources, young people's career horizons should be broadened and their self awareness enhanced. The framework for accomplishing these goals are the phases in a career education program: career awareness, career exploration, and career preparation.*

An expanded conceptualization of career education is contained in "A New Goal for a New Era," a paper presented in March 1972, by Peter Muirhead, U.S. Deputy Commissioner of Education. Muirhead notes that the purpose of career education is the development of a more unifying kind of educational system. It is directed at two fundamental faults of our present system: the lack of occupational relevance and the undesirable distinction that exists between academic and vocational tracks.

Speaking before a Career Education workshop held in New York City in April 1972 Commissioner Marland clarified additional aspects of career education by noting that it

■ *is for every child.*

■ is a way to provide career awareness in the early grades and career preparation in the upper grades that continues at an ever-increasing level of sophistication.

■ must include vocational education because we estimate that nearly all of our school youth should develop salable skills while in school, whether or not they proceed beyond high school, in a different field. Options are always open.

■ is *not only* for children and young adults. It is also for persons of all ages.

■ favors no ethnic group to the exclusion of any other.

■ is not a rigid program from which no State or school district or adult training effort can deviate. Career education is flexible and can be molded to the unique needs of every State and community.

Swanson (8) has described the purposes of career education in the following terms: it is to provide students with

1 *an instructive environment which would allow them to relate their education to the world of work—its scope, its significance, and its opportunities.*

2 *an opportunity to engage in occupational exploration including work experience, specialized instruction, and career decision-making leading toward a preferred life-style and career pattern.*

3 *an opportunity to exit and reenter the educational system or the labor force or to be instructed in both, as needed, in order to make initial or subsequent progress toward specific career goals.*

Swanson further identifies some essential features without which career education could fail to serve its purposes (8):

1 Career education is for all students *It is not an approach to educational "streaming" nor is it an effort to deal more effectively with one dimension of the occupational hierarchy than another. This need to include all students is a feature considered essential to the goals of justice and equality of opportunity in education.*

2 Career education must be included as an instructional objective at all grade levels *From kindergarten through adult and continuing education. Integrated into the regular curriculum, career education is an approach to enriching the traditional disciplines whose primary function is to describe a part of the world's reality, including the world of work.*

3 Career education is intended to provide job-entry skills to all students prior to or upon completion of compulsory school attendance *Twenty percent of those who enter fifth grade drop out before the completion of twelfth grade. Fifty percent of those who enter fifth grade do not pursue post-high school training. Job-entry skills are needed by almost everyone at some stage in career progress—either as an earning opportunity for later stages or as an earning opportunity for an interim stage in career progress. Job-entry skills are an essential feature of career education.*

4 One hundred percent placement is both a feature and a goal of a career education program *Placement may be in a job or in an educational program which is additionally preparatory. Placement as a feature has a double purpose: to insure that career education is goal-oriented for all students, and to insure that the educational system is willing to accept the burden of its own casualties. Implied in the latter is the need for the educational system to engage in successive placements of the same individuals including those who drop out of post-high school educational programs and those who choose to intersperse adult education with work. Placement is a demanding feature of career education. It provides its most important basis for accountability.*

Hoyt et al (9) cite the following key concepts related to career education:

1 *Preparation for successful working careers shall be a key objective of all education.*

2 *Every teacher in every course will emphasize the contribution that subject matter can make to a successful career.*

3 *"Hands-on" occupationally oriented experiences will be utilized as a method of teaching and motivating the learning of abstract academic content.*

4 *Preparation for careers will be recognized as the mutual importance of work attitudes, human relations skills, orientation to the nature of the workaday world, exposure to alternative career choices, and the acquisition of actual job skills.*

5 *Learning will not be reserved for the classroom, but learning environments for career education will also be identified in the home, the community, and employing establishments.*

6 *Beginning in early childhood and continuing through the regular school years, allowing the flexibility for a youth to leave for experience and return to school for further education (including opportunity for upgrading and continued refurnishing for adult workers and including productive use of leisure time and the retirement years), career education will seek to extend its time horizons from "womb to tomb."*

7 *Career education is a basic and pervasive approach to all education, but it in no way conflicts with other legitimate education objectives such as citizenship, culture, family responsibility, and basic education.*

8 *The schools cannot shed responsibility for the individual just because he has been handed a diploma or has dropped out. While it may not perform the actual placement function, the school has the responsibility to stick with the youth until he has his feet firmly on the next step of his career ladder, to help him get back on the ladder if his foot slips, and be available to help him onto a new ladder at any point in the future that one proves to be too short or unsteady.*

Hoyt (10) believes that successful implementation of career education will demand major changes in American education, including:

1 *the creation of a true open-entry/open-exit system of education in which the term "school dropout" becomes obsolete*

2 *the installation of performance evaluation as a primary basis for evaluating educational accomplishments*

3 *the creation of the 12-month school year, the 6-day school week, and the 18-hour school day in which both youth and adults can learn together in courses that run for varying lengths of time under some form of flexible scheduling*

4 *an increased emphasis on a project-activity oriented approach to instruction that will allow greater individualization of instruction and demand relatively small class sizes*

5 *the presence of 12-month contracts for all professional educators that call for part of the time to be spent in the world of work outside of education and/or in other kinds of learning activities*

6 *the creation of comprehensive career guidance, counseling, placement, and follow-up programs that serve both in-school and out-of-school youth and adults*

7 *the creation of methods for granting educational credit to students for tasks performed outside the walls of the school and under supervision of persons who do not possess standard teaching certificates*

The changes suggested by Hoyt (1975 Associate Commissioner for Career Education) represent formidable barriers to the realization of career education in many schools. The effects of inertia and tradition are difficult to overcome, and they emphasize the importance of continued support and motivation of career education by the federal government.

The partitioning of the curriculum into a series of isolated educational experiences is deplored by Marland (11) who urges educators to

☐ *build a new kind of respect in which all talents, all skills, and all kinds of intellectual preparation and training are understood for the important places they individually hold in our complex and inter-dependent society —that is the heart of the career education idea. . . . The apathy and alienation of many of our young people are too profound and too pervasive to be said to be a matter of occupational unpreparedness alone. We have on our hands an entire generation of boys and girls who are rapidly becoming men and women who fail to understand what they are to do when the transition to adulthood is complete. Inculcating that understanding is what career education is all about. . . . If there is a central message in our conception of career education, it is to cry out against this absurd partitioning of the house of education, this separation of subject from subject, of class from class, this false and destructive distinction between the liberal academic tradition on the one hand and the utilitarian-vocational tradition on the other.*

The catalytic effects of career education as a positive force for rebuilding the curriculum are stressed by Burdin (12):

☐ *Career education must be more than band-aids applied to the school. It must begin with study of how such education relates to its societal context and concurrently how individuality may be supported by personally rewarding careers. Career education must help people select and attain careers which lead to both individual fulfillment and societal progress.*
A vigorous purging and rebuilding of the curriculum must be undertaken by laymen, professionals, and students—all participating to the

degree most compatible with motivation, maturity, training, and experience.

The career knowledge base must be broadly applicable—e.g., in depth knowledge about career clusters rather than superficial, unrelated facts about dozens of jobs or about the same 23,000 job titles now delineated. Purging old content and relating the balance to new emphases are required.

Educators must learn how to be sure that understanding, application, and processes—transferable to an inevitably different future—are learned by students rather than acquisition and regurgitation of facts.

The comprehensiveness of the career education concept is aptly illustrated by William C. Miller (13):

☐ *What does career education include? Reading, writing, arithmetic—certainly! What skills could be more appropriate on most jobs? Attitudes and values, effective human relations, study skills—essential characteristics of a good employee. Art, music, foreign language—these will be a part of the total lifework of some pupils. To hear many describe the scope of career education, it can and should embrace all of education.*

The vitality and breadth of the career education movement have simultaneously attracted and perplexed those involved with instructional programs (13):

☐ *To the vocational people, it is an opportunity to extend the ideas they are concerned about into the academic courses. To the counselor, it is a chance to help the curriculum become more relevant to kids. To the parent, it offers hope of an educational program which is more practical, with a payoff upon graduation with a salable skill and a job.*

A somewhat more comprehensive definition is presented by Wesley Smith (14), California Director of Vocational Education:

☐ *Career Education is a comprehensive, systematic, and cohesive plan of learning organized in such manner that youth at all grade levels in the public schools will have continuous and abundant opportunity to acquire useful information about the occupational structure of the economy, the alternatives of career choice, the obligations of individual and productive involvement in the work force, the intelligent determination of personal capabilities and aspirations, the requisites of all occupations, and opportunities to prepare for gainful employment. Career education is the shared and unending responsibility of all professionals in education, and involves input from—and relationship to—all subject-matter disciplines and all supportive educational services. In short, it is a priority objective of public education, with achievement measured by employability in occupa-*

tions, both gainful and useful, that are a reasonable match of both the talent and the ambition of every citizen.

As these quotations suggest, career education means different things to different people. To some vocational educators, career education represents a new phase in traditional programs of skill development; in addition to the development of job skills, it includes personal and social adaptive skills that are essential to directing one's own career life in the face of rapid change. To others, career education is much broader than preparation for one's work role: Keller (15) defines career education as ". . . that part of the school's curriculum and instruction which focuses on the development of individuals for their social and economic roles in life, these roles being the work role, home-community-citizenship roles, as well as the avocational-leisure roles in life."

General educators may interpret career orientation to mean a special unit or course taught by a social studies teacher. But it is also an infusion into each curriculum area at all educational levels of career-oriented activities. To some educators, career education means a chance to explore the real world of work, to get "hands on" experience. But, in addition to hands-on experiences, career education should also assist students to interpret such experiences in terms of their own career self-images. The elementary teacher may see career education as a concept primarily for the high school, but values, aptitudes, interests and self-concepts cannot wait until Grade 10. The businessman may view career education as the school's effort to get students ready to go to work. Although the school is responsible for preparing students for a smooth transition to the adult world, career education may fail without the active support of the home and community, which are "learning laboratories" for the skills of adult living.

Career education has been examined for both its *content* and its *process* objectives. Theories of career development that have emerged over the past several decades have significantly affected the conceptualization of career education. Keller (15) has perceived the process of career development as both transitional and cyclical, including the following phases:

☐ *Awareness (of self and career roles); Exploration (to discover self and career roles); Identification (with career roles); Preparation (for career roles); Career Assessment and Recycling.*

An underlying concept of the role of vocational-technical education in career education is that everyone, at every reasonable level, will attain a degree of occupational skill, whether or not that skill represents the ultimate aspiration of the learner. Career education becomes a developmental process of interfacing the individual's life roles with reality—finding out about, deciding, and preparing for productive participation in life.

Bell's Endorsement
of Career Education

In 1974, T. H. Bell, who succeeded Sidney Marland as U.S. Commissioner of Education, summarized some of the accomplishments and new directions of career education (16). Addressing the National Conference of State Coordinators of Career Education, he pointed out that for the first time in the history of career education

1 . . . *there is a congressional mandate for career education. By enacting Section 406, Title IV, Public Law 93–380 (Educational Amendments of 1974), Congress made career education a law of the land.*

2 . . . *Congress is favorably considering the appropriation of funds earmarked for career education.*

3 . . . *there will be a National Advisory Council on Career Education.*

4 . . . *an active inter-agency team, representing the Departments of Commerce, Labor, and Health, Education and Welfare is studying and making recommendations regarding relationships between education and work.*

In the same address, Commissioner Bell identified a variety of other significant developments that related to the support and growth of career education (16):

1 *Career education continues to find its greatest strength and most dramatic growth at the local level. The Council of Chief State School Officers estimates that almost 5000 of the 17,000 school districts in the U.S. will have career education programs this fall (1974).*

2 *The increasing strength and support for career education evident at the State level is extremely encouraging also. Six State legislatures have enacted career education legislation, and others are now considering it. More than half of the State boards of education have adopted policy statements supporting career education. More than three-fourths of our State departments of education have appointed at least one full-time professional in career education.*

3 *Non-governmental groups continue to support and lend strength to career education. . . . The National Education Association, at its 1974 convention, passed a resolution supporting career education. The support being given by the National Youth Organizations is heartwarming. . . . The Chamber of Commerce of the USA is continuing its strong and positive support. The National Advisory Council on Vocational Education put the title "Career Education" on its Eighth Report.*

4 *The Office of Education has adopted its own position paper on career education . . . the paper contains a generic definition of career education. While it clearly speaks to relationships between education and*

work, it leaves States and local school systems free to develop their own specific career education definitions. The centrality of work—both paid and unpaid—in this definition seems to me essential in expressing a set of goals consistent with both the economic and the humanistic need for work in our society today. The paper emphasizes integration *within education and* collaboration *by the formal education system with both the business-industry-labor-professional-government community and the home and family structure. This emphasis provides us with a solid basis for career education . . . that points us toward a bright future.*

In September 1974, the Secretary of Health, Education and Welfare (HEW) approved a paper titled, "Career Education: Toward a Third Environment." In November 1974, Commissioner Bell of the United States Office of Education (USOE) released a policy paper titled "An Introduction to Career Education," which described the Office of Education's interpretation of the HEW policy on career education. The USOE paper was consistent with the provisions of Section 406 of the Education Amendments of 1974, which provided the first official congressional endorsement of career education. Draft copies of the initial paper were reviewed with a high degree of consensus by career education leaders. The policy paper was subsequently released to state education agencies and to local school systems to assist the development and expansion of career education.

The USOE Policy Paper (17), written by Associate Commissioner for Career Education, Kenneth B. Hoyt, summarizes the conditions calling for educational reform by citing eleven criticisms of present educational systems, and it presents a generic definition of career education:

□ *"Career" is the totality of work one does in his or her lifetime. "Education" is the totality of experiences through which one learns. Based on these two definitions, "career education" is the totality of experiences through which one learns about and prepares to engage in work as part of her or his way of living. "Career" is a developmental concept beginning in the very early years and continuing well into the retirement years. "Education," as defined here, obviously includes more than the formal educational system. Thus, this generic definition of career education is purposely intended to be of a very broad and encompassing nature. At the same time, it is intended to be considerably less than all of life or one's reasons for living.*

Several assumptions are outlined in this paper, which suggest a series of tentative "truths" underlying the planning of career education programs. Other aspects of the position paper include a description of the tasks essential for initial program implementation on the part of classroom teachers, counselors, educational administrators, businessmen, and home and family members. A statement of learner outcomes emphasizes the variability of educational goals from one developmental level to the next. Finally, a number of educational policy changes are advocated to facilitate the systematic adoption and funding of career education at all educational levels.

New Dimensions
of Career Education

Although the roots of career education extend deeply into the past, the dynamics of change have brought about certain identifiable new dimensions. The first, elaborated by Swanson (18), involves the contributions of educational research which, limited by a variety of conditions, allow the following generalizations:

1 Children have a higher capacity for learning and instruction at earlier ages than was heretofore understood This conclusion . . . has resulted in an emphasis on early childhood education. As demonstrated . . . career education can be an important dimension of early childhood education.

2 The achievement of learning goals is in direct proportion to the amount of time invested in teaching and learning by students and teachers, and to the effectiveness of such invested time. . . . If career education is an important educational goal, its importance must have a direct relationship to the investment of student and teacher time.

3 Education is not culturally irrelevant; its subcultural variations are significant. . . . Students worth educating are not socially and culturally homogeneous. Nor are they oriented to any particular segment of the occupational hierarchy. It is increasingly important to note that many of the success related outcomes of the educational process are essentially non-cognitive; they relate to social relations, to the socialization process and to the status-transmitting influence of work roles.

A second new dimension to career education is provided by the sobering realization that there may be limits to the world's possibilities for continuing economic growth. The interacting consequences of continued exponential growth of population, food production, industrialization, pollution, and consumption of nonrenewable resources will, it is contended, lead to the need for zero population growth within 50 years. Discussions of this possibility have not had wide currency in the field of education even though the present group of 12th graders will reach retirement age within those 50 years. What are the long-run implications of the energy crisis? of zero growth or near zero growth for education? Climbing the success ladder was a realistic hope as long as economic expansion permitted the ladder to become longer so that those on the higher rungs could also climb. But zero growth restricts the length of the ladder and invites a conflict that will even more sharply divide the rich from the poor, a conflict that may use the educational system as its battle ground.

A further implication of restricted growth will involve the educational assumptions surrounding student selection. Under conditions of expanding growth, the educational systems reward those individuals and institutions with a high capacity for expansion, and it tends to discourage those that maintain a static or declining role. This basis of selection and reward for expansionism will not function as smoothly in a zero growth situation. Full employment, even with a healthy commitment to the work ethic, may be impossible to sustain without a great deal of underutilized labor. The present inability to control inflation is a symptom of this problem.

What then are the likely consequences of near zero growth for career education? Certainly the new situation will be difficult to accept, and the difficulty will be greater for the poor than for the affluent. Education may get blamed (as it did for Sputnik), and career education may be identified as part of the problem. If career education becomes identified with the least remunerative jobs in a community, the possibility of zero growth will add new hazards to the concept and to its implementation (18).

Principles of
Career Education

For a variety of reasons—the complexity of the concept of career education or the expenses of operationalizing the concept—the conceptualizations of career education need continuing reassessment. This is necessary to assure that they possess the philosophical bases, comprehensiveness, and programmatic structures essential for preparing the learner to successfully perform the several roles he or she may have and/or will have in the future. Putting into operation a program of career education without the broadest possible conceptualization could result in a misjudgment of priorities and a misdirected use of available resources.

A properly planned and executed career education program operates as a vital component within a comprehensive school system. The developmental stages in a career education delivery system include: conceptualization, design, development, pilot testing, revision, field testing, field revision, installation, and diffusion. As this list suggests, career education aims to improve educational outcomes by relating all teaching and learning activities to the concept of career development. Unfortunately, this concept lacks a systematic philosophical base. What may contribute to the ambiguity of the concept is that it really borrows the traditional concepts of education and attempts to synthesize them with a career-oriented approach.

The concept of career education is based on programmatic considerations; it is problem-oriented, but it lacks a comprehensive analysis of the cultural, social, and political factors that are the causes of these problems. A concept of career education is too narrowly perceived when it focuses on only problematic considerations, such as relevance, rational career choices, and preparation-placement.

What is actually taking place in present career education programs is the infusion of career-oriented education into the guidance, curricular, and administrative operations of the school system. This trend is not necessarily negative, but in many programs the overriding emphasis is on the economic role of the individual.

It remains to be seen whether educational performance will be enhanced by a career-oriented curriculum. Many young people with strong career drives lose motivation when they pursue curricula in their desired fields because of other circumstances that mitigate against their academic success. In other words, career education, as vital a concept as it is, does not constitute the totality of education. However, its principles constitute a means of injecting relevance and meaning into education at any level.

From among the varied perspectives of students, teachers, school administrators, educational researchers, parents, employers, public policymakers, and others, the various concepts of career education can be characterized, on their degree of comprehensiveness, into nine categories or levels:

1 Career education focuses on the *performance of manipulative skills* of a practical arts nature, with little, if any, consideration given to the application of those skills to useful employment or to earning a living. Level I is thus activity oriented, present oriented, and it is unidisciplinary in scope.

2 Career education focuses on the *performance of manipulative skills plus the development of cognitive and affective learnings* essential for successful employment in one or more jobs in an occupational cluster. Learning objectives are derived from task-analysis studies. Level 2 is thus job oriented and primarily present oriented. The cognitive and affective learning experiences are provided in such a way as to enable the student to perform the manipulative skills. Education for the cluster will proceed so that a student can leave school by grade 10 and find employment for which he or she has the necessary capabilities. The educational system will be organized to permit the individual to return to school at any age for additional training. Strong emphasis will be given to career (job) awareness and exploration to enable the student to make a wise career (job) selection, prepare for this chosen career (job), and value the dignity of all work. A single field of study provides the manipulative skills and related cognitive and affective learnings essential for the job cluster.

3 Career education focuses on the performance of *manipulative skills plus the development of the cognitive and affective learnings* essential for employment in one or more jobs in an occupational cluster. This level is job oriented and primarily present oriented. It is essentially the same as level 2 except that a multidisciplinary approach provides the manipulative skills and related cognitive and affective learnings. That is, the entire curriculum of the school is integrated, with all learning experiences presented in an occupationally relevant manner.

4 Career education focuses on the performance of manipulative skills plus the development of the cognitive and affective competencies needed for employment in a cluster of occupations plus consideration of the relationships between the individual's "off the job" existence and his or her *life as a worker and as a citizen.* Development of the qualities of leadership and citizenship, and of constructive use of leisure time are provided for. Career education is education for living and for earning a living. It is also concerned with the wise use of leisure time, a satisfactory family life, and participation in community activities. It is learner oriented. It seeks to integrate the student with his or her present and immediate future environment. It is taught in a unidisciplinary mode.

5 Career education focuses on the performance of manipulative skills plus the development of the cognitive and affective competencies needed for employment plus competencies needed for family living, participation in community activities, and aesthetic appreciations. It is *education for living and earning a living* in the present and immediate future. It is learner oriented. It seeks to integrate the student with his or her environment. It differs from level 4 of career education in that a *multidisciplinary approach* is used; that is, the learning experiences are integrated among several subject matter areas.

6 Career education focuses on development of the individual's *capabilities for coping with the present and the future.* It is *education for living and earning a living now and in a future society.* The individual will prepare for employment in existing jobs as well as in occupations that have not yet emerged, in a society that does not yet exist. Because the job does not yet exist, task analysis cannot reveal the specific skills and learnings it will require. As we move toward "knowledge occupations," less emphasis will be given to psychomotor skills, and increasing emphasis will be given to decision-making competencies involving all levels of the occupational hierarchy. This level of careeer education is learner oriented. It is multidisciplinary. Learning experiences will be organized around problems of *social and economic change.*

7 Career education focuses on *individuals in relation to their physical, social, and technological environments.* Concern will be shown for restructuring the learning and work environments to be supportive of individual life styles in a pluralistic society. This level will be primarily *decision-maker oriented*, recognizing that decisions are made by all those affected by them. A technology of behavior will provide insights that support behavioral outcomes.

8 Career education focuses on individuals in relation to their physical, social, and technological environments. This level will be *decision-*

implementer oriented, recognizing that decisions are implemented by those who participate in making them. Learning experiences will aim at development of *leadership behavior that recognizes the need to provide learning and work environments that reinforce life styles and evolving world views.* A technology of behavior will support behavioral outcomes as in level 7.

9 Career education focuses on individuals in relation to their total environment, including the political environment. This level of career education will be *public policy-maker oriented.* Concern will be given to the development of public policies related to the work ethic, pluralism, welfare, support of education, and so on. It will be highly future oriented. A combination of behavioral technology and public policy-making technology will support individual life styles in a pluralistic environment within the framework of evolving world ideas.

To develop and operationalize career education programs from the least comprehensive, level 1, to the most comprehensive, futuristic, humanistic, level 9, will be expensive and talent demanding. Crucial decisions must be made as to how to parcel out the work and how to avoid duplication of effort. However, if our citizens are to prosper in the pluralistic society of the year 2000 and beyond, do we have any other alternative?

Let us turn, at this point, to an examination of some basic models that illustrate the conceptual dimensions of career education in the United States.

Career Education Models

Career education, according to Herr (19), can be seen as the synthesis of two streams of thought about educational purpose. One uses an occupational model as its stimulus; the other uses a career model. The occupational model has been concerned principally with ensuring that students, when they leave school, have highly developed skills in rather narrowly defined occupations. The career model, on the other hand, conceives of the individual as moving through the educational system along a number of pathways that have differing points of entrance to the work system. This model emphasizes the importance of individuals having the skills that will permit them to choose as freely as possible among the multiple occupational opportunities.

The career model is broader than the occupational model. It includes not only the acquisition of occupational skills but also the factors—attitudes, knowledges, self-concepts—that motivate decision-making styles. This model is concerned with helping students develop preferences and execute plans by which they can implement them. Thus the implications for personal growth found in the career model are not confined

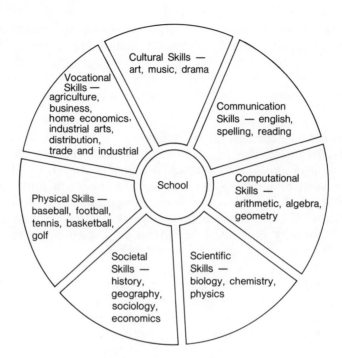

Figure 5.1   The subject-centered curriculum.

only to young people going directly to work. This model maintains that all students, regardless of their ultimate goal beyond high school, need to be helped to find purpose in what they are doing (20).

Most of our school systems currently operate within a subject-centered curricula. A scope and sequence of skills is identified for each subject, and each student is, theoretically, placed on a continuum according to his or her achievement, abilities, and interests, as shown in Figure 5.1. Little progress has been achieved, however, in cutting across subject lines and integrating these subjects into a meaningful whole for the student. Likewise, there has been only limited success in relating much of the content of these existing courses to student goals.

As reflected in Figure 5.2, however, career education is an educational process, a means to an end, the end being the realization of goals of the individual: economic, political, social, and personal. This model illustrates three major principles of career education:

1 There is a continuum of career phases, ranging from career awareness to career preparation, with intermediate stages of career exploration and orientation. Although each phase is identified with a specific time period (K–6, 7–8, 9–10, 11–Adult), there is a progression to the phases, as indicated by the upward arrows. The inverse pyramid indicates the continuous and expanding nature of these phases as individuals grow and mature through career education.

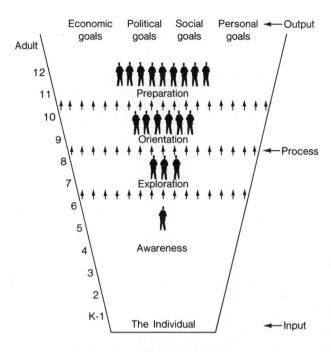

Figure 5.2   Career Education Model.

2 Learning experiences both within and outside the formal school structure should be selected as a *means* of helping the individual to fulfill his
or her economic, political, social, and personal goals. Thus subject matter
is selected for its contribution to the student's goals. Learning experiences of more depth are needed throughout life as individuals set and
reset goals and as their varying personal roles develop.

3 There is a movement toward an individualized approach to learning.
During the awareness phase, activities are planned for both individuals
and groups that focus on general awareness of the world of work, the
values of a work-oriented society, and the role of the individual. At this
level, all students are exposed to the same concepts, although they practice them in a variety of settings.

As students move through the upper phases of career education, they
select clusters, or families, of occupations to explore. As they approach
the preparation phase, choices are narrowed to one cluster, and later
training provides specialized competency within that cluster. Thus career
education becomes more diversified as it advances through the four
phases and as individuals select from and experience the multiple career
options available, both in the roles toward which they aspire and in the
learning experiences available as preparation.

An analysis of federal career education models will serve to set the
stage for a more comprehensive understanding of these concepts.

Federal Models
for Career Education

In 1971 the U.S. Office of Education announced its intention to spend $15 million in the development of four experimental models for career education.* Model 1 was to be school based. Model 2, employer based. Model 3, rural-residential based, and Model 4, home-community based. Initial USOE model conceptualization of career education served as a foundation for Model 1.

School-Based Model

The Center for Vocational and Technical Education (CVTE) was designated in 1971 by the U.S. Office of Education as the prime contractor for the school-based model. The purpose of the project was to develop, test, and install a Comprehensive Career Education Model (CCEM) by restructuring the existing American educational program around career development needs. The USOE model, shown in Figure 5.3, illustrates the relationship of the broad goals of career education (awareness, exploration, and preparation) to the options of further education or immediate job placement.

The object of Model 1 (CCEM) was to develop and test a career education system (K–12) in six school systems (representing varying sizes, geographic locations, and cultural ethnic populations) that would help students to develop (a) a comprehensive awareness of career options; (b) a concept of self that is in keeping with a work-oriented society, including positive attitudes about work, school, and society, and a sense of satisfaction resulting from successful experience in these areas; (c) personal characteristics, such as self-respect, initiative, and resourcefulness; (d) a realistic understanding of the relationships between the world of work and education to assist individuals in becoming contributing members of society; and (e) the ability to enter employment in a selected occupational area and/or to go on for further education.

In conceptualizing the role of career education in a comprehensive school setting, Model 1 drew heavily on theories from the areas of vocational education, guidance, curriculum development, and human growth and development. Eight areas of educational experience were identified as the basic conceptual elements of career education: career awareness, self-awareness, appreciations/attitudes, decision-making skills, economic awareness, beginning competency, employability skills, and educational awareness.

After the elements were identified, the CVTE staff designated terminal

---

* Simultaneously, 52 "mini-models" of career education, funded as exemplary programs under the Vocational Education Act, were activated in local school districts. United States Office of Education Commissioner Marland further allotted $9 million from discretionary funds to the states for vocational research and development focusing on establishment of career education models.

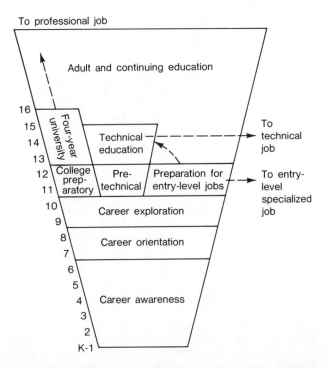

Figure 5.3 USOE comprehensive career education system: school-based model. Source: ERIC Clearinghouse on Vocational and Technical Education, *Career Education Practice*, Information Service No. 65, VT 017 221. Columbus: The Center for Vocational and Technical Education, The Ohio State University, December, 1972, p. 19.

"outcomes" as student-learning goals for each element. These outcomes were designed to equip exiting students with entry-level job skills and to prepare them for further academic or vocational education. The element outcomes were: career identity, self-identity, self-social fulfillment, career decisions, economic understandings, employment skills, career placement, and educational identity. The eight elements and their corresponding outcomes, when placed graphically against the 13 grade levels (K–12), evolved a CCEM Program Goal Matrix, as illustrated in Figure 5.4.

The Model 1 curriculum (K–12) includes all those experiences of the child under the auspices of the school that use both on- and off-campus educational resources to provide the opportunity for, appreciation for, and understanding of the dignity of work and a fulfilling life. It is assumed that Model 1 must:

1 assist youth to choose an individualized personal life style and to establish and discover alternative paths for reaching goals commensurate with that life style

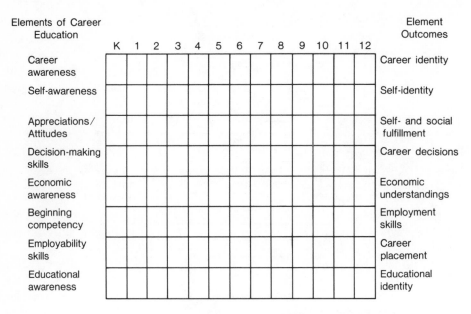

Figure 5.4 Comprehensive Career Education Model: Program Goal Matrix. Source: Center for Vocational Education, The Ohio State University, Progress Report, Project 7–0158, July 20, 1972.

2 prepare students to enter the world of work as contributing members of a productive society

3 assist young people to view education as a lifelong pursuit that is not restricted to schools, classrooms, or traditional institutions of learning

4 assist youth to develop problem-solving skills required to cope with an increasingly cybernated society

The Model 1 curriculum activities have been divided into two subcomponents: the K–6 group, which is responsible for the development and implementation of a career awareness curriculum; and the 7–12 group, which is responsible for the career exploration and career-entry preparation of students in those grades. Individualized instructional packages have been developed by the CVTE staff for the implementation of the Model 1 curriculum.

Employer-Based Model

The objectives of Model 2, the employer-based model (21), are: (a) to provide an alternative educational program for students, aged 13–18, in an employer-based setting; (b) to unify the positive elements of academic, general, and vocational curricula into a comprehensive career education program; (c) to increase the relevance of education to the world of work; and (d) to broaden the base of community participation, particularly by involving public and private employers more directly in education.

Planning studies were conducted at the Far West Laboratory for Educational Research and Development at Berkeley, California, at the Northwest Regional Educational laboratory at Portland, Oregon, and at Research for Better Schools, in Philadelphia, Pennsylvania. Four pilot sites —Philadelphia, Pennsylvania; Charleston, West Virginia; Portland, Oregon; and Oakland, California—were chosen for the employer-based model.

Model 2 advocates year-round operation and open entrance and exit of students, and it offers a new setting for academic studies, which keys them to job experiences provided by a consortium of local employers, such as banks, publishers, travel agencies, hospitals, factories, and so on. Each consortium encourages the cooperation of diverse community groups, such as unions, schools, parents, and employers.

Certain stipulations were identified by the U.S. Office of Education that were to be followed in establishing employer-based models; namely, they must provide for the needs of all students; they must allow students to return to a traditional school setting; and they must provide for college-bound students as well as for those who intend to enter the labor force.

Research for Better Schools, Inc., established a private academic school, the Academy for Career Education, which serves as an excellent example of an employer-based education model. It involves four elements: a management structure, an instructional program, guidance and counseling activities, and an evaluation plan. The central element of the model is the instructional program because the nature of instruction strongly influences the other three elements. This instructional program, more than half of which is conducted by employers, is organized around three educational areas: general education, explorative education, and specialized education.

The general education area of the instructional program uses community resources, both human and physical, to realize its objectives. For example, instruction in the arts is developed in conjunction with the Art Alliance, a professional association of artists in Philadelphia. Lectures, demonstrations, and small-group instruction are provided by the professional artists.

The explorative education area provides students with a broad perspective of the economic system and career opportunities through a structured series of examinations of employer clusters. A student explores a different cluster area each quarter. A cluster is formed by three related employers. For example, the finance cluster includes a bank, an insurance company, and a brokerage house. During the first quarter of the academy's operation, the students explored cluster areas in communication, finance, government, health, manufacturing, research, sales, utilities, and systems and logistics. Each student spent one or two days a week at the employer location. A World of Work seminar, conducted by the local Chamber of Commerce, provided an opportunity for students to share their cluster experiences and discuss their career plans.

The third major area in this career education model is specialized education, which provides for more direct involvement with actual career and life-skills experiences. Career specialization is a work-study plan, which focuses on two related kinds of instruction—an internship, in which a student works on location in an area of particular interest for a short time to develop general job-related skills; and residency, in which a specific job is examined more intensively in an employer setting to allow the student to acquire more sophisticated work skills.

Research for Better Schools, Inc., has identified a list of propositions (22) that have grown out of the experiment in developing an employer-based, experience-centered program:

1 *Career education provides a highly individualized form of education that accommodates the needs of all students and attempts to relate their education to their future life and careers.*

2 *Career education, even when conducted by employers, is not a radical departure from existing forms of education. Rather, the program addresses many traditional content areas in unusual environments, with different kinds of instructors and new techniques.*

3 *The ultimate success of employer-based career education depends on changes in educational custom and law which are in conflict with the employer-based model. These customs include such mistaken ideas as (a) school is a building with a definable space that is the locus of all meaningful learning, (b) students can learn only from someone who has been certified as a teacher, and (c) academic credit must be supervised and certified by the educational bureaucracy.*

4 *Employers and non-profit institutions are uniquely equipped to help students to learn about the world of work as well as the life skills needed by all individuals.*

5 *There are as many reasons for employer participation in the program as there are employers willing to participate—contribution to education, public relations, tax credits, and better trained employees all play a part in the decision of some companies.*

6 *Career education presents an exciting opportunity for progress toward curriculum fusion and program integration.*

7 *An employer-based model holds strong implications for contributing to public education in the future. It can become an alternative high school for some students. It can be adopted as a refinement for a cooperative work-study program. It can contribute to the spread of "open learning" systems. And it may lead to a closer relationship between societal and educational planning.*

8 *The design of an employer-based career education model can be viewed as a research project, a developmental effort, or a demonstration project. Employer-based career education may be viewed as an experiment to examine the extent to which employers are willing and able to contribute to education.*

Rural-Residential-Based Model

The objective of the Mountain Plains Education and Economic Development Program (MPEEDP) is to develop, through action, research, and experimentation, programs that can be implemented on a widespread basis (23). Model 3, the Rural-Residential Career Education Model, is committed to a goal of improving the personal development and employability of individuals in a six-state region. This experimental demonstration activity involves various individuals, agencies, and other resources in preparing adults and children of rural unemployed and underemployed families in Wyoming, Montana, Idaho, North Dakota, South Dakota, and Nebraska for rewarding employment. The private, nonprofit corporation, MPEEDP, with its core management team located at a former Air Force base at Glasgow, Montana, is engaged in a comprehensive research design, from the initial selection of participants through job placement and follow-up, and will train the staff for each state. Program goals, objectives, and philosophy have been detailed, and various reports and conferences on new methods will document the progress of this career education model.

The Montana site makes it possible for low-income families from the six-state region to train for 6 to 18 months. Each member of each family learns new skills, whether for better jobs, more efficient homemaking, or further education. In 1972, over 100 families were in training in Glasgow.

A residential community is but one aspect of the innovative, experimental approach being used in Model 3. Both the career education program and living in the created community are envisioned as providing the rural disadvantaged with learning experiences that may improve their employability. Guiding the research and program development activities is a working definition that views career education as the aggregate of processes by which individuals acquire and develop the goals (values), abilities (knowledge, attitudes, skills, and behaviors), and motivation to: (a) contribute to their own growth and to the growth of their society, and (b) to make prudent use of their personal as well as their society's resources and energies. The ultimate goal of the residential-based model is to determine whether or not low-income rural residents can develop career roles through specially adapted in-house experiences. Obviously the institutional approach at Glasgow will be observed carefully as a potential form of career education for other segments of the population. Plans for the model, drawn by the Mountain Plains Regional Educational Center at Glasgow, involve the use of several program components for disadvantaged families and individuals, including education, family life and community services, area economic development services, health services, and research and evaluation activities.

Home-Community-Based Model

Still in its early stages is the fourth model, a home-community effort that will use television and radio programming to encourage unemployed or underemployed adults to take advantage of local retraining programs. Through the use of the home-based model, the U.S. Office of Education hopes to (a) enhance the quality of the home as a learning center, (b) develop educational delivery systems into the home and community, (c) provide new career education programs for adults, (d) establish a guidance and career placement system to assist individuals in occupational and related roles, and (e) develop more competent workers. The home-community-based model thus features adult education—at home, on the job, in a community center, or wherever it is most convenient or effective.

The Rand Corporation is conducting an in-depth study of successful media-based educational systems as a basis for the USOE prototype for implementing the home-based model. Simultaneously, studies are being made by the Educational Development Corporation of Newton, Massachusetts, to define population characteristics appropriate for a career education television series, to develop an evaluative plan for the series, and to carry out conceptualization and feasibility studies of supporting components for career guidance and home study.

USOE-Conceptualization
of Career Education

Career education, as indicated by USOE guidelines, involves the following characteristics: (a) restructuring of basic subjects around the theme of career development, (b) extensive guidance and counseling for decision making, and (c) studying careers in relation to major fields of occupations so that the students leaving high school will be prepared for either employment in a job of their choosing or additional education in institutions of advanced standing.

Specifically, a comprehensive developmental program in career education from K–12 seeks to (24):

1 *develop in pupils attitudes about the personal and social significance of work*

2 *develop each pupil's self-awareness*

3 *develop and expand the occupational awareness and the aspirations of the pupils*

4 *improve overall pupil performance by unifying and focusing basic subjects around a career development theme*

5 *provide experiences for students to assist them in evaluating their interests, abilities, values, and needs as they relate to occupational roles and career lines*

6 *provide students with opportunities for further and more detailed exploration of selected occupational clusters, leading to the tentative selection of a particular cluster for in-depth exploration at a grade level functionally equivalent to ninth grade*

7 *provide in-depth exploration and training in one occupational area and providing a foundation for further progress, leaving open the option to move between clusters if desired*

8 *provide guidance and counseling for the purposes of assisting students in selecting an occupational specialty for grade levels functionally equivalent to eleventh and twelfth with the following options: intensive job preparation, preparation for postsecondary occupational program, or preparation for a four-year college*

9 *provide every student intensive preparation in a selected occupational cluster, or in a specific occupation, in preparation for job entry and/or further education*

10 *provide intensive guidance and counseling in preparation for employment and/or further education*

11 *ensure placement of all students, on leaving school, in either a job, a postsecondary occupational education program, or a four-year college program*

12 *maintain continuous follow-through of all drop outs and graduates and use the resulting information for program revisions*

Table 5.1 provides a breakdown of the USOE conceptualization of a career education program model by objective, depth and scope, courses or curricula, and location of instructional facilities for each educational level.

In 1974 the U.S. Office of Education issued a policy paper that identified ten concept assumptions that, taken as a whole, can be viewed as representing a philosophical base for current career education efforts (25). These assumptions, that serve to summarize the underpinnings of the career education movement, include:

1 *Since both one's career and one's education extend from the pre-school through the retirement years, career education must also span almost the entire life cycle.*

2 *The concept of productivity is central to the definition of work and so to the entire concept of career education.*

3 *Since "work" includes unpaid activities as well as paid employment, career education's concerns, in addition to its prime emphasis on paid*

Table 5.1 Career Education Program Model (USOE Conceptualization)

Grade	Objective	Depth and scope	Courses or curricula	Location of instructional facilities
elementary (grades K–6)	to develop an awareness of the occupational world	general understanding with unrestricted exposure to all fields of work; guidance and counseling for career development	integrated as part of total program	every elementary school
early secondary (grades 7–10)	to stimulate occupational interest and provide exploratory and prevocational experiences	acquaintance with many specific occupations; opportunities for practical experiences; guidance and counseling for career development continued	continue integrated program and provide separate courses that include experiences related to all fields of work	every middle and high school
late secondary (grades 11–12)	to provide specific training for a grouping of closely related occupations and further exploratory experiences for those needing it	training for job-entry skills; guidance and counseling for career development continued; placement services provided	separate courses with skill development objectives; program offerings will be dependent on student interest and labor demands	high schools, area centers, private occupational schools, and business and industry
postsecondary	to provide advanced specific occupational education and training	in-depth training; many advanced technical offerings; guidance, counseling, and placement services provided	separate courses; offerings dependent on student interest and labor demands	community colleges, state colleges and universities, private occupational schools, business and industry
adult	to provide occupational training, upgrading and/or retraining	training for specific employment needs of individual; job counseling for adults; placement services provided	offerings dependent on demand; many short-term programs	local schools, area centers, community colleges, colleges and universities, private occupational schools, business and industry

employment, extend to the work of the student as a learner, to the growing numbers of volunteer workers in our society, to the work of the full-time homemaker, and to work activities in which one engages as part of leisure time.

4 *The cosmopolitan nature of today's society demands that career education embrace a multiplicity of work values, rather than a single work ethic, as a means of helping each individual answer the question "Why should I work?"*

5 *Both one's career and one's education are best viewed in a developmental, rather than in a fragmented, sense.*

6 *Career education is for all persons—the young and the old; the mentally handicapped and the intellectually gifted; the poor and the wealthy; males and females, students in elementary schools and in the graduate colleges.*

7 *The societal objectives of career education are to help all individuals: (a) want to work; (b) acquire the skills necessary for work in these times; and (c) engage in work that is satisfying for each individual throughout his or her lifetime.*

8 *The individualistic goals of career education are to make work: (a) possible, (b) meaningful, and (c) satisfying for each individual throughout his or her lifetime.*

9 *Protection of the individual's freedom to choose and assistance in making and implementing career decisions are of central concern to career education.*

10 *The expertise required for implementing career education is to be found in many parts of society and is not limited to those employed in formal education.*

State Models for Career Education

Several states have developed far-reaching, innovative programs in career education. In this section we will examine three of these models, from Michigan, Arizona, and Wisconsin.

Michigan Model

William C. Miller, Deputy Superintendent of the Wayne County Intermediate School District, Detroit, Michigan, sees career education as (26) "really a reorientation of most of education toward the relevant and real world of work and the economic sector of our society and culture." Data in Table 5.2 illustrate a sequential approach toward this goal as incorporated in the Michigan Career Education Program Model.

Table 5.2 Michigan Career Education Program Model (26)

Grade	Objective	Depth and scope	Courses or curricula	Location of instructional facilities
elementary (grades K–6)	to develop an awareness of the occupational world	general understanding with unrestricted exposure to all fields of work	integrated as part of total program	every elementary school
early secondary (grades 7–10)	to stimulate occupational interest and provide exploratory and prevocational experiences	acquaintance with many specific occupations, primarily through a study of occupational clusters; opportunities for practical experiences	continue integrated program and provide separate courses that include experiences related to all fields of work	within every local middle and high school
late secondary (grades 11–12)	to provide specialized training for a specific occupation or a grouping of closely related occupations	training for job-entry skills and more advanced training on postsecondary level; counseling for career development	10–30 specialized programs depending on employment opportunities and student interests	local high schools and/or area centers
postsecondary	to provide advanced specific occupational education and training	in-depth training for specific occupations or an occupational cluster; counseling for career development, continued	20–50 programs; many offerings will depend on local demand	community colleges, technical institutes, state colleges and universities
adult	to provide occupational training, upgrading, and/or retraining	training for specific employment needs of individual; job counseling for adults	many (20–50) programs; number of offerings will depend on demand	local schools and/or area centers, community colleges, technical institutes, colleges and universities

Source: Educational Leadership, *Vol. 31, No. 2, November 1973, p. 154.*

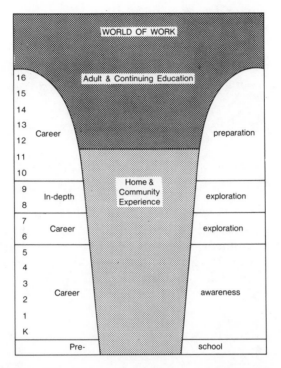

Figure 5.5 Arizona Career Education Model (27).

Arizona Model

Arizona has made great strides in implementing a career education model. At the statewide level, career education is viewed as a vehicle for reorienting the entire system of education; as such, it impacts on all facets of education. It reaffirms the Arizona definition of career education, which states that education and career education are synonymous. It involves all students, all age levels, and all jobs. Figure 5.5 illustrates the Arizona model.

Wisconsin Model

One of the more effective approaches toward implementing career education is underway in Wisconsin. The thrust of the plan is toward integration of career guidance activities into the curriculum. In the Wisconsin experiment, 300 teachers and counselors approached guidance as a cooperative function.

Initially, the State Superintendent of Public Instruction appointed a 35-member career development study committee of teachers, pupil personnel specialists, and school administrators. Over a two-year period, the committee developed and field tested a curriculum-centered career development model. The efforts of the superintendent's study committee resulted in (28):

1 *a definition of the career development process*

2 *a designed conceptual framework for a career development model*

3 *identification of 16 major concepts in career development*

4 *a scope-and-sequence matrix model for program infusion at appropriate grade levels*

5 *several hundred general objectives that would aid in implementing identified concepts*

6 *local workshop organizational plans, resource aids, and program references*

These products were intended to assist local school staffs in designing their own career development programs and to serve as a link for state-wide program continuity. Figure 5.6 illustrates the career development model, and Figure 5.7 provides an example of its application.

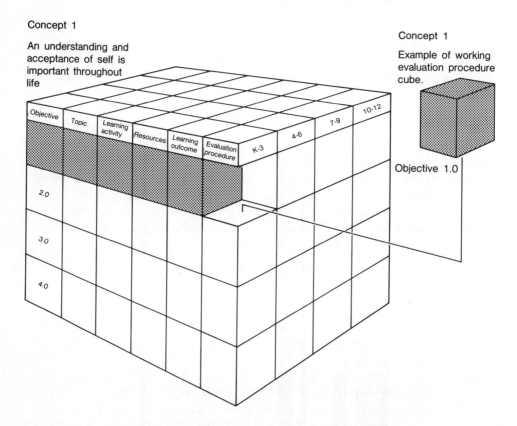

Figure 5.6 Wisconsin Model for Career Development: Vertical and horizontal example for model expansion (29).

The program has been carried out in Wisconsin through state-conducted local workshops for teachers; leadership was provided by members of the superintendent's study committee, who had themselves used the workshop approach to validate in-service methods. (Significantly, after developing the model, members of the study committee saw career development as a *process*, whereas each had previously viewed it as a variety of unrelated programs.)

Because the state model covered only general concepts and objectives, members of each local system staff completed their own district guides, including behavioral objectives, teacher methods, student activities, resource materials, curriculum considerations, student outcomes, and evaluation procedures. This strategy ensured maximal implementation of plans that were uniquely fitted to student and community needs.

Ten pilot workshops involving 35 school districts were held to field test the state guide. Two model-refinement workshops were held after the field test for revision purposes.

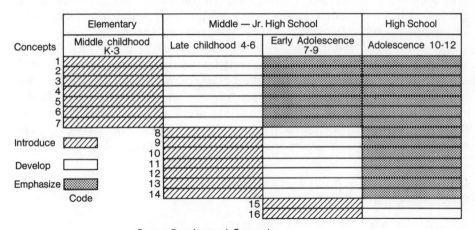

Career Development Concepts

 1 An understanding and acceptance of self is important throughout life.
 2 Persons need to be recognized as having dignity and worth.
 3 Occupations exist for a purpose.
 4 There is a wide variety of careers which may be classified in several ways.
 5 Work means different things to different people.
 6 Education and work are interrelated.
 7 Individuals differ in their interests, abilities, attitudes and values.
 8 Occupational supply and demand has an impact on career planning.
 9 Job specialization creates interdependency.
10 Environment and individual potential interact to influence career development.
11 Occupations and life styles are interrelated.
12 Individuals can learn to perform adequately in a variety of occupations.
13 Career development requires a continuous and sequential series of choices.
14 Various groups and institutions influence the nature and structure of work.
15 Individuals are responsible for their career planning.
16 Job characteristics and individuals must be flexible in a changing society.

Figure 5.7 Wisconsin Career Development Scope-and-Sequence Model (30).

The same basic state format was used at each of the local field-test sites. A general orientation to the process of career development was given, followed by an exacting explanation of the state model. During the first several days, the models, goals, concepts, and objectives were discussed and refined by the whole group. After consensus was obtained, the staff members were broken down into grade cluster groups to begin their writing tasks. Staffs servicing students in grades K–3, 4–6, 7–9, and 10–12 worked together, while group leaders and consultants coordinated their work.

No group could begin to develop a concept for its grade cluster or subject matter unless the preceding grade group had completed its writing task or unless the group was to introduce a concept. The purpose of this procedure was to ensure that a given concept would be constructed developmentally and that there would be no duplication of activities between grades (see Figure 5.7).

Each grade-level group was to expand upon the state goals and general objectives by writing related behavioral objectives for each of the grades within its cluster, as well as corresponding activities, resources to be used, expected outcomes, and methods for evaluation.

The completed product was a very specific set of guidelines for local staff members that would assure a continuous infusion of career development in their districts and individual classrooms. This cooperative planning eliminated duplication between grades and structured the pace of experiences in keeping with appropriate student maturation levels. The results of some 38,000 hours involved in testing the effectiveness of the state guide resulted in several positive actions as reported by Drier (31):

1 *Thirty-five local schools had comprehensive career development guides for local implementation.*

2 *Three hundred classroom teachers, building principals, and school counselors committed themselves to infusing career development activities into their classrooms.*

3 *The field test participants gave practical suggestions for revision that have made the final state guideline draft much more usable for future districts.*

4 *The field-test participants proved that local staffs are capable of model construction, implementation, and commitment.*

Local Career Education Programs

Almost all states and numerous local school districts have now initiated career education programs. For example, the legislatures of Arizona, Florida, and North Carolina each allocated $3 million a year to help school districts convert to career education. Wyoming and Georgia are heavily committed. Dallas is an outstanding example of a city that is converting on its own, and other cities are taking similar action.

The Dallas, Texas, Skyline Center represents an excellent example of the community involvement needed in planning and establishing a career-oriented school. In the planning stages, the business, social, and educational communities of Dallas were involved in recommending the content, scope, and sequence of offerings for this new school. Committees were established in 18 career clusters as a basis for exploring the question: What can a school do to enhance the opportunities for students to enter the field of work represented by your business? One central theme emerged from these planning sessions: Dallas Skyline Center should provide each student with at least three educational options: (a) an opportunity to enter the world of work immediately on graduation from high school with a salable skill; (b) an opportunity to continue his or her education at a trade, technical, or community college; or (c) an opportunity to continue his or her education at a university or professional school. These would represent options available to the student at graduation rather than choices that would have to be made at grades 8 or 9.

While committees were determining the educational specifications, the physical layout of the school was being designed to encourage innovation rather than to simply house the program. Skyline Center is actually three schools in one, built to serve four student bodies. The comprehensive high school serves as a local high school for students within its attendance zones. The Career Development Center serves as an extension for all Dallas high schools, offering study in three-hour clusters. Some students transfer to Skyline full time, whereas others attend half day and return to their local high schools for required subjects. The Center for Community Services offers programs of continuing education for adults and out-of-school youth at night and during the day if space is available.

Prior to the opening of the center, performance-based, criterion-referenced curricula were written for each of the 24 clusters that were implemented during the first year. During the opening months, activities at Skyline were carefully monitored by special evaluation teams.

Several factors have been identified that contribute to the success of the Skyline Center (32):

1 *the involvement of all aspects of the business, professional, and educational community in the design phase of the building*

2 *the creation of three schools in one*

3 *the creation of entrance standards for students wanting to attend— students' reasons for entry must relate to the point that they want more opportunity rather than their inability to achieve in the program at their own high school*

4 *in addition to the normal programs of occupational education, programs of advanced study were designed in every facet of business and* *school life; all the programs were designed to go beyond the opportunities available to students in any other school*

5 *the creation of the Skyline Advisory Board, complete with paid administrative assistance, and the Cluster Advisory Committee to develop fully the partnership between the school and the business community*

6 *the involvement of industry in the preparation and in the execution of the program*

7 *the decision to equip the building with the equipment used by industry rather than equipment that would simulate conditions in industry*

8 *the use of advisory committee members to work directly with students and teachers*

9 *the creation of a research and evaluation group to be a participating member of the development team in Skyline Center*

Summary

The continuous and accelerated nature of change in our society brings about frequent and intensive appraisal of education. Career education is a reflection of the continuing need for changes in public education. Most of the elements of career education are not new but have their roots in early efforts to implant vocational education and vocational guidance in the public schools. New emphasis, however, was given to the career education concept in 1971 by Dr. Sidney P. Marland, U.S. Commissioner of Education, who advocated a "totally new system," involving the blending of academic and vocational programs. Marland outlined only the broad parameters of a new learner-centered system, preferring that states and local school districts develop and refine their own career education plans and strategies. The challenge to spell out essential aspects evoked a wide and generally positive reaction among educators who formulated a diversity of conceptualizations of career education, ranging from an emphasis on earning a living in the narrowest sense, to an emphasis on the individual in relation to the total environment in the broadest sense. The career education movement received further impetus in 1974 when the Office of Career Education was established by Congress. An Associate Commissioner for Career Education was appointed by the new Commissioner, Terrence H. Bell, to give direction to the movement.

There is general agreement in the objectives of career education that would (a) allow all students to relate their education to the world of work; (b) provide an opportunity to engage in occupational exploration, including work experience, specialized instruction, and career decision-making, leading toward a preferred life style and career pattern; and (c) provide automatic exit and reentry to the educational system or the labor force as needed. The transitional phases in career education programs that are most evident are career *awareness*, career *exploration*, career *identification*, career *preparation*, and career *assessment*.

The U.S. Office of Education funded the development of four experimental models for career education: the school-based model, the employer- or experience-based model, the rural-residential-based model, and the home-community-based model. These models are available to assist states and local communities in installing new programs of career education throughout the country. In addition, many states have successfully developed and implemented their own career education models. Among these are Arizona, California, Florida, North Carolina, Oregon, and Wisconsin. Notable among career education efforts by cities is the Dallas Skyline Center for Career Education, which represents an excellent example of community involvement in planning and implementing a career-oriented school. Most current career education models recognize that learning experiences inside and outside the school should be selected as a means of helping individuals fulfill their economic, political, social, and personal roles. The methodology of career education moves away from a group approach toward an individualized approach to learning.

Activities

For review

1 Which of the nine levels of career education presented in the chapter most closely describes your interpretation of the role of career education?

2 Cite several ways in which career education differs from the traditional subject-centered curriculum.

3 Contrast the similarities and differences of vocational education and career education.

4 Briefly contrast the four United States Office of Education career education models as to their objectives and organization.

5 Summarize the contributions of career education to the following roles of the individual: economic, personal, social, political.

6 What the basic reasons for job preparation in terms of occupational clusters as opposed to preparation for a single occupation?

7 The design of a career education model can be viewed as a research project, a developmental project, or a demonstration project. What is your view and why?

8 What two basic elements are emphasized in the generic definition of career education mentioned by Associate United States Commissioner of Education Kenneth B. Hoyt?

For discussion

1 Present the pros and cons of career education that uses an approach such as that employed in the rural-residential-based model.

2 How do you think career education will benefit *you* in the years ahead?

3 What changes do you foresee in teacher education as a result of the career education movement?

4 What similarities and differences do you find in the assumptions underlying career education, as stated in 1972 by Commissioner Marland and in 1974 by Commissioner Bell?

For exploration

1 Interview one or more of the following individuals for his or her definition of career education: an elementary teacher, a high school teacher of academic courses, a high school teacher of vocational courses, a counselor, a principal, a college teacher of academic courses, a college teacher of vocational courses. How do their conceptualizations differ? Why? What implications can be drawn for future implementation of career education?

2 Contrast the basic beliefs of John Dewey and Charles Prosser with the primary objectives of career education as you interpret it.

3 Prepare a job ladder for the occupational cluster that represents your primary career field of interest. Such a ladder will reflect occupations requiring varying levels of preparation and ability.

4 From the current literature, describe one career education model not discussed in the text.

References

1 Gordon I. Swanson, "Facts and Fantasies of Career Education," *The Visitor*, Vol. 69, No. 2, April 1972, p. 2. (Reproduced by permission)

2 Edwin L. Herr, *Review and Synthesis of Foundations for Career Education* (Columbus: ERIC Clearinghouse on Vocational-Technical Education, The Center for Vocational and Technical Education, The Ohio State University, March 1972), pp. 29–30.

3 Sidney P. Marland, Jr., "Career Education Now," in *Vocational Guidance Quarterly*, Vol. 20, No. 3, March 1972, p. 190.

4 Ibid, pp. 190–192.

5 "Position Paper on Career Education," adopted by the National Association of State Directors of Vocational Education, Las Vegas, Nevada, September 1971.

6 Report of the American Vocational Association Task Force on Career Education, December 1971.

7 Keith Goldhammer and Robert E. Taylor, *Career Education: Perspective and Promise* (Columbus: Charles E. Merrill Publishing Company, 1972), p. 6. (Reproduced by permission)

8 Gordon I. Swanson. See Ref. 1, p. 1. (Reproduced by permission)

9 Kenneth B. Hoyt, Rupert N. Evans, Edward F. Mackin, and Garth L. Mangum, *Career Education: What It Is and How to Do It*, Second Edition (Salt Lake City: Olympus Publishing Company, 1974), pp. 5–6. (Reproduced by permission)

10 Kenneth B. Hoyt, "Career Education: Myth or Magic," in *National Association of Secondary School Principals Bulletin*, Vol. 57, No. 371, March 1973, pp. 29–30. (Reproduced by permission)

11 Sidney P. Marland, Jr., "Career Education: A Report," in *National Association of Secondary School Principals Bulletin*, Vol. 57, No. 371, March 1973, pp. 2–4. (Reproduced by permission)

12 Joel L. Burdin, "Career Education: Another Illusion or Opportunity," in *Journal of Teacher Education*, Vol. 24, No. 2, Summer 1973, pp. 82, 153. (Reproduced by permission)

13 William C. Miller, "Career Education and the Curriculum Leader," in *Educational Leadership*, Vol. 31, No. 2, November 1973, p. 153. (Reproduced by permission)

14 Wesley Smith, "Career Education: A Bridge to Relevancy in the Public Schools," Sacramento: California Department of Education, n.d., as quoted in William C. Miller, "Career Education and the Curriculum Leader," in *Educational Leadership*, Vol. 31, No. 2, November 1973, p. 154. (Reproduced by permission)

15 Louise J. Keller, "Objectives for Career Education in Office Education," address to the National Business Education Association, Chicago, Illinois, February 21, 1973.

16 Terrence H. Bell, "Career Education in 1974: A View from the Commissioner's Desk." Address before the National Conference for State Coordinators of Career Education, Center for Vocational Education, The Ohio State University, October 31, 1974. Delivered by tele-lecture.

17 Kenneth B. Hoyt, "An Introduction to Career Education," A Policy Paper of the Office of Education, November 1974.

18 Gordon I. Swanson. See Ref. 1, pp. 2–3. (Reproduced by permission)

19 Edwin L. Herr, "Unifying an Entire System of Education Around a Career Development Theme," in *Career Education: Perspective and Promise*, eds. Keith Goldhammer and Robert E. Taylor (Columbus: Charles E. Merrill Publishing Company, 1972), p. 100.

20 Ibid, p. 101.

21 Keith Goldhammer and Robert E. Taylor. See Ref. 7, p. 8. (Reproduced by permission)

22 Wesley E. Budke, Glenn E. Beattis, and Gary F. Beasley, *Career Education Practice* (Columbus: ERIC Clearinghouse for Vocational and Technical Education, The Center for Vocational and Technical Education, The Ohio State University, 1972), pp. 11–13.

23 Ibid, pp. 14–15.

24 U.S. Office of Education, "Guidelines and Work Statement," RFP–73–21 (Washington, D.C.: U.S. Department of Health, Education and Welfare, February 28, 1973.)

25 Terrence H. Bell and Kenneth B. Hoyt, *Career Education: The USOE Perspective* (Columbus: The Center for Vocational Education, The Ohio State University, 1974), p. 10.

26 William C. Miller. See Ref. 13, p. 154. (Reproduced by permission)

27 *Career Education: Leadership in Learning* (Phoenix: Arizona Department of Education, 1974), p. 6.

28 Harry N. Drier, Jr., "Career Development Activities Permeate Wisconsin Curriculum," in *American Vocational Journal*, Vol. 47, No. 3, March 1972, p. 40. (Reproduced by permission)

29 Ibid, p. 41.

30 Ibid, p. 40.

31 Ibid, p. 41. (Reproduced by permission)

32 B. J. Stamps, "Dallas Skyline Center from Conception to Reality," in *National Association of Secondary School Principals Bulletin*, Vol. 57, No. 371, March 1973, pp. 87–88. (Reproduced by permission)

Chapter 6

Implementing

Career Education:

Issues, Problems,

and Needs

Introduction

In this chapter an examination is made of (a) the role and objectives of career education at the elementary, middle school, secondary, and higher education levels, (b) the implications of career education for the training of teachers, and (c) some of the basic issues, problems, and needs of career education.

Through the Elementary School

If career education is to attain its goals, then it must begin in the elementary school. At this level, students must be helped to become aware of the world of work, of the values of a work-oriented society, and of themselves as individuals and as members of society.

At the elementary level, career education is conceived as a mélange of experiences, such as interpersonal relationships, hands-on creative expression, and problem-solving work. It is most effectively implemented as an integral part of the existing curriculum. Implementing career education does not mean the addition of another course to an already crowded curriculum. Neither does it suggest that the teacher de-emphasize existing substantive content. Rather, the implementation of career education involves the modification of present course outlines to include a career education *emphasis*.

One of the first questions that school administrators ask when considering a career education program is: What concepts should be included? The U.S. Office of Education has funded two curriculum efforts that are specifically directed toward elementary school career education. One outcome of these projects will be the identification of a series of recommended concepts. The two projects, at Eastern Illinois University and at American Institutes for Research, are charged with these responsibilities (1):

1 *develop, evaluate, and disseminate career education curriculum guides that are applicable to any school with grade levels functionally equivalent to K–6 and which result in the integration of positive values and attitudes toward work, self-awareness, development of decision-making skills, and awareness of occupational opportunities in career lines within major occupational fields*

2 *develop, implement, evaluate, and disseminate sample teaching learning modules for the K–6 career education curriculum guides achieved by fusing and/or coordinating academic and occupational concepts and utilizing multimedia instructional tools*

3 *develop, evaluate, and disseminate a design of a K–6 career education instructional system which is adaptable to any elementary instructional program and may serve as an alternative to present career education instructional systems*

Operating on the broad goals for career education, state and local school systems are identifying specific career education objectives that guide the development and implementation of local programs. For example, the *Career Development Guide for the Elementary School*, developed by the state of Maine, identifies these program objectives (2):

1 *introduce the student to the world of work and career opportunities*

2 *establish the relationship of occupational skills to academic skills*

3 *develop, through exploration, a self realization related to abilities and interest for future career selection*

4 *acquaint students with problem-solving techniques as they prepare themselves for the world of work*

5 *encourage the student to understand that career selection is related to the need and abilities of the individual*

6 *develop an understanding and appreciation of the interrelationship of the various careers in the world of work*

Through the Middle School

Exploration is a crucial phase in career education. The skills and knowledge acquired during this phase become the foundation for decision making at succeeding levels. The major thrust at the middle school level is toward having the student explore various occupational clusters and become familiar with the preparation requirements and the educational opportunities available for obtaining the necessary training.

The U.S. Office of Education has identified the following occupational clusters as those into which career education will ultimately be integrated at all levels of the educational program:

Business and Office Occupations
Marketing and Distribution Occupations
Communications and Media Occupations
Construction Occupations
Manufacturing Occupations
Transportation Occupations
Agri-Business and Natural Resources Occupations
Marine Science Occupations
Environmental Control Occupations
Public Service Occupations
Health Occupations
Hospitality and Recreation Occupations
Personal Services Occupations
Fine Arts and Humanities Occupations
Consumer and Homemaking Occupations

Within each cluster, specific occupations may be perceived as existing on a particular rung of a career ladder; thus, occupations may be viewed both individually and in relation to each other within the cluster. During the exploratory phase, the student should examine not only the opportunities available within a cluster of occupations but also the life-style implications of each occupation.

The focus of career education at the middle grade level is evident in the objectives identified for the programs. For example, the Hosterman Junior High School Career Development Committee, in Minnesota, has developed a guide to career development in grades 7–9 as it can be facilitated by English, mathematics, science, and social studies units. They formulated a list of assumptions that underlie the development of clusters of occupations and that can be related to specific subject areas (3):

1 *Career exploration, instead of being a difficult and clumsy addition to the teaching process, can actually become an efficient, effective vehicle for all types of learning.*

2 *Curriculum experiences need to be interdisciplinary or, better still, non-disciplinary in nature.*

3 *The student must be allowed to discover through interesting and meaningful (to him or her) activities that planning for career choices and maintenance is an ongoing process.*

4 *Career development is essentially a process of relating self to occupations.*

Along with an examination of occupational clusters, the exploration phase at the middle grades level should provide opportunities for students to examine themselves, their abilities, and their goals. A strong guidance and counseling component is important in the exploration phase of career implementation because it helps students to realistically correlate information about themselves with occupational choices. As students begin to explore a wide variety of occupations, they are also beginning to make very tentative decisions regarding suitable careers that offer possibilities for a life style that they envision as their own. Two urban school systems, those of Albuquerque, New Mexico, and Philadelphia, Pennsylvania, provide good examples of career education at the middle school level (4).

A federally funded career education project in Albuquerque involved 35 mini-grant programs that were conducted within 24 elementary and middle schools. Among the successful outcomes of the project was the favorable impact of innovative career awareness activities on disadvantaged Indian students, their parents, and the community. Shortcomings of the program were identified as a lack of adequate facilities, time, and funds, and concerns for the future of the program.

Under Title III, Supplementary Centers and Services Program, of the Elementary and Secondary Education Act, a multipurpose project was established in the Philadelphia City School District to serve students in the metropolitan area. The project consisted of five programs: (a) a career development program involving three schools, where special curricula and guidance activities were used to expose children to the world of work; (b) a community schools program involving use of over 20 schools as community centers for the mobilization of social, cultural, recreational, educational, and economic services. The schools provided tutorial and remedial programs, music activities, recreational activities, adult education, and other services to the community; (c) a volunteer training program consisting of the use of volunteers in five schools to assist teachers by tutoring students, performing professional tasks, and contributing talents for enrichment programs; (d) a magnet schools program involving the conversion of six schools to a grade 7–4–4 rather than a grade 6–3–3 organizational plan. Team teaching, individualized instruction, programmed materials, and the use of teacher aides were stressed; (e) an integral plan for evaluation was introduced in relation to programs employing a systems approach. Approximately 12,000 students and 600 teachers participated in the program.

Through the Secondary School

The career-centered curriculum at the high school level represents a continuation of experiences that are similar to those of the awareness and exploration phases at the elementary and middle school levels. At this level, however, emphasis is placed on occupational preparation activities within occupational clusters. In some states the occupational preparation phase is preceded by an intensive career orientation stage at grades 9–10, focusing, as in the Illinois model, on such occupational clusters as business, marketing, and management; personal and public services; health; industrial technology; and agricultural and biological sciences.

Integration or interlocking of content at the secondary level is more difficult to achieve than at the elementary levels for obvious reasons: 1. Teacher preparation is presently aimed toward preparing subject-matter specialists. 2. Most teachers, especially those outside the vocational areas, have little or no work experience outside teaching and generally inadequate knowledge of occupational requirements. 3. Many teachers lack the necessary skills and knowledge of occupational clusters needed to relate the curriculum content to the student's career plans. 4. Many school systems are unable to provide the necessary time for teachers of the various disciplines to plan complementary learning experiences.

Several states have now established career education programs that are beginning to operate effectively at the secondary school level. One such example is the state of Oregon, where career education is based on two assumptions: 1. Secondary schools should be preparatory institutions for all students. 2. A secondary school preparatory program should tie the curriculum to the goals of students in such a way that they are motivated while they are in school and they are also better equipped to choose from among many alternatives as they take that next step, whether it be on-the-job training, apprenticeship, community college, proprietary school, or a four-year college.

Infusing the career-cluster approach into the secondary education program requires many changes. First, high schools must make a definite commitment to move from the present curricular tracking system, which uses such terms as "advanced college prep," "terminal general," or "remedial-basic," to career-cluster tracks. Second, high school curricula will need to be rebuilt around the career-cluster or family-of-occupations concept. Third, specific training for those thousands of technical occupations that do not require a bachelor's degree will largely become the responsibility of postsecondary institutions. And finally, every secondary school and community college must greatly strengthen its guidance and counseling programs.

Increasing numbers of school systems are focusing on revision of secondary school objectives and goals to reflect the integration of curricula that is implicit in career education. The following examples illustrate how secondary career education programs are being implemented at the local level.

In Washington, D.C., exemplary project funds are helping to develop a career education program that stresses community involvement. With assistance from local business, industry, and service agencies, high school seniors who do not plan to enter college immediately are getting occupational skills that will prepare them for rewarding careers following graduation. The school system had initially hoped to recruit 500 seniors for the program, but the publicity campaign with the Board of Trade proved so effective that it had to make room for additional students.

The career-bound program serves grades 6–12 in the Scottsdale, Paradise Valley and Cave Creek School Districts in Arizona. With assistance from career counselors and aides, each school operates programs that have been developed by its teachers and administrators. The objectives of the program (5) are to: (a) integrate career concepts into ongoing teaching; (b) train teachers, administrators, and counselors to increase career education skills; (c) counsel students in the process of developing decision-making skills; and (d) develop and refine curricula that illustrate how to teach the career concepts.

Methods include use of specially trained teachers to demonstrate career materials, disseminate information, and create new approaches for classroom teachers. A resource center is operated by the project, which coordinates all commercial and teacher-made media and lessons, originates news letters and bulletin boards, and ties the diversified project together. Classroom methods include experiences with actual workers, through the use of guest speakers, tele-lectures, tours, and four- to eight-hour visits on a one-to-one basis with the students in an actual work setting. Students gain further insight into the world of work through setting up their own imaginary companies, hosting career days, taking interest surveys, and thinking about how they want to live as adults.

During 1973, approximately 750,000 students participated in over 100 career education pilot projects in every state and territory. By 1974, almost 5000 of the nation's 17,000 school districts had developed active career education programs. Programs were also underway for the development of effective career education for minorities. One of these, along the Continental Divide, will combine educational innovation and space technology. The National Aeronautics and Space Administration plans to launch an experimental satellite over the Rocky Mountains to test satellites as television relays in remote areas. The satellite will test the feasibility of bringing career education into homes and schools on Indian reservations and other remote communities. Eventually the Rocky Mountain states hope to develop a career awareness program for this television transmission. The satellite will carry four audio bands so that the television set will eventually bring in one visual picture with accompanying sound narratives in Navajo, Hopi, Spanish, and English (6).

Other projects involved approximately one million Vietnam-era veterans in 1973. They were enrolled in such career-related programs as the Career Opportunities Program, Talent Search, and Upward Bound, as well as various vocational education and student loan programs.

In summary, career education at the secondary level includes the following objectives: exploring careers within a specific family of occupations; selecting a specific career, making initial preparations, and developing post-high school plans related to it; developing salable skills; continuing development, refinement, and application of basic skills; and developing the attitudes, skills, and understandings that relate to the personal, family, social, and cultural dimensions of one's life.

Through Higher Education

The implementation of career education involves a wide variety of postsecondary career preparation programs and institutions designed to accommodate the needs of adults. Since 1970 higher education has put into effect new and expanded career-oriented programs. The associate degree appears to be replacing the high school diploma as the point of departure for many Americans. The four-year college program acts as a finishing institution with career programs geared to the professional level. The nature and extent of career education in each institution is related to its priorities and purposes. In this section we will examine the contributions to career education that may be made by two-year, four-year, and graduate educational programs.

Two-Year Programs

The two-year programs of higher education have a four-fold career-education responsibility: (a) to provide multiple options in career education; (b) to work with secondary schools and postsecondary proprietary schools in the orderly articulation of career education sequences; (c) to work with the major producer and service units in the economy on such issues as desirable pre- and in-service training and work-study programs; and (d) to maintain constant contact with four-year colleges and universities to negotiate the issues of educational philosophy and academic transfer. The two-year college system may well be the fulcrum of career education. As such it has a responsibility to search for balanced, highest-common-denominator agreements about the meaning and direction of the career education movement.

Four-Year Programs

Four-year baccalaureate programs have many contributions to make to the emerging emphasis on career education. The first is to ensure that career education does not slip into the traditional mold of training solely for the vocations and professions. If career education is to become a truly liberating concept, it must subsume definitions of career that go beyond job competency. Most human beings are awake 112 hours a week; only 40 of those are spent on the job, leaving 72 hours for social and personal matters. Most four-year higher education institutions attempt to feature those aspects of curricula that relate not just to human technology for the economy but to human conditions. Designers of career curricula must catch the spirit of liberal arts education and meld it with vocational and professional training at all levels.

The second contribution four-year colleges can make to career education is to work with their extension divisions and with external degree programs to provide off-campus remedial programs in liberal arts studies for those who wish to broaden their educational horizons. An individual may come to value the liberal arts components of education later in life when the tedium of a particular job becomes oppressive.

A third contribution that the four-year college can make to career education is to devise further means of providing wholeness or unity to the total educational program. This task will involve concerted efforts on a college-wide basis to provide the basis for multidisciplinary programs and experiences.

Higher education institutions view the emerging concept of career education with mixed reactions. While some deplore the democratization and further vocationalism of higher education, others welcome the shift toward practical training. In the long run, the pluralism of higher education is likely to have a mitigating effect on tensions created by the debate about career education.

But higher education in the United States has always been career oriented. Harvard was established in 1636 to train clergy. During the next two centuries a variety of private and sectarian colleges were established for the training of men for spiritual, intellectual, and political leadership. The Morrill Act in 1862 gave thrust to the notion that higher education should be career oriented in specific and practical terms, and it resulted in a mingling of the liberal arts emphases with occupational professionalism. Consequently, such diverse fields as teaching, law, business, medicine, agriculture, and homemaking have been served both by general education and by specifically occupational courses at the undergraduate and graduate levels.

There is some truth to the contention that most general curricula are designed to cultivate humanistic insights and intellectual capacities that are not specific to careers, hence the assumption that preparation for life is more than narrow job training. In addition the status conferred by degree credentials continues to have bearing on career rewards regardless of the specificity or sophistication of college-level education. Yet automation and specialization have led to the fact that eight out of ten jobs in the next ten years will need less than a baccalaureate level of preparation. As the need for technical job skills increases and as the costs of higher education continue to rise, the real and assumed benefits of baccalaureate status may melt away.

The prestigious liberal arts institution tends to deplore these trends toward democratization and further "vocationalization" of higher education. On the other hand, the two-year community college and the comprehensive university and proprietary schools tend to welcome the shift toward practical training. The strength of American higher education is its pluralism, and diverse contributions to the concept of career education can be made by even the highest levels of educational institutions: the graduate professional schools and the graduate programs in the arts and sciences.

Graduate Programs

Graduate professional schools can perform a major role in describing professional careers and in articulating the technical and paraprofessional training needed by those who wish to enter a professional field at a support level rather than at a professional level—the training and certification of paraprofessionals in education is a case in point. Graduate professional schools also bear a heavy responsibility for developing leadership personnel to conduct the research and development aspects of career education.

The quality of intellectual standards involved in research and teaching in graduate schools of arts and sciences has implications for all the professions, ranging from medicine to the newer fields such as oceanography. The multidisciplinary nature of graduate education brings with it a special responsibility to raise profound questions about the social consequences of existing career definitions in order to effect further humanization of the world of work. Thus a graduate school of engineering may work on questions of improving the efficiency of the assembly line, while the graduate school of philosophy raises the question of whether or not the assembly line is compatible with human dignity. All graduate schools must provide in-service and continuing education for those who wish to shift careers or to upgrade themselves within a specific career. They must continue to collect new knowledge while improving their capacity to disseminate to the world of career education the products of their libraries and laboratories.

The response of higher education toward career education has been attentive, partially critical, and partially supportive. What is needed now is a constructive partnership in which all levels of education work together to create a concept of career education that is both technologically sophisticated and humanistically informed.

Teacher Education

What are the implications of career education for teacher education? Is career education but another artificially stimulated movement heading toward oblivion, or can it help to make education more vital for each person and for society? The answers to these questions will be conditioned by the extent to which career education becomes a focus for the preparation of all teachers.

By virtue of its role in a pluralistic culture, the teacher education institution is obligated to examine all alternative paths toward realizing the mission of public education. So it is in the training of teachers that the career education movement will meet perhaps its most severe test. Teacher educators must first be informed about the objectives and scope of career education before they can adequately assess the permanence or impermanence of the concept. Teachers have their own ideas and creative ways of interpreting basic concepts, and their understanding of career education is crucial to successful classroom implementation.

Successful implementation of career education, particularly in the school-based model, requires a cadre of teachers who are familiar with the nationally developed approach to career education. Provision must also be made to train personnel needed in the industrial, home-community, and residential models of career education. Although the burden of staff development for career education is being placed primarily on co-operating schools, the theoretical basis on which these in-service programs are built and the role of these programs in the total effort of teacher education has not yet been made clear.

Future training of career educators must be established as an integral part of current teacher education programs. Models must be flexible enough to turn out individuals capable of undertaking the duties of the career development specialist, who will be responsible for working with all teachers and other personnel as they strive to meet career education goals.

Specific objectives of a career education program to serve personnel needs of the four USOE models should include persons who have developed: (a) the ability to coordinate purposeful learning experiences for youth with viable segments of business-industry, public service, and the family-home unit; (b) sufficient knowledge and experience in vocational guidance and career planning so that advice, direction, and acquisition of resources pertaining to the major occupations can be included in routine classroom activities; and (c) an understanding, appreciation, and experience with typical job classifications, job-entry requirements, and job-placement opportunities in the major occupational clusters.

Needs of pre-service and in-service teachers must be met in any comprehensive plan for training the three types of personnel that will be needed in career education. Staff development opportunities in career education will be needed for the already certified teacher. The pre-service prospective teacher must be given preparation to complement his or her specific teacher education program. A career education specialist, whose prior preparation may or may not be in the professional education area, comprises a third option. The training of all of these personnel would include formal course work and experiences in career development and planning, coordination and public relations, guidance, counseling, and supervision.

Career Education
for Elementary Teachers

What are the implications of career education for training elementary teachers? The elementary teacher spends a considerable length of time, day after day, with pupils, and he or she may be the only adult that many of the students actually observe at work. Thus the teacher is in a unique position to serve as a model of the working adult.

Elementary teachers are asked to demonstrate skills in relating to children, but they should also have the basic management skills needed to plan sensory activities for small groups of children. Diagnosing children's needs, examining instructional resources, relating content from many disciplines of knowledge, and planning for individual as well as social activities—all require a continuous flow of decisions. The teacher who works to make reasons, as well as decisions, visible to the class is helping children learn career development skills; they will learn that being human means being capable of making decisions and living with their consequences.

Elementary teachers will need preparation for involvement with the self-images of young children, particularly as children project themselves into the future. Technical skills in this area will enable teachers to explore a greater variety of adult roles and models, to bring out the historical and affective dimensions of adult lives, and to focus on the career opportunities that appear to meet needs, interests, abilities and values. To help children explore the future, elementary teachers need to plan activities around the following concepts: 1. People change their minds about what they like to do with their time, energies, and resources. 2. Dynamic forces shape business, industrial, and governmental operations. 3. A free society requires that individuals be willing to assume responsibility for part of their own futures. 4. Many of life's activities require cooperation with people of diverse origins, interests, and abilities as well as of varying amounts of individual initiative.

The elementary teacher must understand what support systems are available to the career education curriculum, in particular: (a) community resources, such as local businesses, parent involvement, and school-community liaison services; (b) administrative and technical supports, such as instructional learning centers; and (c) pupil guidance activities and services. For elementary teachers, skills in community development, group dynamics, systems analysis, and human relations will become increasingly important as they become more involved in implementing career development programs.

Career Education
for Secondary Teachers

What are the implications of career education for the training of high school teachers? The readiness and competence of teachers to participate in an organized approach to career planning and decision making is vital to the success of secondary schools in meeting their obligation to help students achieve their developmental tasks. The active involvement of all teachers who are concerned with vocational development should be of immediate concern to school administrators, counselors, and directors of vocational education and of pupil personnel services, because the teacher is in a unique position to reach students in a variety of settings.

Determining what should be taught in the pre-service teacher education setting is logically related to the formulation of objectives, determination of content, materials, instructional aids, teaching strategies, and opportunities for individualized learning. Student involvement might well begin with activities planned for an assessment quarter or as part of orientation to the role of the teacher in the beginning stages of the professional education sequence.

To what extent has the prospective teacher for the high school developed the competence necessary to perform effectively in the classroom, to serve as a group leader, in team with counselors? To what extent does he or she comprehend vocational objectives that might be pertinent for every teacher regardless of subject being taught? Tennyson (7) has suggested the following instructional goals for classroom teachers:

1 *to provide experiences which will enable students to gain a fuller awareness and appreciation of the occupational avenues growing out of the particular subject and the nature of the roles played by workers in these occupations*

2 *to contribute to the student's testing of reality by showing the relationship between the requirements of these vocations and the education or training needed to meet them*

3 *to develop attitudes of respect for and appreciation of the social usefulness of all types of work to which the subject may lead*

Questions such as the following might be used to determine the readiness of potential career education teachers: To what extent do they understand that the concept of career increasingly refers to a sequence of occupations that an individual may occupy in his or her lifetime? Are they aware of the job clusters currently identified for study by the U.S. Office of Education? Do they view current technology as leading to preparation for a life of multiple occupations for many future job seekers? What do they know about entry jobs in their immediate labor-market areas? Have they been exposed to the concept of developmental tasks and life stages? Are they aware of research pertaining to the setting of goals by adolescents of various ability levels? Do they view occupational choices as a process of self-actualization?

A helpful discussion that has implications for the high school teacher is presented by Super (8). He describes the role of the teacher or the counselor as one of helping individual students to understand themselves and their environment and to find satisfying ways of developing their personal resources. He explains the concept of life stages as they relate to adolescence and the need for planned exploration to continue for several years after the termination of formal schooling. He mentions that vocational maturity involves learning to acquire relevant information and to anticipate choices that will have to be made. These needs of adolescents suggest that schools should develop additional methods for teaching students about the possibilities and pitfalls of planning ahead.

Many teacher-training institutions will use a task force or committee approach to assess their short-run and long-run commitments to career education. They will need to answer the question, How comprehensive should a functional program of career education be for the 1970s and beyond? The essentials are likely to involve at least five core areas, in which prospective teachers become acquainted with (a) the concept of career education, (b) where people work, (c) career planning, (d) sources of information, and (e) the role of the teacher in helping students prepare for careers.

Career Education
for In-Service Teachers

In-service teachers seeking to incorporate career education into their classroom teaching will find themselves heavily involved in producing and using relevant, job-oriented course materials. They will also make more extensive use of the community as a source of teaching materials and learning experiences. Staff development is viewed by Drier (9) as a process encompassing six goals:

☐ (a) *insure that all staff involved with the delivery of career education are continually informed of the rationale and methods of infusing career education into the existing program; (b) provide needed assistance to staff regarding any new career education content that is being built into the program; (c) provide ongoing needed assistance to become competent in using specific techniques being designed within the program; (d) provide time and setting to interface with other staff to exchange knowledge, opinions, and questions during the implementation phase; and (e) keep staff advised as to support programs or materials that will assist in meeting their instructional objectives.*

The above goals represent a set of operational considerations that provide the criteria (10) for measuring the success of career education:

1 *There must be evidence of administration and board policy support; staff development must clearly be a priority. The district including the project personnel must assist in the development of a climate and a commitment if career education is to be achieved.*

2 *The program rationale and objectives must be stated clearly; there must be an obvious relationship between what staff are presently doing, and what is to transpire. The related evaluation process should be delineated (including related research and instrumentation).*

3 *Professional and support staff members must know how and when to participate and relate to the program. Participatory-peer structured developmental approach is recommended. There should be multiple avenues for involvement to accommodate different styles, different stages of development, and different entry or achievement opportunities.*

4 *There must be adequacy and coordination of the materials to be used. This is necessary to maximize understanding that minimizes personal risk. Progress regarding support features such as equipment or building modifications should be explicit and timely.*

5 *Relevance and realism for all staff are necessary. This relates to certification, status, attention, time, income, and especially to the ongoing tasks for which the staff members are accountable—knowledge gain, skill acquisition, quality of work, professional role and expertise.*

6 *A reasonable plan for the achievement of the desired objectives must include short- and long-range goals, time frames, stated management expectations and interventions, and processes for program modification. Backup support and/or alternative routes are helpful.*

7 *Leadership and role responsibilities for all staff members should be defined. Leadership should be determined on the basis of competency and accountability rather than status per se.*

8 *Communication flow and feedback must be a part of the process and program. Lack of feedback regarding performance gain or modification causes turbulence and reversion; this includes learners and the community as well as the staff members who are involved. It is more difficult, but also more essential, when interaction involves non-school agencies, businesses, or institutions.*

9 *Sufficient time must be provided—time for change, time for development and accommodation, time within the priority hours for activity. If the program is an add-on, if it occurs only during "off" hours or days, then all of the above elements including support and commitment are negated.*

10 *Support and modification must be observable in all components of the program. A single change or thrust will be rejected or isolated by the routine, ongoing practices and procedures. Professional and personalized staff development programs must be systemic as well as systematic.*

To date no magic formula has been developed by which national priorities or instructional improvements become operational in our schools. As an institution at the crossroads of every significant movement, the schools are subject to multiple and often contradictory values. Both the desire to change and the reluctance to change are always with us, so it becomes a formidable challenge to redirect staff development in any consequential way. No one person is adequate to the task. What is needed is a consortium of all sectors of education, each operating according to the responsibilities assigned, and each supporting the total effort in appropriate ways.

Career Education Centers

As a means of assisting the development and implementation of career education programs in Georgia, the College of Education at the University of Georgia has established an interdisciplinary Center for Career Education. The major purposes of the center are (11):

1 to provide the leadership for the State of Georgia in developing, refining, and demonstrating models for career education in the public schools

2 to provide for the design, development, implementation, and evaluation of curriculums, materials, procedures, and field experiences necessary for Georgia career education models

3 to provide a locus for research studies and the evaluation of content and process in career education

4 to develop in-service and pre-service programs to prepare professional personnel for all phases of the career education program

5 to establish a materials center which will include resources relating to career education and develop means of disseminating materials to those involved in programs of career education

Activities have been planned for institutes and workshops to meet the needs of eight different levels and/or interest areas (11):

Component A *a program to train teams of teachers and counselors to prepare guides for fusing concepts of self and career awareness*

Component B *a program to assist interdisciplinary teams of junior and senior high teachers, from participating clusters, in the preparation of local guides for interlocking their curriculums in order to serve more effectively disadvantaged and handicapped students*

Component C *a program to assist teams of leadership personnel from 19 local school clusters in the preparation of a local management guide for implementing a program of comprehensive career education*

Component D *a program to assist teams from each of the 19 school clusters to prepare a local guide for job placement*

Component E *a program to prepare prevocational teachers to conduct mini-prevocational programs in agriculture, business education, home economics, and industrial technology*

Component F *a program to prepare prevocational teachers to conduct the "World of Construction" programs in their respective school environments*

Component G *a program to prepare prevocational teachers to conduct the "World of Manufacturing" programs in their respective school environments*

Component H *a program to prepare post-secondary instructors to operate learning evaluation laboratories*

An Appraisal of Career Education

An appraisal of the theory and practice of career education reveals both strengths and weaknesses. This section identifies some of the primary issues and problems as they have evolved in the early years of the career education movement.

Issues and Problems

In December 1971, at its annual meeting in Portland, Oregon, an American Vocational Association (AVA) task force raised four major issues (12) as a basis for a recommended AVA position regarding career education:

Issue 1   Leadership of career education *The relationship of career education to all of education can clearly be identified . . . There is an issue concerning the agencies and professional associations that can and should give the leadership to development and management of career education.*

The suggested AVA position *Career education clearly is concerned with career choice and preparation for employment; therefore, the agencies and associations providing direction to vocational education should give leadership to career education. The national level of administrative responsibility for career education rests with the U.S. Office of Education in an expanded and improved Bureau of Adult, Vocational and Technical Education. AVA should take the leadership role by sponsoring a national forum with broad representation from major educational and other related groups to develop guidelines, establish legislative goals, and define the role of various programs in relation to career education.*

Issue 2   Financing of career education *New developments in education cannot be initiated without consideration of the additional costs for both development and implementation at the national, state, and local levels. Such additional costs may come from new funds or from reallocation of existing funds. Career education will be effective to the extent that funding permits broad vocational education programs that are available throughout the entire life span of its clientele. The Vocational Education Amendments of 1968 provide only enough funding to pilot new developments at this time; additional funding will be required to facilitate the necessary changes.*

The suggested AVA position *AVA should take the leadership in identifying and promoting legislation that will authorize categorical funding for all segments of career education, including vocational education. Full funding of the Vocational Education Amendments of 1968 should be a continued goal of AVA. Additional legislation should be encouraged to achieve the funding levels necessary for further expansion of vocational education and the total career education program.*

Issue 3   The role of vocational education in career education *The placement and importance of vocational education in the total context of career education is of concern to many vocational educators. Will there continue to be programs of vocational education that concentrate on intensive occupational preparation?*

The suggested AVA position *AVA should reaffirm a commitment to a broad definition of vocational education and should support the retention of vocational education as a significant and identifiable component of career education.*

Issue 4   The role of AVA in career education *Career education is a relatively new concept to the lay public as well as to many educators both within and outside the American Vocational Association. Should AVA assume the responsibility of communication and, if so, how should this be done?*

The suggested AVA position *AVA should and must assume this responsibility. Suggested ways include:*
(a) Conduct institutes for AVA members that would report programs of career education and develop national, state, and local leadership; (b) focus on career education at future AVA meetings in general sessions, divisional and departmental meetings; (c) prepare and distribute publications on career education to vocational educators, school administrators, and the lay public; (d) collect and interpret data for developing and promoting career education legislation; (e) promote a White House Conference on Career Education; and (f) provide visibility within the AVA organizational structure for emerging aspects of career education.

In 1973, John R. Ottina, Acting Commissioner of Education, summarized some of the issues involved (13):

☐ *Were we bent upon an anti-intellectual azimuth that would deny the historic meaning of the liberal arts? Were we so pre-occupied with occupational fulfillment that we endangered the ultimate educational ideal of personal, social, emotional, and humanistic fulfillment? Were we thoughtlessly extolling the virtues of technical education (such as in the community colleges) to the corresponding implied disparagement of the liberal arts institutions? Were we seeking to track minority students into "blue-collar" jobs at a time when the college doors were being opened wider? Were we accentuating the "work ethic" at a time when some young people believed they had found a nobler motivation than economic gain?*

One thing comes through in these kinds of questions. We have not been using the English language to best advantage. We have not been communicating as well as we should have and have tried to. The answer to each of these questions, at least as we in the Office of Education have visualized and conceptualized career education from the outset, is a resounding "NO." Career education was never intended to devalue a liberal arts education or to stress occupational preparation at the expense of personal and humanistic development. And it is certainly not an approach designed to track minority students into blue-collar jobs, to deny them the advantages of a college education, or to place undue emphasis on the work ethic. The truth lies in the absolute reverse of these negative assumptions, and there is a touch of irony in the fact that a reform effort such as career education is being identified with the very wrongs it is trying to right.

Career education simply says that every student should be aware of all sorts of career options, that the son of the motel manager may want to follow in his father's footsteps but should also know that he has the ability and opportunity to become a forester or oceanographer or attorney. How many careers do most teenagers know about, beyond those in which family and the parents of friends are involved? A recent study shows that even school-sponsored field trips tend to focus on museums and art galleries, with almost no exposure to places where people pursue their careers. So an important aspect of career education is to broaden the thinking and career-selection process for every student.

If he selects a career that requires a four-year or two-year college degree, then college is an essential step in his career development and his high school preparatory work and guidance counseling should lead him in this direction. But our young people should not be encouraged to go to college just for the prestige and so-called status that a college education provides. Higher education is costly and time-consuming. It should be directed not only at expanding young minds but also at giving them the skills to compete in rewarding careers.

If anything, the union card of the 1970s for the majority of young people is not a four-year degree, just as it is not a high school diploma. The Department of Labor says that by the end of the decade four out of every five jobs will not require a four-year degree. What often gets lost is the other half of this projection—that most of these jobs will require training beyond high school. In other words, the new technologies and service industries have created a new middle ground of job opportunities that call for one or two years of training beyond high school, but do not require a four-year college degree. Blue-collar jobs as we have known them in the past are fast disappearing. All this says we need to stop indoctrinating our young people with the notion that any career aspiration not based on an academic or professional degree is somehow demeaning,

somehow unworthy of becoming one's life goal. To continue this fal-
lacious idea is a disservice to our young people.

Criticisms of Career Education

Critics of career education have raised a number of concerns about the
theory and practice of career education. Professors Robert J. Nash and
Russell M. Agne of the University of Vermont identify what they regard as
three questionable assumptions of career educators about the teaching-
learning experience (14). They then explore the ramifications of these
assumptions for teacher-education reform.

---

1 Career educators assume that because specialization is the key to occupational success, then the learning experience itself must be highly specialized.

Professors Nash and Agne point out that excessive specialization of education around job clusters is restrictively utilitarian and that students gain
insight only into the nature of the marketplace and so neglect the in-
tuitive, spiritual life of the arts, humanities, and religion. Similarly, they
advance the view that teacher-education reform risks excessive specialization in its emphasis on practical, demonstrable, measurable competencies (14).

☐ *To alleviate the catastrophes of "career overload," teacher educators*
will have to provide a vision of life for prospective teachers where human
beings are continually learning to integrate all kinds of knowledge—lib-
eral, spiritual, instrumental, expressive, political, scientific, and sexual.
We might develop paratactical models for enabling persons to . . . iden-
tify professions barren of personal growth possibilities.. . . and to
receive new ideas and experience throughout their lives without becoming
paralyzingly overloaded or indiscriminately selective.

Is it possible that people will become more obsessed with jobs and
economics and less with constructing a truly democratic, participating
social order?

---

2 Career educators assume that learning must take place in one sequential
order.

It is suggested that the rationale that views career education in terms of sequential stages is merely an administrative convenience for doling out training in stages over periods of time for increased educational productivity and lower unit-cost learning. Similarly, performance-based teacher education is seen as an administrative device to keep track of and control over a student's progress through teacher-determined stages. Rigid sequencing in conjunction with external vocational goals and behavioral objectives can be an overwhelming learning impediment for some students. Introspection, experimentation with different forms of affiliative relationships, and withdrawal from institutionalized learning represent different forms of student disengagement from the educational structure. Teacher education should do more, it is contended, than give lip service to the rhetoric of "individual differences."

---

3 Career educators assume that a specific body of skills and knowledge should be required of all students.

The current emphasis on designated marketable skills—vocabulary, mathematical, and attitudinal competencies, appears to Nash and Agne to be incomplete and shortsighted because the knowledge and behaviors that will be required in the future have yet to be determined. The emphasis on maintaining the economic system as it is could be viewed as effecting a deadening standardization in learning (15): "Strikingly absent from career education programs thus far is training in skills which enable people to become more probing, analytical, and politically astute." Teacher educators, it is suggested, will have to encourage students to explore and challenge not only their own value systems and those of the corporate state, but also the underlying ideological purposes of their studies—with the objective of making explicit the sociopolitical values imbedded in the infrastructure of each curriculum (15). This can only happen when students understand the structural realities of the institutions where they will work and when they can effectively consider and act upon workable alternatives to those institutions (16).

Although the criticism of exclusionary organizations is admirable, educators must still recognize the realities of all corporate systems: Workers in today's world perceive a direct relationship between their work and their worth, and this perception arbitrarily designates some careers as high or low in status. In spite of their own efforts to replace teaching credentials with teaching performance, career educators are still in danger of perpetrating, it is suggested, a meritocracy of professions: Workers will continue to make status designations about their jobs based on the number of years spent in training, the extent of their technical skills, and the financial supremacy of some clusters over others. From a teacher education standpoint, the deinstitutionalization and despecialization of careers is suggested. Nash and Agne advanced the belief that educators can change the traditional meaning of work by stressing what both the individual and the society require in order that each may realize its best possibilities. The reconceptualization of work involves two basic questions: How will a career best fit my life style? and, How can I help to create a society where every single human being can live a satisfying, autonomous, and creative life? The key to personal fulfillment in the future will be the ability to undergo a variety of work experiences and still be able to integrate the diverse facets of existence through continuing education and personal reflection.

Fallacies and Fantasies

Swanson expresses the following judgments (17), which he labels "fallacies and fantasies" in career education. They serve to raise some of the fundamental concerns related to the implementation of the concept.

1 *Except at a temporary stage of installation, career education cannot be implemented at a single level of education. The concept requires movement elements which expand and extend beyond the elementary and secondary years. The purposes of career education . . . cannot be achieved by a partial program of career education.*

2 *The organization and structural problems of American education are still too formidable to accommodate a majority of students in programs of career education. The major cities of the North and East have opted for specialized vocational high schools, thus leaving the remainder of the schools rather badly organized to provide for the job-entry skill requirements of career education. The skill center or the area vocational school concept is not well distributed across the country. The capacity of the educational establishment to accommodate career education is thus very limited, a problem which is not attacked by any of the forms of career education.*

3 *Career education which does not rely upon expanded vocational and adult education opportunities will be both a fallacy and a hoax. Career decision-making which is not followed by career training opportunities cannot survive as a part of programmed career education. Worse, if career education is followed by placement in the least remunerative jobs of the community with no opportunity for retaining or upgrading, then career education will be identified with sustained poverty rather than sustained opportunity. An expansion of vocational and adult education is essential to the survival of the concept of career education.*

4 *The costs of implementing career education have been grossly underestimated. Current appropriations are providing for some exemplary elements of a limited number of partial programs. Full implementation* *of career education for only its vocational training and placement aspects would cost from 10 to 15 multiples of current state and federal appropriations.*

5 *Career education is not an emphasis which is unique to the American scene. It is a statutory program in Sweden with an operational history of more than five years. It has functioned in the USSR for more than three years as a combined school and employer-based program. As an employer-based form, it functions in England as a type of adult education. It is being advanced by UNESCO under the rubric of "lifelong education." With a variety of interpretations, career education is a world-wide movement.*

Conflicting attitudes toward current American social problems may represent either the instabilities of social crisis and cultural confusion or the formulation of a more meaningful future through intelligent action. Particularly in the field of education, both the despairing critics and the hopeful reformers are in obvious conflict today. Thus, career education—the education of the masses for democratic participation in redesigning their own future—is becoming a major force for educational reform and also for the redirection and stabilization of social forces. Career education programs will increasingly contribute to the economic, political, and cultural life styles of our future society. Knowledge and understanding of the bases of career education are imperative for redesigning such programs. The present American infatuation for the instantaneous and the accelerated is dangerous. It may be significant that the Greek word for "instant" derived from the verb meaning "to waste or to ravage." Human development cannot be instant, biologically or psychologically. A new career educational sequencing is needed in which learning becomes a form of continuing growth and life, not just achieving some marketable skill.

A number of social issues and dilemmas have contributed to the need to improve our educational system. These include (a) changing meanings of work, (b) the changing structure and composition of the labor force, (c) problems associated with institutional drop outs, (d) problems associated with separating students into college-bound and employment-bound curricula, (e) the information-deficit dilemma, and (f) special needs of minority and disadvantaged populations. Career education has the potential for unifying the curriculum, better meeting individual and societal needs, and dealing with some of these social, psychological, and economic issues.

✳ Needs of Career Education

In the planning and implementation of career education programs, a number of problems have been encountered. Advance planning and attention can do much to overcome obstacles characterized by the following.

1 *There is a need to identify gaps between career education model objectives and existing career education curriculum materials.*

This problem is being overcome by efforts at the local, state, and national levels to develop career education modules for middle and high school students.

2 *In those career education programs which include the need for students to concentrate on occupational skills and awareness, teachers of the academic disciplines will not be easy to persuade that occupational preparation should provide the focus of instruction.*

Because the emphasis on career education came from the top of the educational establishment instead of from within the ranks of teachers, the process of acceptance may be somewhat slower.

3 *Premature concentration on occupational skills at the middle grades level may increase the tracking problem.*
↳ PLACING ONE INTO A PROGRAM

Hopefully, career exploration at the middle school level will result in broader horizons for young people; it would be unfortunate if the result were premature "freezing" of occupational interests.

4 *If curriculum modules are to be the vehicle for implementing career education, a comprehensive plan for articulating them must be developed in each system.*

Teachers and guidance personnel (if these functions are to remain separate in the future) must be trained in academic, job, and "life" counseling. This process will be time consuming and expensive and must be coordinated at a high level.

5 *The assumption that the school is the appropriate agency to develop entry-level job skills ignores many aspects of socioeconomic, political, and cultural reality.*

6 *The legitimate contemporary concerns of minority groups and of women constitute a problem deserving careful attention in the development of realistic career education models.*

7 *There is already in evidence a need to develop priorities among the objectives of career education.*

8 *Effective criteria for the design, development, testing, revision, field testing, installation and diffusion of overall career education programs and instructional materials is needed now.*

Very few educational materials are effectively evaluated before being disseminated. Procedures used to validate and modify career education modules must be well planned. Sufficient time should be spent in conceptualizing an overall evaluative scheme that is realistically related to development and implementation in the individual school system. Provisions for feedback and subsequent revision of materials and practices is vitally needed.

9 *The high degree of visibility and high expectations of career education on the one hand, coupled with ambiguity in the conceptualization of the concept itself, inertia of the academic community to accept the career focus, the unpreparedness of teacher educators and teachers, and the ineffective instructional delivery systems, on the other, could result in career education's becoming a negative educational example, a "white elephant," unless the federal government is willing to provide a long-range commitment to see it through before priorities shift to a new and different effort.*

Many of the problems related to programs funded with "soft" money relate to the requirement to have "something to show" as soon as possible; this is often accomplished to the detriment of high-quality efforts that might have long-range impact on the school curriculum.

10 *Conceptualizations of career education are needed which will foster experimentation in alternative models aimed at educating individuals with differing lifestyles in the context of a changing economic, social, and political environment.*

Will career education concern itself with futurist projects of a society that requires less and less work from individuals? includes a variety of life styles? views the work ethic and unemployment somewhat differently from the traditional taxpayer? concerns itself increasingly with equalizing opportunities for minorities? strives to eliminate sex stereotyping in educational materials, occupational experiences, and role models? places more importance on avocations, recreational needs, and continuing education as a concomitant of sociological and technological change? finds itself faced with the need for better communication and human relations skills?

11 *Increased opportunities for realistic work experience outside the classroom will be needed by academic teachers.*

Career education programs increasingly assume that neither students nor educators can learn what they need to know about work or about relationships between education and work by insulating themselves from the world of work outside of education.

12 *A stronger philosophical base is needed for career education—one which will effectively relate to economic, social, political, and scientific changes in our society—in order to solidify the concept of career education.*

The assumptions and hypotheses underlying career education must be straightforward and clearly understood. An effective career education model should also be psychologically sound.

13 *The planning process should include an input from the "customers" of career education.*

Involvement of students, parents, businessmen, and other members of the community should not be slighted in the planning stage. In view of the multidisciplinary nature of career education, the participation of more elementary and secondary teachers with recent teaching experience is needed on career education project teams to secure needed perspective.

14 *Vehicles for dissemination and diffusion of career education project materials must be built into all programs so as to insure proper application and performance.*

It is possible that an "each one teach one" procedure, for example, could help to make practices and materials more easily transferable to other school districts.

15 *The relationship to the present curriculum of many materials appearing under the career education label appears superficial.*

The integration of the vocational and the academic spheres is difficult and must be approached carefully if permanent effects are desired. More effort is needed by educators to find out what is really working in career education at the grass-roots level.

16 *On the basis of need, constraints, and curriculum objectives, one must question the notion encountered in specific career education programs that high school students should continue to be trained for specific jobs.*

Although there may be some valid exceptions, the career-cluster curriculum is based on the concept that occupations can be classified into logically related groups having identical or similar work-performance requirements. Furthermore, a manageable number, about 15 to 20, of these occupational groups or families will be representative of the spectrum of labor needs and opportunities in our economy.

17 *Coleman (18) has called our present society "information rich and experience poor." Career education projects should spell out the need for students to be active participants in the learning process.*

The role of experience in schooling, and the contribution of career education to it, should be developed more fully in existing projects.

18 *School personnel need to identify and examine materials and practices related to the goals of career education that appear to be working at a high pay-off level since these represent an investment already made.*

The management question of "buy or make" could often be resolved by many school systems in favor of buying materials where they have been developed in higher education, in proprietary education, in the armed forces, in apprenticeships, in Manpower Development and Training Act programs, in elementary-secondary education, as well as through regular commercial channels.

19 *The utilization of a systems approach to the restructuring of educational curricula can optimize the chances for success of career education.*

Alternate educational means, such as community and business resources, peers and paraprofessionals, computer games and media, life experiences, and role models provide available options for realizing system outcomes.

The following summarization of the needs of career education (19) has been offered by U.S. Commissioner of Education T. H. Bell.

1 *We must balance Federal funding for career education with State and local initiative in ways that will continue to make career education, like all good education, primarily a State and local matter. Let us be sure that career education never becomes a massive Federal effort that in effect bribes school systems to change. The original initiative for career education came from the grass roots. It is vital that this initiative not be lost.*

2 *We must communicate career education expertise in ways that will enhance and stimulate local initiative and creativity rather than stifle it. One of the most valuable lessons career education has taught us is that both teachers and students are smarter, more innovative, and more creative than traditional approaches to education have allowed them to be. A second valuable lesson has been the great interest and enthusiasm of the business-labor-industry-professional-government community in joining with the schools and with the home and family structure in a truly collaborative effort to make education, as preparation for work, a major goal of all who teach and all who learn.*

3 *We must make special efforts both to improve the quality of career education and to evaluate its effectiveness. Unless we do so, the great initial enthusiasm we have seen will quickly diminish. The promises of career education are attractive, but those promises need to be backed up by results.*

4 *We must expand the settings in which career education operates. While it has been remarkably well received at the K–8 level, we still have much to do to make career education a reality in most senior high schools. Career education should be evident on the campus of every community college and four-year college and university in the country. Our teacher education programs need to clearly reflect the career education emphasis and point of view. There is much to do before we can say we have met this challenge.*

5 *Finally, we must increase our efforts to provide meaningful and effective career education to special groups—including the physically and mentally handicapped, the gifted and talented, minorities, low income persons, and females. It is eminently appropriate to emphasize that career education is for* all. *However, it is a major challenge to convert this promise into an effective reality.*

Concept of Infusion

Career education is most effectively implemented at each educational level when programs are planned that exemplify the principle of infusion. Infusion refers to a process of penetrating or instilling, so the infusion of career education into existing curricula means that the concepts are interwoven or integrated into existing courses. An infusion strategy for career education should be based on at least five principles: 1. Educational leaders must be convinced of career education's value as a conceptual framework. 2. Career education should be integrated into the present curriculum, not treated as a separate additional program. 3. Every teacher should be a career education teacher even though this would require extensive in-service training. 4. Community involvement is an essential part of career education. 5. Teacher involvement is important in the early planning and curriculum development efforts.

Many states have developed program guides for the implementation of career education. Typical of these guides, which are intended to familiarize interested persons with the implementation of career education, is that produced by the West Virginia State Department of Education (20). It includes (a) a definition of career education; (b) the goals and objectives of the program; (c) a list of concepts on which career education is based; (d) suggested steps for developing a career education program; (e) components of career education, which include the school, community, and family; (f) developmental procedures governing implementation; (g) suggested learning activities for elementary, secondary, and programmatic schemes; and (h) evaluation techniques.

The career education seed has been planted. The strength of the idea, when combined with concerted backing of administrators at a top policy-making level in the educational establishment, provides a better than average chance that it will make a major impact on American education.

Local communities and state departments of education have moved rapidly in providing support, and a number of broadly-conceived career education teaching materials are being developed, many of which are performance based and learner centered. Career education is in many respects a "search for meaning" as related to the modern school curriculum. It must be commended on its integrative aspects and on the quality of its commitment to the field of education.

Federal Role in Career Education

At the national level, the U.S. Office of Education (USOE) and the National Institute for Education (NIE) have stressed their continuing commitment to career education. In 1972, when NIE officially came into being, career education model development was an important area of emphasis. In 1973 the National Council on Educational Research, NIE's policy-making body, approved the relationship between education and work as one of five priority areas. The four career education models (school-based, employer-based, rural-residential-based, and home-based) described in Chapter 5 were implemented under the direction of NIE. But new federal legislation was in the offing that would put career education clearly on its own.

Education amendments of 1974. Title IV, Section 406 of Public Law 93–380 gave federal recognition to career education. In this act, Congress enumerated three basic policies that gave new impetus to the concept of career education (21):

1 *Every child should, by the time he has completed secondary school, be prepared for gainful or maximum employment and for full participation in our society according to his or her ability.*

2 *It is the obligation of each local educational agency to provide that preparation for all children (including handicapped children and all other children who are educationally disadvantaged) within the school district of such agency; and*

3 *Each State and local educational agency should carry out a program of career education options which are designed to prepare each child for maximum employment and participation in our society according to his or her ability.*

These three policies were to be implemented by (21):

1 *developing information on the needs of career education for all children*

2 *promoting a national dialogue on career education designed to encourage each State and local educational agency to determine and adopt the approach to career education best suited to the needs of the children served by them*

3 *assessing the status of career education programs and practices, including a reassessment of the stereotyping of career opportunities by race or by sex*

4 *providing for the demonstration of the current career education programs and practices by the development and testing of exemplary programs using various theories, concepts, and approaches with respect to career education*

5 *providing for the training and retraining of persons for conducting career education programs and*

6 *developing State and local plans for implementing career education programs designed to insure that every child has the opportunity to gain the knowledge and skills necessary for gainful or maximum employment and for full participation in our society according to his or her ability*

In order to carry out these policies, Congress established within USOE an Office of Career Education headed by a director reporting directly to the Commissioner of Education. Dr. Kenneth H. Hoyt was appointed the first Associate Commissioner of Career Education. A comprehensive definition was adopted by Congress, which depicted career education as an educational process designed to (22):

1 *increase the relationship between schools and society as a whole*

2 *provide opportunities for counseling, guidance and career development for all children*

3 *relate the subject matter of the curricula of schools to the needs of persons to function in society*

4 *extend the concept of the education process beyond the school into the area of employment and the community*

5 *foster flexibility in attitudes, skills, and knowledge in order to enable persons to cope with accelerating change and obsolescence*

6 *make education more relevant to employment and functioning in society*

7 *eliminate any distinction between education for vocational purposes and general or academic education*

The act authorized the Commissioner of Education to make grants to state-level educational agencies to enable them to develop state plans for the development and implementation of career education.

A National Advisory Council for Career Education was created. It consisted of (a) the heads of nine top-ranking federal educational agencies, among them, the chairman of the National Advisory Council for Vocational Education; and (b) twelve public members broadly representative of the fields of education, arts, humanities, sciences, community service, business and industry, and the general public. The public members were to be appointed by the Secretary of the Department of Health, Education and Welfare. Duties of the council were to include advising the commissioner relative to the development and implementation of career education, evaluating the effectiveness of programs in meeting the needs of career education, and determining the need for further legislation in order that all citizens may benefit from career education. The council was required by law, in cooperation with the commissioner, to conduct a survey and assessment of the current status of career education programs, projects, curricula, and materials in the United States and to submit a report to Congress by November 1, 1975. The report was to include recommendations of the council for new legislation designed to accomplish the policies and purposes of career education. An authorization of $15 million for each fiscal year from 1975 through 1978 was written into law to enable the commissioner to carry out the law's career education provisions.

Career education tasks: Initial implementation Kenneth B. Hoyt, Associate Commissioner for Career Education, believes that the assumption of new roles, on the part of some staff members, can be accomplished in most educational systems with no serious loss in total institutional productivity (23). To the greatest extent possible, initiation of comprehensive career education programs would be undertaken utilizing existing personnel and existing physical facilities. While the emphasis and methodology would vary considerably from one educational level to another (e.g., the emphasis on vocational education will be minimal at the elementary school level), the following kinds of tasks are essential, in the U.S. Office of Education view, for initial implementation of a comprehensive career education effort:

A All classroom teachers will

1 devise and/or locate methods and materials designed to help pupils appreciate the career implications of the subject matter being taught.

2 utilize career-oriented methods and materials in the instructional program, where appropriate, as one means of educational motivation.

3 help pupils acquire and utilize good work habits.

4 help pupils develop, clarify, and assimilate personally meaningful sets of work values.

5 integrate, to the fullest extent possible, the programmatic assumptions of career education into their instructional activities and teacher-pupil relationships.

B In addition to A above, some teachers will be charged with:

1 providing students with specific vocational competencies at a level that will enable students to gain entry into the occupational society.

2 helping students acquire job-seeking and job-getting skills.

3 participating in the job placement process.

4 helping students acquire decision-making skills.

C The business-labor-industry community will:

1 provide observational, work experience, and work-study opportunities for students *and* for those who educate students (teachers, counselors, and school administrators).

2 serve as career development resource personnel for teachers, counselors, and students.

3 participate actively and positively in programs designed to lead to reduction in worker alienation.

4 participate actively in part-time and full-time job placement programs.

5 participate in career education policy formulation.

D Counseling and guidance personnel will:

1 help classroom teachers implement career education.

2 serve, usually with other educational personnel, as liaison contacts between the school and the business-industry-labor community.

3 serve, usually with other educational personnel, in implementing career education concepts within the home and family structure.

4 help students in the total career development process, including the making and implementation of career decisions.

5 participate in part-time and full-time job placement programs and in followup studies of former students.

E The home and family members where pupils reside will:

1 help pupils acquire and practice good work habits.

2 emphasize development of positive work values and attitudes toward work.

3 maximize, to the fullest extent possible, career development opportunities and options for themselves and for their children.

F Educational administrators and school boards will:

1 emphasize career education as a priority goal.

2 provide leadership and direction to the career education program.

3 involve the widest possible community participation in career education policy decision making.

4 provide the time, materials, and finances required for implementing the career education program.

5 initiate curriculum revision designed to integrate academic, general, and vocational education into an expanded set of educational opportunities available to all students.

Summary

Career education efforts at the elementary school level have focused on activities designed to help pupils to become *aware* of the world of work and of the values of a work-oriented society and to become aware of themselves as individuals and of their potential roles in society. *Exploration* of various occupational clusters is emphasized at the middle grades and junior high school level. At the high school level, career education emphasizes occupational *preparation* activities within occupational clusters. Programs of higher education have a responsibility to provide *multiple options* in career education, to work with high schools in articulating the career education sequence, and to provide pre- and in-service training and work-study programs. Some universities have developed multidisciplinary career education centers to provide leadership in developing and demonstrating models and as a means of training teachers for career education in the public schools. A key factor in the success of career education at the local school level is the active involvement of all who are affected in planning, implementing, and evaluating the program.

Career education is faced with many issues and problems; for example, there is the ambiguity of the concept itself and the question of who should provide leadership to develop and manage it. There are gaps between career education objectives and existing materials. Academic teachers are not easily convinced that job preparation should provide the focus of instruction. The unpreparedness of teacher educators and teachers and the lack of effective instructional delivery systems provide obstacles to a smooth transition to career education. Financial, organizational, and structural problems of American education handicap the educational system in accommodating career education. Despite these problems, career education has already made a strong impact on the public school system. There is much evidence of concerted action at all levels to bring about change and to set education on a new course.

Strong and definite leadership for the career education movement has emerged at the national level. Within the U.S. Departments of Commerce, Labor, and Health, Education and Welfare there is a growing consensus as to the crucial importance of work as a focus for educational efforts. Other evidence of the growth of career education includes the creation by Congress of an Office for Career Education, the adoption by the Office of

Education of its own position paper on career education, and the widespread actions of states and local school districts in activating career education programs at all levels.

Activities

For review

1 Explain the primary functions of career education at the following levels: elementary, middle grades, high school, college.

2 Identify five obstacles to immediate and future implementation of career education in our public school system. How can these obstacles be overcome?

3 Summarize the three policies relating to career education as specified in Title IV of the Educational Amendments of 1974.

4 What are the primary duties of the National Advisory Council for Career Education?

For discussion

1 Who should be in direct charge of career education at each level of the educational ladder: (a) the regular teacher(s), or (b) a specialist in career education? Why?

2 Should career education be taught (a) as a separate curriculum or series of courses, or (b) integrated into existing courses at all educational levels? Explain your answer.

3 Several members of the community have expressed an opinion that career education is not needed for the college-bound student. How would you justify career education for *all* students?

4 It has been said that the two-year college system may well be the fulcrum of career education. What reasons can you cite to support this statement?

5 At what level of the educational continuum would you expect to find most opposition to career education? Why?

6 How do the tasks described by Hoyt as essential for initial implementation of a comprehensive career education effort differ from those presently performed by educators and members of the business community?

For exploration

1 The superintendent of Brentwood School Systyem, which has decided to develop a career education program, has retained your services as a consultant. He has asked you to outline a procedure for converting the school program to career education. From the data furnished you, it is apparent that the school has emphasized college preparatory programs even though the system has a heavy enrollment of students who do not go on to college. Describe the delivery system you would recommend.

2 Select a school with a successful career education program. Write the administrator for details of the program, including its objectives, organization, and activities. Prepare a report that reflects the outstanding features of the program.

3 Select a student at one of the following levels: elementary, middle grades/junior high, high school, area technical school or community college, college, or graduate school. Explore his or her interest and concern about occupational opportunities. How do career interests differ at the various age levels?

4 Your librarian has asked you for the names of ten publications you would recommend for addition to the school library collection on career education. Identify the titles after consulting your colleagues for their suggestions.

5 Assume that you are an administrator in a local school system that is planning to incorporate career education in grades K–12. Outline a staff development plan to prepare teachers for the change.

6 Prepare a report describing the current scope and progress of career education in the school where you are employed or one in which you would like to work.

References

1 Janet Sutherland, "Career Education: Curriculum Development for the Elementary School," in *Business Education Forum*, Vol. 28, No. 5, 1974, pp. 29–30.

2 Charles W. Ryan, *Career Development Guide for the Elementary School* (Augusta, Maine: Bureau of Vocational and Adult Education, State Department of Education, July 1971).

3 Hosterman Junior High School Career Development Committee, *Career Development* (Robbinsdale, Minnesota: Independent School District 281, Robbinsdale Area Schools, August 1971).

4 U.S. Department of Health, Education and Welfare, Office of Education, Bureau of Elementary and Secondary Education, *Pacesetters in Innovation: Pace Projects to Advance Creativity in Education*, OE–20103–67, Comprehensive Program for Innovation, Philadelphia City School District (Bethesda, Maryland: ERIC Document Reproduction Center Service, 1967), pp. 26–27.

5 *Career Education: Leadership in Learning* (Phoenix, Arizona State Department of Education, n.d.), p. 19. (Reproduced by permission)

6 U.S. Department of Health, Education and Welfare. See Ref. 4.

7 W. Wesley Tennyson, "The Teacher's Role in Career Development" (Washington, D.C.: National Vocational Guidance Association, 1965), as quoted in Milton Kiesow, "Career Education for High School Teachers," in *Journal of Teacher Education*, Vol. 24, No. 2, Summer 1973, p. 104.

8 Donald L. Super, "Career Development," in *Psychology of the Educational Process*, eds. Dantz and Bare (New York: McGraw-Hill Book Company, 1970), as quoted in Kiesow, "Career Education for High School Teachers," in *Journal of Teacher Education*, Vol. 24, No. 2, Summer 1973, p. 105.

9 Harry N. Drier, Jr., "In-Service Preparation: Key to Career Education Delivery," in *Implications of Career Education for Teachers' Preparation*, eds. Anna M. Gorman and Joseph F. Clark (Columbus: Center for Vocational and Technical Education, March 1972), p. 165.

10 Ibid, pp. 167–168.

11 Calfrey C. Calhoun, "New Approaches and Trends in Business Teacher Education in the South," in *National Association for Business Teacher Education Review* (Washington, D.C.: National Business Education Association, 1973), pp. 19–20. (Reproduced by permission)

12 American Vocational Association Task Force on Career Education, Portland, Oregon, December 1971.

13 John R. Ottina, "Career Education Is Alive and Well," in *Journal of Teacher Education*, Vol. 24, No. 2, Summer 1973, p. 85. (Reproduced by permission)

14 Robert J. Nash and Russell M. Agne, "A Case of Misplaced Relevance," in *Journal of Teacher Education*, Vol. 24, No. 2, Summer 1973, p. 88. (Reproduced by permission)

15 Ibid, p. 90. (Reproduced by permission)

16 Ibid, p. 91. (Reproduced by permission)

17 Gordon I. Swanson, "Facts and Fantasies of Career Education," in *The Visitor*, Vol. 59, No. 2, April 1972, pp. 3–4. (Reproduced by permission)

18 James S. Coleman, "How Do the Young Become Adults?" in *Phi Delta Kappan*, Vol. 154, No. 4, December 1972, pp. 226–230.

19 Terrence H. Bell, "Career Education in 1974," tele-lecture to National Conference for State Coordinators of Career Education, Center for Vocational Education, Ohio State University, Columbus, Ohio, October 31, 1974.

20 West Virginia State Department of Education, "A Guide for the Development of Career Education" in *Abstracts of Research Materials in Vocational and Technical Education*, Vol. 6, No. 3 (Columbus: The Center for Vocational Education, 1973), p. 461.

21 "Educational Amendments of 1974" Public Law No. 93–380 (Washington: Government Printing Office, 1974), p. 68.

22 Ibid, p. 69.

23 Terrence H. Bell and Kenneth B. Hoyt, *Career Education: The USOE Perspective*, (Columbus: The Center for Vocational Education, The Ohio State University, 1974), pp. 13–15.

Chapter 7

Career

Guidance

in

Vocational Education

Introduction

In the late 1890s the United States changed from an agrarian to an industrial society, a movement that brought about changes in our educational system as well as in the economy. This movement toward industrialization resulted in both a decrease in the need for child labor on farms and an increase in the need for formally trained workers. The passage of child labor laws, which brought a halt to the kind of child exploitation portrayed in the novels of Charles Dickens, resulted in an increased emphasis on formal schooling. Children and youth lost their direct contact and their first-hand knowledge about the world of work and the influence of their parents as vocational counselors also decreased. As Shaw has stated (1):

□ . . . *as older patterns of family guidance changed, as the length of public education increased, as demands for more highly educated workers grew, and as the number of educational and occupational alternatives exploded in need, the need for more formal means of assisting young people to make choices became apparent.*

The individual credited with having the strongest influence on early vocational guidance is Frank Parsons. His theory of vocational choice, proposed at the beginning of the twentieth century, has continued to influence vocational guidance to the present day. According to Parsons, the wise choice of a vocation involved three factors (2):

□ . . . (a) *a clear understanding of yourself, your aptitudes, abilities, interests, ambitions, resources, limitations, and their causes; (b) a knowledge of the requirements and conditions of success, advantages and disadvantages, compensations, opportunities, and prospects in different lines of work; (c) true reasoning on the relations of these two groups of facts.*

The outcome of vocational guidance, using Parsons's theory, was the matching of an individual to an occupation that was most suitable. This emphasis on the matching of the two sets of data, individual traits and job factors, illustrates the fact that Parsons viewed guidance as an event that took place in a person's life rather than a process.

The work of Parsons and of others who expanded and elaborated on his ideas became known as the *trait-and-factor theory*, which subsequently formed the basis for the development of several popular instruments currently used in vocational guidance. These include the Strong Vocational Interest Blank, the Kuder Preference Record, the Differential Aptitude Test, and the Guilford-Zimmerman Aptitude Survey.

Developmental
Theory and Career Guidance

After the 1950s the emphasis in counseling shifted away from an occupational choice to an analysis of *why* and *how* a person chooses a particular occupation.

Super and Ginzberg, leaders of the developmental period, advanced the theory that vocational development is a lifelong process. They shifted the focus of vocational guidance from the concentration on a single occupational choice at some point in time to a recognition that vocational development is a process that takes place over a period of time. The *developmental theory* thus involves an understanding of vocational behaviors occurring at different life stages. Super redefined vocational guidance as (3):

⊠ *the process of helping a person to develop and accept an integrated and adequate picture of himself and of his role in the world of work, to test this concept of reality, and to convert it into a reality, with satisfaction to him and to society.*

Since the turn of the century, theories underlying vocational guidance have resulted in major changes in its practices (4):

1 *The single occupational-choice-at-a-point-in-time focus of the early practitioners of career guidance has given way to a broader, more comprehensive view of the individual and his or her development over the life span.*

2 *The specific age focus of traditional career guidance is not valid. Instead of the notion that a permanent occupational choice is made at some point, usually during late adolescence, we now understand that occupa-*

tional choice is a process which takes place over a period of time and is a result of a combination of interacting determinants.

3 *Career guidance activities are important over the life span of the individual; therefore, educational personnel at all levels, kindergarten through adult, have a part to play. When viewed as a continuous process, career guidance is a program in the mainstream of education rather than an ancillary service.*

4 *People at work are no longer seen only as objects through which occupations are analyzed and classified. Rather we now understand that a work setting can be used as a medium to help people better understand themselves.*

5 *Career guidance is more than a simple process of matching people to jobs; it is a complex process of human development and should be treated as a major educational goal.*

The emerging programs of career education draw on the developmental theory of vocational development, building on the classifications of the life span made by Havighurst, Ginzberg, Super, and others.

What is the relationship of the guidance function to the current developments in career education? Career education has become a number one priority within the U.S. Office of Education, and career guidance has been identified nationwide as an aspect of high priority within the framework of career education. As Kehas notes (5): "The issue in career education is not how one organizes the world of work but rather how one organizes his developing self in relation to work."

It is an underlying goal of career education to enable every person to make *informed* choices about his or her career. Every person has certain career options, and the real question is whether or not that person is able to perceive those options and to make effective decisions regarding them. Being able to make wise decisions about available options is the result of knowledge. As O'Hara has suggested (6): "Students must have knowledge of the elements involved in the educational and vocational actions they are about to take."

As opposed to the earlier concept of guidance, in which the counselor assisted the individual to assess his or her aptitudes in the light of skill requirements for specific jobs, career guidance is concerned that each individual *understand* the process of decision making and the gradual unfolding of vocational possibilities and consequences. It is concerned not with matching individuals and jobs but rather with providing the individual with the tools needed to arrive at decisions in light of the options that are available.

Ginzberg points out (7) that persons with higher incomes have more opportunity than the poor to make mistakes and recover from them in career planning. Youth from higher income families can remain in school for longer periods and can revise their career plans if they become dissatisfied with their initial choices. They learn about themselves, their strengths, interests, values, and limitations as related to the world of work in a process that begins at birth and extends over a long period, with input from family, friends, peers, and society at large.

For the poor, however, many paths have been closed or narrowed at birth by family or neighborhood poverty, minority status, poor schooling, and the like. The job-exploration process is considerably shortened among the disadvantaged because early in life they frequently must settle for a job—a way to support themselves and their families.

We have said, then, that an individual moves along one of a number of pathways as he or she progresses through the educational system and into the world of work. Moreover, these pathways depend on a number of factors—economic, social, psychological, and educational—as well as on the decisions made by the individual.

Career guidance, as a vital component of career education, is concerned with providing individual students with the tools to make informed choices. To choose a career is to select from among available alternatives. The individual learns to narrow the field of choices by discarding the undesired options.

If we accept the importance of decision making in career development and the fact that the ability to make effective decisions is crucial to the healthy development of every human being, then we must ask ourselves whether learning to make good decisions should be left to chance or should be taught. Such decision-making skills can be taught in varying degrees of sophistication beginning in the elementary grades. But the optimal time for formal decision-making training seems to be in the middle school years before attitudes become too firmly fixed.

Decision-making skills closely parallel the steps in scientific problem solving (8), including (a) how to identify the decision to be made; (b) how to identify the alternatives to the decision and where to find information about each alternative; (c) how to predict one's success in each alternative; (d) how to estimate the degree to which each alternative will accord with one's own values, interests, and abilities; and (e) how to construct a plan of action. Without training, an individual usually completes the first two steps in the process, but less frequently is each of the remaining completed.

McBrien recommends the use of the Miller and Tiedeman Cubistic Model in teaching decision-making. This model, which encompasses problem conditioning, psychological states, and self-comprehension, aims at making learners become aware of their decision making as they experience it. The following training objectives are recommended by McBrien (9):

1 *The learner can identify the parts of the decision-making activity*

(a) *Awareness of the exploration stage can be demonstrated by naming a future decision with its anticipated outcome.*

(*b*) *Awareness of the crystallization stage can be demonstrated by naming several alternatives to the choice. Alternatives should include those with disadvantages.*

(*c*) *Awareness of the choice stage is demonstrated when the learner selects, and names, the best alternative (for him). Since the activity is related to training, the learner is not expected to implement his decision.*

(*d*) *Awareness of the clarification stage is demonstrated when the learner, over time, contemplates his decision. The learner will articulate both his actions leading to choice, and his consideration of the consequences of the choice.*

2 *The learner can use the decision-making skills in interaction with a peer*

(*a*) *As a peer teacher, the learner can label the stages that his pupil proceeds through while the pupil is involved in making decisions.*

(*b*) *The peer teacher can identify decision points for his pupil. He will use these experiences to aid his pupil in improving decision-making skills.*

(*c*) *The peer teacher can label the decision-making style of his pupil.*

3 *The learner is aware of and can articulate his decision-making style*

(*a*) *In a peer group the learner articulates activity while proceeding through the stages of a decision he made.*

(*b*) *In peer group discussions the learner reports both success and problems with his decision making.*

(*c*) *The learner reports fewer impulse choices and more planned decisions.*

During the first part of the training, the language of the process of decision making is taught. A primary objective is the mastery of the vocabulary associated with the process. After this stage, students can practice identifying activities as they encounter choice (decision-making) points.

The second phase involves peer teaching. The process of assisting other students in developing decision-making skill is designed to accomplish two objectives for peer teachers: they teach others about planned decision making and, perhaps more importantly, reexamine their own decision making. Low-risk decisions based on the daily activity of the student are the learning materials used in this step rather than prepared materials, role-playing, or case studies. "Learning to make planned decisions as decision points are experienced is the main goal." (9)

During the third phase, the individual functions independently; that is, making decisions with awareness. Weekly discussion groups in which peers discuss both their positive and negative decisions is the recommended means of implementing this stage. As McBrien notes (9): "The intent is that the activity of articulating one's decision experiences will enhance individual awareness of decision-making style."

The task of developing career guidance programs to facilitate career education is not an easy one. Just as the present curriculum and organization of most schools will require revision and staff retraining and updating to implement career education, so will modification be required in the present practices of counseling. One obvious change will be the moving away from one-to-one counseling toward more involvement with group work with teachers. At the present student-counselor ratio (over 500 to 1), a high school student sees a counselor on the average only two to four times a year for less than 20 minutes per session. A second change will be a better balance between counseling the non-college-bound and college-bound students. Although counseling in this country grew out of vocational counseling, it has allowed itself to lose contact with its roots.

One must be careful, however, to assure that the term "career guidance" does not apply only to those students who are planning to seek employment on leaving high school or to those planning to enroll in a postsecondary program such as the vocational-technical school or community college. Career guidance must include all students, regardless of the occupation or kind of training they choose.

Some of the weaknesses of present career guidance as reflected in the literature have been summarized by Willingham (10):

1 *Counselors are not adequately trained and lack the specialized knowledge to perform the many diverse tasks involved in educational and occupational counseling.*

2 *Counselors have limited authority and relatively low status in school systems.*

3 *Career guidance is a minor commitment of most counselors who prefer personal counseling and guidance for college.*

4 *Counselors spend most of their time on administrative, clerical, and disciplinary duties.*

5 *Guidance is often regarded as a costly fringe service which is usually undersupported and is subject to cuts in times of economic stress.*

6 *Guidance services as now constituted lack relevance and practical value.*

7 *Present guidance programs tend to focus on adding to general happiness—they lack specific realistic goals.*

8 *Available occupational information is inadequate and uninteresting to students.*

9 *Counselors are isolated from the rest of the school staff; vocational guidance is given in bits and pieces; and vocational and academic guidance are given separately.*

10 *Counselors have insufficient understandings of the special needs of ethnic minorities.*

Brown, Feit, and Forestandi have suggested (11) that Lundquist and Chamley's 3 Cs problem-solving model provides an excellent framework for examining the role of counselors in career education. Three basic assumptions underlie this model. First, counselor activities can be classified under three general topics: counseling, consultation, and coordination: The *counseling* component is the direct involvement of the counselor with the student, providing specific assistance. *Consultation* is a less intense process in which the student receives help indirectly from the counselor, usually through a third party. *Coordination* usually involves the marshaling of available resources in an effort to assist large numbers of students. The second basic assumption is that the role of the counselor is flexible, depending on determinants such as expertise, personality, and other environmental factors. The third assumption is that the needs of the student are the basis from which all the counselor's functions grow. Table 7.1 illustrates how a counselor might initiate his or her role in career education through the framework of the 3 Cs model.

Career development is an ongoing, continuous process. Therefore, it is important that systematic guidance activities be initiated in the elementary grades and that they continue through the postsecondary level.

Career Guidance
at the Elementary Level

Beginning in kindergarten, career development should focus on expanding the perceptual base of the individual with relation to self, education, and the world of work. Experiences should be planned that help students to develop positive self-concepts—finding out who they are, how they are alike and different from others—and healthy interpersonal relationships. In addition to the self-related goals, elementary career guidance should focus on developing a broad occupational information program that will serve as a foundation for career decisions in the future. The career guidance emphasis at this level, as reflected in the career education models in Chapter 5, is an awareness level, not a time when definite occupational choices should be made.

Use of the team approach to career guidance at the elementary level is essential for success. Effective programs do not operate solely within the confines of the counselor's office, but rather they permeate the entire educational process. One way of encouraging total school involvement is through the use of a guidance committee, including counselors, teachers, students, and administrators. Parents and representatives from the local business community can also make valuable contributions to such a committee. The use of advisory committees is not new to vocational educators who, through the years, have recognized the contributions of lay persons and other educators to vocational education.

Table 7.1 Potential Functions of the Counselor in Career Education (12)*

Function/Grade	Student	Family	Community	School
coordination K–6	may help students with activities related to self help and helping others, ie, students teaching students	may aid family in recognizing how the home and school may foster career awareness, ie, PTA	may help the community to design agencies to foster student development, ie, big brother program	may coordinate the school's field trips and other activities related to career awareness
7–9	may help students in placement for occupational awareness	may aid family in recognizing how home and school may foster career awareness	may obtain sites for placement for career exploration	may aid teachers in developing teaching units dealing with careers that cross subject lines
10–12	may help the student to conduct a community occupational survey	may aid family in recognizing how home and school may foster career awareness through educational awareness	may aid in career choice implementation by placement activities within the community	may develop internships for career exploration
consultation K–6	may assist students to be "co-counselors" in assisting other students	may aid families in promoting adaptive behavior in children	may aid in the development of community resources, ie, service clubs, which promote student development	may aid teachers in developing skills to promote positive classroom behavior
7–9	may help students gain skills in assisting other students in their career exploration	may aid parents in identifying experiences that will foster career development	may assist business and industry to identify and provide career exploration opportunities	may aid teachers in developing skills in use of group processes in promoting student growth and development

10–12	may help students to develop a placement plan to aid in career development	may aid students who are having adjustment problems by working with the parents	may develop feedback mechanisms between the community and schools so that programs can be evaluated and improved	may help teachers understand the implications of subject matter to the student's career choice
counseling K–6	may facilitate development of appropriate interpersonal skills, attitudes, and behavior			
7–9	may aid students in understanding themselves			
10–12	may help students to make appropriate educational and/or career choices			

It should be noted that the activities listed within each box should not necessarily be restricted to the grade level in which they appear; ideally, many of the functions should continue throughout the education process.

In designing career activities for elementary guidance programs, several characteristics of the learning habits of elementary pupils should be kept in mind:

1 Imitation is a major method of learning As Campbell et al have stated (13): "Children use role modeling as a basis for developing their own behavior." A career guidance technique is to bring into the child's world adults who represent a variety of role models, thus exposing the child to occupational roles outside his or her immediate environment.

2 Learning is enhanced through physical activities because verbal skills are still in the process of being developed A visit to an elementary school, especially during the children's play periods or free time, will demonstrate the importance of physical activities as learning techniques. From early years, children engage in role-playing activities as they play doctor, nurse, teacher—modeling the roles they know about. Through planned, play-type experiences, including dramatics, role-playing, games, and simulations, students can effectively explore the occupational world.

3 Concrete rather than abstract concepts are more readily learned Children, especially at the early elementary levels, experience difficulty in attempting to think in abstractions. Therefore, guidance activities should be planned that give children the opportunity to learn through direct experience.

Career Guidance at the Middle School Level

The exploration level follows the awareness level in the career education models and basically corresponds to the middle school years within the educational framework. Matheny believes (14) that

□ . . . *urging middle school youth to make vocational decisions would appear untimely, but furnishing them with opportunities to explore work both as observers and as participants would seem highly desirable. Exploring broad occupational areas contributes to the student's understanding of the nature of work, the characteristics of workers, the differences in work settings, and his own preferences and distastes.*

As at the elementary level, career guidance at the middle school level is most effective when it is a product of the total school program. Whenever possible, community resources should be used in conjunction with school activities to offer realistic career development experiences for students. The objective of these experiences is to promote an understanding of the skills needed in a job, not to teach specific job skills. Games, problem-solving exercises, and other stimulation activities are increasingly available to supplement or, in some cases, to replace first-hand, on-the-job exploration. Developing decision-making skills, described earlier in this chapter, is also an important objective for the middle school level.

The Program of Education and Career Exploration (PECE), underway in several Georgia schools, incorporates group guidance as a vital part of exploratory work experiences. After experiencing a work role, students are encouraged to share the following items with other students (15): (a) their observations of job performances and job conditions; (b) how they felt about themselves while performing or observing the work; (c) what personal needs they feel would be met or prevented by such work; (d) what aptitude they feel they might have for such work; and (e) how they think one goes about preparing for such work.

These kinds of follow-up activities incorporate the dual objectives of examining self in relation to work. By the time they have completed the middle grades, students should have a good idea of the *types* of jobs that interest them and should be able to make *tentative* choices of one or more job fields.

In summary, career guidance objectives for the middle school level should include the following (16): (a) exploring the relationship between student characteristics and occupational and educational requirements; (b) learning the processes involved in planning and implementing occupational goals; (c) learning educationally and vocationally related behaviors; and (d) beginning to develop tentative plans for the future.

Career Guidance
at the High School Level

The high school years are significant in our society. During this time the student is expected to make important decisions concerning the future. Should he or she enter the labor market on completion of high school, or before? Should he or she go for further training in vocational-technical school, in a community college, or in a university? Through programs of career awareness and exploration, students have narrowed their area of interest and have begun developing skills within occupational clusters of their choice. Career guidance assumes an important role as a conditioner of occupational preferences at the secondary level.

Hansen suggests some basic assumptions that might undergird a secondary career guidance program (17):

1 *that an integrated cross-disciplinary program of career guidance as part of the regular school curriculum, grades K–12, is more consonant with new and emerging contemporary knowledge about career development*

2 *that it is possible to plan a series of vocationally relevant experiences which have meaning for the career development of adolescents, and that*

certain kinds of appropriate experiences can be defined for students at various levels of their growth

3 *that the curriculum needs to be interpreted broadly to include kinds of experiences that extend beyond the school walls and beyond traditional subjects*

4 *that an integrated program has as its goal not to encourage the student to make a specific vocational choice but rather to foster an understanding of the process of decision-making—the relevant factors in self and society and the variety of potentialities which might be fulfilled*

5 *that an effective program of career guidance must involve the cooperation of total staff and community in planning meaningful experiences to meet the emerging needs of students*

Several goals may be identified as appropriate for the implementation of career guidance at the secondary level: (a) to continue practice and refine expertise in decision-making skills introduced in the middle grades; (b) to acquaint students with a variety of options available during high school and after high school; (c) to assist students in evaluating short-term and long-term effects of selecting various options; (d) to assist students in evaluating occupational opportunities in relation to self needs, interests, values, and aptitudes; (e) to train students to locate and use information such as employment bulletins and school catalogues; (f) to help students to interpret and evaluate occupational and/or educational information. To realize these goals, counselors will need to employ both group and individual guidance activities, using direct and indirect contact, thereby expanding the role of counseling at the secondary level.

In most career education models, students select two or three occupational clusters for in-depth exploration, and then they begin preparation in one of those clusters. An interesting alternative to this approach— examining clusters *vertically*—is a *horizontal* examination of job clusters; that is, an examination of a job cluster that would include functional job groupings related to a person's abilities, achievement areas, and personal aspirations. In the vertical approach the jobs that are examined are related by similar identifications and field characteristics. In the horizontal approach, a student might consider a group of jobs that are, professionally, almost totally unrelated, as compared with normally classified, or vertical, job clusters. Thus each student would develop a set of job clusters that, because of personal abilities or aspirations, he or she wishes to explore.

An important aspect of career counseling at the secondary level is job placement and follow-up. It has been a logical outcome of vocational education and should be expanded to become an important ingredient of career education. Several principles serve to reinforce the development and operation of a successful job placement program:

1 One centrally located office or center should be established to disseminate job information for the entire student body.

2 Job placement programs should be designed to serve all students, including early school-leavers as well as graduates, as they seek employment.

3 As a part of the total school program, job placement should be coordinated with other components such as the instructional and work-study programs.

4 The staff of the job placement program should develop and maintain a close working relationship with employers of the community.

5 The job placement program should include periodic follow-up to evaluate effectiveness of present programs (including its own) and to determine emerging needs.

In describing student follow-up in Baltimore, Buckingham reports (18) that all students placed in full-time jobs are followed up at the end of the first three months and again at the end of the first year. In addition, each employer is sent a questionnaire at the end of six months on which he or she evaluates the employee as to efficiency and attitude. Constructive criticism of school programs is also requested on the questionnaire. In addition, the worker is asked to report back so that the schools can determine what program adjustments may be desirable.

Such follow-up programs provide important input to the school program by (a) indicating needed curriculum revisions; (b) identifying areas for staff development and growth; (c) pointing up equipment and facilities needed for career education; (d) evaluating the effectiveness of instructional methods and procedures; (e) providing additional information about the requirements and opportunities of various jobs; and (f) evaluating the effectiveness of placement programs.

Follow-up activities are helpful in assisting individuals to acquire jobs, and they provide an effective summative evaluation of instructional programs. They are of little value, however, if the process of follow-up ends with the collection and tabulation of data. It is only when the data are examined in light of program objectives and when teachers, students, counselors, administrators, and advisory council members *use* data for program improvement that follow-up activities take on real meaning.

Career Guidance at
the Postsecondary Level

Until recently, career guidance has been primarily concentrated at the high school level, and as such it has culminated with the student's leaving school or graduating. However, research has pointed up a need for career guidance to continue at the postsecondary level. Many students who are enrolled in community colleges or vocational-technical schools have postponed specific career decisions and are in need of career counseling. Other students of this age range, though not in school, have graduated from high school without making career decisions, even though they may be seeking employment. Garbin found that individuals who enter the world of work following their high school years encounter work adjustment problems that interfere with their progress. Cooley and Lohnes reported that vocational plans tend to stabilize considerably after high school (19).

The emerging role of postsecondary education, especially in vocational-technical schools and community colleges, presents a challenge to counselors. It is not unrealistic to anticipate that most of the citizens of our society will benefit from some form of postsecondary education in the near future. The open-door policy of the two-year post-high-school institution has resulted in the attendance of a heterogeneous group of students, with widely different needs, values, interests, abilities, and achievement levels. The Educational Amendments of 1972 determined that equal access to postsecondary education for all citizens was a national goal.

The community college, or junior college, serves a wide range of students through its multiple programs. At least six major services may be identified: (a) transfer programs—two-year programs for students planning to transfer to four-year colleges or universities; (b) occupational training—pre-employment training, retraining, or updating of skills of present and potential workers; (c) adult basic education—programs of basic survival skills for persons of less than eighth-grade education; (d) adult civic education—high school equivalency programs (General Educational Development Programs); (e) workshops, seminars, and special-interest mini-programs for various groups within business-industry and the community; and (f) avocational and cultural education—instruction in a wide range of leisure activities.

Consequently, student personnel services at the postsecondary level are confronted with a student population consisting of recent high school graduates, minority groups seeking new educational opportunities, women seeking new or updated skills to enter or reenter the labor market, and older workers seeking retraining for jobs changed by technology. Other enrollees include school drop outs who are deficient in basic education, various groups from business and industry who are enrolled in mini-courses, workshops, and seminars, and individuals of all ages and walks of life who enroll in a variety of courses for personal interest and development.

Career guidance at the postsecondary level is a function of a broader area, Student Personnel Services, which is concerned with total student development. Because a community college must be responsive to the needs of the society it serves, and must offer many levels of learning experiences to its heterogeneous population, it requires a strong student personnel program. The activities of the student personnel program, including career guidance, may be classified into fourteen functions, as follows (20):

1 Precollege information *Disseminating information by brochures, counselor visitations, on-campus visits, conferences; direct correspondence, etc., to encourage college attendance, to note special features of the college, to foster understanding of requirements for admission and for special curriculums, to develop proper attitudes, and to contribute to student decision making and planning; giving of information pertinent to interpretation of tests and other data, and offering educational and occupational service to applicants prior to formal admission.*

2 Registration and records *Designing registration forms and data processing procedures; effecting class changes and withdrawals, recording instructors' grades; providing transcripts and, where possible, machine scheduling of students into classes; maintaining accurate, functional records to be compiled into a cumulative file reflecting educational, psychological, physical, and personal development.*

3 Appraisal *Obtaining, organizing, and evaluating significant background information such as transcript and test interpretations, individual case studies, interviews with students, staff inquiries, etc., to determine admission and curriculum eligibility to effect proper placement and to assist students toward the self-knowledge needed for decision making and planning; measuring of aptitude, interests, values, achievement, and personality factors of students, as well as assessing the pervasive characteristics and tone or climate of the institution; evaluating of past records and testing in the skills of reading, listening, speaking, composition, and mathematics to assure proper placement of students in courses of varying levels of difficulty.*

4 Counseling *Providing professional service to students in clarifying basic values, attitudes, interests, and abilities; assisting in all phases of decision making, formulating vocational-educational plans; identifying and resolving problems interfering with plans and progress; and providing appropriate sources for more intensive and deep-seated personal problems; giving of information pertinent to selection of courses, occupational prerequisites, transfer requirements, effective study methods, academic progress, availability of resource agencies, and other such areas of concern to students.*

5 Orientation *Giving information associated with induction into college, attitude development, effective study skills, test interpretation, vocational decision, and educational planning; providing of occupational information toward narrowing of vocational choice (basic curriculum decisions and planning are contingent upon possession of maximum occupational information made available through comprehensive libraries, brochures and references, seminars, consultation services, faculty advisement, and particularly through regional occupational information centers); provid-*

ing experiences which will acquaint students with the physical and social environment of the college, its procedures, regulations, and staff resources, and to facilitate their adjustment to and use of college and community resources.

6 Remediation *Offering formalized activities designed to remedy academic deficiencies in reading, writing, listening, computing, and study skills that obstruct the student's progress toward his goals.*

7 Cocurricular activities *Arranging for cultural activities, sponsoring of clubs and organizations, advising student publications, organizing vocational and other special interest groups, developing and managing a program of intercollegiate and intramural athletics; advising student government organizations, providing training in formal and informal group processes, conducting leadership training programs, and supervising intercollegiate student government conferences and all other significant aspects of citizenship training.*

8 Health Services *Determining health and physical condition of the students, reviewing health records, health counseling, establishing a referral system, apprising parents, and other systematic and periodic checks on the health and physical well-being of students made possible by the employment of a public health nurse.*

9 Financial assistance *Providing information on loans, scholarships, part-time jobs, and budget management; soliciting funds, securing government grants, and developing other resources of financial assistance for students while attending the junior college or upon transfer; and giving information and assistance to students seeking financial support.*

10 Placement services *Assisting students in obtaining employment while attending college or upon termination of enrollment.*

11 Housing *Planning and directing activities related to housing provided or approved by the college; using the residence hall for the development of social amenities, social grace, and concern for moral and ethical conduct.*

12 Food services *Designing of the food services to foster student-faculty contact, to contribute to community solidarity, and to develop social skills; supervising and administering this student facility.*

13 Research and evaluation *Planning, gathering, and analyzing data that are related to the student personnel functions and needed in making decisions regarding college facilities, curriculums, courses, budgets and policies; and preparing reports to persons needing such information; developing and executing plans for periodic and systematic evaluations of the student personnel program.*

14 Community services *Providing off-campus vocational and educational counseling and other student personnel services to out-of-school youth and adults.*

Trends in Career Guidance

An examination of the impact of career education on postsecondary education suggests that several changes are taking place in the career counseling function of student personnel services:

1 use of the computer to assist student and counselor in more readily obtaining career information for simulated activities as well as for obtaining career information

2 released time for counselors to gain first-hand experience in new and emerging occupations

3 more effective counselor assistance in assessing individual learning styles and in aiding instructors to plan the most effective learning activities for students

4 increased use of games, simulation, and troubleshooting as tools in helping students to make appropriate career choices as well as to develop decision-making skills

5 operation of community guidance centers; Bushnell suggests (21) that by the end of the decade most community colleges will be operating community guidance centers that will assist adults in career planning, personal development, and education planning.

Evaluating Career Guidance

Evaluation should be a planned part of a total career guidance program to determine the extent to which program objectives have been realized, both collectively and at each instructional level. Herr and Cramer suggest the following procedures for evaluating a career guidance program within a systems approach (22):

1 *formulate the broad goals of the vocational guidance program*

2 *classify these goals so that an economy of thought and actions can be achieved. Decide which developmental stages require which guidance processes for implementation*

3 *define objectives in behavioral terms*

4 *suggest situations where the desired objectives and behaviors might be observed*

5 *develop or select appraisal techniques, such as standardized tests, monitoring instruments, questionnaires, etc.*

6 *gather and interpret performance data and compare these data with the stated objectives*

The evaluation plan for each career guidance program is unique; that is, it is designed to assess the effectiveness of a program that was established for a particular school setting. Although general guidelines such as the above may be helpful, each school must design its own system in relation to its objectives.

The significant elements of career development are the skills that enable each individual to use his or her capabilities freely and responsibly in ego-involved activities that contribute both to individual fulfillment and to society's progress. Also involved is clarification of the personal values and attitudes that motivate an individual to gain task skills and to want to contribute and be constructive. These skills involve knowledge not only of specific tasks but also of the ways such tasks are combined interdependently in occupations. Career guidance is thus concerned with fostering self-understanding, so that the individual can use such understanding to make the best choices from among available courses of action.

Summary

Vocational guidance, as we know it today, has been affected by changes in our educational system as well as in the economy itself. Historically, several theories of vocational counseling have given direction to the process of career guidance. The first of these was the *trait-and-factor theory*, generally attributed to the work of Frank Parsons in the early part of the twentieth century, which viewed guidance as an event that matched an individual's traits to the job factors.

During the 1950s the emphasis in counseling shifted away from an occupational choice to an analysis of *why* and *how* a person chooses an occupation—the *developmental theory*. Leaders such as Super and Ginzberg advanced the idea that vocational development is a lifelong process involving an understanding of vocational behaviors occurring at different life stages. The focus on a single occupational choice at a point in time gave way to a broader, more comprehensive view of the individual and his or her development over the life span. Career guidance became recognized as a complex process of human development, best treated as a major educational goal.

Theories of career guidance today, as opposed to earlier concepts in which the counselor assisted the individual in assessing aptitudes in the light of skill requirements for specific jobs, is concerned that each individual understand the process of decision making and the gradual unfolding of vocational possibilities and consequences. It is designed to provide the individual with the tools needed to arrive at decisions based on available options. Decision-making skills, as a facilitator of career choice, are taught in varying degrees of sophistication beginning in the elementary grades. Such skills closely parallel the steps in the scientific method of problem solving. Decision-making models, such as that proposed by Miller and Tiedeman, aim at making learners aware of their decision making as they experience it.

The career guidance emphasis at the elementary level is designed to promote an awareness of many types of occupations. Learning is enhanced through role-playing activities in which young children simulate the world of work. At the middle school level, the emphasis shifts to exploring broad occupational clusters, the characteristics of workers, the differences in jobs, and the student's own preferences. At the high school level, the student is encouraged to select two or three occupational clusters for in-depth exploration and then to begin preparation in one of those clusters.

The heterogeneity of student population at the post-high-school level has resulted in an increased need for career guidance. At this level, career guidance normally operates as a function of the broad area of Student Personnel Services, which includes precollege information, registration and records, appraisal, counseling, orientation, remediation, cocurricular activities, health services, financial assistance, placement services, housing, food services, research and evaluation, and community services. Career guidance at the post-high-school level has been facilitated by the use of computers, games, simulation, and guidance centers.

An effective evaluation plan for a total career guidance program possesses both formative and summative dimensions. It is based on the broad goals of the vocational guidance program, and its objectives are defined in measurable terms so that assessment can be made continuously and effectively. It uses a variety of reliable appraisal techniques, such as standardized tests and questionnaires, to assess individual skills, personal values, and attitudes. It always interprets performance data against the stated objectives of the career guidance program.

Activities

For review

1 Explain the contribution made by Frank Parsons to vocational guidance.

2 Compare the trait-and-factor theory with the developmental theory of counseling.

3 Outline the steps involved in the decision-making process.

4 Explain how counselor activities are related to the 3-Cs model.

5 What is the role of counseling in programs such as PECE (Program for Education and Career Exploration)?

6 In what ways are the high school years crucial for the student?

7 Which functions of the Student Personnel Services are related to career guidance? Explain your answer.

8 Explain the basic procedures involved in evaluating a career guidance program.

For discussion

1 How is guidance related to career education?

2 Recall a decision that you made recently. What steps did you follow in arriving at your decision?

3 Under what conditions would one-to-one counseling be advisable? Under what conditions would group counseling be advisable?

4 The team approach to career guidance at the elementary level is essential for success. Why is this particularly true at the elementary level?

5 Discuss the differences between horizontal and vertical job clusters. Under what conditions would you recommend the use of each?

6 What are the principal uses of follow-up data for a counselor?

7 Justify a guidance program at the postsecondary level.

8 Explain how you would set up a job placement program in your school.

For exploration

1 Interview a counselor to find out the different kinds of tasks that counselors perform.

2 Formulate a set of objectives that might be appropriate for career guidance at the elementary level.

3 Examine the current literature and prepare a list of games and materials that would be appropriate for use in career guidance at the middle school level.

4 Compare the goals identified for career guidance at the secondary level with goals of the guidance-counseling program at a secondary school of your choice.

5 Write an article on the importance of job placement and follow-up in career guidance.

6 Visit a community college or area vocational-technical school. Describe the student population served by this institution.

7 Construct an instrument that you might use for student follow-up purposes.

References

1 M. C. Shaw, *School Guidance Systems* (Boston: Houghton Mifflin Company, 1973), p. 12.

2 Frank Parsons, *Choosing a Vocation* (Boston: Houghton Mifflin Company, 1908), p. 5.

3 Donald E. Super, "Vocational Adjustment: Implementing a Self-Concept," in *Occupations*, Vol. 30, November 1952, p. 92.

4 Norman C. Gysbers, Harry N. Drier, Jr., and Earl J. Moore, *Career Guidance* (Worthington, Ohio: Charles A. Jones Publishing Company, 1973), pp. 6–7. (Reprinted by permission of the publisher)

5 Chris D. Kehas, "Guidance and the Process of Schooling: Curriculum and Career Education," in *The School Counselor*, Vol. 21, No. 2, November 1973, p. 111.

6 Robert P. O'Hara, "Guidance for Career Development," in *Guidance for Education in Revolution*, ed. David R. Cook (Boston: Allyn and Bacon, 1971), p. 195.

7 Eli Ginzberg, "A Critical Look at Career Guidance," in *Manpower*, Vol. 4, No. 2, February 1972, p. 3.

8 Kenneth B. Matheny, "Facilitating Career Development in the Middle School," in *Contemporary Concepts in Vocational Education*, ed. Gordon F. Law (Washington, D.C.: American Vocational Association, 1971), p. 244. (Reproduced by permission)

9 Robert J. McBrien, "Decision-Making Training Essential for Career Education," in *Clearing House*, October 1973, pp. 86–87. (Reproduced by permission)

10 Warren W. Willingham, *Career Guidance in Secondary Education* (New York: College Entrance Examination Board, 1972), pp. 12–14, as quoted in T. Anne Cleary, "New Directions for Career Planning," in *Essays on Career Education* (Portland: Northwest Regional Educational Laboratory, 1973), p. 47. (Reproduced by permission)

11 Duane Brown, Stephen Feit, and Robert Forestandi, "Career Education: The Counselor's Role," in *The School Counselor*, Vol. 20, No. 2, January 1973, pp. 193–196. (Copyright 1974 American Personnel and Guidance Association. Reprinted with permission)

12 Ibid, p. 195.

13 Robert E. Campbell, Garry R. Waltz, Juliet V. Miller, and Sara F. Kriger, *Career Guidance: A Handbook of Methods* (Columbus: Charles E. Merrill Publishing Company, 1973), p. 19.

14 Kenneth B. Matheny. See Ref. 8, p. 242. (Reproduced by permission)

15 Ibid, p. 244. (Reproduced by permission)

16 Robert E. Campbell et al. See Ref. 13, p. 27.

17 Lorraine S. Hansen, "A Practitioner Looks at Career Guidance in the School Curriculum," in *Vocational Guidance Quarterly*, Vol. 16, No. 2, December 1967, p. 99.

18 Lillian Buckingham, "Job Placement as a School Program," in *American Vocational Journal*, Vol. 47, No. 3, March 1972, p. 64.

19 Robert E. Campbell et al. See Ref. 13, p. 38.

20 Charles C. Collins, *Premise: Planning Student Personnel Facilities* (Washington, D.C.: American Association of Junior Colleges, 1967). (Reproduced by permission)

21 David S. Bushnell, *Organizing for Change: New Priorities for Community Colleges* (New York: McGraw-Hill Book Company, 1973), p. 96.

22 Edwin L. Herr and Stanley H. Cramer, *Vocational Guidance and Career Development in the Schools: Toward a Systems Approach* (Boston: Houghton Mifflin Company, 1972), p. 273.

Part 3

Operational Dimensions

of Vocational Education as

a Component of

Career Education

Chapter 8

Institutions

Providing

Vocational-Technical

Education

Introduction

How, when, and where do we acquire the knowledge, skills, and attitudes necessary to perform in the world of work? Although every chapter in this book provides information necessary to answer this question, this chapter concentrates on describing *where* and *when* such learning is provided. *How* knowledge, skills, and attitudes necessary to perform at work are acquired is discussed in Chapter 10.

It is important to keep in mind that where one acquires the abilities to perform in a particular vocation depends on many factors. Some people who have had no formal preparation are able to perform in their vocations more successfully than others who have had considerable education and training. Such people are said to be "gifted" or to have a special "knack" to do the work. Other people require a great deal of preparation to be able to perform. Some people are ready to enter the world of work at an early age, sometimes long before they complete their formal education. Others do not give any thought to earning a livelihood until they have completed all their formal education.

It is the purpose of this chapter to review some of the major institutions in the United States that provide vocational-technical education of less than the baccalaureate degree. Emphasis is placed on the various levels of the public educational systems, because they appear to be assuming more and more responsibility in preparing people to enter the world of work through the concept of career education. The roles in vocational education of business and industry, government, labor unions, professional and civic organizations, religious organizations, and other agencies are discussed in this chapter. In addition, the objectives of specific areas of study in vocational education, such as occupations in business and distribution, agri-business, home economics, trade and industry, and health fields are reviewed.

Public Educational Institutions

What is the responsibility of public educational institutions in preparing individuals for work? Because people have different needs and because different vocations require different kinds and lengths of preparation, just when and where vocational preparation should begin is an open question. But the objectives of all levels of education, kindergarten through adult, should be structured to provide relevance to vocational preparation. How to do this at each level of career preparation is described in the following sections.

Elementary School

It was established in Chapter 4 that the purpose of career development in relation to vocational education in elementary grades is the same as it is in relation to general education. The individual during these years of rapid development is made aware of the types of work one might pursue, the various life styles and work environments, the relative earning power and types of training required for different vocations. Educational objectives at these levels should be structured so that the individual can begin to acquire knowledge and attitudes, and to some extent skills, in performing certain work tasks.

Even in nursery school, activities can be structured in preparation for later vocational competency. Moustakas and Berson (1) include in their objectives of the nursery school the following statement:

□ *The nursery school must be concerned with the enhancement of the child's individuality, and the development of attitudes, interests, understandings, and beliefs which will enable the child to be a happy, secure, contributing member of society. To reach these goals the nursery school must have an emotionally warm, friendly, relaxed atmosphere.*

The general education objectives expressed in this statement deal primarily with the affective domain, with the importance of attitudes. The activities that children engage in at this level should thus focus on respect for all individuals and for all types of work—professional and nonprofessional.

The objectives of the kindergarten are similar. The Florida State Department of Education includes among its kindergarten objectives (2) those listed below. The child will learn to:

1 *use materials freely and constructively which may result in increasing initiative, creative power, independence and motor coordination*

2 *develop motor skills and coordination through play with appropriate apparatus. This improved motor control is reflected by better handling of*

classroom equipment—blocks, pencils, scissors, crayons, as well as other equipment

3 *express himself freely within a group situation and be stimulated to independent thinking in organizing and communicating his ideas.*

Activities in the kindergarten should be developed around the three learning domains—cognitive, affective, and psychomotor. The kindergarten pupil should learn to use the tools of work—scissors, crayons, hammers, paper, wood, cloth, and so on. Although adult tasks are not normally performed, kindergarten children are made aware of different vocations in which one might use these tools, through stories, field trips, and visits by workers representing all types of occupations.

The Educational Policies Commission of the National Education Association included in its statement of the purposes of education a list of objectives concerning economic efficiency. Preparation for meeting these objectives must by necessity begin in the elementary school. The Commission states (3):

□ *It is important that children should learn that each may properly enjoy the fruits of civilization only by doing his part in the work of the world. Work should be regarded as something to be sought, enjoyed, and respected rather than as something to be avoided, suffered, and despised. . . . Even the younger children can learn the necessity of contributing effort to a common cause.*

Six of the objectives stated by the commission are directly concerned with work, while the other four are concerned with the need for individuals to possess knowledge, skills, and attitudes necessary for them to be wise consumers. It is generally conceded that vocational education that does not include all such learnings is incomplete. The commission's objectives for economic efficiency follow (4):

1 *Work: The educated producer knows the satisfaction of good workmanship.*

2 *Occupational Information: The educated producer understands the requirements and opportunities for various jobs.*

3 *Occupational Choice: The educated producer has selected his occupation.*

4 *Occupational Efficiency: The educated producer succeeds in his chosen vocation.*

5 *Occupational Adjustment: The educated producer maintains and improves his efficiency.*

6 *Occupational Appreciation: The educated producer appreciates the social value of his work.*

7 *Personal Economics: The educated consumer plans the economics of his own life.*

8 *Consumer Judgment: The educated consumer develops standards for guiding his expenditures.*

9 *Efficiency in Buying: The educated consumer is an informed and skillful buyer.*

10 *Consumer Protection: The educated consumer takes appropriate measures to safeguard his interests.*

The extent to which the elementary curriculum can be planned to meet these objectives depends on many factors. It is certainly not to be expected that when students complete the sixth grade they are "educated" and have therefore successfully achieved these objectives to the extent of their adult needs. Rather, they should have successfully achieved them so that they can continue to build on them. These objectives are appropriate at all levels of education.

The objectives of elementary school programs are necessarily general in nature with respect to vocational education. Just as the "home" prepares the child to enter school at either the nursery school, kindergarten, or first grade level, the elementary school prepares the child to enter the junior high or middle school, where objectives take on more specificity. As stated by Jarvis and Rice (5):

☐ *A vital curriculum objective of the elementary school is to initiate instruction which helps children understand the world of work and stimulates their interest in thinking about tentative vocational choices. In the elementary years, teachers can help children develop responsibility, punctuality, thoroughness in work, and intellectual and social skills which are requisite for attaining vocational success in adult life.*

Middle School

With respect to career education, we have already identified the objective of the middle school years as being that of career exploration, which would build on the career awareness experiences of elementary school. As a part of the career exploration phase, students might take short vocational courses, in which they would be introduced to the range of knowledge, skills, and attitudes needed by individuals to perform in selected occupational areas. With limited hands-on experiences, they would be able to examine themselves in terms of their aptitude for acquiring and developing such abilities.

Educational objectives of the middle school years act as a bridge between those of elementary school and of high school. As Bossing and Cramer (6) state, it is the objective of the middle or junior high school:

□ *to make available sufficient personal interest explorations to initiate a clear understanding of the industry and culture of the adult world*

to provide experiences designed to develop appropriate attitudes and values necessary for living in a democracy as an individual member and as a contributor to the common good

In a statement of objectives for secondary education, Davis says (7):

□ *Secondary education should provide educational experiences that will help students equip themselves with the skills, knowledge, understandings, and attitudes necessary for earning their own living.*

These statements of objectives for middle school and the high school show that the middle school years are transitional ones. The vocational objectives at this level are both more specific than they are at the elementary level yet much more general than is the case at the high school level.

It is suggested (8) that during the middle school years the student:

□ *. . . can be aided in his learning by making systematic studies of several classes of jobs which interest him so that he can find out whether they are open-ended or dead-end; what training is required for entrance; what later training, if any, is helpful in promotion; where these training opportunities can be had; and what prerequisites there are to obtaining the training. If there are persons in the community who hold such jobs, students should talk with them and, where possible, sample units of instruction that illustrate such training programs. Several hours each month could be used fruitfully in helping students carry on systematic exploration of occupations and jobs that seem attractive to them so that career choices will not be superficial, educational and training needs will be anticipated, and students can learn how to continue life planning over the years.*

In junior high school economic orientation and occupational preparation should reach a more sophisticated stage with study by all students of the economic and industrial system by which goods and services are produced and distributed. The objective should be exposure to the full range of occupational choices which will be available at a later point and full knowledge of the relative advantages and the requirements of each.

Although the objectives of vocational education during the middle school years are more specific than they are at the elementary level, they are still not directed toward preparing students for job entry skills; rather they are intended to be exploratory in nature. Even at this intermediate level of vocational education, however, it is quite possible that some students can be identified as needing job-entry level training that is usually left to the responsibility of grades 10 through 12.

Thompson offers the following statement to describe the objectives of vocational education at the middle school level (9):

□ *A generalized objective for vocational education at the middle school is to have each individual obtain a broad, fundamental understanding of the world of work as well as a personal sense of his ability to control and manipulate this world. The youngster is to express himself in and become sensitive to the problems in the world of work. This can be done at this level by having the students work with materials, which are the vehicles for the induction of changes in learners, changes that are behavioral as well as cognitive.*

Hoyt et al (10) are much more specific in their objectives of vocational education at the junior high school level:

1 *Every junior high school student should be able to explore his occupational interests and aptitudes from among the broadest possible range of occupational areas.*

2 *Every junior high school student should see clearly the relationships between the academic content he is being asked to master and his tentative occupational choices.*

3 *As many junior high school students as possible should acquire some real work experience.*

4 *Junior high school students should be provided with some basic vocational skills which they can use as building blocks in their later career education development.*

5 *Occupational choice options should be kept open for all junior high school students while each should be simultaneously encouraged to make tentative personal commitments to one or more broad occupational areas at some broad level of competence.*

6 *Junior high school students should be provided with sufficient knowledge about and experience in the various vocational education areas open to them at the senior high and post-high school level so that these students can really choose from among them.*

7 *Those students who express an intention to leave the formal educational structure, at least for awhile, near the end of the junior high school years, should be provided with a set of salable vocational skills that they can use in obtaining employment.*

8 *Vocational exploratory programs should be provided in such a way that academic learnings in traditional junior high school areas will be enhanced rather than de-emphasized.*

Exploratory activities should include opportunities to examine occupational training in the areas of the traditional vocational subjects of agricultural education, business and office education, distributive education, health education, trade and industrial education, and technical education. Although these activities should be designed to keep all occupational options open, they should also provide opportunities for students to make tentative occupational choices.

High School

At the high school level, the objective of vocational education is to prepare an individual for initial employment. Vocational programs should thus be based on the needs of individuals enrolled in the programs and on the labor needs of the community. Vocational education should be a part of the objectives of any high school, even those whose primary objective is to prepare students for college. Traditionally, high schools have placed emphasis on preparation for college regardless of the needs of individuals for preparation for work immediately upon graduation from high school. The comprehensive high school has as its objectives dual programs designed to prepare students for college entrance and to prepare students for work immediately upon graduation. With increasing emphasis being placed on career education, greater importance is given to the philosophy that every student who is graduated from high school should have at least one vocational skill that he or she can use following high school, regardless of ultimate career objective.

Whether or not a school provides vocational education in none, one, or all of the vocational fields depends on the needs of the students and the community. In the sections that follow, objectives of each of the traditional vocational fields at the high school level—agricultural education, business and office education, distributive education, health occupations education, home economics education, and trade and industrial education—are reviewed.

Agricultural education As discussed in Chapter 2, the passage of the Smith-Hughes Act in 1917 inaugurated a period in which vocational education focused on the training of farmers. The Federal Board for Vocational Education, in its 1931 report, proclaimed that "the primary aim of vocational agriculture is to train present and prospective farmers for proficiency in farming." Subsequent editions of the publication reaffirmed this aim (11).

However, contemporary programs, which are outgrowths of the Vocational Education Act of 1963 and the Vocational Education Amendments of 1968, emphasize broadened objectives, including: (a) preparation and advancement in *any* occupation involving knowledge and skill in agriculture; (b) occupational exploration, guidance, and counseling; and (c) development of abilities essential for effective citizenship.

Roberts (12) lists seven major objectives of vocational agriculture to meet the aim of training present and prospective farmers for proficiency in agriculture:

1 *make a beginning and advance in farming*

2 *produce farm commodities efficiently*

3 *market farm products advantageously*

4 *conserve soil and other natural resources*

5 *manage a farm business effectively*

6 *maintain a favorable environment*

7 *participate in rural leadership activities*

Designed primarily for secondary school students, these objectives may be adapted to other levels of instruction in vocational agriculture.

An example of specific objectives in agricultural education is provided by the Omaha Public Schools (13):

1 *to develop an appreciation of the role of agriculture on the part of all students. This would involve units of agricultural information in elementary grades, exploratory and pre-vocational junior high courses for girls and boys, and courses in general agriculture such as economics and livestock and livestock products*

2 *to prepare persons for off-farm agricultural employment*

3 *to provide a course in agricultural science professions for seniors*

4 *to contribute to the solution of agricultural-rural migrant adjustment problems*

5 *to provide facilities for training and retraining of workers, including adults, in agricultural industries*

These objectives go far beyond the vocational aspects of the subject and provide all students with the opportunity to become knowledgeable about agriculture as a part of their general education.

As is true in all fields of education, the nature of agricultural education is changing. Hunsicker (14) describes the transitions in vocational agricultural education:

☐ *The transitions are leading to an entirely new concept of vocational education in agriculture. The name "Agricultural Education" or "Vocational Agriculture" which has, for a half century, connoted chiefly production agriculture, such as farming and ranching, is giving way to the broad concept of Vocational Education for Agribusiness Occupations, increasingly referred to as "Agribusiness Education." This new title includes the preparation of individuals for employment in both agricultural production and the off-farm related businesses. The word "agribusiness" was inserted for the first time in the 1966 edition of major dictionaries and glossaries. The definition not only provides the authority but also establishes the*

*occupational range for which training in this field is needed. The new title
"agribusiness" is now defined as (a) a blend of agriculture and business,
and (b) a combination of the producing operations of a farm (ranch,
greenhouse or nursery) and, in varying degrees, the services associated
with them; the manufacturing and distribution of farm equipment, fertilizers and supplies; the processing, storage, marketing and distribution
of farm commodities including food and fiber; and the conservation, pres-
ervation and use of renewable natural resources.*

Business and office education Business education has been a part of
this country's educational system from its earliest years, with training in
accounting, commercial law, and business arithmetic included in the
early high school curriculum. In present-day curricula, business education
is recognized as having both general and vocational education objectives.
It has been defined as education that will equip the student with skills
necessary to perform particular functions in an office or data processing
occupation; it will also provide him or her with the understandings and
knowledge needed for handling personal affairs and for using the services
of the business world.

A review of the major objectives of business education helps to develop
an understanding of its role in the school program. The *vocational objective* relates specifically to the preparation of students for initial employment, to upgrading existing skills, and to retraining in new and/or related
business and office occupations. The *exploratory objective*, aimed primarily at the middle grades and early high school, provides opportunities
for students to gain information about careers in business. The *occupational intelligence objective* recognizes that all citizens should have an
intelligent understanding of the various areas of work in which they earn
a living. The *economic-understanding objective* is related to developing
economic literacy in all citizens. The *consumer education objective* serves
a dual role; it promotes the discriminating use of services and resources
by consumers and a corresponding understanding of the consumer viewpoint and how best to serve the consumer. The *personal-use objective* relates to those business courses designed to prepare students for proper
execution of their personal business affairs. The *semi-vocational objective*
recognizes that many business skills lead to advancement in professions
or occupations other than those directly related to business. The *college
preparation objective* recognizes that high schools have an obligation to
provide background preparation in business as well as to develop skills
that provide students with tools to cope more effectively with college
demands.

Changing objectives in business education are reflected in a review of
the philosophical statements in *This We Believe about Business Education in the High School* prepared by the Policies Commission for Business
and Economic Education. The first statement, published in 1961, was
written by twelve national leaders in business education, who represented
two of the most prestigious organizations in the field—the National Busi-

ness Education Association and Delta Pi Epsilon, a national honorary fraternity. The commission's first statement described the purposes of business education in the following manner (15):

☐ *Business education is concerned with two major aspects of the education of youth:*

A *the knowledge, attitudes, and nonvocational skills needed by all persons to be effective in their personal economics and in their understanding of our economic system*

B *the vocational knowledge and skills needed for initial employment and for advancement in a business career*

We believe that

1 *Business education has an important contribution to make to the economic literacy of every high school boy and girl.*

2 *Business education must provide an adequate program of vocational preparation for those boys and girls who will enter business upon completing high school.*

3 *Business education courses should be available as electives to those high school students planning to go to college and should be accepted by the colleges and universities as meeting part of the college entrance requirements.*

Within ten years a third organization had been added to the sponsorship of the Commission—the American Vocational Association. The Commission's second statement regarding the role of business education in the high school reflected the increasing importance of vocational preparation through business education (16):

☐ *Major statements of the purpose of education in America have identified a need for business education. Business education achieves its goals through—*

specialized instruction to prepare students for careers in business

fundamental instruction to help students assume their economic roles as consumers, workers, and citizens

background instruction to assist students in preparing for professional careers requiring advanced study

In an effort to satisfy the needs of all students, secondary schools should provide sound programs of business education that provide instruction for and about business.

We believe that

. . . Business education is an effective program of occupational instruction for secondary students desiring careers in business.

. . . Business education has an important contribution to make to the economic literacy of all secondary school students.

. . . Business education is desirable for students who plan programs requiring postsecondary and higher education in business.

A complete reading of the two statements reveals only one mention of the word "career" in the first statement and repeated use of the word in the second statement, clearly indicating a change in the attitude of business educators. They are no longer preoccupied with the academic acceptability of business education at the secondary level; they are more concerned with the need for business education to provide all students with the necessary knowledge, skills, and attitudes for them to function effectively as business and office workers and as citizens. Another difference in the two statements that indicates a change in attitude on the part of business educators is the orientation of the second statement around the needs of individuals, the business community, and the community at large, suggesting the need for a flexible curriculum to meet those needs. In comparison, the earlier statement describes a rather rigid and highly structured subject matter curriculum.

The Policies Commission for Business and Economic Education has prepared a number of statements reflecting the objectives, roles, and needs of business and office education. Its first pamphlet, "A Proposal for Business-Economic Education for American Secondary Schools," was directed to school administrators. Its purpose was to assure that administrators were focused on the need to begin, to continue, or to reinforce business education programs in the secondary schools. Since then, the commission's statements have reflected changing attitudes of business educators. "This We Believe about Implementing Individualization of Instruction in Business Education" is a statement that reveals a new focus on the part of business educators—on the needs of students as individuals rather than on a desire to teach certain subjects or to gain acceptability from peers in doing so.

The objectives of business education in the high school should be written collectively by business teachers, with the advice of students, other teachers, school administrators, and representatives of the business community. The objectives should reflect the philosophy of the school and business community being served. Depending on the overall objectives of the school, the business education curriculum may need to be developed in such a way that it meets one, two, or all of the following objectives:

1 to prepare students for careers in business

2 to help students assume their economic roles as consumers, workers, and citizens

3 to assist students in preparing for professional careers requiring advanced study

Distributive education Distributive education is charged with the responsibility of preparing persons for employment in marketing, so it is concerned with activities such as selling, buying, transporting, storing, promoting, financing, research, and management. Instruction in distributive education is offered at the high school, postsecondary and adult levels; it includes preparatory and supplemental training to prepare persons for initial employment as well as to update existing skills or provide new ones.

The Distributive Education Publications Committee of the American Vocational Association describes the purposes of distributive education as follows (17):

☐ *The major purpose of distributive education is to prepare people for employment in distribution. Three goals, which describe the responsibility and functions of distributive education, are generally accepted.*

The first goal, to offer instruction in distribution and marketing, emphasizes the educational contribution of distributive education. This primary aim provides instruction, which is essential for entrance or advancement in distributive occupations, for youth and adults, regardless of their previous educational achievements, their social, economic, cultural, or ethnic backgrounds.

The second goal, to aid in the improvement of the techniques of distribution, is economic in nature. Our high standard of living is based upon the efficient distribution of goods and services. Distributive education makes a further economic contribution in terms of human resources by helping to provide people with the wide range of competencies necessary for successful employment.

The third goal is a social one because distributive education has a commitment to help prepare workers who understand their responsibilities to society—workers who will strive to secure equal rights and opportunities for all, and who will recognize that only through proper work habits and responsibile actions can a fine and competitive society be maintained.

The objectives of distributive education have changed since it was first introduced to the secondary school program in Boston in 1912. At that time, the objective was to provide cooperative training in retail store work for the purpose of improving the lot and quality of work of sales personnel (18). During its early years it was often under the supervision of persons in business education, trade and industrial education, and agricultural education.

With the passage of the George-Deen Act in 1936 and later through the George-Barden Act of 1947, distributive education became officially recognized as a part of reimbursed vocational education. Training under these acts, however, was limited to employed persons above the age of sixteen and to cooperative plans in the high school distributive programs. Major provisions of the Vocational Education Acts of the 1960s included removal of the employment requirement for participation, thus enabling schools to develop preparatory programs. Postsecondary programs were stressed under these acts.

Health occupations education Health occupations education is becoming a viable program at the secondary school level. Traditionally, preparation for work related to health occupations has been left to hospitals, private schools with advanced programs requiring a high school diploma for admission, higher education institutions, and other agencies. With these institutions unable to meet the increasing need for preparation of medical workers at reasonable costs, demands are being made more and more on public education systems, including the secondary school. It is now recognized and accepted that there are many paramedical tasks that can be learned and performed by high school age individuals.

What are the objectives of such a program? Sands (19) discussed the four main issues in health care that have influenced the development of health occupations education at the secondary level. They are, "unequal availability of health care, questionable quality of health care, skyrocketing costs, and responsibility for or control of health services." It should be the objective of secondary health occupations programs to help cope with these issues.

Rachel K. Winer, Chief of Health Occupations, Division of Occupational Education, Massachusetts Department of Education, proposes a curriculum in health occupations designed to meet these varied needs (20):

☐ . . . *many health needs require minimal basic skills which may be meaningfully presented to secondary school students in an occupational-education continuum allowing for numerous career options. . . . A health-career continuum becomes meaningful to the student by exposing him to a variety of experiences in the world of work. . . . Exposure to health occupations along this continuum provides the student with a variety of options for seeking the particular work role from which he will derive ego satisfaction. Should exposure to a particular discipline yield poor performance or negative attitudes, he can move horizontally in the continuum to another option.*

Winer further describes the purposes of the Massachusetts program (21):

☐ *The program in health careers at the secondary level permits the student to choose from the previously mentioned two major options, in either of which he may enroll in a health continuum where exposure to a variety of semi-specialized skills builds up in vertical fashion. Or, he may choose a single elective in the program, for he can pick up or drop any one of the health occupation courses and still remain in his regular program of study. Even if he chooses the single elective the student becomes qualified for employment as a nurse's aide in a nursing home or primary care facility. . . . At the completion of each grade after the ninth grade, the student in the health career continuum does have a salable skill and is employable.*

. . . the ninth grade student receives a concentrated introduction to the world of work in health occupations.

At the tenth grade, students who choose to continue in the program elect nursery school aide/child care for a 20-week period, followed by a dietary aide program in the second semester for another 20-week period.

. . . At the eleventh grade the program is designed to prepare the student to function as a nurse's aide, hospital assistant, or health service assistant. . . .

At the twelfth grade level, the student has three options: medical assistant aide, dental assistant aide, or work-study program. The purpose of these twelfth grade courses is to equip students with a beginning salable skill, that is, the qualification to function as an aide in a doctor's office, clinic, or medical library, or as a ward or unit clerk in a health agency. . . .

The student acquires the facility to maintain patient records, handle forms for Blue Cross/Blue Shield and Medicare, and prepare case histories. He gains skills in telephone communication, medical communication, initial medical transcription and other office tasks. . . .

A further option for the graduate is entrance, with advanced standing, into a postsecondary . . . program. . . .

For students who do not elect to enter the health career continuum, a choice of any one program except those at the twelfth grade level is possible as an elective.

The program designed to meet these objectives is shown in Figure 8.1. A similar program described by Hill (22) is designed

☐ *to help students set realistic career goals and give them the necessary training and education to either move into post high school career programs or enter the labor market as unlicensed assistant health workers. The curriculum was planned to include instructional content common to all health occupations, an indepth study of health careers, and on-the-job skill development.*

Home economics education Technological advances in our society and the resulting changes in agriculture, business, and industry have been

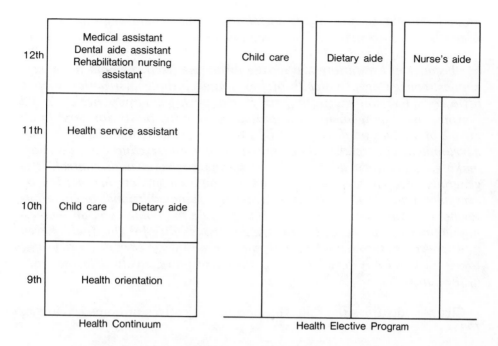

Figure 8.1 A program in health careers for secondary schools (21).

reflected in twentieth-century family life. The primary responsibility of the home is no longer the provision of food, clothing, and shelter or the rearing, education, and employment of its members. Increasing numbers of women are employed at some time during their lifetime, with about three out of every five serving in multiple roles of homemaker, wife, mother, and wage earner. This fact suggests the importance of joint programs in occupational areas such as home economics, business education, health occupations, and distributive education to prepare women for their multiple roles.

Reflecting the changing roles of women in society, the objectives of vocational home economics have been expanded (23) to include an increased emphasis on management; greater concern for educating the individual for self-understanding and for family membership; a lessening, but not the abandonment, of manipulative skills; and education for assuming the dual role of homemaker and wage earner.

The new directions for home economics are described by Hatcher and Halchin in the following statement (24):

□ *The charge to home economics for the seventies is to help all people to improve their quality of life. All people is not to be loosely interpreted. . . . The signs of the times as manifested in the identification of discriminatory practices involving sex, race, age, religion, and ethnic back-*

ground, and the accompanying social action and federal legislation, have added impetus to making home economics more generally available to groups of people and individuals who have been neglected, not willfully, but because of limitations within the discipline itself. The old home economics, consisting principally of foods and clothing instruction with a little consideration given to family relationships, family health, child rearing, and management, was limited in its potentiality for serving all people of all ages in all walks of life. With increased emphasis on human development and relationships, nutrition, consumer education, decision-making, concern for adequate housing, and environmental control, it is generally recognized that the home economics concepts are needed by everyone. Then, too, a shift in sex roles has some additional implications for home economics. Women working outside the home (and an increasing number of them are) are carrying responsibility for the dual or even multiple roles of homemaker, wife, mother, and wage earner. By the same token men and boys are becoming more and more involved in the work of the home.

Girtman identifies the following specific objectives of home economics (25):

1 *to improve the quality of family living and to help youth and adults develop the abilities needed for the occupation of homemaking*

2 *to prepare individuals for gainful employment in occupations involving home economics knowledge and skills*

3 *to provide preprofessional education for students who will enter colleges and universities*

4 *to help prepare individuals for responsible citizenship, with special emphasis on consumer responsibility*

5 *to help transmit the American culture from one generation to another and to develop heritage appreciation*

These objectives reflect both the general and vocational education emphasis of home economics education.

Industrial education Vocational industrial education is considered to be the broadest of all the vocational fields, with training programs designed to prepare skilled and semiskilled workers in a wide range of trade and industrial occupations. The U.S. Office of Education has defined trade and industrial education (26) as (a) any craft, skilled trade, or semiskilled occupation that directly functions in the designing, producing, processing, fabricating, assembling, testing, modifying, maintaining, servicing, or repairing of any product or commodity; and (b) any other occupation, including service occupations that are not covered above, which is usually considered to be technical, or trade and industrial in nature.

Roberts (27) uses the term "vocational industrial education" to include machine shop, carpentry, electrical appliance servicing, millwork and cabinet making, radio servicing, sheet metal, auto mechanics, printing, air conditioning, barbering, practical nursing, foundry, needle trades, plastics, plumbing, upholstering, and watchmaking.

Trade and industrial education is concerned with preparing students at the secondary and postsecondary levels to (a) make wise career choices; (b) attain the attitudes, skills, and knowledge necessary for job entry employment; and (c) upgrade existing skills or retrain for a new job in a wide range of semiskilled, skilled, and technical occupations.

Roberts (28) describes the following objectives as basic to the establishment of the vocational industrial education program:

1 *to provide instruction of an extension or supplemental type for the further development of performance skills, technical knowledge, related industrial education, safety, and job judgment for persons already employed in trade and industrial pursuits*

2 *to provide instruction of a preparatory type in the development of basic manipulative skills, safety judgment, technical knowledge and related industrial information for the purpose of fitting persons for useful employment in trade and industrial pursuits*

Industrial arts education In December 1973, industrial arts was added to Public Law 92–318 and officially became part of the group of vocational education programs eligible for federal aid. Industrial arts is defined in the *Federal Register* as (29):

□ *those education programs which pertain to the body of related subject matter, or related courses, organized for the development of understanding about the technical, consumer, occupational, recreational, organizational, managerial, social, historical, and cultural aspects of industry and technology including learning experiences involving activities such as experimenting, designing, constructing, evaluating, and using tools, machines, materials, and processes which provide opportunities for creativity and problem solving and assisting individuals in the making of informed and meaningful occupational choices.*

In the Vocational Education Act the following objectives are identified for industrial arts instructional programs:

1 to assist individuals in the making of informed and meaningful occupational choices by

(a) providing occupational information and instruction pertaining to a broad range of occupations

(b) providing laboratory experiences in shops and laboratories in business or industry to acquaint students with jobs

(c) providing guidance and counseling for students enrolled in the industrial arts program

(d) employing industrial arts teachers who have qualifications as provided in the state plan

2 to prepare individuals for enrollment in advanced or highly skilled vocational and technical education programs by

(a) providing individuals with occupational information and exploratory experiences for enrolling in such programs

(b) providing occupational information and exploratory experiences directly related to current practices in industry

Historically, industrial arts has been recognized as part of the general education experiences of students from the elementary level through college. In 1968 an industrial arts planning committee recommended the following objectives, which are applicable at all grade levels with appropriate materials and methods (30):

1 *to develop an insight and understanding of industry and its place in our culture*

2 *to discover and develop talents, aptitudes, interest, and potentialities of individuals for the technical pursuits and applied sciences*

3 *to develop an understanding of industrial processes and the practical application of scientific principles*

4 *to develop basic skills in the proper use of common industrial tools, machines, and processes*

5 *to develop problem-solving and creative abilities involving the materials, processes, and products of industry*

Postsecondary Schools

Prior to World War II, postsecondary education was limited to those persons who indicated potential for entering a profession, thus excluding large segments of the population. Since that time, the number of junior/community colleges and vocational-technical schools has greatly expanded, providing more advanced occupational preparation for existing and emerging jobs. Programs for the retraining, upgrading, and updating of persons presently in the work force are important components of postsecondary vocational education.

The postsecondary institutions focus not only on the preparation of individuals for entry-level jobs but also for middle-level positions. Gillie (31) describes the middle-level position as one whose occupational functions demand "(a) some cognitive skills in addition to the manual type proficiencies, and (b) preparation for both the cognitive and manual aspects of the job by specially designed programs offered by area vocational-technical schools, various types of proprietary schools, and community junior colleges."

Area vocational-technical schools may indeed be the most rapidly growing institutions in vocational education. Designed to serve the vocational training needs of residents in a particular area, they offer full-time and part-time day and evening programs in numerous vocational, technical, and trade areas. These schools are designed to meet the occupational and educational needs of both high school graduates and drop outs; of beginning workers, of former workers reentering the labor market, and of present workers.

The objectives of junior/community colleges are more diverse and geared to community needs. They include terminal vocational education programs, terminal general education programs, preprofessional or transfer programs, as well as short courses, training programs for specialized groups, and adult or continuing education.

Increasing numbers of four-year institutions are providing vocational education through four-year and non-degree programs. Many colleges and universities provide vocational education through extension and continuing education programs. For years, agricultural education and agricultural extension personnel have conducted adult education programs.

For students with little or no previous vocational training, the objectives of each vocational field are basically the same as those identified for secondary programs; that is, providing entry-level skills. Students entering with prior training or experience, however, may wish to move vertically up the career ladder by acquiring more advanced, specialized training. For example, a student completing a stenographic program at the secondary level may enroll in a program for medical secretaries at the postsecondary level. Other students may elect to move horizontally, acquiring a broad base of knowledge in related areas, such as from accounting to data processing.

Other Institutions

In addition to the public schools there are other institutions that provide vocational and technical education. For example, many private schools—operated by individuals or by large business and industrial firms —offer such educational experiences. They might operate at the secondary and or postsecondary levels and might offer programs in various occupational areas, such as business, barbering, and cosmetology. The objectives of these institutions are generally much narrower than those of the public schools, concentrating specifically on the knowledge and skills required to perform specific work tasks rather than on making the student a better citizen or a wiser consumer.

Business and industrial firms also provide vocational and technical training, either in the form of on-the-job training or through cooperative efforts with schools, public or private, or with government. On-the-job training is usually provided for individuals in order to increase their productivity, promotability, employment stability, or their on-the-job safety. Evans (32) expands on the reasons why employers conduct such training:

1 *Almost all employers are extremely cost conscious, and one of the obvious major components of cost is productivity of each worker, from the president of the company down to the lowest level of unskilled worker. Productivity is influenced by skills, knowledges, and attitudes, and hence training programs are used to increase skills; to increase knowledge about the job, the company, the industry, and the economic system, and to change attitudes toward fellow workers and management. A single training program may have all three goals, but more commonly one goal is emphasized.*

2 *Programs to enhance promotability are heavily concentrated on supervisory and management personnel. Job rotation training, which familiarizes the supervisor with many different parts of the firm, and many other types of training are used. If a worker must be promoted because of his increased seniority, it is obviously advantageous to the employer to have him ready for the new position if at all possible. Even more important is the need to have supervisors and managers ready to step into posts of increased responsibility when the need arises.*

3 *When an effective employee leaves, a variety of costs are incurred. The employee must be terminated, and a new employee must be recruited, screened, and trained. Each of these steps is expensive. Job satisfaction is one of the major ways of reducing turnover, and training can be one factor which increases job satisfaction.*

4 *Poor safety records are expensive in terms of insurance costs and decreased confidence on the part of workers and of the community.*

Many firms conduct formal, highly structured orientation programs for new employees, which introduce them to the firm and acquaint them with its organizational structure. Company policies that affect the new employee are introduced, such as those regarding payroll and fringe benefits. Specific knowledge and skills that the new employee will need to perform on the job might also be taught. Many orientation programs go far beyond the objectives discussed here; but when they do, they are primarily structured for management-level employees.

To overcome the shortages of skilled workers in many areas, the federal government has provided funds to private industries to subsidize training programs. These programs might be conducted independently, on company property, or in cooperation with private or public schools.

Labor unions also conduct vocational and technical training programs both to train workers for specific job skills and to control the availability of such trained personnel. This limiting function is designed to assure that the job market will not become flooded with individuals with specific skills and thus cause the salary scale to depreciate. In addition, training is available through professional associations, such as the Administrative Management Society; through agencies, such as the national Institute of Life Insurance and the Young Men's Christian Association; through the military; and through various church groups. Each branch of the military, for example, conducts training programs in many vocational areas in order to assure that there are qualified persons to conduct the extensive military operations. In addition, the serviceman or woman gains knowledge and skills that can be used later to earn a living in civilian life. In this way, qualified individuals are encouraged to go into certain occupations in industry once they are discharged. These are only a few of the ways that individuals acquire vocational and technical training outside the framework of the public schools.

Summary

Public educational institutions provide activities for vocational development of individuals at all levels. Although general educational development is the primary focus of the nursery school and kindergarten years, activities are included that are intended to develop positive attitudes toward the dignity of work and toward the need to become a contributing member of society. Children are given activities designed to develop motor skills, communication skills, and creativity. At upper levels of the elementary grades the individual should be made aware of the requirements and opportunities of many jobs, professional and nonprofessional.

As the bridge between elementary school and high school, the middle school should provide opportunities for the individual to explore several occupational clusters. Students should be given opportunities for self-analysis and for hands-on experience in order to determine work interests and abilities in the various occupational clusters. Promotion opportunities and life styles relating to each field should be examined. Vocational activities should be structured so that academic learnings are enhanced by them. Although tentative occupational choices might be goals at this level, all options for occupational decisions should remain open.

The objective of vocational education at the high school level is to prepare the individual for entry level employment. The individual should select a single cluster of skills, in a field that is relevant to the community, and participate in activities designed to develop entry level skills. In every vocational area the objectives should be designed to provide the individual with necessary knowledge, skills, and attitudes preparatory to actual employment or to more advanced study.

At the postsecondary level, objectives should be designed to give individuals job entry-level skills, additional training, and/or retraining to advance in their occupation. Junior colleges, community colleges, four-year colleges and universities, as well as postsecondary vocational schools provide vocational and technical education. Such education may or may not carry college credit; it may be part of the regular school curriculum or it may be operated as continuing education for adults. An important objective of vocational education at the college level is to prepare teachers of vocational education.

Private institutions and business and industrial firms also provide vocational education, which is usually much more specialized than that offered in public institutions. Labor unions also conduct vocational and technical training programs to train workers for specific job skills and to control the availability of trained personnel.

The objectives of vocational education vary considerably with the level at which the instruction is offered, the objectives of the institution, providing the instruction, and the objectives and needs of the individuals and communities being served. At the lower levels (elementary and middle school) the objectives are general in nature. At the high school level they become more specific with respect to vocational training, but they continue to include general education goals. Objectives of public education institutions are oriented more to the needs of the individual and the community, whereas the objectives of business, industry, and labor are oriented more to their respective needs.

Activities

For review

1 What are the objectives of vocational education at the elementary school level? the middle school level? the high school level? Relate the objectives at each level to career education and general education.

2 Distinguish among the objectives of vocational education at the secondary level: in a college preparatory school, a comprehensive school, and a vocational school.

3 What factors are important in deciding what occupational areas are to be included in a vocational curriculum at the preparation level?

4 What are the vocational and/or general education objectives of the following vocational areas at the secondary level?

(a) agricultural education

(b) business and office education

(c) distributive education

(d) health occupations education

(e) home economics education

(f) industrial arts education

(g) trade and industrial education

5 When should the preparation phase of vocational education begin in a student's curriculum?

6 Compare the role of vocational education in the postsecondary vocational-technical school and in the junior/community college.

7 Distinguish between industrial arts and vocational industrial arts.

8 Distinguish between the objectives of vocational-technical education in postsecondary schools that do not offer the baccalaureate degree and in four-year colleges and universities.

9 What kinds of institutions provide vocational and technical education other than public schools? What are the objectives of each?

For discussion

1 Where, when, and how does an individual acquire knowledge, skills, and attitudes necessary to perform as a technician, artisan, secretary, carpenter, electrician, dental assistant, receptionist, and so on?

2 Many children rule out or eliminate many types of job opportunities for consideration before they even begin school. What can be done in grades K–6 to combat this?

3 This chapter has indicated that each individual should strive to be a "contributing member of society." What does this mean? How does an individual know when he or she is a contributing member? How do the schools help an individual to be a contributing member?

4 Career education in the middle school/junior high school is focused on exploration. However, if potential drop outs are identified, specific objectives should be met to develop job entry level skills. How can students be identified as potential drop outs, and what steps should be taken to help them develop a salable skill?

5 "Every student who is graduated from high school should have at least one vocational skill that he or she can use on leaving high school regardless of a future career objective." Do you agree with this statement? Why or why not? Is this statement without exceptions?

6 Discuss objectives of vocational education that would be appropriate to all individuals at every level of education.

7 This chapter makes a statement, with which many authorities agree, that the middle or junior high school years are a bridge between elementary school and high school. Do you agree or disagree with this statement? Explain.

8 Discuss the advantages and disadvantages of training individuals for work in public institutions prior to employment and on-the-job training by industry.

9 How do labor organizations influence vocational objectives of public institutions?

10 How does the federal government influence vocational objectives of institutions?

11 How do private business and industry influence vocational objectives of institutions?

12 List and discuss factors that influence the varying needs that individuals have for vocational development and preparation. Include personal and family factors, community factors, private and industrial business factors, and governmental factors.

13 "All levels of education, kindergarten through adult, should be structured to provide relevance to vocational preparation." Does this statement mean that every individual should be prepared for a vocational competency requiring less than a baccalaureate degree? Explain.

14 Explain how the cooperative plan program and the project plan program could be combined to aid in individualized instruction in your occupational area.

15 Do you agree or disagree with the statement that training can be one factor that increases job satisfaction? Explain.

For exploration

1 It has been stated in this chapter that the objectives of vocational education have changed over the years. Study the objectives of each of the areas listed below. Compare the objectives today with those of ten, twenty, thirty, or fifty years ago. How have the objectives changed? What influences have been primarily responsible for bringing these changes about? Document your responses.

(a) agricultural education

(b) business and office education

(c) distributive education

(d) health occupations education

(e) home economics education

(f) industrial arts education

(g) trade and industrial education

2 Identify the institutions in your community that are preparing individuals for the world of work. What are the objectives of these institutions? How do the objectives of the institution relate to the objectives to prepare individuals for work? How are these objectives met?

3 Identify the institutions in your community that are retraining individuals so that they can better perform their work, prepare for promotion, or prepare for another job. What are the objectives of these institutions? How do the objectives of the institution relate to the objectives to retrain individuals? How are these objectives met?

4 Identify *jobs* that are done in your community that require special knowledge, skills, and attitudes of workers performing them. Where did the individuals performing these jobs acquire the necessary knowledge, skills, and attitudes? Did they acquire them in the most economical way for themselves? for their employers? for the community? What is the rate of turnover in these jobs? Is the demand for individuals with these special skills being met satisfactorily?

5 Visit the employment-unemployment bureaus, public and private, in your community or in some community to which you have access. Talk with the manager to determine the extent of unemployment in the community, the reasons for unemployment, and what is being done in the community to improve the situation. Can you relate unemployment and the reasons for it to the objectives of institutions that are or could be preparing individuals for vocations? Is the community doing what it should or as much as it can to prepare individuals for work? Are institutions in the community that are responsible for the welfare of the community doing what they should be doing to prepare individuals for work?

6 Each of us has a responsibility to see that every citizen in our community has the right kind of opportunity for vocational development and preparation. Below is a list of institutions that might prepare individuals for vocational development. Visit the ones found in your community or in some community to which you have access. Talk with administrators, teachers, and students to determine the extent to which vocational development and preparation is made a part of the curriculum. What are the objectives of the institution? What are the objectives of each program designed to carry out the objectives of the institution? Do the objectives include vocational development and preparation? Ask to see the written objectives and the curricula designed to carry out the objectives, if they are available. Ask to see syllabi or outlines of specific activities that are undertaken to meet the objectives of vocational development and preparation. You might want to construct an instrument to use in collecting these data prior to your visit.

(a) nursery schools and kindergartens, public and private

(b) elementary schools (at all levels), public and private

(c) middle schools and high schools, public and private

(d) vocational-technical schools, secondary and postsecondary

(e) community and junior colleges, public and private

(f) four-year colleges and universities, public and private

(g) churches

(h) YMCA and YWCA

(i) labor organizations

(j) civic agencies, such as civic-sponsored craft groups

(k) governmental agencies

(l) private industrial and business firms and organizations

(m) hospitals

7 Using the following criteria, evaluate the vocational programs in your community to determine whether or not they are meeting their objectives:

(a) Has the community need for each of the vocational programs been based on local surveys?

(b) Are the students being adequately trained to gain employment on completion of the program, as evidenced by follow-up studies on graduates?

(c) Are the physical facilities and equipment adequate and up-to-date?

(d) Are the curricula constantly being revised?

(e) Do the students have access to and receive adequate counseling pertaining to vocational education?

(f) How do the students react to vocational training?

(g) Are the attitudes of the academic teachers toward vocational education positive?

(h) Are vocational teachers constantly upgrading their skills, methods, and techniques by attending workshops, seminars, college classes, or returning to the world of work for on-the-job experience?

8 If you have not read the books listed below or are not familiar with the taxonomy of educational objectives—cognitive, affective, psychomotor— check out the books from your library and study them carefully to learn how to structure educational objectives in this way. Try to involve yourself in a class or group discussion so that you can become familiar with such educational objectives. Try to involve yourself in structuring objectives into these categories. Define the terms: cognitive domain of learning, affective domain of learning, and psychomotor domain of learning.

B. S. Bloom et al, *Taxonomy of Educational Objectives, Handbook I: Cognitive Domain* (New York: David McKay Co., 1956).

D. R. Krathwohl et al, *Taxonomy of Educational Objectives, Handbook II: Affective Domain* (New York: David McKay Co., 1964).

Elizabeth J. Simpson, *The Classification of Educational Objectives, Psychomotor Domain* (Urbana: University of Illinois Press, 1966).

9 Examine the vocational objectives for some educational institution in your community or in a community to which you have access. If the objectives have not already been categorized into cognitive, affective, and psychomotor domains of learning, attempt to do so yourself. If they have already been so categorized, see if you agree with the way they have been structured. What is the purpose for structuring educational objectives into the three domains of learning?

10 Resolved that it should not be the objective of elementary (middle) schools to prepare individuals for vocational development. Rather, the objective of these levels of education should be to prepare individuals to reason and to appreciate learning so that they can advance to high levels of learning and cultural development. Debate this issue, supporting your position with documentary evidence from highly influential individuals— educators and laymen.

11 One of the leading groups in the United States that have influenced the thinking of educational leaders and laymen has been the Educational Policies Commission. This commission has been active for many years and is sponsored by the National Education Association of the United States and the American Association of School Administrators. The documents they write are published by the National Education Association. They have influenced the objectives of education primarily through these documents, which they publish when they see a need. They express their philosophy about what education is and what it should be, using input from a wide audience. Go to your library and check out some of these documents. Read, study, examine, and discuss with others the ideas expressed by the commission on the objectives of education. How does your philosophy and the philosophy of your school and community relate to the ideas expressed?

12 Interview a personnel manager in one or more industries in your community to determine:

(a) whether or not the industry has a systematic form of on-the-job training

(b) what items receive the most emphasis during the training period

(c) how extensive the training program is

(d) whether every new employee is required to participate in the training program

(e) whether new employees who have had related vocational training prior to employment receive higher wages than those without such related training

13 Survey a third-grade class (or some other elementary class) in your community to determine what career each of the students wants to enter and why. Report the results to the class.

References

1 Clark E. Moustakas and Minnie P. Berson, *The Nursery School and Child Care Center* (New York: Whiteside, Inc., 1955), p. 18.

2 *A Guide for Organizing and Developing a Kindergarten Program in Florida*, Revised Bulletin 53A (Tallahassee, Florida: State Department of Education, January 1955), p. 9.

3 Educational Policies Commission, *The Purposes of Education in American Democracy* (Washington, D.C.: National Education Association, 1938), p. 92.

4 Ibid, p. 90. (Reprinted with permission)

5 Oscar T. Jarvis and Marion J. Rice, *An Introduction to Teaching in the Elementary School* (Dubuque, Iowa: Wm. C. Brown Company Publishers, 1972), p. 49.

6 Nelson L. Bossing and Roscoe V. Cramer, *The Junior High School* (Boston: Houghton Mifflin Company, 1965), pp. 52–53.

7 E. Dale Davis, *Focus on Secondary Education: An Introduction to Principles and Practices* (Chicago: Scott, Foresman and Company, 1966), p. 56.

8 Sterling M. McMurrin, ed., *Functional Education for Disadvantaged Youth* (Lexington, Massachusetts: Lexington Books, D. C. Heath and Company, 1971), pp. 11–12, 35. (Reprinted by permission of the publisher)

9 John F. Thompson, *Foundations of Vocational Education, Social and Philosophical Concepts* (Englewood Cliffs, N.J.: Prentice-Hall, Inc., 1973), p. 243.

10 Kenneth B. Hoyt, Rupert N. Evans, Edward F. Mackin, Garth L. Mangum, *Career Education: What It Is and How to Do It*, Second Edition (Salt Lake City: Olympus Publishing Company, 1974), pp. 88–89.

11 J. Robert Warmbrod and Lloyd J. Phipps, *Review and Synthesis of Research in Agricultural Education* (Columbus: Center for Research and Leadership Development in Vocational and Technical Education, 1966), p. 2.

12 Roy W. Roberts, *Vocational and Practical Arts Education: History, Development, and Principles*, Third Edition (New York: Harper & Row Publishers, 1971), p. 158.

13 James T. Horner, "Agricultural Education from Kindergarten to Senior High School," in *The Agricultural Education Magazine*, Vol. 42, No. 11, May 1970, p. 286.

14 H. N. Hunsicker, "Transition in Agricultural Education," in *The Agricultural Education Magazine*, Vol. 45, No. 5, November 1972, p. 103.

15 Policies Commission for Business and Economic Education, *This We Believe about Business Education in the High School* (Washington, D.C.: National Business Education Association and St. Peter, Minnesota: Delta Pi Epsilon, 1961).

16 Policies Commission for Business and Economic Education, *This We Believe about Business Education in the Secondary School* (Washington, D.C.: National Business Education Association and St. Peter, Minnesota: Delta Pi Epsilon, 1970).

17 Distributive Education Publications Committee, *Distributive Education & You* (Washington, D.C.: American Vocational Association, March 1970), pp. 2–3.

18 Kenneth B. Haas, "The Origin and Early Development of Distributive Education—Parts I, II, and III, in *The Origin and Development of Distributive Education*, ed. Susan S. Schrumpf (Hightstown, N.J.: McGraw-Hill, Inc., 1972), p. 9.

19 William F. Sands, "The Health Care Crisis: Can Vocational Education Deliver?" in *American Vocational Journal*, Vol. 46, No. 9, December 1971, p. 24.

20 Rachel K. Winer, "Rung by Rung up the Health Career Ladder," in *American Vocational Journal*, Vol. 48, No. 7, October 1973, p. 47.

21 Ibid, pp. 48–49.

22 E. Joy Hill, "Kentucky Pacesetters for Health Careers Education," in *American Vocational Journal*, Vol. 47, No. 5, May 1972, p. 32.

23 Hester Chadderdon and Alyce M. Fanslow, *Review and Synthesis of Research in Home Economics Education* (Columbus: Center for Research and Leadership Development in Vocational and Technical Education, 1966), p. 2.

24 Hazel M. Hatcher and Lilla C. Halchin, *The Teaching of Home Economics*, Third Edition (Boston: Houghton Mifflin Company, 1973), pp. 48–49. (Reprinted by permission of the publisher)

25 Carolyn J. Girtman, "The Program, the Teacher, and FHA," in *American Vocational Journal*, Vol. 43, No. 3, March 1968, p. 26.

26 *Administration of Vocational Education—Rules and Regulations*, Vocational Education Bulletin No. 1, U.S. Office of Education (Washington, D.C.: U.S. Government Printing Office, 1966), p. 46.

27 Roy W. Roberts. See Ref. 12, pp. 281–282.

28 Ibid, p. 271.

29 *Federal Register,* Document 73–24594. U.S. Government Printing Office, filed November 20, 1973.

30 Industrial Arts Policy and Planning Committee, *A Guide to Improving Instruction in Industrial Arts* (Washington, D.C.: American Vocational Association, 1968), pp. 9–11.

31 Angelo C. Gillie, Sr., *Principles of Post-Secondary Vocational Education* (Columbus, Ohio: Charles E. Merrill Publishing Company, 1973), p. 15.

32 Rupert N. Evans, *Foundations of Vocational Education* (Columbus, Ohio: Charles E. Merrill Publishing Company, 1971), pp. 207–208.

Chapter 9

Organization

of Vocational

and Technical

Education

Introduction

□ *All countries have organizational mechanisms of some sort (usually ministries of education) for planning and administering the regular education system. But relatively few have any organized way of seeing to it that employing establishments throw their full weight into the task of training qualified personnel to meet their own needs and to promote the country's development. Nor is there usually any organized way of promoting desirable linkages between the employment system and the education system so that each will aid the other in their particular responsibilities for OET [occupational education and training]. Likewise lacking, in the usual case, are organized means for joint planning and for enlisting mutually reinforcing efforts of the education system and employing establishments and also of the numerous other institutions . . . [engaged in occupational education and training]. (1)*

These words point up a problem that is so complicated it staggers the imagination. Since its beginnings the United States has wrestled with the problem of establishing responsibility for education and of providing competent structures for carrying out that responsibility.

This organizational problem has affected vocational as well as academic education. Staley (2) has recommended the following structure for an occupational training organization: an autonomous, quasi-public entity with a governing body representing:

1 *employers, public and private*

2 *workers, through representatives of trade unions and professional associations*

3 *government agencies concerned, usually the labor and education ministries, but also perhaps other ministries or agencies concerned with manpower, planning, economic affairs, industry, commerce, or agriculture*

4 *special education and training institutions or development services ac-*
tively engaged in work related to the OTO's [occupational training or-
ganization] functions.

Getting such an organization established and functioning in our society is a difficult task, even though it would undoubtedly result in much
increased efficiency, by bringing together all the segments of society that
are involved in occupational education and training. Many national conferences have been held on this issue, resulting in various recommendations and resolutions to alleviate the problem. But then each participating agency has been left on its own to develop its programs as it sees fit,
with no established means of coordinating or comparing efforts. Burkett
(3) points up the hopelessness of comprehensive manpower planning at
the national level and suggests that the situation cries out for a coordinated effort that can be successful.

The purpose of this chapter is not to propose a national plan; rather,
it is to outline national efforts, as well as state and local organizational
efforts, for vocational and technical education in the United States. Although these efforts are undergoing constant reorganization, the changes
are slow enough and the need to understand them is great enough that we
must become well acquainted with these efforts. Knowing the influences
working on organizational structures is essential to understanding, evaluating, and improving the administrative leadership and thus the quality
of vocational and technical education. Examining "what is" provides a
basis for making improvements.

National Efforts

Although there is no one organizational structure at the national level
that is solely responsible for vocational and technical education, the
United States Office of Education in the Department of Health, Education
and Welfare of the executive branch of the federal government has traditionally been looked to for leadership in educational development, including vocational education and now career education. The Education
Amendments of 1972 established one new department to share this leadership, the National Institute of Education. Also, the United States Department of Labor provides national direction for vocational and technical
education. Although this department has long been involved with the support of vocational training, the Comprehensive Employment and Training
Act of 1973 (Public Law 93–203) extended its role. This Act (4) assigned
to the Secretary of Labor the responsibility of encouraging and supervising the development and administration, at state and local levels, of programs to provide job training and employment opportunities for economically disadvantaged, unemployed, and underemployed persons so that
they could compete for, secure, and hold jobs. But, for purposes of this
discussion, our primary attention will be on the Office of Education and
within that office the Bureau of Occupational & Adult Education, which is

in effect the operating branch of the federal government for vocational education.

There is a long list of other national organizations that are influential in the area of vocational and technical education. They include professional organizations such as the following: American Vocational Association, National Education Association, National Business Education Association, American Industrial Arts Association, American Home Economics Association, National Association for Practical Nurse Education and Service, American Occupational Therapy Association, Board of Certified Laboratory Assistants, Council of Dental Education, American Medical Association, American Registry of Radiologic Technologists, The Vocational Industrial Clubs of America, Inc., Future Business Leaders of America, Inc., Future Homemakers of America, Future Farmers of America, Distributive Education Clubs of America, Future Secretaries of America (National Secretaries Association; International), Office Education Association, Future Data Processors, National Association of Secondary School Principals, and National Science Foundation. Other agencies exerting influence nationally include such organizations as the AFL-CIO, Joint Council on Economic Education, American Association of Colleges for Teacher Education, National Council for the Accreditation of Teacher Education, National Congress of Parents and Teachers, National Association of Manufacturers, United States Chamber of Commerce, and National Retail Merchants Association. In addition there are many agencies from business and industry that are influential, and there are many agencies and commissions that grow out of or are affiliated with organizations already mentioned.

United States Office of Education

The Education Division of the Department of Health, Education and Welfare is composed of the United States Office of Education and the National Institute of Education. Inasmuch as the major responsibility for education has traditionally been left to the state governments, the influence of the United States Office of Education has been limited. It has traditionally acted as a clearinghouse for educational information, collecting statistics on the condition of education, disseminating the information to the school systems, and promoting efficient methods of teaching. But with the increase in federal legislation, in federal funding, and thus in the need for controls, the influence of the United States Office of Education has increased dramatically in the last two decades. It is now charged with administering the far-flung and multifaceted education programs funded by the United States government. But even so, particular care has been taken to avoid federal control of education; the historic tradition of vesting primary responsibility for education in local governments has been upheld.

As is the case for any organization, the organizational structure of the United States Office of Education is not static. Its structure changes as the educational needs of the nation change, as determined by Congress

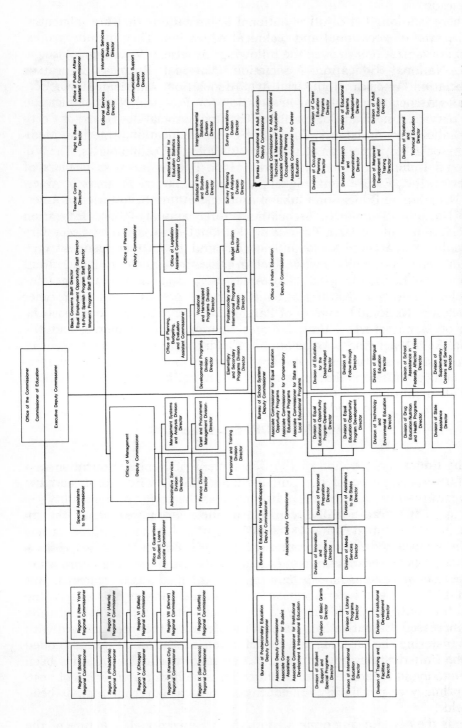

Figure 9.1 United States Office of Education. Source: Deputy Commissioner for Management, Education Division, Office of Education, Department of Health, Education and Welfare, June 1, 1974.

and the President. However, to understand the role of the federal government in vocational education, it is necessary to discuss the organization of this office. The office is headed by a commissioner of education. There are ten regional commissioners, one each for the nation's ten regions. The office has five main divisions: the Bureau of Postsecondary Education, Bureau of Education for the Handicapped, Bureau of School Systems, Office of Indian Education, and Bureau of Occupational & Adult Education, each headed by a deputy commissioner. In addition, there are administrative and planning offices as well as special interest areas that are not controlled by the five main divisions. The relationships among the various components of the Office of Education are shown in Figure 9.1.

Vocational and technical education is the responsibility of the Bureau of Occupational and Adult Education, which is headed by a deputy commissioner and three associate commissioners—one for adult, vocational, technical, and manpower education; one for occupational planning; and one for career education. The bureau is divided into seven divisions: Occupational Planning, Career Education, Research and Demonstration, Education Systems Development, Manpower Development and Training, Adult Education, and Vocational and Technical Education. The organizational structure is shown in Figure 9.2. It is this unit in the Office of Education that administers occupational, vocational, and career education programs for the United States Office of Education. The Division of Occupational Planning provides leadership and technical assistance in the development of occupational education programs. The Division of Career Education coordinates all career education programs within the Office of Education; it develops objectives and plans for the program, provides technical assistance, and administers assigned programs of grants and contracts. The Division of Vocational and Technical Education administers grants and contracts and provides technical assistance in these areas.

National Institute of Education

Created by the Education Amendments of 1972, the National Institute of Education was formed to carry out the following policies (5):

☐ *The Congress hereby declares it to be policy of the United States to provide to every person an equal opportunity to receive an education of high quality regardless of his race, color, religion, sex, national origin, or social class. Although the American educational system has pursued this objective, it has not yet attained that objective. Inequalities of opportunity to receive high quality education remain pronounced. To achieve quality will require far more dependable knowledge about the processes of learning and education than now exists or can be expected from present research and experimentation in this field. While the direction of the education system remains primarily the responsibility of State and local governments, the Federal Government has a clear responsibility to provide leadership in the conduct and support of scientific inquiry into the educational process.*

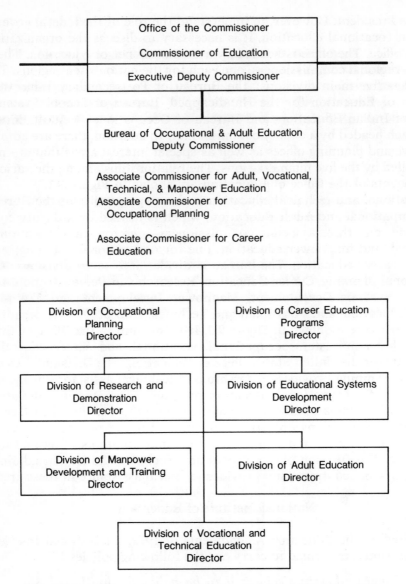

Figure 9.2 Bureau of Occupational and Adult Education, Office of Education. Source: Deputy Commissioner for Management, Education Division, Office of Education, Department of Health, Education and Welfare, June 1, 1974.

The Congress further declares it to be the policy of the United States to:

1 *help to solve or to alleviate the problems of, and promote the reform and renewal of American education*

2 *advance the practice of education, as an art, science, and profession*

3 *strengthen the scientific and technological foundation of education*

4 *build an effective educational research and development system*

The amendments further provide that the institute shall consist of a National Council of Educational Research and a director of the institute. The council is composed of fifteen members appointed by the President, by and with the advice and consent of the Senate, the director, and such other ex officio members who are officers of the United States as the President may designate. The council establishes general policies for and reviews the conduct of the institute. It advises the assistant secretary of the Education Division of the Department of Health, Education and Welfare and the director of the institute on the development of programs to be carried out. It also makes recommendations for strengthening educational research, improving methods of collecting and disseminating the findings of educational research. The director is authorized through the institute (6):

□ . . . *to conduct educational research; collect and disseminate the findings of educational research; train individuals in educational research; assist and foster such research, collection, dissemination, or training through grants, or technical assistance to, or jointly financed cooperative arrangements with, public or private organizations, institutions, agencies or individuals; promote the coordination of such research and research support within the Federal Government; and may construct or provide (by grant or otherwise) for such facilities as he determines may be required to accomplish such purposes. As used in this subsection, the term "educational research" includes research (basic and applied), planning, surveys, evaluations, investigations, experiments, developments, and demonstrations in the field of education (including career education).*

It is important to note that the wording of the amendments specifically includes career education as an area of concern by the institute. The act authorized to be appropriated $550 million to carry out the institute's functions during the period from July 1, 1972 through June 30, 1975.

The organizational structure of the National Institute of Education is shown in Figure 9.3. In addition to the director, deputy director, and the National Council on Educational Research, who report to the Assistant Secretary for Education, the chart shows organizational components falling into three categories: support, planning and evaluation, and program implementation (7). The *support* component is administered by an office of external relations, an office of public information, an adviser to the institute, and an office of administration. The *planning and evaluation* component includes an office of human rights and an office of planning and management. The *programs* component includes an office of research, office of programs, and office of dissemination and resources.

NIE conducts three basic activities:

1 *Research* NIE supports research concerning the relationship of education and work. These include studies of the changing economic and noneconomic returns to individuals and society from the investment in education, and policy analyses examining assumptions about the match

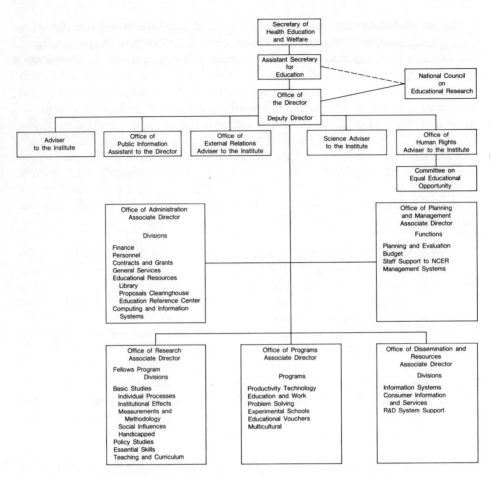

Figure 9.3 National Institute of Education. Source: Office of Public Information National Institute of Education, Department of Health, Education and Welfare, *NIE: Its History and Programs*, February 28, 1974, p. 13.

between educational experience and world of work experience. These studies assist students, parents, teachers, school boards, administrators and legislators in making the many decisions they face regarding the improvement of educational practice.

2 *Program development* Based on the findings of research and policy analyses, NIE supports design and development projects, from the pre-kindergarten to adult levels, to evaluate a range of suggested improvements. While ultimately intended for implementation within state and local educational settings, these developmental activities characteristically are too high risk or too expensive for states and localities to undertake. The outcomes generally will be programs and ideas which have proven themselves successful, but will from time to time include the finding that proposed solutions or improvements do not improve education.

3 *Dissemination* NIE has the mandate to improve educational practice by learning how best to assist states and localities in applying the results of R&D activities. NIE is developing a variety of ways to provide information on products from its successful R&D. On a limited scale it is providing appropriate technical assistance to help school districts, colleges and other institutions utilize career education products.

As a newly created branch of the federal government, the institute's operating role is not clearly defined. It is currently involved in research, development, and dissemination activities in all areas of education, including career education. However, its only contact with actual program implementation is through pilot tests or field tests of materials developed through institute-sponsored projects. Its future role might well be determined by the effect its current efforts have on developing activities.

Professional Organizations

There are a number of professional organizations that are concerned with promoting vocational education, its programs, research, and legislation. Many of the organizations, such as American Home Economics Association, National Vocational Guidance Association, and National Business Education Association, are concerned specifically with one field of vocational education. Two organizations which encompass all of the vocational areas are briefly described.

American Vocational Association The American Vocational Association, (AVA), is a national organization with state affiliates, composed primarily of teachers, supervisors, teacher educators, administrators, and counselors. Divisions have been established in these areas: Administration, Agriculture, Business and Office, Distributive, Guidance, Health Occupations, Home Economics, Industrial Arts, Manpower, New and Related Services, Technical, and Trade and Industrial. Special organizations are maintained for members in most of the divisions.

Officers of AVA include president, past president, vice presidents of the 12 divisions, and an executive director. The expansion of the organization to include vice presidents in twelve areas, as opposed to six a decade ago, is an indication of responsiveness to growth, changes resulting from legislation, and special needs relating to vocational education.

AVA promotes research through its various divisions and committees. It carries on a program of publication and provides leadership in promoting national legislation relating to vocational education. *American Vocational Journal*, published monthly, September through May, is the official organ of this organization which presently has a membership of over 55,000.

National Education Association The National Education Association (NEA), with state and local affiliate groups, is the nation's largest professional organization for teachers, supervisors, teacher educators, administrators, and counselors, and educational secretaries in all fields of education. NEA maintains numerous divisions, associations, councils, and commissions. Many of these have active organizations which hold local, state, and national meetings, publish journals, yearbooks, and other volumes of interest to their members. Like AVA, the NEA is actively involved in research, publication, and promotion of legislation relating to education. The headquarters of the organization, with over a million members, is in Washington, D.C.

Duplication of effort For practically every type of vocational and academic program, there is one or more national organizations that exert influence on that program. Such efforts may tend to strengthen programs, by virtue of analysis from different points of view, or they may tend to weaken programs, through lack of cohesion. Duplication and multiplicity of effort in national organizations is exemplified in business education, an area in which many national organizations exert an influence. Some effort is made to provide means for these organizations to work together, but for the most part they work independently and thus weaken the effect they might have if more unity were achieved. The National Business Education Association, probably the strongest national group working to improve all levels of business education, has some of its efforts duplicated by the Business and Office Education Division and the National Association of Teachers for Business and Office Education of the American Vocational Association as well as by the American Assembly of Collegiate Schools of Business.

State Efforts

The organization of vocational education at the state level is more unified than it is at the national level because the Vocational Education Act of 1963 required that each state have its own state plan. Even though the various state organizations are uniquely different, having a "State Plan," as specified by the Vocational Education Act of 1963 and subsequent amendments, tends to unify the various state influences.

In addition, it is much easier to influence individuals within the confines of a limited geographical area, such as a state, than it is to pull the various nationwide influences together.

Each state has an administrative unit to plan, organize, supervise, and administer education, including vocational education. Whereas the federal government's role has been largely advisory, fact finding, and information disseminating in nature, the state government's role has been much more administrative and supervisory. The state government supervises local programs closely and sets specific standards to which each local unit must adhere for approval. But as is true at the national level, the state-level organizational structure of vocational education is not static; it changes to meet changing needs within the state and to meet changes that are reflected in federal legislation.

There are significant differences in philosophies within the various states for the administration and control of vocational education. Wisconsin has a unique program that emphasizes vocational education at the postsecondary level, with little emphasis in the high schools. In Ohio, the State Division of Vocational Education has primary responsibility for secondary school programs, whereas postsecondary programs are under the direction of the State Board of Regents. California's program includes a well-developed community college system, which provides free, postsecondary vocational education within commuting distance of 90 percent of the State's residents. Colorado has a state board for vocational education and community colleges, which administers both secondary and postsecondary education.

The vocational and technical program in Mississippi provides educational experiences in both the secondary schools and postsecondary junior colleges. The program is administered by the State Board of Education—a pattern that is followed by many states. The organizational chart for the Vocational-Technical Division of the Mississippi State Department of Education is shown in Figure 9.4, as taken from the state plan. This chart indicates the state director of vocational-technical education to be the executive officer responsible for vocational education. He or she reports to the assistant state superintendent, who in turn reports to the state superintendent of education, whose responsibilities include vocational education as well as all phases of public education of less than baccalaureate-degree level. It should be noted that the state superintendent reports to the Mississippi State Board of Education. The state plan specifies (8):

☐ *The Mississippi State Board for Vocational Education is the sole agency responsible for the administration of the State Plan and for the supervision and the administration thereof by local educational agencies, and has the sole and all necessary power to cooperate with the U.S. Office of Education in the administration of vocational and technical education under the State Plan.*

The state plan also quotes a portion of the Mississippi Code of 1942, which specifies that the State Board of Education shall constitute the State Board for Vocational Education. Although there are some disadvantages to this organization, it does tend to facilitate action. As the executive officer of the State Board of Education, the state superintendent is responsible for the administration of the state's vocational education programs. The staff of the vocational division is also responsible to the State Board through the executive officer (9).

In Mississippi, the State Board is composed of three members: the state superintendent, the state attorney general, and the secretary of state. Each is elected to office by popular vote (10). The composition and method of acquiring members of state boards of education varies widely from state to state.

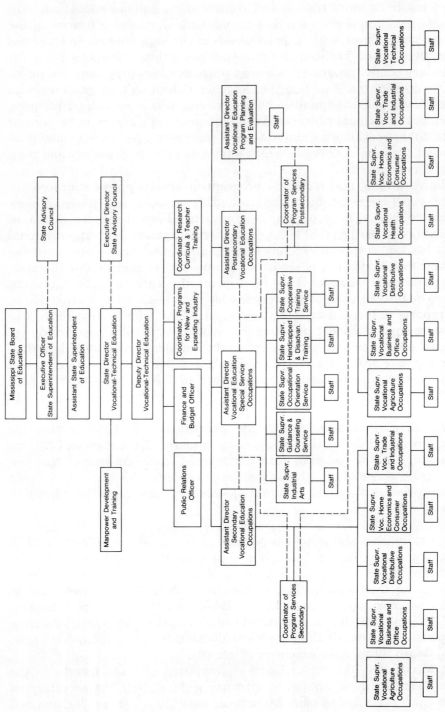

Figure 9.4 Organizational chart for vocational-technical education in Mississippi. Source: 1975 Mississippi State Plan for Vocational Education.

The Vocational Division of the Mississippi State Department of Education has four sub-units for administrative and supervisory purposes, each headed by an assistant director. The units are: Secondary Programs, Postsecondary Programs, Special Services, and Vocational Education Program Planning and Evaluation. The purpose of Secondary Programs is to administer and supervise the state's secondary vocational programs, which include components in Agriculture, Business and Office Occupations, Distributive Occupations, Home Economics and Consumer Occupations, and Trade and Industrial Occupations.

The Postsecondary Programs unit administers and supervises postsecondary vocational programs, including components in Agriculture, Business and Office Occupations, Distributive Occupations, Health Occupations, Home Economics and Consumer Occupations, Trade and Industrial Occupations, and Technical Occupations. The purpose of the Special Services unit is to administer and supervise Industrial Arts, Guidance and Counseling, Occupational Orientation, Handicapped and Disadvantaged Training, and the Cooperative Training Service. Each of these units provides consultative and technical assistance to local educational agencies in planning and carrying out programs. The fourth unit, Vocational Education Program Planning and Evaluation, has the responsibility of planning and evaluating programs. In addition, there is a Public Relations office, a Finance and Budget office, an office of Programs for New and Expanding Industry, and an office for Research, Curricula, and Teacher Training.

The relationship among the federally required state advisory council, the state superintendent of education, and the state director of vocational education is also illustrated in Figure 9.4. The Mississippi State Advisory Council is composed of fifteen members appointed by the governor. The Vocational Education Amendments of 1968 (11) require representation on such state advisory councils as follows: persons who are (a) familiar with vocational needs and problems of management and labor in the state; (b) from community and junior colleges and other institutions of higher education, area vocational schools, technical institutes, and postsecondary or adult education agencies; (c) familiar with, although not directly involved in, the administration of state and local vocational education programs; (d) familiar with programs of technical and vocational education, including programs in comprehensive secondary schools; (e) representative of local educational agencies and school boards; (f) representative of labor and vocational education agencies in the state, including representation from the Comprehensive Area Manpower Planning System of the state; (g) representative of school systems with large concentrations of academically, socially, economically, and culturally disadvantaged students; (h) knowledgeable or experienced with respect to the special educational needs of physically or mentally handicapped persons; and (i) representative of the general public, with knowledge of the poor and disadvantaged, who are not qualified for membership under any other category.

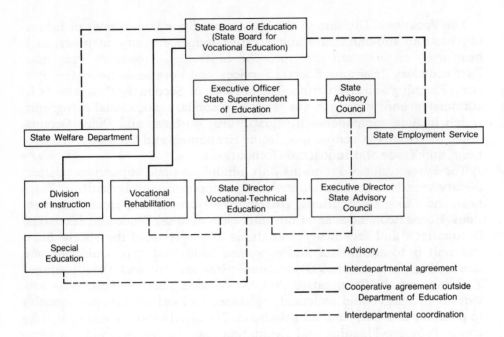

Figure 9.5 Relationships between the vocational division of the Mississippi State Department of Education and other state agencies. Source: 1975 Mississippi State Plan for Vocational Education.

The Amendments further require that the State Advisory Council (a) advise the State Board on the development of policy matters arising in the administration of the state plan; (b) evaluate vocational education programs, services, and activities assisted under this title and publish and distribute the results; and (c) prepare and submit an annual evaluation report of the effectiveness of vocational education programs, services, and activities, recommending any necessary changes.

An example of the relationship that might be required between the state administrative unit for vocational education and other agencies is illustrated in Figure 9.5. Cooperative agreements are maintained by the Division of Vocational Education of the Mississippi State Department of Education with the Mississippi Welfare Department and with the Mississippi Employment Service. The state plan calls for a liaison committee with representatives from both agencies and local institutions to provide a continuous discussion of information available and actions necessary to meet objectives. The agreement with the State Employment Service requires the State Board and local vocational agencies to (12):

1 *make available to the Mississippi State Employment Service information regarding training programs being planned in the public schools and junior colleges of the State*

2 *collaborate with the Mississippi State Employment service in determining needs for vocational and technical programs*

3 *cooperate with the Mississippi State Employment Service in providing counseling, testing, and placement service*

4 *provide lists, including occupational qualifications, of students having completed various vocational-technical programs to the Mississippi State Employment Service*

5 *provide lists of the schools and classes that are being conducted by the local educational agencies*

6 *provide Mississippi State Employment Service a list of vocational technical dropouts; qualifications at the time of termination will be included*

The Mississippi State Employment Service is required to (12):

1 *provide information regarding job opportunities in the communities and elsewhere to the State Board and local educational agencies*

2 *provide information regarding job requirements of occupations to the State Board and local educational agencies*

3 *cooperate with the State Board and local educational agencies in giving aptitude tests and other assessment instruments*

4 *cooperate with the State Board in conducting studies to collect information not otherwise available about jobs in fields of work for which vocational training is deemed to be practical*

5 *provide the State Board with information in regard to exceptional persons available for training*

6 *give special attention to counseling, testing, and placement services to school dropouts*

7 *assist in placement of students who have left or completed training*

Close coordination between the Mississippi Welfare Department and the Vocational Education Division of the State Department of Education assures that vocational education funds are used more effectively to train the disadvantaged. The Vocational Education Division also maintains working agreements with the state's institutions of higher education to see that there are adequate programs to prepare teachers and adequate facilities and personnel for curriculum research and development. The Vocational Division supervises these activities as well as vocational programs and activities at the local level.

Although the organizational charts for state-level vocational education administration do not show career education as a function of the Division

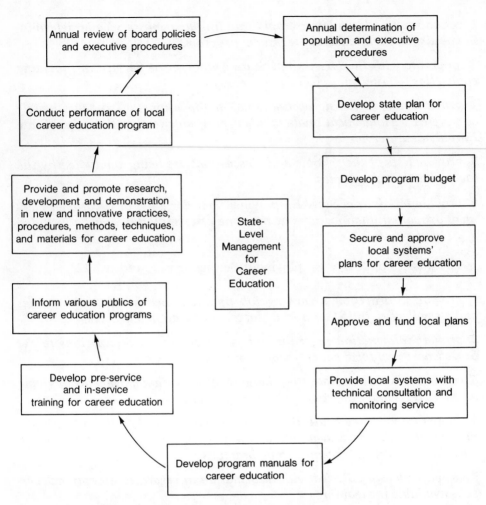

Figure 9.6 Cycle pattern of functions for state-level management of career education (14).

of Vocational-Technical Education, this unit of the State Department of Education has assumed the responsibility for administering career education for the state. The argument for this organizational structure is presented by Bottoms (13):

□ . . . *one important level of [the educational management] system is the state department of education. . . . there are elements of the state level management system that can make it possible for the concepts of career education to become operational in schools and in the lives of students.*

. . . the leadership for it must extend beyond vocational education to involve all segments of the educational community; however . . . the leadership thrust for career education within the state department of education . . . should be the vocational education division.

Figure 9.6 illustrates the cycle pattern of functions for state-level management of career education. This model, as conceived by Bottoms, depicts the evolving nature of the concept of career education. The Division of Vocational Education in the State Department of Education is visualized as the vehicle through which these changes are managed. Bottom's illustration clearly shows the relationship between the State Department and the local school system, where the goals and objectives of vocational and career education become realities.

Local Efforts

The organization of vocational education at the local level is influenced by its organizational counterparts at the state and national levels. The influence of the federal government is brought about primarily through legislation that affects the state organization, which in turn establishes guidelines and controls that affect local organization. Such influence over local units is effected by the federal and state governments' control of funds, which are issued on the basis of the local units' compliance with established guidelines.

It seems important at this point to define what is meant by local level. It might refer to a county-wide system of vocational education, a city-wide system, or even a combination city-county system. It might involve one school, a number of classes taught in a number of places in a city or county, or it might even occur within the physical facilities of the State Department of Education. With all these different possibilities, it seems most appropriate to think of local level as applying to those conditions where vocational education brings learner and teacher together in a single administrative system, even though a single administrative system might comprise two or more subsystems. A local-level system thus generally includes all programs that are administratively prepared as a local plan to be submitted for approval to the State Department of Education.

In the following pages, we will discuss local-level organization of vocational education in the public schools and consider the facilities used to carry out the programs. We will first discuss college preparatory school organization and facilities, then the comprehensive school and the vocational school.

Organization and Facilities
in College Preparatory Schools

In college preparatory schools, vocational teachers are likely to report to the school principal just as all other teachers do. There will not be a full-scale program of vocational education, but there might be selected programs designed to help the college-bound student. For example, typewriting is a skill that may prove valuable both in course preparation and as the source of part-time employment while the student is in college. The fact that it might help him or her earn a living later on is incidental. For the college preparatory school, the same kind of reasoning would apply to classes in home economics, industrial arts, and other vocational areas.

Career education exists in the college preparatory schools only as it applies to the college-bound student. Guidance and counseling are therefore designed to help students make choices for college entrance; little attention is given to ultimate career decisions. As a result, many students in the college preparatory school enter college with no conception of their future career.

As a result of this focus, facilities for vocational education in the college preparatory school are limited. There will probably be few schools that do not offer typewriting, home economics, or industrial arts. But the quality of the equipment will depend on the financial situation of the school and the interest and competence of the teacher.

Organization and
Facilities in Comprehensive Schools

Comprehensive schools are organized to meet the needs of both the college preparatory student and the vocational student. Vocational curricula theoretically receive as much attention as academic curricula, depending on the kinds of jobs that secondary-school graduates are being prepared to fill. The vocational program, as well as other programs, might be loosely organized under a *head*. Such organization provides vocational teachers a framework through which curricula can be developed by teachers in the particular vocational field; it also provides a structured arrangement for determining school objectives that are in agreement with student and community objectives. In large schools, where enrollment in several vocational areas requires more than one teacher in each area, there should be a head for each area as well as a head for the total vocational program. The head teacher reports to the principal, who in turn reports to the superintendent.

The layout of the up-to-date physical plant of the comprehensive Valdosta High School in Georgia is shown in Figure 9.7. A two-winged diamond-shaped plant designed to serve a comprehensive curriculum, the objectives of the school include preparing individuals for college or for work immediately following graduation. Although one diamond wing is primarily for academic courses and the other for vocational courses, the plant is actually designed so that subject matter areas are in the physical areas best suited to them. For example, note in Figure 9.7 that home making is located in the academic wing with science, math, social studies, foreign language, and English, whereas art and music are located in the vocational wing with business education, driver education, and trade and industrial education.

Each subject area in this "open" school takes up the equivalent space of one to five or six classrooms in a traditional school. Areas are designed to accommodate the latest equipment, materials, and teaching techniques. Facilities in each area are designed to accommodate large-group instruction (open space planning), small-group instruction, and individualized

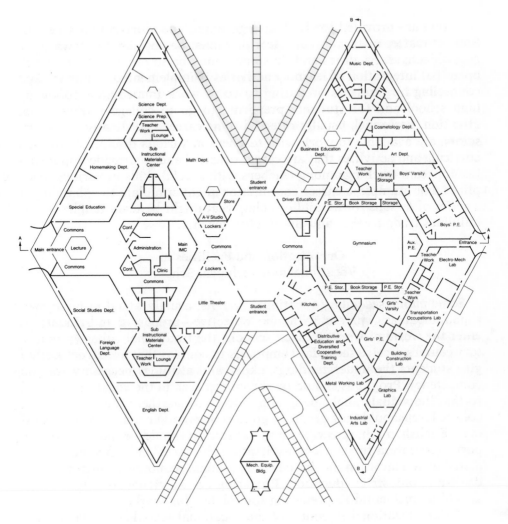

Figure 9.7 Physical plant of the Comprehensive High School, Valdosta, Georgia. Source: Superintendant of Schools, Valdosta, Georgia.

instruction. Students can work independently, and teachers can easily move from tutorial-type instruction to team teaching. Flexibility and adaptability are key characteristics of this plant.

The planners envisioned that individuals would be able to proceed at their own level of progress in their own area of interest and aptitude and at the same time have opportunities to interact with students in other areas of interest.

Career education in the comprehensive high school takes on a much broader meaning than is the case in the college preparatory school. It includes preparation for careers requiring college education and for careers not requiring a college education. The organizational structure of school personnel must thus be such that career counseling, guidance, and instruction are provided for both college-bound and work-bound students. Subject matter instruction and learning must be coordinated toward career objectives. Facilities and personnel must be so organized and developed that integration of learning activities is implemented. Guidance and counseling for students preparing to go to work immediately following high school and for students preparing to go to college receive equal attention. Personnel, usually referred to as career coordinators or counselors, are available to work with teachers in various disciplines to plan curricula and activities that are career oriented and to provide opportunities for team teaching among teachers with special skills in various disciplines. For example, a career coordinator might stimulate the planning of a series of lessons for a buildings class that might be team taught by the buildings trade teacher and the English teacher.

Organization and Facilities in Vocational and Technical Schools

Some public secondary vocational schools, usually found in large metropolitan areas, operate with one objective—preparing individuals to enter the world of work. In such schools, the traditional college preparatory courses receive secondary emphasis to courses that are structured to give students the understandings, skills, and attitudes necessary for job competency. Programs should be structured even in the vocational school so that individuals might be qualified to continue their education at the college level should they decide to go to college rather than to work. However, English, math, science, and social studies should be planned to support preparation for work in agriculture, business and office education, distributive education, health education, home economics education, and trade and industrial education. Preparing an individual to enter college should be incidental to preparing him or her for work.

The organizational structure of the vocational school is similar to that of the college preparatory school and the comprehensive school. Where there is more than one teacher in a vocational area, a head teacher should be designated. The head teacher usually reports to the school principal, who reports to the superintendent. The superintendent reports to the Board of Education, which reports to the people of the community being served by the school. The superintendent might be elected to the position or appointed, and he or she might or might not be a member of the Board of Education, which establishes policies under which schools operate. The Board is sometimes responsible to the people and so might be elected by popular vote. Or the Board might be appointed by a governing body of the community being served by the schools.

A school participating in federally funded programs is required to have an overall advisory committee of community leaders to help determine policy with respect to objectives, curricula, finances, and other matters. In addition, each occupational area is required to have a craft committee to advise teachers in planning, organizing, and conducting the program.

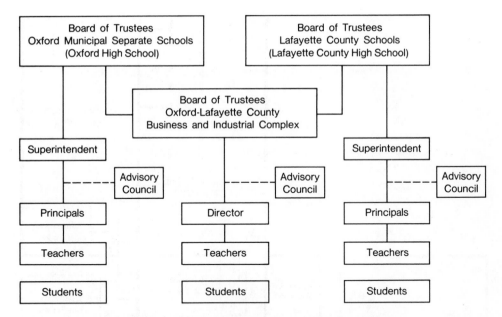

Figure 9.8 Vocational education in Lafayette County, Mississippi. Source: Adapted from the Local Plan for Vocational Education for the Oxford Municipal Separate School District and the Lafayette County School District.

Frequently, a vocational and technical secondary school serves one or more high schools. An example of such a school is the Oxford-Lafayette County Business and Industrial Complex located in Oxford, Mississippi. This school serves two high schools, each under separate administration. Figure 9.8 shows the relationships among the organizational structures of the three schools.

Oxford High School is governed by a Board of Trustees as part of the Oxford Municipal Separate School District in Lafayette County (so designated because it includes the geographical city limits of Oxford as well as some outlying areas of the county, which are administratively organized as part of the city schools). The Board is made up of five members, three of whom are appointed by the Oxford City Council and two of whom are elected by the registered voters in the outlying areas.

Lafayette County High School is governed by a Board of Trustees elected by the registered voters in the county on a rotating basis.

Oxford-Lafayette Business and Industrial Complex is governed by a Board of Trustees made up of six members, three from each of the two Boards of Trustees of the school systems being served.

Vocational students spend half of the school day at their parent high schools, taking general education courses on a traditional schedule of 50-minute periods. The other half of the student's school day is spent on a block schedule at the complex, preparing for work in a specific vocational

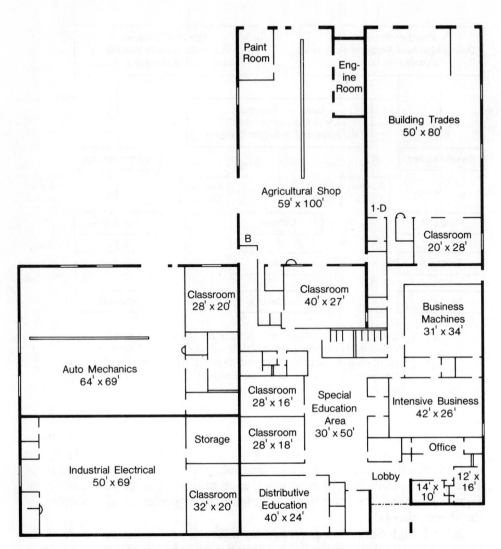

Figure 9.9 Floor plan for Houston Vocational Center,
Houston, Mississippi. Source: Superintendent of schools,
Houston Separate School District.

area. In addition, each of the parent schools being served by the complex
has vocational programs, some of which receive funds under the state
plan for vocational education. For example, distributive education, which
is reimbursed, is taught in Oxford High School rather than in the complex. Both parent schools also offer non-reimbursed secretarial courses.

Teachers in the Oxford-Lafayette County Business and Industrial Complex are responsible to the director who is responsible to the Board of
Trustees of the complex. The director has equal status with the principals
of the two parent schools. The principals report directly to their respective superintendents who report to their respective Boards of Education.

Three advisory councils are maintained; one for each of the two high schools and one for the Business and Industrial Complex. Members of the councils for the parent schools are appointed by the respective superintendent for an indefinite term. Members of the council for the complex are recommended by the director and appointed by the Board. They advise the schools on employment trends and needs in the community, make suggestions for improvement of vocational programs, and serve as public relations liaisons. They are also involved in preparing the local plan for vocational education. Each member on the advisory councils serves as a member of the craft (advisory) committee in his or her occupational area.

Facilities in vocational schools necessarily depend on the kinds of programs to be operated, the organization of these programs, and the availability of funds. Figure 9.9 illustrates plant facilities of vocational centers established to serve parent schools (as compared to Figure 9.7, which shows plant facilities of the vocational program in a comprehensive school). Such facilities must be designed to accommodate specific programs, but they must also be flexible enough to be adapted easily to other vocational uses.

The kinds of vocational programs to be found in vocational schools should be determined by the needs of the students and the community to be served. As an illustration, one would think that, in the primarily rural setting of Lafayette County, agricultural education would be a major program in the vocational complex. In the initial stages of planning, agricultural education was included. It remained in the planning until a survey was taken of students who would be using the facilities. Not one expressed an interest in vocational agricultural education, so the program was dropped from the curriculum before the facility was completed.

Summary

Organization of vocational and technical education for public educational institutions at the local level is affected by a number of factors generated at the national level, the state level, and the local level.

At the national level the most influential factor is the role the federal government assumes, a role that is expanding through increased funding of state and local vocational education programs. The administration of funds is primarily a responsibility of the United States Office of Education. Although the major activity of the federal government has traditionally been that of collecting and disseminating information, it is now supervising vocational activities and conducting research that affects local-level programs. Other national factors affecting vocational education are professional and nonprofessional organizations. Such organizations affect programs through policy statements and through activities such as making project grants.

At the state level the most influential factor is the role of the state government, operating through the State Department of Education and the State Board of Vocational Education. Political and social attitudes of the people of the state toward vocational education influence the organizational structure. Organization at the state level is much more unified than at the national level. Goals and objectives at the state level are more easily defined because of the smaller geographical area and the more homogeneous nature of the needs being served. Each state receiving vocational funds from the federal government is required to prepare a State Plan for Vocational Education under guidelines established by federal legislation.

At the local level the most influential factors are the needs of the people in the community being served and the willingness of the community to provide for those needs. The kinds of organizational structures are numerous and varied, but there is usually an elected or appointed Board of Education that establishes policy. This policy is administered by officials most often identified as superintendents, who are members or ex officio members of the board. Individual schools are administered by principals and/or directors. Vocational programs are found in comprehensive schools, which also provide programs to meet the needs of the college-bound student, and are increasingly located in vocational complexes adjacent to the comprehensive school or on a separate campus. Vocational high schools are found in large metropolitan areas; their primary objective is to prepare individuals for work immediately upon graduation. The vocational school is responsible for all phases of education and does not look to another school for general education. In the college preparatory school, vocational courses are secondary to the basic purpose of the curriculum, and are intended to aid the college-bound student.

Organization and facilities change as goals, objectives, curricula, and activities are reexamined and as new technological developments are made. Examples of school plants have been discussed in this chapter to illustrate the need for flexible learning areas that provide for a wide variety of activities, both academic and vocational. The plant, equipment, and supplies must be adequate to provide learning activities for students with varying abilities, interests, and aptitudes.

Activities

For review

1 What factors influence the organization of vocational and technical education at the national level? state level? local level?

2 Describe the organizational structure of vocational education at the national level.

3 What are the major functions of the United States Office of Education and the National Institute of Education?

4 In what bureau of the United States Office of Education is vocational and technical education located? Name the other bureaus. Name the seven divisions of the bureau in which vocational and technical education is located.

5 What federal legislation created the National Institute of Education?

6 Is vocational education more unified or less unified at the state level than it is at the national level? Explain.

7 Describe the organizational structure of vocational education at the state level.

8 What are the criteria set forth in the Vocational Education Amendments of 1968 for the composition of a State Advisory Council for Vocational education?

9 What are the responsibilities of a State Advisory Council as set forth in the Vocational Education Amendments of 1968?

10 What state agencies might be involved in vocational and technical education other than the State Department of Education?

11 Define the term *local level* with respect to the organization of vocational education.

For discussion

1 Discuss the need for and the problems involved in joint planning between the employment system and the educational system in organizing and actuating vocational and technical education in the United States.

2 Do labor organizations influence the organization of vocational education? Explain.

3 Discuss the feasibility of establishing a national agency responsible for developing a national program of vocational education, with goals, objectives, activities, and procedures for implementing the program throughout the United States. Who would make up this agency? How would it function? What would be its relationship with states and local-level programs? What would be the advantages of such an agency? the disadvantages? What kinds of problems would be encountered?

4 Compare the extent of the federal government's control over vocational education with that of the state government.

5 Discuss the advantages and disadvantages of providing vocational education in each of the following types of schools:
  (a) college preparatory school
  (b) comprehensive school
  (c) vocational school

For exploration

1 Study the constitution and by-laws of the American Vocational Association. Is the organization planned to provide the most effective leadership for your occupation? Are all segments of vocational education adequately represented? Is the association organized to bring about the most effective influence and leadership? How are offices determined? What are their duties and responsibilities? What projects and services are rendered to members? Be prepared to report on the organizational structure to the class. Invite an active leader in the American Vocational Association to talk to your class about the role of the association in vocational education.

2 Study the constitution and by-laws of your state's vocational association; follow the same procedures that are called for in Item 1 above.

3 Study the constitution and by-laws of the national organization for teachers in your occupational speciality. Follow the same procedures for this organization that are called for in Item 1.

4 Study the constitution and by-laws of the state organization for teachers in your occupational specialty. Is there more than one? Follow the same procedures for this organization that are called for in Item 1.

5 Study the organization of vocational education at the state level in your state. How does it compare with the organization discussed in this chapter? What is the make-up of your State Board of Vocational Education? How are members placed in office? Are they elected? appointed? Be prepared to present your findings to the class. Invite a state vocational leader to talk with your class about the role of the state in vocational education.

6 Study the organization of vocational education in your community. How does it compare with the organizational structures discussed in this chapter? What is the make-up of the governing body of vocational education in your community? How are members placed in office? Are they elected? appointed? Be prepared to present your findings to the class. Invite a local leader to talk with your class about the organization of vocational education in your community.

7 How should the physical facilities needed to carry out the objectives of vocational education in a local system be determined? Research the literature in your college library on physical facilities for vocational education. Study physical plants (buildings and grounds) and equipment, furniture, teaching materials, and so on, required in your occupational specialty. If possible, visit one or more vocational facilities. Talk with administrators and teachers. What do they think is good about their facilities? What is bad? Why? Compare what you see and hear with what you find in the literature. How do you account for differences?

8 Explore the advantages and disadvantages of having school officials (superintendents and members of Boards of Education) elected and appointed. Take a position and be prepared to defend this position in class. Invite an official who is elected and one who is appointed to come to the class to discuss how they feel about this issue.

9 Invite a vocational education official to come to the class to discuss the purposes, similarities, and differences between an advisory council and a craft committee.

10 Write to the Commissioner of Education of the United States Office of Education for an updated organizational chart showing the organizational structure of vocational education at the national level. Compare the updated chart(s) with the charts in this chapter. Be prepared to present and to discuss the changes in class.

References

1 Eugene Staley, *Planning Occupational Education and Training for Development* (New York: Praeger Publishers, 1971), p. 152.

2 Ibid, p. 153.

3 Lowell A. Burkett, "It's Impossible, Period," in *American Vocational Journal*, Vol. 46, No. 3, March 1971, pp. 25–27.

4 "Comprehensive Employment and Training Act of 1973," Public Law 93–203, *United States Statutes at Large*, 1973, Vol. 87 (Washington: Government Printing Office, 1974).

5 "Education Amendments of 1972," Public Law 92–318, Section 405, June 23, 1972, United States Congress, pp. 93–94.

6 Ibid, p. 95.

7 Office of Public Information, National Institute of Education, *NIE: Its History and Programs* (Washington, D.C.: Department of Health, Education and Welfare, United States Government, 1974).

8 *1975 Mississippi State Plan for Vocational Education* (Jackson, Mississippi: Mississippi State Department of Education, 1974), Part I, p. 1.

9 Ibid, pp. 1–2.

10 Ibid, p. 2.

11 "Vocational Education Amendments of 1968," Public Law 90–576, Section 104(b)(1), United States Congress (Washington: Government Printing Office, 1968).

12 *1975 Mississippi State Plan.* See Ref. 10, Part II, pp. 10–11.

13 Gene Bottoms, "State Level Management for Career Education," in *American Vocational Journal*, Vol. 47, No. 3, March 1972, p. 89.

14 Ibid, p. 90.

Chapter 10

Curriculum

Structure and Strategy

in

Vocational Education

Introduction

The curriculum, originally conceived as consisting of a series of courses leading toward a definite goal or objective, should be regarded as all of the educational experiences that an individual encounters under the direction of the school. The vocational component of the curriculum is a body of prescribed educational experiences under school supervision designed to prepare the individual for a role in society and to qualify him or her for a trade or profession.

Providing an adequate curriculum is the most important function of the school system. Numerous factors affect the curriculum, including the administrative policies of the school, philosophy of the school, teacher competence, school equipment and facilities, findings of educational research, instructional materials, school personnel policies, parent-teacher relationships, federal, state, and local laws, community culture and environment, socioeconomic trends, and public opinion and support.

Approaches to
Curriculum Development

A variety of approaches have been used in curriculum development, including (a) *Activity or Job Analysis Approach*, which determines needed skills for adult use; (b) *Adult Needs Approach*, which prepares the learner for adult life; (c) *Student Needs Approach*, which attempts to satisfy essential needs of individuals; (d) *Creative Values Approach*, which encourages each individual to develop latent abilities; (e) *Current Practices Approach*, which surveys the best practices in present curricula and incorporates them into the new curriculum; (f) *Educational Shortages Approach*, which readjusts the curriculum if students do not reach desired standards; and (g) *Interest Studies Approach,* which takes its direction from analysis of the interests of individuals and groups.

Teske Program Planning Model

Dr. Philip R. Teske, vocational agriculture teacher educator, and U.S. Office of Education vocational program planning specialist and research advisor, developed a comprehensive model for curriculum design that has been successfully used in vocational education. The model, shown in Figure 10.1, is a comprehensive one that is well adapted for use in planning a total curriculum or any one or a combination of its individual components. The Teske model illustrates a sound approach toward systematic development, implementation, and revision of vocational curricula.

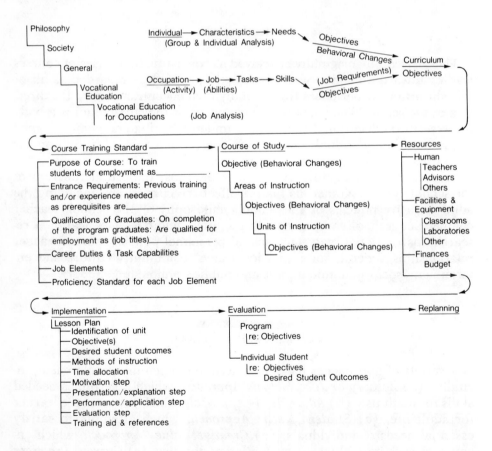

Figure 10.1 Program planning flow chart (1).

NOBELS- (national studies)
new office business education learning systems
-1970-71- identified office occupations

Foundations of
Curriculum Development

needs assesment

The aims and objectives are the most important factors in the school program because all other factors (equipment, materials, methods, and so on) depend on the teachers' beliefs regarding what should be done. Tentative aims should be determined early in the process of curriculum development because they (a) locate the ends toward which effort should be directed; (b) act as guiding principles throughout a course of action; (c) serve as criteria for the selection of materials to be presented to students; and (d) serve as standards by which the outcomes of instruction may be finally evaluated.

The selection, organization, and presentation of subject matter should follow a psychological order; that is, activities, experiences, and materials should be planned and then taught at the time when the need for their use is most apparent. Among the criteria for selection of subject matter are the following: 1. Subject matter should be related to the student's interests. 2. It should make a definite contribution to the student's objectives. 3. It should give the learner that development which is most helpful in making decisions and in meeting and controlling life situations. 4. It should be assembled primarily for the needs of the learner, not according to content and boundaries of existing subject matters.

A thorough study of the curriculum should involve the following:

1 philosophy of the school

2 objectives of the program

3 relation of curriculum to community and occupational life

4 characteristics, growth and development of target population

5 learning theory

6 student-teacher planning

7 student-teacher relationships

8 articulation among the divisions of the school system, home, community, industry, professions, and higher education

9 organization, time, schedule, grade allocation or level

10 general scope and sequence of the curriculum

11 content, activities, and experiences

12 sample units, modules and operation sheets

13 methods, forms, records, classroom management

14 instructional materials, including equipment, supplies, and multimedia

15 building facilities necessary to carry out curriculum objectives

16 plans for evaluating and testing

17 materials for students and teachers

Principles of
Curriculum Construction

Traditionally, the following procedures have been used in curriculum development:

1 Consult with students, parents, teachers, and the school guidance counselor in order to determine the interests, needs, and abilities of the students

2 Conduct job analyses to determine

(a) number and type of jobs available in employment area

(b) necessity for, amount, and type of training

(c) employment conditions

(d) additional training necessary for advancement

*3 Conduct surveys to determine

(a) probable number of students who will be enrolled in the program, in relation to community size

(b) probable number of jobs that can be filled each year

(c) employment trends in area for which training is planned _(local community)_

(d) pupil mobility

4 Set up advisory committee to work cooperatively with school administration and vocational teachers in building an effective and realistic program; this advisory committee should include

(a) employers

(b) outside curriculum specialist

(c) nonbusiness representative

5 Include in the content of the curriculum the following elements

(a) technical job information

(b) vocational skills

(c) occupational intelligence

(d) integration of job information, job skills, and occupational intelligence to complete the job preparation and make the student a finished worker

(e) development of attitudes, appreciations, and personality

6 "Sell" the proposed program to ensure

(a) a favorable attitude by the administration, faculty, parents, and students

(b) the ability of the school to support the program in terms of equipment and teaching personnel

7 Make decisions concerning

(a) selection of students—based on interest, aptitude, and ability

(b) credit or recognition for satisfactory completion of course

(c) standards of achievement

(d) length of the course

(e) transfer of credit should student be unfitted for such work

(f) type of work experience—simulated, directed, cooperative, or otherwise

(g) the portion of the total program to be taught by the laboratory method and the portion to be mastered by outside study

(h) the method of instruction—individual, class, or both

(i) the method of learning—"learning by doing" or discussion, question-answer method

8 Draw up guides for evaluating effectiveness of program, looking especially at

(a) achievement (accomplishment of changed behavior) versus objectives

(b) relevance of subject matter

(c) effectiveness of teaching methods

9 Provide for study and revision through

(a) occupational surveys

(b) changed social and economic conditions

(c) follow-up studies of students placed

(d) research, both formal and informal

(e) discovery of new and relevant resource materials

(f) periodic check-up on all facets of program

Modern Curriculum
Design Using Systems Approach

A systems approach to curriculum development is a rational, problem-solving method of analyzing the educational process and making it more

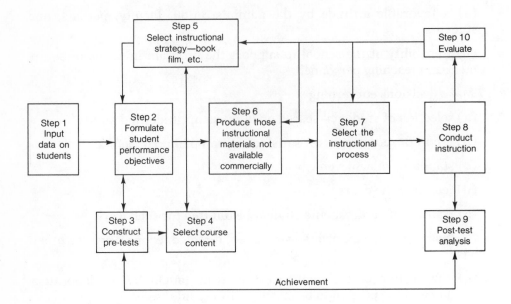

Figure 10.2   A systems approach to curriculum design: Strategic areas.

effective. The system is this process taken as a whole, incorporating all of its aspects, including the students, teachers, curriculum content, instructional materials, instructional strategy, physical environment, and evaluation of instructional objectives.

Educational effectiveness is defined in terms of desired changes in student behavior, and it is tested accordingly. Implicit in this definition of effectiveness is the understanding that these changes will be achieved within the context of minimal cost and feasible allocation of resources without imposing unacceptable limitations on any other elements within the total system. Systems analysis attempts to increase educational effectiveness by clarifying educational objectives with great precision and then by redesigning the entire educational process in order to ensure student achievement of these objectives. Both the student and the teacher know exactly what is expected on completion of an instructional unit. General statements of purpose become operational only when they are specified in terms of behavioral changes in skills, knowledge, attitudes, and values on the part of the student, as shown in Figure 10.2.

Flow-Chart Explanation

Step 1   Gather input data on students   Exactly what is known about the population of students for whom this curriculum will be developed? New tests will be developed to supplement the existing information provided by currently standardized tests and school records. Results of these tests will enable the project committee to establish more accurately the level of skill development, knowledge, and attitudes that each student will bring to the classroom. A full-time school psychologist will assist the committee in acquiring relevant information about these students and in handling special problems as they arise.

Step 2   Formulate student performance objectives All course, unit, and lesson objectives will be stated in terms of student performance. Students will know exactly what is expected of them and how they will be evaluated. The objectives are concerned with skill development in reading, writing, listening, speaking, and viewing; and with knowledge of the concepts developed in five thematic units—self-identify, the family, the family of man, the hero, and the future.

Step 3   Construct pre-tests Each student will be pretested to determine to what degree he or she has already mastered the unit objectives. The results of each pre-test will enable the teacher to diagnose learning requirements and to prescribe the proper learning packet.

Step 4   Select course content Course content will be selected only after the objectives have been determined and on the basis of the contribution it will make toward helping the student achieve the stated objectives.

Step 5   Select the instructional strategy Once the content has been chosen, the media considered most suitable for its presentation will be selected, to include printed materials, films, audiotape, filmstrips, and other audiovisual media.

Step 6   Produce those instructional materials not available commercially Although a great variety of instructional materials are available commercially, many cannot match specific teaching objectives. Therefore, a media production and duplication center should be established locally to help develop the kinds of materials necessary to ensure achievement of the objectives.

Step 7   Select the instructional process After the objectives, content, and media have been chosen, the instructional process thought to be most effective will be determined. This learning environment includes large-group instruction, small-group interaction, independent research, or individualized instruction.

Step 8   Conduct instruction As the function of the teacher in this curriculum differs from that of his or her more conventional role as dispenser of information, there will be little "talk and chalk." The new function of the teacher will be to diagnose learning problems, to prescribe the best learning sequences, to conduct small-group discussions and train the students to engage independently in similar discussions, and to assist via individual conferences.

Step 9   Analyze post-test On completion of the instructional units and after consultation with the teacher, the student will be tested. If there is a significant gain between the pre- and post-test scores, the student will then go to the next learning sequence.

Step 10   Evaluate Every phase of the instructional process will be constantly evaluated so that more effective procedures and strategies can be developed. This ongoing evaluation is the key element in the entire process. It will be performed in conjunction with leading consultants in the field and will provide the necessary data to revise the course, unit, and lesson objectives. The students who participate in the pilot program will be involved throughout the entire evaluation process by means of interviews, attitude surveys, and questionnaires.

Models for Curriculum Design

One of the major problems confronting vocational educators is that of developing and maintaining curricula that are attuned to the rapid social and technological changes in society. Since the early 1960s, the rate of change has been accelerating. Thus, maintaining a relevant curriculum is a continuing task for vocational educators at all levels. Techniques, content, and methods that have served satisfactorily in the past are not adequate to present and emerging needs.

Each generation has debated the question of what should be taught in the schools. The following discussion reviews some of the basic characteristics of curriculum models as they have been practiced.

Subject-Centered Curriculum

A traditional organizational pattern that has been widely used at the secondary level separates students into two or three separate tracks—college-bound, general, vocational—an organizational pattern that has tended to penalize all students. The college-bound students are directed toward those courses that will enhance their performance on standardized tests, such as college entrance exams, and in college courses. However, there is little opportunity for them to acquire entry-level employment skills or to learn about the business and industrial community and how it functions. In contrast, students enrolled in the vocational track develop employment skills, but they have limited opportunity to develop basic competencies needed in present-day society or to enroll in college preparatory courses that would allow them a later option for college training. Students in the general programs often graduate without occupational preparation or specific plans for the future.

The most common organization of content within the traditional curriculum is the isolated-subject, a curriculum in which individual subjects are stressed. Consideration is given to the vertical arrangement of courses, but little attention is given to horizontal relationships of courses offered during a particular year or semester.

Core Curriculum   *freshman year*

Traditionally, curricular offerings at the high school and college level have been divided into those courses required of all students, those required of some students, and those electives required of no students. The group of separate subjects required of all students is commonly known as the core. Establishing a common core that is required of all students is common practice in high schools and colleges. Generally, vocational education subjects are not included as part of the common core required of all students, but are treated as electives.

Other types of core curricula emphasize the separate subjects but provide for informal and formal correlations among the subjects around a theme. Alberty, in his discussion of the six types of core curricula, suggested that the Type V core provides the most promising curriculum design for transforming general education in the high school into a program suited to the challenging times in which we live (2).

The Type V core, known as the adolescent needs or problems core, is concerned with treating broad categories covering areas in which students are likely to encounter problems. The content of the Type V core is not a fusion of two or more subjects; rather, it consists of materials from whatever fields have a bearing on the solution of student problems. Thus, fields such as vocational education, which have heretofore not been regarded as part of general education, are included in the development of appropriate teaching-learning units. This organizational pattern makes use of large blocks of time and encourages the use of problem-solving techniques and decision-making skills in attacking problems (3).

Cluster-Based Curriculum

Through the years vocational education has tended to be organized around a single-occupation concept. That is, within a given vocational area, a student would select one occupation and follow a planned program in preparation for it. Today we live in an age that is characterized by mobility and the changing nature of jobs. Persons who are prepared with a broad base of skills that apply to more than one occupation tend to have more flexibility in adapting to the needs of the labor market. Thus, the cluster concept evolved as an alternative to the single-occupation concept.

The cluster concept is based on the premise that certain occupations have common learning and skill requirements and that students who have mastered these skills have more employment options. There are critics, however, who point out that such an approach may not develop the depth required for specialized job performance in single occupations.

During the 1960s, several projects were funded by the U.S. Office of Education in which clusters were identified in areas such as building trades, child care, mechanical technology, merchandising, and office occupations. In the project, "Identification of Task and Knowledge Clusters Associated with Performance of Major Types of Building Trades Work," ten trades were selected for study: bricklaying, carpentry, cement finishing, electrical work, iron work, painting, plastering, plumbing, roofing, and sheet metal. From the analysis of data, seven clusters of knowledge widely used in the ten building trades were identified: construction types, methods, and materials; tools and machines; mathematics; science; communication; safety; and worker welfare. Specific skills and knowledge were identified in each cluster (4).

In a project at the University of South Florida under the direction of Calhoun, twelve units of instruction were found to be common to the functional aspects of business and office education: computational skills, filing, grooming, human relations, keeping records, mail handling, office machines, problem-solving, processing forms, proofreading, telephone, and typewriting (5).

(not included) Organic Curriculum

In the late 1960s, Morgan and Bushnell proposed a curriculum design that would lead to options permitting the maximum self-actualization of each individual. Students leaving school either before or following graduation would have useful tools for employment. For example, a student might enter college and pursue a professional degree program; he or she might enter a community college or technical school for advanced occupa-

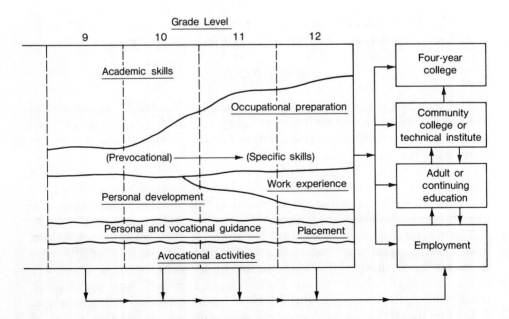

Figure 10.3 Organic curriculum options (6).

tional training. The student would have entry-level skills, which would permit access to the labor market, or he or she might continue training through adult education.

Figure 10.3 illustrates the options available in an organic curriculum (6). A key feature in the organic curriculum is that the student is able to decide which option to take after graduation instead of three or four years before. The organization of this curriculum design was based on a systems concept, hence the name "organic," or systemic.

The first step in implementing the organic curriculum model is to identify the behavioral requirements needed for entry into the several postsecondary options. The next step is the construction of a high school program that will provide students with the skills and knowledge needed to attain these objectives.

The following objectives are characteristic of an organic curriculum (7):

1 *emphasize the articulation between academic and vocational learning for the purpose of fusing the two programs; employing vocational preparation as the principal vehicle, the inculcation of basic learning skill could be made more palatable to many students who otherwise would have difficulty seeing the value of a general education*

2 *expose the student to an understanding of the "real world" through a series of experiences which capitalize on the universal desire of youth to investigate for himself; abstract, verbal principles would be acquired through nonverbal stimuli, such as seeing, feeling, manipulating, and even smelling*

3 *develop a core of generalizable skills related to a cluster of occupations rather than just those related to one specialized occupation*

4 *orient students to the attitudes and habits which go with successful job performance*

5 *provide a background for the prospective worker by helping him to understand how he fits within the economic and civic institutions of our country*

6 *make students aware that learning is life oriented and need not, indeed must not, stop with their exit from formal education*

7 *help students cope with a changing labor market through developing problem-solving ability and career strategies which can lead to an adequate level of income and responsibility*

8 *create within the student a sense of self reliance and awareness which leads him to seek out appropriate careers with realistic aspiration levels*

The financial costs of such a curriculum discouraged all but the most enthusiastic supporters. Nevertheless, the organic curriculum became a forerunner of current career education concepts.

Competency-Based Curriculum

—task performed at a specific standard

One of the more recent trends in vocational education at all levels is competency-based instruction. A competency-based program is one that specifies the desired objectives or competencies in an explicit form, identifies the criteria to be applied in assessing the learner's competencies, and holds the learner accountable for meeting these objectives. Such a program, however, must be based on two major technologies that only recently became available to education. The first of these is a systems design that permits the employment of a sophisticated management schema. Only through such a management plan can the program really be controlled, evaluated, and renewed. The second technology is the modularization of the instructional program. The individualization of the program has been made possible through the development of learning modules whose use permits self-pacing by students and instructors.

Traditionally the competencies needed for employment have been defined ambiguously. An examination of curriculum and courses of study at the high school, technical school, junior college, and college/university reveals that indicators of expectancies are stated in terms of required courses and time spent in them, such as one year of cosmetology, three quarters of shorthand, one year of horticulture. In competency-based education programs, the demonstration of competencies replaces course "passes" and specific amounts of time spent in class as indicators of subject mastery. In other words, in a traditional program, the time is held constant and the achievement varies. In competency-based programs, the time varies and the competencies are more nearly constant.

The absence of clearly defined expected outcomes hampers the instructional process. Even when sufficient time is provided, the lack of specific criteria makes it difficult to measure whether the programs (courses) have resulted in desired outcomes.

Two conditions must be met if competency-based programs are to be implemented: (a) identification of specific competencies and (b) procedures for assessing competencies in terms of appropriate criteria.

The systems-oriented curriculum-instruction design process can be construed as a series of functions that must be performed to achieve the objectives of the subsystem. Each function includes identifiable processes and products. The functions are:

1 specification of assumptions, tasks, goals and objectives

2 generation and selection of objective criteria

3 identification and design of assessment strategies

4 specification of instructional philosophy

5 development of instructional strategies

6 selection and/or development of instructional resources

7 development of feedback mechanisms

Individualized Instruction *(part of competency-based curriculum)*

Contemporary curriculum designs are characterized by a trend toward learning that is student centered rather than teacher centered. Objectives, which are based on task analysis, communicate the anticipated outcomes to the learner. The emphasis in instructional programs has shifted away from concern for the group norm toward concern for the individual. Individualized instruction thus requires that vocational educators make decisions that are relevant to each student.

Basically, a curriculum model for individualized instruction includes the following elements:

1 selection and sequencing of instructional tasks and objectives

2 development and/or selection of instructional materials and activities needed for teaching each objective, or for achieving each objective

3 evaluation for placing each student at the appropriate point in the curriculum

4 plan for developing individualized programs of study

5 procedure for evaluating and monitoring individual progress

The term *individualized instruction* is frequently used in education and has numerous interpretations. It is characterized by at least three levels of sophistication, thus allowing considerable flexibility in designing programs.

■ *Level one—Self-paced* The simplest form of individualization to implement is one in which students are expected to acquire the same skills and knowledge with the same material, but the rate or pace at which each student progresses through the material varies.

■ *Level two—Alternate modes* The next level of individualization consists of providing more than one instructional mode for acquiring each competency. For example, this level involves the use of a variety of instructional modes for presenting the same concepts—tapes (auditory), sound-slides or filmstrips (auditory-visual), print (visual), and so on.

In the initial stage the teacher usually recommends the mode that each student should follow, based on observation and knowledge of the student's ability and learning style. In the next stage, two or three alternate modes are identified, and the student is allowed to choose the one he or she wishes to use. The final stage in level two (same competencies for all students, but different routes and rates) permits students to determine on their own the instructional mode best suited to their individual styles of learning.

■ *Level three—Independent learning* One of the most important goals in education is to help each student acquire the competencies necessary to become an independent learner, one who can assume personal responsibility for learning. If the teaching-learning process is teacher-centered, if students are limited to what the teacher explains or demonstrates, if students never learn "how to learn" or how to become independent learners, then students are severely handicapped when they leave school. The changing nature of jobs makes it imperative that students know how and where to acquire necessary new skills, they must not be limited by what the instructor knows or presents in the classroom.

After leading the student through the first two stages of individualization, the teacher is now ready to introduce level three, in which the learner selects the competencies to be acquired, the instructional modes to be used, and determines the length of time to be devoted to each.

There are, of course, many basic competencies that all students must master and which the student cannot elect to omit. However, at the application level, students who demonstrate sufficient maturity can embark on independent learning.

Open-Access Curriculum

In the early 1970s, a number of key ideas triggered an interest among educators in what has become known as the *open school*. These ideas stemmed generally from a realization that change had created a wide gap between the theory and practice of curriculum design. The bases for educational reform, founded in social, philosophic, economic, and psychological developments of the times, have been discussed elsewhere in this text. New knowledge served as a basis for questioning old practices and served to establish new assumptions about the role of education. The volume of new knowledge brought with it a realization of the impossibility of education's "being all things to all people." The possibility of attacking any discipline from a variety of entry points gained credibility when it became apparent that pupils could not only learn things out of sequence but they could move at a faster pace and increase their apparent capacity for knowledge in the process. The publication of Bruner's *The Process of Education* (8) stimulated a reconsideration of the *structures* of knowledge in all fields and raised serious questions regarding previously held assumptions concerning curriculum scope-and-sequence patterns. The creativity movement paved the way for acceptance of the idea that virtually anything may be taught, on some level, to children of any age. Knowledge and learning viewed from this perspective emphasized the need for building within each learner a competence in "learning to learn" and extended relearning throughout a lifetime of encounters with relativistic, changing "truth."

The open school, as a form of curriculum design, represents an innovative approach to making education serve the learner. Although in operation, at this point, in a relatively few schools, it possesses potential for wider use as problems connected with its implementation are solved. The open school is characterized by:

1 an assumption that all students will succeed if the formula for success is established for each student individually

2 creation of large clusters of content as a substitute for proliferation of lesser courses

3 multiple entry points to each large body of content, beginning with the outer (exploratory) area and proceeding toward the more certain knowledge at the center

4 open-exit, which allows students who leave school to make use of job-entry skills as early as the eighth or ninth grade level

5 de-emphasis of *teaching* and emphasis on *learning*—students in direct charge of their time for up to half their schedule, supported by teacher-counselors

6 in-depth learning in the form of personalized intensive study in large blocks of time—continuity scheduling as opposed to repetitive, sequential, short-term exposure

7 assignment of large groups of students (150–200) to teams or "mini-schools" for large blocks of time to permit discretionary grouping and scheduling

8 differentiation of teacher role in such a way that each has a unique, contributory task based on values, preferences, and interpersonal relations

9 location of teaching services (corresponding to consolidated academic areas such as science, arts) in large open-space arrangement containing decentralized library (learning center)

10 use of individualized, multimedia instructional packages to facilitate individual progress learning

The open-access curriculum rejects the isolated-subject schedule, the idea of tracking students, grouping in the school's master schedule, sequencing content beyond absolute essentials, permitting more than one-fourth of the curriculum to be defined as a core of common learnings, labeling any legitimate body of knowledge as a "frill," use of behavioral changes in students or teachers as an exclusive measure of program effectiveness, "intellectual closure" as a primary teaching method, restricting what the student learns to what the teacher knows, requiring teachers to work alone and unassisted by related specialists or unchallenged by competing disciplines or philosophies.

Open-school advocates rely heavily on involvement of students, teachers, administrators, members of the school board, and the community to gain acceptance. Visitations to schools in the "open" design and in-service experimentation are an important part of the process of adoption. Frequently the computer is used to program individual student data such as test scores, personality traits, strengths and weaknesses, to differentiate teacher roles, and to provide individualized curricula based on computerized data. Careful planning and the acceptance of key publics are vital to the success of the open school.

The teacher is the key to the potential success of the open classroom. Teachers must understand the open classroom concept personally and then develop the desire to explore it. They must be encouraged to try many different avenues with their students, including a variety of teaching techniques. They must be provided with an abundance of instructional materials, many of which they have developed themselves. Such an approach will result in many teachers customizing education for their students as well as for themselves.

Vocational and other teacher education programs are likewise indispensable to the success of the open school. Those programs, which are themselves in a competency-based format, will be able

1 to help teachers understand and internalize the concepts of open education: teaming, non-gradedness, continuous progress, and unified media

2 to provide intensive training in techniques of open education: contracts, learning centers, individualized packets.

3 to show teachers how to individualize instruction in the content areas

4 to provide training in management techniques of open education: scheduling, organizing, recordkeeping, control and management, parent involvement, and reporting

5 to help teachers identify the proper use of media in the schools of the future

6 to help teachers identify and provide a unique learning experience for students

The open-access classroom is being used in many vocational programs where individualized instruction is emphasized. In one school, all business education courses are taught by a team of three instructors in a classroom laboratory that operates daily during all class hours. Students may schedule their courses at any period their schedules permit, with the help of an advisor. All three instructors are available to teach any course to individuals or small groups.

This flexible-scheduling feature permits many more students to enter the business program than was possible under the fixed-class schedules of previous years. Instructors can increase the number of students they can efficiently teach from a previous level of 100 to as many as 300.

All courses are taught on a completely individualized basis, with emphasis on individual interests and abilities. Work programs for each student replace the large-group lecture methods of the past. Many more opportunities for personal career counseling are possible between individual students and the instructor. During unscheduled study periods, students use the lab and its facilities to work on project assignments with the help of an instructor who is always on duty in the laboratory.

A similar example may be found in home economics education. Within a large laboratory, equipment and materials relating to various specializations are grouped together. For example, the Foods Learning Center may be located at one end of the laboratory, whereas learning centers related to clothing, child care, or arts and crafts are arranged throughout the lab. Such an open-space arrangement facilitates individual and/or small-group instruction in several learning centers simultaneously. Instructional teams (teachers and aides) work cooperatively with students in formulating and realizing their objectives.

Curricular Needs Assessment

Although there would be no disagreement among vocational educators over the importance of maintaining a relevant curriculum, actually putting such a curriculum into effect is difficult. Vocational education, more than any other area in the school, is probably better attuned to the needs of its students and of the business and industrial community because of its use of such techniques as advisory committees, cooperative work programs for students, internships in business and industry for teachers, and identification of specific skills needed for employment; however, there remains a need for systematic efforts in curriculum revision.

One strategy for curriculum updating is the use of needs assessments. A need may be defined as a discrepancy between what is desired and what exists. The greater the discrepancy observed, the greater or more critical the need.

Consider this example: Suppose an analysis of test data reveals that students enrolled in a given vocational area score lower than the school norm (or total vocational norm) in mathematics. A survey of students, parents, teachers, and business/community leaders reveals agreement on the need for students to improve their math skills because this is one of the basic skill components of vocational programs. A need has now been defined. The test data provided evidence of *perceived level* of performance; the survey data revealed a *desired level*, which is higher than the current level.

The example shows that two types of needs are generated by the assessment process—felt needs and validated needs. Felt needs reflect the ideas, attitudes, and beliefs of people; that is, the students, staff, parents, community/business leaders. Validated needs are generated from relevant data (or hard data) gathered about current conditions in the school—student enrollment in vocational education, available instructional materials, library resources, test results, and so on. These are the facts on which a successful needs assessment depends. For vocational education, systematic needs assessments serve

1 to gain support for a quality program by involving staff, students, parents, community/business leaders in identifying the student needs the program should fill

2 to identify critical student needs most likely to benefit from concentrated improvement programs

3 to identify those student needs that students, staff, parents, and community/business leaders value as having highest priority

These procedures may be used to determine the critical needs and the priority among them:

1 determine the desired student outcome objectives that the school seeks to achieve

2 collect, analyze, and interpret data that reflect the extent to which the objectives are now being achieved

3 using the identified needs as a basis, and with the help of an advisory committee, develop a questionnaire to which students, parents, teachers, business/community representatives might respond by

(a) indicating omission of major needs

(b) indicating extent of agreement with identified needs

(c) indicating which needs are most critical

The Vocational Education Family

Vocational education today consists of a number of interrelated fields, programs, and curricula, with the primary objective of preparation for gainful employment. The distinction between vocational and general education is rapidly being replaced by an educational system, reflected in career education, that integrates both vocational and general education aspects through curricular programming.

In the following section, attention is turned to the unique contributions of the fields that comprise the vocational education family. A brief treatment of the nature of each field, its enrollments, curricular content, trends, and employment opportunities is provided.

Agricultural Education

During the past quarter century major changes have taken place in the field of agriculture. Advances in science and technology have transformed agriculture into a complex industry. In addition, along with the increase in the total population of the nation, there has been a decrease in total farm workers needed to produce food to meet increasing consumer needs. The decrease in numbers of farm workers has been accompanied by an increase in the number of off-farm workers engaged in the agricultural supply, services, and marketing areas. To provide for these changing educational needs, the scope of agriculture education programs has been extended to include training in agribusiness, natural resources, and environmental protection.

Two decades ago, the vocational agriculture curriculum was essentially the same throughout the nation. In keeping with expanding on-farm and off-farm occupations and vocational agriculture objectives, subject matter is now adapted to individual needs and interest within local school districts.

The content of the instructional program in agriculture has been classified as follows by the U.S. Office of Education in Handbook VI, *Standard Terminology for Curriculum and Instruction in Local and State School Systems* (9):*

01.01 Agricultural Production

01.02 Agricultural Supplies and Services

01.03 Agricultural Mechanics

01.04 Agricultural Products (Processing, Inspection, Marketing)

01.05 Ornamental Horticulture

01.06 Agricultural Resources (Conservation, Utilization, Services)

01.07 Forestry

As can be seen from this classification, the majority of opportunities are in the nonfarm occupations. The employment outlook points to a continuation of this trend, with the number of farm workers expected to decrease and the significant source of job openings being job replacements. The replacements, however, will need to be more highly trained than their predecessors because of improvements in technology and the mechanization of farm operations.

The curriculum in agricultural education includes courses related to both farming and nonfarming occupations. The trend at the high school level is to offer basic instruction, including units such as plant science, animal science, soil science and agricultural mechanics, and occupational exploration during the first two years. In the last two high school years, specialized courses such as agricultural mechanics, forestry, and ornamental horticulture are offered. Because persons entering occupations in

* This taxonomic source has been used throughout this chapter to classify occupations within the various vocational fields.

agricultural businesses and industries need vocational competencies other than technical agriculture, programs of study frequently incorporate content from other vocational areas, such as from business education, distribution and marketing, and trades.

Full-time and part-time postsecondary programs provide the student with opportunities to specialize in the various phases of vocational agriculture listed in the preceding USOE classification. Short-term specialized programs are also offered for adults.

In 1928 the Future Farmers of America (FFA), a youth service organization for present and former students enrolled in vocational agricultural programs, was organized. Its major aims and purposes include leadership and character development, opportunity for self-expression, cooperation, service, and sportsmanship. There are four types of membership in FFA—active, associate, collegiate, and honorary—with four grades of active membership ranging from Green Hand to American Farmer. In 1969 girls were first eligible for membership in FFA on the national level. The organization publishes an official magazine, *The Future Farmer*.

Business and Office Education

Of all the vocational education fields, business and office education was next to last to receive federal funding (only industrial arts was later). Not until the Vocational Education Act of 1963 were federal monies provided for this field. Even today, not all business education programs are classi-

Table 10.1 Public Secondary School Enrollment by Subject Areas: 1948–1949, 1960–1961, 1970–1971

Subject area	1948–49		1960–61		1970–71	
	Number	Percent of total	Number	Percent of total	Number	Percent of total
1	2	3	4	5	6	7
Total enrollment, grades 7–12	6,907,833	100.0	11,732,742	100.0	18,406,617	100.0
English language arts	7,098,770	102.8	12,972,236	110.6	25,852,165	140.5
Health and physical education[1]	7,794,671	112.8	12,081,639	103.0	22,193,800	120.6
Social sciences	6,981,980	101.1	11,802,499	100.6	19,659,790	106.8
Mathematics	4,457,987	64.5	8,596,396	73.3	14,137,090	76.8
Natural sciences	4,031,044	58.4	7,739,877	66.0	12,772,195	69.4
Music	2,484,201	36.0	4,954,347	42.2	6,559,452	35.6
Business education	3,186,207	46.1	4,667,570	39.8	[2]7,314,194	39.7
Industrial arts	1,762,242	25.5	3,361,699	28.7	5,397,074	29.3
Home economics	1,693,825	24.5	2,915,997	24.9	[2]5,282,850	28.7
Foreign languages	1,234,544	17.9	2,576,354	22.0	4,729,282	25.7
Art	1,219,693	17.7	2,383,703	20.3	4,350,685	23.6
Agriculture	373,395	5.4	507,992	4.3	[2]789,102	4.3
Vocational trade and industrial education	369,794	5.4	344,704	2.9	[2]1,141,638	6.2
Distributive education	[3]	[3]	38,363	.3	[2]295,633	1.6
Other	111,053	1.6	106,467	.9	[2]232,736	1.3

[1] Includes driver education and ROTC.
[2] Includes occupational programs as well as individual courses. These programs may represent enrollment in 2 or more courses.
[3] Data not reported separately.

NOTE.—Percentage may exceed 100.0 because a pupil may be enrolled in more than one course within a subject area during the school year. Data for 1970–71 are based upon a small sample survey.

SOURCE: U.S. Department of Health, Education, and Welfare, Office of Education, *Patterns of Course Offerings and Enrollments in Public Secondary Schools, 1970–71.*

fied as "reimbursed" programs, so it remains somewhat difficult to obtain an accurate picture of total business education enrollments, especially at the secondary level.

This difficulty in determining exact enrollment figures can be clearly demonstrated by comparing the enrollment figures cited by the U.S. Department of Health, Education and Welfare in the *Digest of Educational Statistics*, 1973 edition, which reported 7,314,194 enrollments in secondary business education and 1,395,909 enrollments in federally funded business-office education classes at the secondary level for 1970–1971 (Tables 10.1, 10.2). It should also be noted that secondary school enrollments in business education alone in those years almost equaled the total combined enrollments in home economics, agriculture, trade and industrial education, and distributive education, as shown in Table 10.1.

Table 10.2   Enrollment in Federally Aided Vocational Education Classes, 1966–1972

Level and type of program	1966	1967	1968	1969	1970	1971	1972	Percent change, 1971 to 1972
1	2	3	4	5	6	7	8	9
All programs	**6,070,069**	**7,047,501**	**7,533,936**	**7,979,366**	**8,793,960**	**10,525,660**	**11,710,767**	**11.3**
Secondary	3,048,248	3,532,823	3,842,896	4,079,395	5,114,451	6,506,375	7,278,523	11.9
Postsecondary	442,097	499,906	592,970	706,085	1,013,426	1,148,312	1,336,191	16.4
Adult	2,530,712	2,941,109	2,987,070	3,050,466	2,666,083	2,870,973	3,096,053	7.8
Special needs	49,002	73,663	111,000	143,420	¹805,384	¹1,423,710	¹1,635,782	14.9
Agriculture	**907,354**	**935,170**	**851,158**	**850,705**	**852,983**	**845,085**	**896,460**	**6.1**
Secondary	510,279	508,675	528,146	536,039	550,823	562,141	603,324	7.3
Postsecondary	5,987	8,093	11,036	15,816	23,381	28,418	34,924	22.9
Adult	390,388	413,454	305,357	290,336	278,779	254,526	258,212	1.5
Special needs	700	4,948	6,619	8,514	¹69,087	¹94,138	¹100,226	6.5
Distributive	**420,426**	**481,034**	**574,785**	**563,431**	**529,365**	**578,075**	**640,423**	**10.8**
Secondary	101,728	151,378	175,816	184,206	230,007	241,119	262,730	9.0
Postsecondary	15,833	21,003	44,824	60,718	82,160	85,859	102,844	19.8
Adult	301,116	303,783	349,730	307,976	217,198	251,097	274,849	9.5
Special needs	1,749	4,870	4,415	10,531	¹47,272	¹61,877	¹63,703	3.0
Health	**83,677**	**115,109**	**140,987**	**175,101**	**198,044**	**269,546**	**336,652**	**24.9**
Secondary	9,793	16,734	20,952	23,207	31,915	43,300	59,466	37.3
Postsecondary	36,496	54,135	64,592	91,922	102,515	137,943	177,466	28.7
Adult	37,065	42,721	52,865	56,603	63,614	88,303	99,720	12.9
Special needs	323	1,519	2,578	3,369	¹20,179	¹39,953	¹48,708	21.9
Home economics	**1,897,670**	**2,186,992**	**2,283,338**	**2,449,052**	**2,570,410**	**3,129,804**	**3,445,698**	**10.1**
Secondary	1,280,254	1,475,235	1,558,004	1,670,347	1,934,059	2,416,207	2,630,997	8.9
Postsecondary	2,652	3,506	4,395	13,490	44,259	52,792	68,604	30.0
Adult	602,363	685,225	677,478	718,817	592,092	660,805	746,097	12.9
Special needs	12,401	23,026	43,461	46,398	¹233,000	¹526,518	¹665,350	26.4
Office	**1,238,043**	**1,572,335**	**1,735,997**	**1,835,124**	**2,111,160**	**2,226,854**	**2,351,878**	**5.6**
Secondary	798,368	985,398	1,059,656	1,122,198	1,331,257	1,395,909	1,507,664	8.0
Postsecondary	165,439	192,639	225,182	218,448	331,001	335,198	360,245	7.5
Adult	271,149	389,194	443,481	482,160	448,902	495,747	483,969	-2.4
Special needs	3,087	5,104	7,678	12,318	¹197,359	¹287,231	¹294,491	2.5
Technical	**253,838**	**266,054**	**269,832**	**315,311**	**271,730**	**313,860**	**337,069**	**7.4**
Secondary	28,865	27,614	36,286	31,833	34,386	36,163	38,820	7.4
Postsecondary	100,151	97,156	104,746	130,564	151,621	177,718	189,468	6.6
Adult	124,730	140,431	127,418	151,714	85,723	99,979	108,781	8.8
Special needs	92	853	1,382	1,200	¹13,373	¹23,511	¹28,332	20.5
Trades and industry	**1,269,051**	**1,490,807**	**1,628,542**	**1,720,859**	**1,906,133**	**2,075,166**	**2,397,968**	**15.6**
Secondary	318,961	367,789	421,719	458,554	692,396	809,140	952,283	17.7
Postsecondary	115,539	123,374	137,732	174,201	261,182	309,812	356,879	15.2
Adult	803,901	966,301	1,030,723	1,042,362	952,555	956,214	1,088,806	13.9
Special needs	30,650	33,343	38,368	45,742	¹182,642	¹265,894	¹275,219	3.5
Other	.....	.....	**49,297**	**69,783**	**354,135**	**1,087,270**	**1,304,619**	**20.0**
Secondary	.....	.....	42,317	53,011	309,608	1,002,396	1,223,239	22.0
Postsecondary	.....	.....	463	926	17,307	20,572	45,761	122.4
Adult	.....	.....	18	498	27,220	64,302	35,619	-44.6
Special needs	.....	.....	6,499	15,348	¹42,472	¹124,588	¹159,753	28.2

¹ Disadvantaged persons included in distribution by level above.

SOURCES: U.S. Department of Health, Education, and Welfare, Office of Education, annual reports on *Vocational and Technical Education;* and unpublished data.

Learning experiences in business and office education are designed to lead to employment and/or advancement of individuals in occupations related to the facilitating function of the office. "'Facilitating function," as used here, refers to the expediting role of the office occupations as the connecting link between the production and distribution activities of an organization. Included are a variety of activities, such as recording and retrieval of data, supervision and coordination of office activities, internal and external communication, and the reporting of information.

The U.S. Office of Education has classified the business and office education instructional program into nine areas:

14.01 Accounting and Computing Occupations

14.02 Business Data Processing Systems Occupations

14.03 Filing, Office Machines, and General Office Clerical Occupations

14.04 Information Communication Occupations

14.05 Materials Support Occupations

14.06 Personnel, Training and Related Occupations

14.07 Stenographic, Secretarial and Related Occupations

14.08 Supervisory and Administrative Management Occupations

14.09 Typing and Related Occupations

The business curriculum, aimed at realizing both vocational and general education objectives, is usually divided into two areas of instruction:

1 Basic or general business This comprises those courses that contribute to the primary understandings and knowledge needed by all students. Examples include Introduction to Business, Basic Business, Business Law, Economics, Economic Geography, Consumer Problems, Business Management, Business Principles, and Business Psychology.

2 Vocational business education This comprises those courses that equip students with entry-level skills in the various business and office occupations. Examples include Advanced Typewriting, Bookkeeping, Accounting, Shorthand, Office Machines, Office Practice, Cooperative Business Education or Vocational Office Training.

Data Processing is one of the most rapidly growing aspects of business education. It may be classified as vocational business education, especially at the postsecondary level. Courses related to this phase of the business curriculum include Key Punch, Introduction to Computers, Unit Record-keeping, Basic Computing Machines, Computer Mathematics, COBOL, and Computer Programming.

The business function in our society continues to expand, and as it does, it develops new jobs, uses new machines, and designs new systems. The broad occupational categories in the field of business include:

1 *Clerical* clerk typist, file clerk, shipping and receiving clerk, dispatcher, information clerk, office machine operator, title searcher, switchboard operator, post office clerk, receptionist

2 *Secretarial* stenographer, court reporter, executive secretary, legal or medical secretary

3 *Bookkeeping and accounting* credit analyst, estimator, auditor, bank teller, bookkeeping machine operator, cashier, tax specialist, junior accountant, treasurer

4 *Data processing* systems analyst, programmer, computer and console operators, keypunch and coding equipment operators, tape librarian, project planner

5 *Management* administrative assistant, budget management analyst, administrative secretary, clerical and office supervisor, chief clerk, credit and collection manager, personnel manager

6 *Business teaching* middle school or high school level, vocational-technical schools, independent business schools, community and junior colleges, college or university level, educational assistant, training specialist, school supervisor or administrator

One of the most recent developments in office occupations is word-processing systems, in which secretarial jobs are organized according to functions related to correspondence and to administrative support. Administrative and corresponding secretaries are the primary specialists in the word-processing center. Remotely located, linked by recorders and dictation devices, and supported by automated typing and copying equipment, these information-production professionals now require a new set of tools and facilities (frequently linked to a computer) to provide administrative services. Similar dramatic changes are occurring in other aspects of the office occupations.

Several youth organizations are available to students enrolled in business and office education. The largest of these is Future Business Leaders of America (FBLA) with its collegiate counterpart, Phi Beta Lambda. FBLA offers three levels of active membership: assistant, supervisor, and leader. The programs and activities of FBLA are aimed at helping students to prepare for business careers, increasing understanding of the business education program, and developing leadership abilities. The official publication of FBLA is the *Future Business Leader*. Future Secretaries Association (FSA) is an international student organization for prospective secretaries designed to promote interest in secretarial careers. A similar organization for students interested in electronic data processing is Future Data Processors (FDP), sponsored by the Data Processing Management Association. Several colleges also sponsor chapters of Pi Omega Pi, a youth organization for business and office education. One of the newest organizations is the Office Education Association (OEA), founded in 1967 for office occupations students. Students who are members of FBLA, FSA, and FDP may also join OEA.

Distributive Education

Distributive Education has become increasingly important in recent years due to the role of marketing and distribution in the economic growth of the nation. As technological advances are made, as society becomes more complex, as changes occur in product-consumer relationships, distributive education must adjust. Distributive education is thus concerned with creating and managing change in the area of marketing and distribution, but the real task is to bring about change that will best serve the customer.

The content of distributive education may be classified into five areas of competency, including marketing competency, technology competency, social competency, basic skill competency, and economic competency. These areas are included, in varying degrees of difficulty or concentration, in programs ranging from the high school through the adult level.

Jobs within the distributive area fall within one of the following occupational categories, as identified by the U.S. Office of Education:

04.01 Advertising Services	04.10 Home Furnishings
04.02 Apparel and Accessories	04.11 Hotel and Lodging
04.03 Automotive	04.12 Industrial Marketing
04.04 Finance and Credit	04.13 Insurance
04.05 Floristry	04.14 International Trade
04.06 Food Distribution	04.15 Personal Services
04.07 Food Services	04.16 Petroleum
04.08 General Merchandise	04.17 Real Estate
04.09 Hardware, Building Materials, Farm and Garden Supplies	04.18 Recreation and Tourism
	04.19 Transportation

Occupational opportunities in marketing and distribution range from basic jobs, usually filled by graduates of high school programs, to top management positions, usually filled by college graduates. Present and projected employment opportunities in the distributive field are strong.

Students enrolled in distributive education classes at the high school and post-high school levels are eligible for membership in Distributive Education Clubs of America (DECA). Organized in 1947, DECA is primarily concerned with leadership development. There are three types of membership: active, associate, and honorary. In addition to the student organization, there is an adult organization, DECA, Incorporated, which was established to serve as the legal body for the student organization. The official publication of DECA is *The Distributor.*

High school instruction is organized either under the *cooperative plan* or under the *project plan.* The cooperative plan involves a combination of classroom instruction and supervised on-the-job training. The project plan combines classroom instruction with coordinated laboratory experiences. The distributive education curriculum at this level provides pre-employment courses, generally offered at grades 9 and 10, focusing on topics such as introduction to the nature of business, job interviews, and an introduction to the field of distribution. Technical and related instruction, correlated with the cooperative training, is offered during the last two years.

Distributive education at the postsecondary level is concerned primarily with specialized areas of distribution and marketing for students preparing for specialist and middle management positions. Postsecondary programs, which combine class experiences plus internship, include such courses as human relations, mathematics, communication, marketing, management, and supervision. Whereas the primary focus of high school and postsecondary programs is on preparation for employment, adult programs are designed for those seeking greater job proficiency and specialized skills as well as for those desiring entry-level skills. Consequently, both general and specialized courses are offered in the adult program. According to Donnell (10):

□ *The qualifications for a retail employee are undergoing greater changes than ever before. The sheer increase in sales volume, coupled with escalating costs, is forcing a revisualization of business. The computer is taking a prominent role. The increased complexity of business will require better educated employees, not only to handle the computer-related activities, but also to serve a more alert citizen.*

Numerous factors may be identified that contribute to the changes in the distributive occupations. Samson (11) lists six factors that he considers to be of primary importance in influencing change, including archaic material handling, new life styles of consumers, electronic computers, changing business structure, job creation for the disadvantaged, and the service emphasis.

Health Occupations Education

Labor problems in the health occupations have mounted over the past decade. A number of factors may be identified as contributing to the demand for health services, including population growth, rising income levels, increased awareness of the importance of health education, expanded health insurance coverage, and government financing of health care for the aged and low-income families. One solution for meeting increasing labor demands is the training of technicians and aides at less than professional level to remove the more routine duties from the professional medical worker.

A limited number of programs in practical nursing were in operation after the Smith-Hughes Act of 1917, under which nursing was broadly defined as a trade and thus included under the trade and industrial provisions of the act. Health occupations were first mentioned in federal legislation in the George-Barden Act of 1946, in which funds were made available for teaching practical nursing. A decade later the Health Amendments Act established this area as a new subsystem within vocational education. As a result, programs in practical nursing were developed at the secondary and postsecondary levels. The Vocational Education Act of 1963 and the subsequent Vocational Education Amendments of 1968 allowed states considerable flexibility in developing health occupations programs.

Not only are the numbers of health workers increasing sharply, but new occupations and specialties are continually emerging in medicine, dentistry, and nursing. Techniques for the regulation of workers in health occupations have been developed and administered, either by appropriate professional organizations or by legally constituted authority in the respective states, as a means of safeguarding the public against unqualified and/or unscrupulous persons. Therefore, regulatory practices such as licensing, certification, and/or registration in certain of the health occupations have been established.

The U.S. Office of Education includes the following classification of instructional programs in its taxonomy of the health occupations:

07.01 Dental

07.02 Medical Laboratory Technology

07.03 Nursing

07.04 Rehabilitation

07.05 Radiologic

07.06 Opthalmic

07.07 Environmental Health

07.08 Mental Health Technology

07.09 Miscellaneous Health Occupations Education

There are a wide range of job opportunities in the health occupations. Approximately 250 job titles are listed in the *Dictionary of Occupational Titles*, including a variety of technicians, nurses, aides, office assistants, and maintenance workers. Job requirements vary within these occupations, with most preparation programs ranging from one to four years. Instructional programs in health occupations education are found at both high school and postsecondary school levels. The majority of the programs, however, are at the postsecondary level and involve a combination of classroom instruction and supervised field experience.

Some of the more common health occupations are practical nurse, assistant, and technician. Practical nursing programs generally are twelve months in length and involve classroom work and supervised hospital experiences. The curriculum includes topics such as first aid, family life, geriatric nursing, needs of children, the human body, nutrition, medication and treatment, and human relations.

Health occupations assistants work in various occupations, such as dental, medical laboratory, occupational therapy, and medical office. Training programs and curricula are designed for the specific occupation; for example, the curriculum for laboratory assistants includes hematology, bacteriology, serology, parasitology, chemistry, and blood banking, whereas the curriculum for medical office assistants focuses on topics such as typewriting, accounting, filing, records management, communication, medical terminology, and instruments.

Health occupations technicians apply technical knowledge to a specific health occupation; thus they work primarily with instruments. A number of technical occupations are related to health occupations, including dental laboratory technicians, dental hygienist, medical technician, optical technician, and X-ray technician. Specific curricula and supervised laboratory experiences are designed for each specialization.

The development of new programs for extending nursing roles to include work that would otherwise be performed by a physician is one of the most important current trends in the nursing profession. Other trends include the use of health teams (paramedics) to replace the doctor and nurse as the sole health workers, thus allowing the physician to use his or her professional skills in a more efficient manner.

At the present time there is no specific youth group serving the health occupations, but the feasibility of establishing such an organization is being explored.

Home Economics Education

Home economics comprises the related courses or units of instruction that are organized to enable students to acquire knowledge and develop understanding, attitudes, and skills relevant to (a) personal, home, and family life; and (b) occupational preparation using the knowledge and skills of home economics. The subject matter includes concepts that are drawn from the natural and social sciences and humanities as well as those that are unique to the field.

Home economics classes are offered at high school, postsecondary, and adult levels, with the majority of enrollments being at the high school level. Federal aid for home economics began with the Smith-Hughes Act of 1917, with programs for home and family living. The Vocational Education Act of 1963 and the Vocational Education Amendments of 1968 and 1972 placed more emphasis on training for gainful employment.

The U.S. Office of Education taxonomy of occupations identifies two major instructional areas in home economics education:

09.01 Homemaking: Preparation for Personal, Home, and Family Living; these programs are not specifically directed toward preparation for gainful employment

09.02 Occupational Preparation: Care and guidance of children; Clothing Management, Production and Services; Food Management, Production and Services; Home Furnishings, Equipment and Services; and Institutional and Home Management and supportive services

Home economics instruction includes a combination of directed projects, course offerings, and related group experiences in areas such as home management, family economics, family health, family relations, child care and development, nutrition, clothing, and textiles. Home projects are an essential part of home economics instructional programs, as are occupational experiences a component of all vocational programs. The content of home economics curricula lends itself to a variety of organizational patterns and curriculum models, thus allowing students to select topics or areas of concentration for personal and professional use.

Hill (12) suggests that home economics educators should be alert to situations such as the following: a reversal of present trends toward care of children outside the home; an acceleration of communal living; invention of new food products; and development of yet-unknown designs for urban living. Home economics educators have a major responsibility for instruction to help all workers make consumer decisions that will be compatible with individual goals and community welfare. They need to join with business educators and social science educators, other fields with a particular responsibility for consumer education, to develop a more effective consumer program in the public schools. Emphasis needs to be given to such areas as the influence of consumer decisions on environment, consumer protection, the effects of international trade practices and tariffs on quality and cost, and the ethics involved in buying services.

The home economics youth organization, Future Homemakers of America (FHA), was founded in 1945 and is open to any individual who has taken or who is taking a course in home economics. FHA is concerned with developing cooperative and intelligent leadership and with helping individuals to improve personal, family, and community living. FHA offers three degrees of achievement: Junior Homemaker, Chapter Homemaker, and State Homemaker. The official FHA publication is *Teen Times*.

Trade and Industrial Education

A relevant program in industrial education, as in all vocational education, is one that is attuned to current and projected trends in business and

industry. To be so attuned, industrial educators must maintain a close relationship with business and industrial leaders and workers and must see that changes are reflected in the curriculum.

Industrial education is offered at high school, postsecondary, and adult levels in part-time and full-time programs, with the largest enrollment being in adult programs. Curricula are aimed at preparing persons for initial employment, at upgrading their existing skills, and at retraining them in a new or related occupation. The increasing number of comprehensive high schools throughout the nation has resulted in an increase in industrial education programs at the secondary level.

Instruction in trade and industrial education is provided in (a) basic manipulative skills, (b) safety judgment, and (c) related areas such as mathematics, drafting, communications, and science, as required to perform successfully in a given occupational cluster. Instructional programs are aimed at developing attitudes and concepts basic to all industrial occupations in addition to developing specific skills and knowledge applicable to the various occupational clusters. Supervised work experience is an integral part of many programs, whereas simulated laboratory experiences are an alternative in other programs.

Vocational industrial occupations are found in a variety of job categories, such as manufacturing, construction, mining, transportation, and public utilities. Industrial education programs had their beginning in 1917, with the passage of the Smith-Hughes Act, and were expanded through the George-Barden Act of 1946, the Vocational Education Act of 1963, and the 1968 and 1972 Vocational Amendments.

The wide range of occupations covered in industrial education is evident in the U.S. Office of Education classification of instructional programs, as indicated below:

17.01 Air Conditioning

17.02 Appliance Repair

17.03 Automotive Services

17.04 Aviation Occupations

17.05 Blueprint Reading

17.06 Business Machine Maintenance

17.07 Commercial Art Occupations

17.08 Commercial Fishery Occupations

17.09 Commercial Photography Occupations

17.10 Construction and Maintenance Trades

17.11 Custodial Services

17.12 Diesel Mechanics

17.13 Drafting

17.14 Electrical Occupations

17.15 Electronics Occupations

17.16 Fabric Maintenance Services

17.17 Foremanship, Supervision, and Management Development

17.18 General Continuation

17.19 Graphic Arts Occupations

17.20 Industrial Atomic Energy

17.21 Instrument Maintenance and Repair

17.22 Maritime Occupations

17.23 Metalworking

17.24 Metallurgy

17.26 Personal Services

17.27 Plastic Occupations

17.28 Public Service Occupations

17.29 Quality Food Occupations

17.30 Refrigeration

17.31 Small Engine Repair, Internal Combustion

17.32 Stationary Energy Sources Occupations

17.33 Textile Production and Fabrication

17.34 Leathermaking

17.35 Upholstering

17.36 Woodworking

Some states classify their postsecondary occupational programs into two main categories: technical and trades. Technical programs consist primarily of two-year programs in such areas as engineering technology, office-related technology, nursing, and forest technology. Trade education generally consists of one-year programs in curricula such as auto mechanics, drafting, welding, practical nursing, and machine shop. The following discussion provides a more detailed treatment of the concept of technical education.

Technical Education

As our technology becomes increasingly complex, engineers and scientists have to become more highly trained, demands that are also reflected in training programs for technicians. Instructional programs must of necessity be flexible, responding to the changes brought about by technology.

The majority of programs in technical education are located in public and private postsecondary institutions. Junior colleges, vocational-technical schools, technical institutes, engineering schools, and technical high schools offer instructional programs of a technical nature.

The main thrust of technical education can be traced to the 1940s, when the U.S. Office of Education recognized and proclaimed the need to train technicians who would work on jobs that required more limited competencies than those of a professional engineer but more than those needed by skilled mechanics. As industry mushroomed during and after World War II, there were increasing demands for technical workers.

The definition of technical education is still somewhat unclear, with technical institutes, colleges, and vocational-technical schools formulating their own objectives. McMahon (13) suggests that "preparation for a technical occupation requires an understanding of, and ability to apply, those levels of mathematics and science appropriate to the occupation. And in those occupations that can be properly defined as technical, the mathematics and science required is more advanced than that required for a middle-type craft or skilled-trades occupation." Such a definition tends to view technical education as a level of training as well as an occupational field.

Technical curricula include preparation in supporting sciences and mathematics in addition to an emphasis in the field of technical specialization, such as in electronics, mechanics, chemistry, or aeronautics. Instructional programs generally combine classroom instruction, laboratory experiences, and supervised work experiences. The U.S. Office of Education classifies instructional programs of technical education as follows:

16.01 Engineering-related Technology

16.02 Agricultural-related Technology

16.03 Health-related Technology

16.04 Office-related Technology

16.05 Home Economics-related Technology

16.06 Miscellaneous Technical Education

Technicians are frequently employed in direct support of the professional engineer. For example, the engineering technician is capable of assisting in engineering functions such as designing, developing, testing, and modifying of products and processes; production planning, writing reports, and preparing estimates; analyzing and diagnosing technical problems that involve independent decisions; and solving a wide range of technical problems by applying his or her background in the technical specialties.

There is no national youth organization exclusively for students in technical education. Secondary students enrolled in vocational industrial education (trade, industrial, or technical courses) are eligible for membership in the Vocational Industrial Clubs of America (VICA). Organized in 1965, VICA provides four types of membership: active, professional, associate, and honorary. Six national goals have been identified by VICA: professional growth, community understanding, safety, teacher recruitment, cooperation, and good public relations. Educators recognize the importance of VICA, and of all vocational service organizations, as a significant teaching tool in realizing the objectives of the various occupational programs.

Industrial Arts Education

Prior to 1973, industrial arts was recognized primarily as general education for students. It offered opportunities for exploring various vocational areas and for instruction in leisure time activities and home-repair skills. Through the past half century, industrial arts curricula have included a variety of units, such as woodworking, drafting, metalworking, plastics, graphic arts, power mechanics, and electronics. Instructional units are frequently organized around four levels: introductory, basic, intermediate, and advanced, as offered at the middle and high school levels.

After the inclusion of industrial arts as a federally reimbursed field of vocational education, the curriculum was expanded to include transportation, construction, graphic communication, and American industry. Not all courses in industrial arts can (or perhaps should) be reimbursed through vocational funds because they do not all fit into the pre-vocational or vocational categories.

Vocational Education Enrollments

Enrollments in federally aided vocational education programs have steadily increased, as shown in Table 10.2. Several factors have steadily contributed to this growth, including (a) increased numbers of students attending school at all levels, (b) decreased drop-out rates, (c) increased job opportunities in the trade and technical fields, (d) increased availability of training programs, especially at the postsecondary and adult levels, and (e) increased numbers of comprehensive high schools.

Total enrollments in secondary vocational education programs more than doubled between 1966 and 1972, whereas postsecondary enrollments were more than three times greater in 1972 than in 1966.

A further comparison of federally aided vocational education enrollments, as shown in Table 10.3, indicates that by 1972 total enrollments had increased by 40 times the 1920 totals, when the only federally aided

Table 10.3   Enrollment in Federally Aided Vocational Classes, 1920–1972

Fiscal year	Type of program								
	Total	Agriculture	Distributive occupations	Home economics	Trades and industry	Health occupations	Technical education	Office occupations	Other programs
1	2	3	4	5	6	7	8	9	10
1920	265,058	31,301	.....	48,938	184,819	.....	.....	.....	.....
1930	981,882	188,311	.....	174,967	618,604	.....	.....	.....	.....
1940	2,290,741	584,133	129,433	818,766	758,409	.....	.....	.....	.....
1942	2,624,786	605,099	215,049	954,041	850,597	.....	.....	.....	.....
1944	2,001,153	469,959	181,509	806,605	543,080	.....	.....	.....	.....
1946	2,227,663	510,331	174,672	911,816	630,844	.....	.....	.....	.....
1948	2,836,121	640,791	292,936	1,139,766	762,628	.....	.....	.....	.....
1950	3,364,613	764,975	364,670	1,430,366	804,602	.....	.....	.....	.....
1952	3,165,988	746,402	234,984	1,391,389	793,213	.....	.....	.....	.....
1954	3,164,851	737,502	220,619	1,380,147	826,583	.....	.....	.....	.....
1956	3,413,159	785,599	257,025	1,486,816	883,719	.....	.....	.....	.....
1958	3,629,339	775,892	282,558	1,559,822	983,644	27,423	.....	.....	.....
1960	3,768,149	796,237	303,784	1,588,109	938,490	40,250	101,279	.....	.....
1962	4,072,677	822,664	321,065	1,725,660	1,005,383	48,985	148,920	.....	.....
1964	4,566,390	860,605	334,126	2,022,138	1,069,274	59,006	221,241	.....	.....
1966	6,070,059	907,354	420,426	1,897,670	1,269,051	83,677	253,838	1,238,043	.....
1968	7,533,936	851,158	574,785	2,283,338	1,628,542	140,987	269,832	1,735,997	49,297
1970	8,793,960	852,983	529,365	2,570,410	1,906,133	198,044	271,730	2,111,160	354,135
1971	10,525,660	845,085	578,075	3,129,804	2,075,166	269,546	313,860	2,226,854	1,087,270
1972	11,710,767	896,460	640,423	3,445,698	2,397,968	336,652	337,069	2,351,878	1,304,619

SOURCES: U.S. Department of Health, Education, and Welfare, Office of Education, annual reports on *Vocational and Technical Education*; and unpublished data.

programs were agriculture, home economics, and trade and industrial education. This table illustrates the cumulative effects of an expansion in vocational education funding, as new programs were added to the reimbursed group.

Vocational education, as a component of career education, should be an integral part of the curriculum, from kindergarten through the adult level, with meaningful objectives at each instructional level. Such objectives should be based on established principles of learning theory. Table 10.4 contains a summary of the underlying purposes of vocational education at each instructional level as well as desired student outcomes.

Table 10.5 illustrates in more detail how the intent or purpose of vocational education at the various levels is realized. At the elementary level, students are introduced to the world of work and become acquainted with various occupations found in the immediate and broader community. During the middle years (grades 7–9), students are oriented toward and explore occupational families and may make a tentative choice of a preferred occupational cluster. At the high school level, students enroll

Table 10.4   Intent of a Developmental Vocational Curriculum

Intent	Level	Desirable outcome
orientational	grades K–6	student acquires positive attitude toward work, school, and increased knowledge of self in relationship to work
exploration and employability	grade 7	student makes tentative choice of broad occupational areas or of several occupational clusters for further exploration
exploration, employability, and job preparation	grade 8	student makes specific choice of occupational cluster for in-depth exploration and for acquiring employability skills
exploration, employability, and job preparation	grade 9	student makes choice of occupational cluster for entry-level job preparation and for further exploration
job preparation, employability, exploration, job entry, and job adjustment	grades 10–12	student prepares for and satisfactorily enters an entry-level job or seeks further education and/or job preparation
job preparation, job entry, adjustment, and exploration	postsecondary	student prepares and satisfactorily enters a specific technical or skilled occupation
job preparation, upgrading, job entry adjustment, progression, and exploration	adult	student prepares for and satisfactorily enters a new occupation or updates and upgrades competence in existing occupational field

Source: American Vocational Journal, *Vol. 46, No. 3, March 1971, p. 22.*

Table 10.5 Developmental Vocational Curriculum: Kindergarten through Adult

Grades K–6	7	8	9	10–11–12	12	13–14	Adult
world of work curriculum	program of education and career exploration	six to twelve-week prevocational courses	one year prevocational courses	preparatory courses in multi-occupations	education or job placement	preparatory courses in a specific occupation	preparatory and upgrading courses
		service → service health service public service personal service food service	→ health and personal service public service food service	→ paramedical personal service public service food service	→ job placement and follow-through service	→ practical nursing medical lab technology cosmetology law enforcement food preparation	specialized training for a short-or long-term nature for upgrading or for entrance into new occupations
fuse career-oriented activities into existing curriculum		home economics (related) clothing and textile child care home and institutional management food and nutrition	→ home economics related occupations	→ child care clothing and textile* institutional management	preparatory education in specific occupation through cooperative education, early or advanced placement in post-secondary education, and specialized secondary labs	clothing construction and alteration child development home furnishing and equipment	

business → organizational

business → business office data processing business contact management and finance → office data processing → office data processing → data processing accounting clerk-typist secretary

→ sales and distribution → sales and distribution → marketing management

→ management and sales

technology → transportation communications construction manufacturing → transportation* communications construction manufacturing → transportation* graphic arts construction* drafting and design metal working electronics electro-mechanical* → auto mechanics commercial art carpentry electrical technology instrumentation drafting and design machine shop electrical appliances

outdoors

expression of ideas → agriculture and natural resources production horticulture agri-business forestry wildlife and recreation → general agriculture → environmental control occupations → production agriculture horticulture* forestry recreation and wildlife agri-business* → environmental control occupations → farm equipment agri-marketing forestry harvesting technology ornamental horticulture

→ pollution control technology

cooperative education

* Sales would be offered as an option for each course with asterisk.
Source: American Vocational Journal, *Vol. 46, No. 3, March 1971, p. 23.*

for longer periods in job-entry preparation in this chosen cluster. Postsecondary and adult programs focus on preparatory work and on the upgrading of skills of a specialized nature for a specific occupation. The table does not attempt to include all available courses or areas of concentration within the vocational fields, but it depicts the gradual movement from general to specialized training as the learner progresses from one developmental level to another.

Evaluation of Vocational Curricula

Evaluation of the effectiveness of a curriculum may consist of formative observations or summative measurements. Evaluation of a formative nature seeks to determine the degree of student mastery of a given task, and it attempts to pinpoint gaps in student learning as a basis for movement toward mastery. Formative evaluation (through achievement tests, observations, or other means) is closely related to diagnostic evaluation, which seeks both to discover causes for learning deficiencies as a basis for correction and to place the student properly at the beginning of instruction. Formative evaluation is useful in the process of curriculum construction, teaching, and learning, for the purpose of improving any of these three processes. Summative evaluation, on the other hand, is directed toward an overall judgment or assessment of the degree to which larger outcomes of a vocational course, curriculum, or program have been realized. Further purposes of summative evaluation relate to grading students' work and reporting to parents or administrators.

A good vocational curriculum is systematically planned and evaluated, reflects adequately the aims of the school, maintains balance among these aims, promotes continuity of experience, arranges learning experiences flexibly, uses the most effective learning experiences and resources available, and makes maximum provision for evaluating the success of both the program and the learner. Students, teachers, parents, employers, and advisory committees make valuable inputs into the evaluation of vocational curricula. However, the ultimate criterion of a curriculum's effectiveness is the success of the former student on the job. A more extensive discussion of the evaluation of the total program of vocational education is contained in Chapter 14.

Summary

The curriculum of a school may be regarded as a product of its environment. It is affected by community culture, by laws, by the philosophy of society, and by socioeconomic trends. Although a variety of techniques have been developed for constructing curricula, vocational educators draw heavily on activity and job analysis. Objectives are, in a sense, the most important factor in planning the curriculum because they determine what will be done. Traditionally, curriculum planning in vocational fields has relied on community surveys to determine what employers needed in the work force. More recently, however, the emphasis in job preparation has shifted so as to place more emphasis on developing the capabilities and meeting unique needs of individuals.

Selection and organization of experiences and curriculum materials should follow a developmental psychological order. The modern method of curriculum building uses a systems approach, which emphasizes the development of precise educational objectives and the re-design of the educational process to ensure appropriate student achievement of objectives. A systems approach to total curriculum design involves (a) gathering input data on students; (b) formulating student performance objectives; (c) constructing pre-tests; (d) selecting course content; (e) selecting instructional strategy; (f) developing instructional materials; (g) selecting the instructional process; (h) conducting instruction; (i) analyzing post-test results; and (j) evaluating student learning.

Numerous models or designs have been used over the years in the attempt to keep curricula relevant. The *subject-centered curriculum* groups students on the basis of their objectives into college preparatory, general, and vocational programs. The *core curriculum* design advocates a large block of time in which all students employ problem-solving techniques to solve felt problems and to meet needs. The *cluster-based curriculum* in vocational education is based on the premise that certain related occupations have common learning and skills requirements and that students who have mastered these skills have more options available for employment.

The *organic curriculum* has been proposed as a design that would provide a student with a variety of options after high school. It emphasizes the integration of academic and vocational learning and more field-centered experiences. The *competency-based curriculum* specifies the desired outcomes in explicit form, identifies the standards to be applied in assessing learner competencies, and holds the learner accountable for meeting those outcomes. Such *systems-oriented curriculum* provisions are based on a procedure that includes (a) specification of assumptions, tasks, goals, and objectives; (b) generation and selection of objective criteria; (c) identification and design of assessment strategies; (d) specification of instructional philosophy; (e) development of instructional strategies; (f) selection and/or development of instructional resources; and (g) development of a feedback mechanism. Competency-based curricula make heavy use of *individualized* approaches, which adjust the pace of learning to the learner, vary the instructional modes, and promote independent learning.

Most recent in the list of curriculum design strategies is the *open-access curriculum*, which creates large clusters of content to replace lesser courses; emphasizes easy access and exit; de-emphasizes traditional teaching in favor of active involvement of the student in learning; uses large blocks of time, large open instructional spaces (classrooms without walls), and multimedia instructional packages. Needless to say, these models or designs are not mutually exclusive but rather have some features in common. The open lab in vocational education is a relatively recent adaptation of the relatively old idea of individualized instruction.

Needs assessments constitute a strategy for updating the curriculum and staff of the school by generating two types of data from appropriate publics: *felt needs* are generated from students, staff, parents, and the community; *validated needs* comprise hard data gathered internally about current conditions in the school—enrollments, materials, resources, test results, and so on. Needs assessments constitute a valuable tool for identifying critical needs of the school, for improving the quality of the instructional program, and for gaining support for education.

The vocational education family consists of a number of interrelated fields, programs, and curricula, including agricultural education, business and office education, distributive education, health occupations education, home economics education, trade and industrial education, technical and industrial arts education. A brief treatment of content and employment opportunities in each field is provided in this chapter. Vocational education enrollments in federally aided programs have steadily increased. The integration of vocational and career education concepts is being reflected in the fusion of career-oriented activities into existing curricula at all levels. Vocational education uses both formative (informational, diagnostic) and summative (terminal assessment) forms of evaluation in order to improve curricula.

Activities

For review

1 Explain the steps in Teske's curriculum planning model and illustrate how they apply to your field.

2 What criteria would you use in selecting subject matter to implement a curriculum?

3 Compare the procedure in the systems-based curriculum model and the Teske curriculum model. How are they alike? How are they different?

4 Identify some basic principles of curriculum construction that have traditionally been used in vocational education.

5 Identify each of the following curriculum models and specify the advantages and/or disadvantages of the use of each in vocational education:

> Subject-centered curriculum
> Core curriculum
> Cluster-based curriculum
> Organic curriculum
> Competency-based curriculum
> Open-access curriculum

6 What is *needs assessment* and what is its role in vocational education?

7 Discuss the effects of automation and technology on each of the vocational education fields, with regard to the nature of the field, employment trends, and curriculum.

8 For each of the vocational fields, identify the primary federal legislative act that provided initial funding of the program.

9 Name the youth organizations associated with each vocational field. What contributions do these groups make toward realizing the goals of vocational education?

10 Explain and/or differentiate three levels of individualization of instruction and give specific examples for implementing each.

For discussion

1 What are the components that make up an instructional system?

2 What will be the role of vocational education within the broader career education scheme? Will all students be provided with employable skills at the end of high school or whenever they exit school? What "employability" skills should be taught to ensure maximum future adaptability and potential?

3 Is it realistic to propose that every high school student be equipped with an entry-level job skill? Is it possible, for example, for a student to enter the health occupations at an assistant level and move up the career ladder to become a physician? Are there more direct ways of assuring student mobility and advancement?

4 Vocational education has a negative image among some educators and members of minority groups. How can vocational education demonstrate that it deserves the prestige accorded the academic subject areas and that it offers hope for all groups?

5 The centrality of work in determining an individual's future life style is well known. However, how can educators prepare people for work roles and also accommodate those for whom a career may not be the sole or major determiner of life style?

6 Career education challenges the concept that the basic function of the school is the transmission of knowledge. However, this challenge does not negate the importance of providing a base of knowledge and skills to support an individual's preparation for a career and to enable him or her to deal effectively with problems. What bodies of knowledge are of the most importance? How can a truly interdisciplinary curriculum be developed?

7 Identify several factors that you think have contributed to the continuous increase in vocational education enrollments. What trends do you predict for the future of vocational education at the secondary level? At the postsecondary level?

8 Identify the problems that might be encountered, both at the secondary and postsecondary levels, in implementing the (a) core curriculum, (b) competency-based curriculum, (c) organic curriculum, (d) open-access curriculum.

9 What role should parents and students play in curriculum construction?

10 Which curriculum model would best fit your vocational field, school, and community needs? Justify your choice.

11 Compare the curriculum organization and content of vocational education in the 1960s with the changes suggested by career education models at the elementary, middle, high school, and post-high school levels.

12 What are some of the means through which the principles and concepts of open schools and individualized instruction could be implemented in a traditional school setting?

13 Select three or four of the forces affecting curriculum as listed below. Briefly discuss how each has affected (a) education in general, and (b) vocational education in particular:

(a) Sputnik

(b) technological developments

(c) attack on poverty

(d) civil rights movement

(e) rising aspirations of populace

(f) growing prosperity

(g) rising educational level of populace

(h) more extensive and accessible performance records

(i) change in methods and content of education

(j) change in social setting and social functions of educational institutions

(k) Vocational Education Act of 1963

(l) Elementary-Secondary Education Act

(m) National Defense Education Act

(n) move from rural-agrarian to urban-industrial society

(o) mobility of the population

(p) more extensive and wider variety of current instructional materials

(q) rise in humanism

(r) rise of controversy over cognitive man versus mentally healthy man

(s) shift in character of job openings

(t) expanding bank of current scientists and scientific data

(u) more leisure time

(v) speed in communication of ideas and data; mass media explosion

(w) increasing imperative that all possess reading skill

(x) demands for involvement in decision processes

(y) space exploration

(z) accountability

For exploration

1 Examine the course offerings of a vocational-technical school or junior college in one of the vocational fields. Compare this listing with the instructional areas identified by USOE. Which instructional areas are included in the curriculum you reviewed?

2 Under the Vocational Education Act of 1963 and the Amendments of 1968 and 1972, monies were allocated for programs for the disadvantaged and handicapped. Interview a vocational education instructor at a post-secondary institution and find out what provisions are being made for recruitment, instruction, placement, and follow-up of these students.

3 Construct a needs assessment instrument that could be administered to teachers, parents, students, administrators, and business community representatives. Administer the instrument to a sample of these groups and prepare a report of the findings to share with the class. Did the groups tend to agree? Which groups were most diverse in their views about the needs of the schools? How could you use this data in curriculum planning and revision?

4 Prepare a diagram of an open-space laboratory that would be ideal for your vocational area in your school setting.

5 Read several definitions of curriculum and select or adapt one with which you most nearly agree.

6 Select a vocational field, preferably one other than your own area of concentration, and prepare a report on its history and development.

7 Prepare a speech that you might give to seventh- or eighth-grade students on job opportunities in your vocational field. Include employment trends, educational prerequisites, and major changes—both present and projected.

8 Interview a student enrolled in a cooperative occupational program in a field other than your own. What is the student's impression of the program? What types of experiences are being provided on the job? How is the classroom instruction related to the on-the-job experiences? You may wish to tape record the interview and share it with the class.

9 Select one youth organization with which you are unfamiliar. Interview a student member and find out his or her impressions of the contributions of the club to its individual members, the department, and the school.

10 Interview an industrial arts instructor and prepare a report for the class about the changes in the program resulting from federal funding.

11 React to each of the following points as it relates to individualized learning in vocational education. Is each point true or false?

(a) the teacher makes the assignment—the student does the work at his or her own pace

(b) levels replace grades

(c) provisions are made for large-group, small-group, and individual teaching

(d) team teaching necessitates curriculum revision

(e) nongradedness can function without change of facilities

(f) individualization of instruction significantly improves achievement levels of students

References

1 Philip R. Teske, "Models for Curriculum Design" (unpublished paper), 1969.

2 Harold Alberty, *The Core Program in the High School* (Cincinnati: South-Western Publishing Company, 1955), p. 25.

3 Ibid, p. 24.

4 William A. Bakamis, Robert E. Kuhl, Edwin K. Hill, Beverly Swarthout, Dale L. Nish, *Identification of Task and Knowledge Clusters Associated with Performance of Major Types of Building Trades Work* (Pullman: Washington State University, 1966), pp. 2, 12.

5 Calfrey C. Calhoun, Project Director, *Purpose Centered Curriculum for Florida Office and Business Education* (Tampa: University of South Florida, 1970).

6 Robert M. Morgan and David S. Bushnell, "Designing an Organic Curriculum," in *National Business Education Quarterly*, Vol. 35, No. 3, March 1967, p. 11. (Reproduced by permission)

7 Ibid, pp. 12–13.

8 Jerome S. Bruner, *The Process of Education* (Cambridge, Mass.: Harvard University Press, 1960).

9 U.S. Office of Education, "Standard Terminology for Curriculum and Instruction in Local and State School Systems." State Educational Records and Report Series: Handbook VI (Washington, D.C.: Government Printing Office, 1969).

10 Edward S. Donnell, "Consumers and Youth, Keys to the 70's," in *American Vocational Journal*, Vol. 45, No. 2, February 1970, p. 33.

11 Harland Samson, "The Changing Nature of Distributive Occupations," in *The Emerging Content and Structure of Business Education*, eds. Ray G. Price, Charles R. Hopkins, and Mary Klaurens (Washington, D.C.: National Business Education Association, 1970), p. 60.

12 Alberta D. Hill, "Don't Stop! But Look and Listen," in *American Vocational Journal*, Vol. 46, No. 4, April 1971, p. 43.

13 Gordon G. McMahon, "Technical Education: A Problem of Definition," in *American Vocational Journal*, Vol. 45, No. 3, March 1970, p. 23.

Chapter 11

Research

and

Vocational-Technical

Education

Introduction

The function of educational research in our preparation for the future is generally accepted as crucial and, in the long run, indispensable. Traditionally, research in vocational and technical education has lagged behind educational research, which, in turn, has not kept pace with research in business and industry. For many decades vocational educators were preoccupied with the organization and implementation of programs in order to keep ahead of insatiable demands for job training. Most research was thus related to the developmental aspects of program planning and evaluation, and little attention was given to the theoretical bases of programs. Until the sixties, most of the theoretical research in vocational education was done in the form of master's theses and doctoral dissertations. Federal legislation of the early 1960s, however, triggered a national awareness of the need to expand such research and to unify the scattered fragments of already existing research into a concerted, organized effort.

In few areas of the educational spectrum have new knowledge, research, and development occurred more dramatically than in the vocational subjects in the 1960s and 1970s, if one accepts the term "vocational" as the umbrella under which may be included all education and preparation for occupations, and careers. Few areas of formal education have contributed more to the advent and development of the technologies (or, conversely, have been more affected by them) than have the various vocational fields. The technician frequently is employed in direct support of the professional and applies his or her specialized background to the solution of a wide range of supporting technical problems. Likewise, the products and inventions from fields such as agriculture, business and industry, and health have improved the productivity of the technician.

In this chapter we will deal with the focus of vocational research and with four types of research that have made a contribution to vocational education. Research competencies of vocational education teachers, supervisors, and teacher educators are reviewed. Attention is given to the identification of research centers and organizations along with the special problem of disseminating the results of research. General problems related to vocational education research and problem areas needing investigation are discussed. Special sections are devoted to analysis of research, funding of research, preparation of research proposals, and examples of current vocational education research.

The Focus of Vocational Research

Despite the apparent lack of vocational research until the 1960s, vocational education pioneered in the use of community occupational surveys, recommendations of local advisory committees, and occupational analyses. It is unlikely that those responsible for any other aspect of the secondary education program have planned their program on as sound a research base as that of vocational education. Brandon (1) uses a paradigm developed by Clark and others and makes some adaptations for vocational research. Evans in particular emphasizes the categories of (a) investigation of educationally oriented problems, (b) classroom experimentation, (c) field testing, and (d) demonstration and dissemination, but with the reservation that unless the results of research in basic scientific investigation are known to vocational researchers, their work will be seriously handicapped or completely worthless.

In the context of reporting research performed in vocational, technical, and practical arts education, Wenrich and others (1) point out that research is highly compartmentalized, that industrial sociologists and psychologists are not aware of work done in vocational and practical arts education, and that there are glaring deficiencies in the treatment of principles of teaching and learning and curricular experimentation. They further indicate the need for research that deals with the sociological and psychological implications of work, with specific community labor needs, and with the organization and administration of the vocational education program.

There are numerous other suggestions about needed research, many of which are concerned with funded research and so have categories of priorities that the funders will recognize. This practice of "prioritizing" research is quite typical of the federal agencies, as necessitated by controlling legislation, by the recommendations of advisory committees, or by the ultimate decisions of administrative officers. Private foundations also tend to support research of a particular viewpoint or orientation. It is evident that state educational agencies with the research coordination units acquired under the amended Vocational Education Act have also framed priority lists in compliance with the federal agency or with their own designs and purposes.

Brandon (1) identifies three prevalent positions among vocational educators with respect to research priorities. At one end of a continuum, practitioners (teachers, administrators, supervisors) wish to see more of the applied and action-type research, with more actual practitioners conducting or directing the research. Research results, accordingly, would be quickly interpreted, disseminated, applied, and evaluated. At the other end of the continuum, scholarly researchers advocate more basic research related to the psychological and social foundations of education. They indicate a need for much more freedom, fewer earmarks and priorities, more long-term grants, and fewer obligations to interpret and apply research findings.

A third voice, smaller yet not necessarily weaker, is heard from the advocate of interdisciplinary research, who demands the involvement of educators, economists, engineers, and others in vocational-technical research. Such an approach would thus involve numerous research methodologies. Research related to the economics of education in general and to vocational education in particular illustrates this approach. Current efforts in cost-benefit analysis, systems analysis, operations analysis, and information management and analysis for decision making are all related to this trend in research and research administration.

Obviously, research activities from these three positions, as well as from others, will continue. That their extreme positions must be reconciled is quite clear if research and development are to contribute to the meaningful education of youth and adults for vocational and career education.

Types of Educational Research

Educational research in vocational education may be classified into four basic types, each of which serves its unique function in the development and improvement of vocational education. *Basic research* is primarily concerned with producing scientifically exact knowledge, whereas *applied research* starts with the facts and propositions established in basic research and tests them in actual situations. *Research and development* programs focus on projects that result in finished products, such as textbooks and supplementary print and nonprint materials; these projects are usually too demanding, expensive, and time-consuming to be completed by one individual. *Action research* is concerned with obtaining specific knowledge about a particular group of respondents with results that are not generalizable to other situations.

Research Competencies

Vocational education teachers, supervisors, and teacher educators perform different functions and have varying responsibilities that require special research competencies.

Vocational Education Teacher

There are certain basic skills and knowledge that teachers need to possess, whether they are interested in conducting research or in implementing research findings. Specifically, they should be able to (2):

1 *use the language of research*

2 *locate sources of resource information*

3 *recognize the commonly used modes of research in education*

4 *enunciate a research problem*

5 *formulate well-constructed hypotheses, tentative solutions or predictive statements which incorporate theory into testable form*

6 *develop the research design for solving the problem*

7 *execute research with precision so that its purposes can be accomplished*

8 *draw conclusions that are based on accurate and valid interpretation of the findings*

9 *use the techniques and tools of research*

Vocational Education Supervisor

In addition to the research competencies recommended for the teacher, vocational education supervisors should also demonstrate competencies in (3):

1 *identifying instructional and curriculum developments that are believed to be sound*

2 *disseminating, communicating, and interpreting the findings of research to teachers*

3 *assisting teachers in identifying problems in vocational education and in developing scientific procedures for solving them*

4 *allocating and directing teachers to research sources so that they may use effectively the services of consultants and technicians*

5 *initiating and organizing institutes for the training and updating of teachers in the methods and techniques of research*

6 *preparing research proposals for submission to funding agencies*

7 *reporting to research centers and universities needed research in the area of vocational education*

Vocational Teacher Educator

It is generally assumed that vocational teacher educators will engage in research as part of their duties and responsibilities. Thus, they should demonstrate the competencies suggested for teachers and supervisors. They should also develop additional sophistication in the following areas (4):

1 *educational measurement*

2 *the disciplines that illuminate education, i.e., psychology, philosophy, anthropology and sociology*

3 *theory-based investigation*

4 *communicating effectively with colleagues so that problems of consequence will be identified and appropriate plans for action will be recommended*

5 *research methodology sufficient to permit effective communication with the research specialists on problems of design and analysis*

6 *research design*

7 *statistical analysis*

8 *use and capabilities of the computer as a research tool*

9 *preparing research proposals for funding*

10 *generating, guiding, and directing student research*

Translating Research into Practice

The translation of research findings into classroom practice is, in most instances, a slow process. For example, it may take one or more years to complete a research study, some time to write the report, from two to six months for journal editors to review it, and then, after acceptance, a lag of six months to a year before it is published. Thus, there may be a gap of 18 months to two years from the time a research report is completed until its publication.

A significant development that is helping to alleviate this problem is the creation of the Educational Resources Information Center (ERIC), which is an acquisition, storage, retrieval, and dissemination system for education. There are nineteen ERIC Clearinghouses throughout the nation, each responsible for a particular educational area. The ERIC Clearinghouse for Vocational and Career Education is currently at Northern Illinois University, DeKalb, Illinois. In addition to the ERIC Clearinghouses, the U.S. Office of Education has funded research and development centers and regional laboratories, which are concerned not only with the production of educational research but also with its dissemination and implementation.

One method of dissemination used by ERIC is *Research in Education,* a monthly publication made up of resumés and indexes. The resumés highlight current research reports, curriculum studies, instructional materials, conference proceedings, speeches, position papers, and bibliographies. The content of each issue is indexed according to subject, author, institution, and accession numbers. Documents that are summarized in *Research in Education* are available from the ERIC Document Reproduction Service in microfiche or hardcopy.

Another source of current information is Abstracts of Instructional and Research Materials (AIM/ARM), compiled and published several times each year by the Center for Vocational Education, Ohio State University, Columbus, Ohio. Each publication is divided into three subsections: abstracts, subject index, and author index. In addition to resumés of completed projects, the publication also includes abstracts of projects in progress. Documents cited in AIM/ARM are generally available in full text or in microfiche either from the publisher or the supplier.

The research consumer should also investigate the series of review and synthesis of research papers in vocational and technical education and related fields published by the Center for Vocational Education. These publications assist in identifying substantive problems and methodological approaches for researchers, and they provide practitioners with a summary of research findings. This series includes *Review and Synthesis of Research* in the various content areas of vocational education as well as in problem areas common to all the content fields. Recent releases include the following areas of interest: *Curriculum Development, Business and Office Education, Industrial Arts Education, Technical Education, Trade and Industrial Education, Administration of Vocational and Technical Education, Distributive Education, Home Economics Education, Placement and Follow-Up of Vocational Education Students, Vocational Education in Rural Areas,* and *Cooperative Education.*

The reevaluation of vocational education by the Panel of Consultants and the supportive position adopted by the American Vocational Association were primary influences leading to the establishment of research centers in vocational-technical education at Ohio State University and at North Carolina State University. The Center for Vocational Education is located at Ohio State University. Its seven purposes include three objectives related to research plus the study of the role of vocational and technical education, the improvement of leadership, foreign assistance, and retrieval of information. The center cooperates with the Education Research Information Center (ERIC) of the U.S. Office of Education. It became the first official clearinghouse for vocational and technical education, a function that has since been contracted to another institution.

An active effort at the University of Wisconsin includes three research focuses that are intimately related to vocational and technical education.

These include the Industrial Relations Research Institute, the Center for Studies in Vocational and Technical Education, and the Institute for Research on Poverty. The activities of the Wisconsin center are an example of those research efforts funded by private foundations, in this case, the Ford Foundation.

There are several centers on the international level that are active in vocational and technical education. The International Education Act is an American effort to provide for a center of this nature. The International Labour Organisation (ILO), with headquarters at Geneva, Switzerland, maintains centers for vocational training and research. The center at Geneva puts out a training periodical and has a continuing abstract service, both available by subscription directly from ILO, Geneva, or from its Washington, D.C., office. A more recent establishment of the ILO is the International Centre for Advanced Technical and Vocational Training, at Turin, Italy, which began its operation in 1965. It is a forum for study and research by (a) the fellows in the center, in the form of study and evaluation; and (b) various organizations interested in the different aspects of economic development, of a sociological, psychological, or pedagogical nature. Languages of instruction are English, French, and Spanish.

Annual reports of the U.S. Department of Labor's Office of Manpower Policy, Evaluation and Research (OMR), as illustrated in *Manpower Research Projects*, provide valuable reading for researchers in vocational-technical education. OMR's research program has covered the social, cultural, educational, and economic aspects of unemployment and the underutilization of labor. Much of its research has centered on the young, the nonwhite, the poorly educated, the handicapped, the older worker, and those in chronically depressed communities, regions, and industries. In its role as a coordinator of research in the Labor Department, OMR was instrumental in the passage of an amendment that authorized the Secretary of Labor to make grants to strengthen labor programs in colleges and universities and to stimulate the study of labor problems. This action has been implemented through the small-grants program and an institutional-grants program, the latter to support long-term programs of research, to provide technical assistance to organizations interested in labor policies and programs, to recruit and train needed research personnel, and to develop interdisciplinary research concerned with the use of human resources. Many doctoral students have received research support through the small-grants program.

The National Science Foundation's interest in the education of scientific and engineering personnel has led to some research activities on its part and to its cooperation with others in studies that relate to the engineering technician. It cooperated with the U.S. Employment Service in examining technical occupations in research, design, and development. Its grant and contract studies are usually reported in the literature and in its *Publications of the National Science Foundation* in "Manpower and Education Studies."

The various military services are very active in research that is invaluable to vocational and technical education. Training, testing, curriculum construction, personnel research and analysis, and many other activities are being conducted on a large scale in various branches of the military. Ready access to military research information is now possible through (a) the computerized Defense Documentation Center; its publication, the *Technical Abstract Bulletin*, provides brief research descriptions and numbers by which copies of research reports may be ordered; and (b) the Clearinghouse for Federal, Scientific, and Technical Information, which provides information retrieval. Its semimonthly journal, *U.S. Government Research and Development Reports*, is available from the U.S. Department of Commerce.

In 1963 the Ford Foundation and its Fund for the Advancement of Education became interested in vocational and technical education in the United States. The status of its support program is reported in *Ford Foundation Grants in Vocational Education*, published periodically by the foundation. The report indicates that grants are supporting work in four categories in secondary schools, technical institutes, community colleges, research organizations, universities, and teacher education institutions in: (a) curriculum improvement, (b) research, development, and information, (c) vocational-technical teacher education, and (d) cooperative work-study education. The foundation supports work at the University of Wisconsin and at the American Institutes for Research.

Graduate students are now, under the Vocational Education Act and the fellowship provisions of the Education Professions Development Act, producing studies related to the total field of vocational and technical education. For the most part, however, the subject matter of graduate education is not structured to produce research of this nature. Acknowledged weaknesses are in dissemination, application, and evaluation. But numerous completed projects and others currently in progress are worthy of examination.

In spite of all of these research efforts, adequate study of new and emerging occupations and their educational implications is not taking place. Instead, there is undue emphasis on the industrial and engineering technician and relatively little on the emerging occupations in agriculture, business and distribution, and health and medicine. This indicates that public school curriculum planners may be generally content to develop existing programs in depth, but at the expense of experimental programs to train people for promising new occupations and to awaken student interest. There is one bright note in this picture, however, in USOE's funding of the development of curricula and materials in 15 occupational clusters, reported elsewhere in this chapter.

Research conducted by state agencies, regional educational laboratories, curriculum development centers, and consortia is now beginning to increase. Several interesting new agencies now include research among their objectives. Among these are: (a) the new federal regions of education; (b) the regional consortia of educational laboratories of state agencies and universities; (c) the state research coordinating units; (d) the five curriculum development centers; and (e) the Educational Commission of the States, which established a sounding board for educational discussion and an inquiry base for the improvement of education.

At the international level, vocational-technical research has been far less actively undertaken than has instruction itself, although an increasing receptiveness toward research appears to be emerging. This attitude is not reserved to the developed countries of Western Europe, the Soviet Union, Japan, or the few countries that have received the bulk of foreign assistance. The developing countries in Latin America and Southeast Asia are also interested in research in vocational and technical education. The Agency for International Development of the U.S. Department of State assists hundreds of active projects throughout the world. Similar projects are supported on a smaller scale by UNESCO, the United Nations Educational, Scientific and Cultural Organization.

Problems in
Vocational-Technical Research

Brandon (5) has identified a number of general problems relative to research in the vocational and technical fields. First, vocational and technical administrators are frequently not "research prone"; that is, they are often inexperienced as to the problems of organizing, operating, and evaluating a research program. The sensitivity between researcher and administrator is always present, because the former wishes to study what he or she pleases, and the latter wishes to direct the attention and study to demonstrable ends. A desirable balance is thus difficult to maintain. Second, research in vocational and technical education is of relatively recent origin. Before some degree of sophistication could be achieved in and among the various specializations of this field, considerable research had become interdisciplinary. Regardless of the merit of the interdisciplinary involvement, communication and understanding are highly problematical. Research techniques, methods, and the terminology and jargon of one discipline are not always well understood or readily acceptable to workers in another discipline. This condition is clearly reflected in the economics of vocational education. No doubt the economist has justifiable interest in the analysis of expenditures and benefits if they are related to the decision-making process. The educator, on the other hand, cannot tolerate the hanging of a price tag on the many intangible purposes and contributions of educational programs. Again, if research is to be interdisciplinary in nature, it will need to be accompanied by education at many levels and not restricted to any one of the disciplines, even if the necessity of such education is not immediately evident to those who are counting the costs. Third, the ratio of supply to demand of research personnel is critically out of balance in the vocational and technical areas. Hopefully, the increased availability of funds for the preparation of research personnel is a step in the right direction.

To what extent can research help to solve the problems of vocational education? Through the years vocational educators have recognized that research is one means of helping to provide answers to problems at the local, state, and national levels.

Tyler (6) describes several functions of educational research that should help the vocational educator to recognize the role of research in answering questions and finding the solution to problems:

1 *to provide answers to operational questions*

2 *to assess educational programs, practices, and materials*

3 *to build up a body of information about the educational enterprise*

4 *to provide the outlook, stimulation and guidance for innovation*

5 *to develop valid theory about educational processes*

The following problems are typical of those that have been, and should continue to be, researched in vocational education:

1 If vocational education systems are to be evaluated and their efficiency improved, it is important to begin by clarifying the objectives, both generally and specifically; that is, what is expected from each level—national, state, local—and from each school, department, and course?

2 In the design of instructional content and method, what relative weight should be given to such educational objectives as the acquisition of concrete knowledge, problem-solving abilities, openness and tolerance, ability for cooperation, creativity, and so forth? What particular pedagogical techniques are most effective for attaining each objective?

3 Persons with the required mental abilities and motivation can likely succeed in many occupations. There are also many jobs in which persons with limited abilities can be successful if given the proper training. Can appropriate strategies be developed for selection and training of persons for those specific occupations in which limited skills are sufficient?

4 Other areas of concern include studies in methodology and prognosis. Which students learn most effectively by which instructional technique? Are some teachers more effective with certain methods of instruction than with others? Does the content determine the instructional method to be used? Can we predict a student's likelihood of success in a specific subject or occupation?

Participants at the National Conference of Research listed the following items as critical problem areas for most states (7): (a) the methodology of curriculum development; (b) the formation of broad labor policies; (c) the relative efficiency of various organizational structures for guiding occupational education; (d) building curriculum for the disadvantaged; (e) teacher education processes; (f) student selection procedures and devices; (g) the development of an informational system that will keep practicing teachers up to date; (h) the indexing of staff and personnel throughout the state who are competent in research techniques; and (i) the extent of vocational education in the private sector.

An AVA publication (*Research and Implementation in Vocational Education*, 1969) identified six topics relating to vocational teaching that call for investigation: philosophical foundations of vocational education; the process of vocational instruction; the preparation of professional personnel; reorganizing the high school curriculum; postsecondary vocational development; and vocational guidance and career development.

If vocational educators are to use educational research to improve classroom practice and to find answers to problems in the field, then they must realize that:

1 educational practices need to be continually challenged, evaluated, and redesigned

2 to effect progressive change, schools and departments need the ability to adapt meaningfully to proven innovative practices

3 the most crucial single factor is the competence of the teacher; little progress can be made until more professionally competent and committed teachers give priority to their role as agents for change

4 research and development, to change vocational education for the better, must involve researchers, educators, and citizens working together to build a profession of education relevant to the times

Analysis of Research

The consumer of research should be able to analyze a research report, determining its strengths and weaknesses as well as its applicability to his or her own situation. The following questions (8), answered on a scale of one to five, are examples of those a consumer of research might raise in the process of critical analysis.

Clarity

1 How clear is the purpose of the study or what the researchers are attempting to do?

2 How explicit are the researchers as to whether the study is attempting to (a) describe, (b) classify, (c) show relationship, (d) test a hypothesis?

3 How explicit are the basic assumptions of the researchers which are indicated?

4 How well defined or how understandable are the terms used in the report?

5 How explicitly are the limitations of the study stated?

Comprehensiveness

1 How adequately is the population and sample utilized in the study described?

2 How adequately are the possible variables affecting the study accounted for?

3 How adequately are the procedures or methods of data gathering described?

Other considerations

1 To what extent did the researchers discuss the validity, or appropriateness and reliability, or consistency of the instruments or coding procedures of the study?

2 To what extent is the situation in which the research was conducted similar to that which you might accept as real or natural?

3 To what extent were you able to differentiate among results, conclusions, and implications in the study?

4 To what extent do the measures, instruments, attitudes, inventories, test scores, validity and reliability describe what the research is attempting to demonstrate: i.e., better teaching, better learning, or the relationship among several variables?

5 On the basis of the above questions, is the study strong or weak?

Sources of Funding for Educational Research and Development

Educational research cannot prosper unless it receives adequate financial support. Table 11.1 indicates U.S. Office of Education (USOE) appropriations for research and training of researchers from 1957 to 1970. In 1957, total USOE appropriations for research and training were only $1 million, whereas in 1970 they were more than $110 million—over a hundredfold increase in 13 years. Fiscal year 1966 is significant, for in that year USOE made its largest dollar increase in support of educational research—from $36 million to over $100 million. Since 1970 the dollar figures have shown a tendency to decline.

Although the U.S. Office of Education and the National Institute of Education are the largest sources of funding for educational research, other government and private agencies play an important role. These other agencies include the National Science Foundation, National Institute of Mental Health, National Institute of Child Health and Human Development, Department of Defense, other federal and state agencies, and private foundations. Financial support for educational research of all kinds is shown by sponsoring agency in Table 11.2.

Table 11.1   Appropriations for Research and Training:
U.S. Office of Education (in thousands of dollars)

Fiscal year	Cooperative research	NDEA* Title VI	NDEA Title VII	Vocational research	Library research	Handicapped research	Totals
1970	$88,900	$2,500	—	$ 1,100	—	$18,000	$110,500
1969	76,077	—	—	11,375	—	15,000	102,452
1968	66,467	3,000	4,400	13,550	3,550	11,000	101,967
1967	70,000	3,100	4,400	10,000	3,550	8,100	99,150
1966	70,000	2,800	4,000	17,750	—	6,000	100,550
1965	15,800	2,250	4,963	11,850	—	2,000	36,863
1964	11,500	1,800	5,000	—	—	1,000	19,300
1963	6,985	1,800	5,000	—	—	—	13,785
1962	5,000	2,000	4,755	—	—	—	11,755
1961	3,357	2,000	4,700	—	—	—	10,057
1960	3,200	4,000	3,000	—	—	—	10,200
1959	2,700	2,500	1,600	—	—	—	6,800
1958	2,300	—	—	—	—	—	2,300
1957	1,000	—	—	—	—	—	1,000

* National Defense Education Act.

Source: U.S. Office of Education, Bureau of Research, Educational Research and Development in the United States (Washington, D.C.: U.S. Government Printing Office, 1969), p. 158.

Despite the long-range increase in the level of financial support for educational research and development, the total remains low. In fiscal 1968, the total estimate (9) of $192 million, expended for educational research and development by the U.S. Office of Education and all other agencies, constituted only one-third of 1 percent of the total education expenditures of $54.6 billion. Most industrial companies, by comparison, expend from 3–5 percent of their budget on research and development. Francis Chase (10), who has made an extensive study of the problem, recommends that support be increased until at least 1 percent of national expenditures for education are devoted to research and development.

With this brief background of funding support, let us examine the ways in which the federal government has sponsored various types of educational research and development.

National Center for Educational Research and Development

Until 1970 most of the federal support for educational research was administered by the U.S. Office of Education, a division of the Department of Health, Education and Welfare. Various agencies within USOE support research activities. In 1969 the Bureau of Research was reorganized and

Table 11.2 Financial Support for Educational Research and Development, by Sponsoring Agency: United States, Fiscal Year 1968

Agency	Amount of support
Total	$192,290,000
Office of Education	101,967,000
National Science Foundation	23,326,000
National Institute of Mental Health	11,860,000
National Institute of Child Health and Human Development	8,377,000
Office of Economic Opportunity	12,800,000
Department of Defense	6,046,000
Other Federal agencies (Labor, Commerce, Children's Bureau, Agriculture, Social Rehabilitation Service, Food and Drug Administration, Interior, National Endowment for the Arts, and National Endowment for the Humanities)	6,725,000
Private foundations	7,344,000
All other (State agencies, higher education institutions, professional and academic associations, etc.)	13,845,000*

Includes estimates for State and local government agencies.

Source: U.S. Department of Health, Education, and Welfare, Office of Education, Bureau of Research, Educational Research and Development in the United States, July 1969.

became the National Center for Educational Research and Development (NCERD). The new title was intended to reflect the USOE commitment to research and development as an approach to improving American education. The center contained five divisions: (a) Educational Laboratories, (b) Elementary and Secondary Education Research, (c) Comprehensive and Vocational Education Research, (d) Higher Education Research, and (e) Information Technology and Dissemination.

The Division of Comprehensive and Vocational Education Research was formed to support research related to vocational education at the high school and junior college levels. It was composed of branches for basic research, instructional materials studies, and studies on organization and administration. An additional branch, the Career Opportunities Branch, was established to support research concerned with identifying and developing careers in new and growing subprofessional fields.

NCERD was dismantled in a USOE reorganization in 1972. Its research responsibilities were absorbed largely by the Bureau of Occupational and Adult Education.

National Research and Development Centers

Two research and development centers were authorized under the Vocational Education Act of 1963 to stimulate national interest in research in vocational and technical education. One of these, the Center for Vocational Education, is located at Ohio State University. Its activities have included a wide range of projects of national scope, including the contract for the federally funded Comprehensive Career Education Model. The Center for Occupational Education is located at North Carolina State University. Its activities have, in some measure, focused on the unique problems of vocational and technical education in the Southern region of the United States.

National Institute of Education

In 1972, at the request of President Richard M. Nixon, Congress created the National Institute of Education (NIE). Operating within the Department of Health, Education and Welfare and independent of USOE, NIE was created as a vehicle for supporting educational research and development. Its first director, Thomas Glennan, developed an organizational structure composed of the following units:

1 *The Office of Research Grants* was vested with responsibility for stimulating research in five study areas: human development, social thought and processes, learning and instruction, objectives and evaluation, and the educational system.

2 *The Office of Research and Exploratory Studies* was charged with a broad range of policy research issues, including exploratory studies leading to program commitments in curriculum and instruction and responsibility for assessment of regional educational laboratories and research and development centers (formerly a USOE responsibility).

3 *The Office of Programmatic Research and Development* was named to administer major research and development initiatives undertaken by NIE, including short-range programs oriented toward development and demonstration as well as toward integrated programs of longer duration.

4 *The Office of Research and Development Resources* was formed to improve the effectiveness of educational research, including a research program on the research and development system itself, in addition to training and dissemination services for linking the institute with the research and development community.

5 *The Office of Planning and Management* was charged with five major responsibilities: planning and evaluation, budget, management systems, organization development, and staff support to the National Council on Educational Research.

6 *The Office of Administration* was given responsibility for five divisions: grants and contracts, finance, general services, personnel, and information resources.

The National Council on Educational Research is responsible for formulating general policies for the Institute. They advise the Director of NIE on program development; recommend improved methods of collecting, disseminating, and implementing education research findings; and submit annual reports to the President and Congress on the Institute's activities, education research, and education in general.

Congress intended that the National Institute of Education would exercise a major role in directing educational research and development at all levels. But from the beginning, the new agency encountered difficulty in securing funding. In its first year, NIE saw its budget reduced from a recommended $162 million to $75 million. The fiscal 1975 budget, which was submitted by NIE to the Congress, totaled $162 million.

Research priorities established by the National Council on Educational Research directed NIE's efforts toward: (a) basic research into the learning process; (b) problems of education for the disadvantaged; (c) educational financing; (d) improving the education of educators; (e) linkage between research and development institutions and schools and universities; and (f) emerging approaches to education: continuing education, nonformal and extra-institutional education, and the relationship of public and nonpublic education.

The NIE was authorized (11) ". . . to assume responsibility not only for the development of educational materials and practices, but also for their dissemination (previously vested in the Office of Education) to students, teachers, administrators, and other potential users."

Bureau of
Occupational and Adult Education

The primary vehicle for the national planning and direction of programs of vocational and technical education is the Bureau of Occupational and Adult Education within the U.S. Office of Education in Washington, D.C. One of the ways in which the bureau seeks to improve and extend vocational education is through its discretionary programs. Under authorization of the Vocational Education Amendments of 1968 (Public Law 90–576), the Bureau provides contract and grant support to vocational education for (a) applied research and training projects (Part C, Section 131 (a)), (b) exemplary demonstration projects (Part D, Section 142 (c)), and (c) curriculum development and coordination projects (Part I). The purpose of these complementary efforts is to improve and extend the vocational education process at the elementary-secondary, postsecondary, and adult levels, to promote the development and diffusion of vocational education curriculum materials, and to demonstrate the results of these efforts to educators and the public, including new ways to create a bridge between school and the world of work for young people. The bureau's Division of Research and Demonstration administers these three programs.

Projects and programs supported by the bureau are carried out through individual contract or grant awards, which are made in response to proposals submitted by colleges and universities, by state and local education agencies, by other public or nonprofit private agencies or institutions, as well as by profit-making groups. Competitions for new grant awards, including priority or program statements, are announced in the *Federal Register*. Request for Proposals (RFPs), which result in contracts, are announced in the *Commerce Business Daily* when proposals are being sought for a specific product.

Various groups advise the Bureau of Occupational and Adult Education concerning the establishment of priorities for the applied research, exemplary demonstration, and curriculum programs each fiscal year. Counsel is sought from the Research Committee of the National Advisory Council on Vocational Education, from the National Network for Curriculum Coordination in Vocational-Technical Education, from the National Research Coordinating Unit Directors Association, and from other groups or individuals concerned with improving the quality of vocational education.

Programs The Vocational Education Amendments of 1968, authorizes federal assistance to states to maintain, extend, and improve existing programs of vocational education. Among other things, the states are to develop new programs of vocational education so that persons of all ages in all communities will have ready access to vocational training or retraining that is of high quality, realistic in the light of actual or anticipated employment opportunities, and suited to their needs, interests, and ability to benefit from such training.

1 *Research and training in vocational education* Part C, Section 131 (a) of the act authorizes the Commissioner of Education to make contracts and grants to support (a) research in vocational education; (b) training programs designed to familiarize persons involved in vocational education with research findings and successful pilot and demonstration projects in vocational education; (c) experimental, developmental, and pilot programs designed to test the effectiveness of research findings; (d) demonstration and dissemination projects; (e) the development of new vocational education curricula; and (f) projects in the development of new careers and occupations.

2 *Exemplary programs and projects in vocational education* Part D, Section 142(c) of the act authorizes the Commissioner of Education to make grants and contracts to stimulate, through federal financial support, new ways to create bridges between school and earning a living for young people who are still in school, who have left school either by graduation or by dropping out, or who are in postsecondary programs of vocational education. Such programs or projects may, among others, include those that (a) are designed to familiarize elementary and secondary school students with the broad range of occupations for which special skills are required and with the requisites for careers in such occupations; (b) will give students educational experiences through work during the school year or in the summer; (c) will provide intensive occupational guidance and counseling during the last years of school and for initial job placement; (d) are designed to broaden or improve vocational education curricula; (e) will provide for exchanges of personnel between school and other agencies, institutions, or organizations participating in activities to achieve the purpose of this subpart, including labor agencies and industry; (f) will increase the educational attainment of young workers released from their jobs on a part-time basis; and (g) will motivate and provide preparation for potential vocational education teachers at the secondary level.

3 *Curriculum development in vocational and technical education* Part I of the act authorizes the Commissioner of Education to make grants and contracts to (a) promote the development and dissemination of vocational education curriculum materials for use in teaching occupational subjects, including curricula for new and changing occupational fields and for those in public service; (b) develop standards for curriculum development in all occupational fields; (c) coordinate efforts of the states in preparation of curriculum materials and prepare current lists of curriculum materials available in all occupational fields; (d) survey curriculum materials produced by other agencies of government, including the Department of Defense; (e) evaluate vocational-technical education curriculum materials and their uses; and (f) train personnel in curriculum development.

Eligibility For each of the three programs previously described, grants or contracts may be awarded in the following categories to agencies or institutions (individuals are not eligible applicants): (a) institutions of higher education; (b) State Boards for Vocational Education; (c) local education agencies; (d) other public or private agencies or institutions, including profit-making organizations. Applications from local education agencies requesting support under Part C (applied research and training programs) and Part D (exemplary or innovative demonstration projects) must be approved by the appropriate State Board for Vocational Education. Under Part D of the act, when an applicant is other than a State Board for Vocational Education or a local education agency, a case must be made that such a grant or contract will make an especially significant contribution to attaining the objectives established for exemplary programs and projects in vocational education. Under Parts C and D, profit-making organizations are eligible for contracts but not grants. All others eligible as applicants may be awarded grants or contracts, with the latter instrumentality generally restricted to the procurement of a particular product as solicited in the *Commerce Business Daily.*

Preparation of Research Proposals

The use of project proposals as vehicles for the development, implementation, and funding of new educational programs has become standard practice. As a result, proposal writing is a valuable skill for both the teacher and administrator. In this section, we look at the mechanics of preparing a proposal. Suggestions are made relative to the various components and procedures, including the rationale, related research, objectives, hypotheses, design, evaluation, dissemination, facilities, personnel, and budget.

Practical Considerations
Prior to Proposal Writing

Some of the factors that will influence the timing of proposals are the following:

1 Availability of funds at the funding level Some agencies commit the bulk of their funds long before the end of the fiscal year in June, so that an application submitted in May, for example, does not have much of a chance during that fiscal year. On the other hand, sometimes there are monies left over in June, which may cause accelerated action on proposals already submitted by that time.

2 Personnel availability Many districts have had great difficulty finding project directors and other important project staff if they have not begun their search early enough. New job hunting begins in the winter, and most regular staff are committed by April or May.

3 Local budgeting For those projects that require cooperative support at the school district level or matching funds, provisions must be made for this consideration in the budget. Budgets are approved at different times of the year, but most are drawn up in the winter and voted on or otherwise approved in April or May. If a proposal requires local funds, this circumstance must be known before budget time.

4 Student schedules Although school is in session from September to June, neither of those months is worth much as far as instructional programs are concerned. Therefore, the beginning date for a project directly affecting students over several months should be between October and February.

5 Procedural delays Proposals cannot be written in a day nor can approval on most projects be obtained in a week. Considering all the factors involved in preplanning, consultation, obtaining local approval, revision, incorporation of state and national suggestions, and preparation of manuscript, a district will need months to bring a proposal to final form.

Review procedures on some kinds of research projects at the USOE or NIE require from two to six months. If state approval is also needed, an additional few weeks should be added in. After approval, two or three days are taken up in notifying the congressman, so he or she can pass the information on to the newspaper. Then negotiation of budgets may require four to six weeks.

Writing the Proposal

Application and proposal forms vary in complexity, from the "fill-in-the blank" type to the proposal for a competitive research grant that will be scrutinized by panels of specialists. The writing of research proposals has become a high art. Every foundation and agency that dispenses research funds requires a statement of the nature of the proposed project. Sometimes it is required that these statements adhere rather rigidly to a standard format; in other instances the format is quite flexible.

In the actual writing of a research project proposal in which careful account must be made of rationale, procedures, and evaluation, these sections will usually be included:

1 rationale, statement of the problem

2 review of the literature

3 objectives

4 hypotheses

5 the design

6 procedures

7 evaluation

8 dissemination

9 facilities

10 personnel

11 budget

Not all components are relevant to all agencies, but it is important to keep in mind the nature and requirements of each. Also, the format of experimental, pilot, and developmental proposals may vary considerably depending on the scope of the project.

For several reasons, it is not possible to give complete instructions on how to design a research proposal. Each project varies from others in such ways that different procedures are needed in every case. A thorough analysis of research design and statistical analysis would take several hundred pages. Moreover, within each project and design there are alternate paths that may be taken. However, there are points of similarity in most proposals, and some of the major points are outlined in this section.

Rationale, statement of the problem The rationale section should explain why the project is needed and the general theory on which the procedures rest. The outline of the statement of the problem may run somewhat as follows:

1 State the problem in terms intelligible to someone who is generally sophisticated but who is relatively uninformed in the area of the problem.

2 Define and delimit the specific area of the research.

3 Indicate the broad questions or hypotheses to be tested.

4 Indicate briefly the significance of the study.

5 Include a single clear statement of the purpose of the research.

The section on significance is often the one that the researcher finds hardest to write. The following suggestions should prove helpful:

1 Indicate how your research will refine, revise, or extend existing knowledge. This applies both to content and method.

2 Almost all studies have two potential audiences, practitioners and professional peers. Statements relating the research to both groups are in order.

3 Indicate what the research means for your institution.

Review of the literature Almost every proposal includes a review of the literature, which serves at least two purposes:

1 It demonstrates to the reader that the writer has a comprehensive grasp of the field and is aware of recent developments.

2 It explains how the study will refine, revise, and/or extend what is currently known about the problem.

It is not easy to decide where to put the review of literature because it can describe research related to all phases of the project, from rationale to procedures. Probably the best place is after the rationale. The review is an essential part of the proposal, for it serves to convince the reader that the investigator is not duplicating previous research on the same subject and it shows that the investigator is aware of the findings of related research. The review should show (a) the uniqueness of the proposal, (b) previous discoveries, if any, related to the proposed research, and (c) gaps in previous research to be filled in by the proposed project.

As a starter, the uninitiated reviewer may wish to look for related research in sources such as the *Encyclopedia of Educational Research*, the *Review of Educational Research*, the *Education Index*, the *Psychological Abstracts*, the yearbooks of professional associations in the vocational service areas, specialized books and periodicals, research available through ERIC microfiche, the *Research in Education* Abstracts, *Abstracts of Instructional Materials* (AIM), and *Abstracts of Research Materials* (ARM).

The organization of the review will vary according to the purpose of the project, but one possible sequence is: (a) historical reviews of the topic in brief style, as in the *Review of Educational Research;* (b) a sufficiently detailed summary of several closely related experiments so the reader can understand procedures and results; and (c) analysis of previous research, showing its relevance to the current proposal.

Objectives, hypotheses, questions Research seeks to test hypotheses or to answer questions. Hypotheses are stated when the researcher wants to test the implications of a theory. In instances where a theory cannot be stated, it is appropriate to ask questions or to pose objectives. The reader of the proposal should be able to connect a particular objective with activities in the procedure section. He or she should also be able to judge whether the evaluation method will indeed determine whether the objectives have been obtained.

Procedures (design, treatment, and evaluation) As the instructions from the USOE or the NIE imply, projects vary so much that no suggested prescription for procedural design will be universally useful. Most proposals, however, contain the following sections:

1 *Design* This section should make it clear whether the basic technique employed is that of a controlled experiment, a case study, an opinion survey, or whatever. In the case of the experiment, it must be shown that the project staff will be able to identify and control variables such as treatment, control procedures, and the like.

2 *Population* In the case of a design calling for the study of subjects, these persons should be described in terms of their age, sex, training, special characteristics relative to the study, and the method to be used to select the population as a sample of a larger group.

3 *Treatment* If there is a subject population and its members are to be taught in some special way or given an experimental treatment, the procedure must explicitly describe what will be done to the experimental group and to the control group. One common weakness to avoid is the brief reference to the control group as receiving "conventional instruction"; more detail is needed.

4 *Instrumentation* Instrumentation is a point at which many research designs break down. Fundamentally sound ideas can fail to produce fruitful findings if instruments not relevant to the variables are used. The writer should be careful to describe the instruments to be used in the study and the process of development, if the instruments are to be constructed.

5 *Sampling* The sample should identify the population to which the results will be appropriate and the type of data to be collected.

6 *Data collection* The proposal should include the general plans for collecting the data plus the anticipated time schedule.

7 *Data analysis* The analysis of data usually involves some type of statistical treatment. The proposal should thus specify the statistical or analytical procedures to be used and the tools, such as a computer program, that are to be employed.

Evaluation The evaluation section is commonly the weakest part of proposals. It may be helpful to define the term "evaluation" as that process by which some persons pass judgment on the degree to which the aims of an enterprise were successfully achieved. This judgment is usually based on the collection of data and then by its analysis and interpretation.

In this section the investigator should explain as explicitly as possible how he or she will determine the degree to which the objectives of the project have been realized (instrumentation, data collection, and data analysis are discussed above). Strengthening the evaluation section means paying closer attention to basic procedures such as (a) listing objectives in measurable form; (b) describing the method of collecting data; and (c) outlining the techniques of interpreting the data.

Dissemination Another of the weaker sections of many proposals, the dissemination part should clearly indicate a workable plan for spreading project information to other organizations to aid them in the process of imitation. Possible techniques include demonstration, publicity in professional publications and in news media, state education department publicity, lectures and reports at conventions, and the final report that can be made available through ERIC microfiche or hard copy. The criteria for judging dissemination plans include clarity, validity, pervasiveness, impact, timeliness, and practicality.

Facilities Granting authorities are naturally interested in knowing whether a local district has the building, equipment, laboratories, etc., necessary for the successful conduct of a project. The proposal should include a description of pertinent facilities, such as space available, subjects available, staff talent, sources of consultative help, data processing center, library and instructional media resources.

Personnel The agency also wants to know who the people are who will conduct the project activities. Of course, these people may not be known at the time of application—another argument for appointing a local person as project director in advance. A description of a person's background includes his or her education, professional experience, publications, and honors. This is no time to be modest, because the reviewing field readers and/or consultants are wary of persons without degrees and college affiliations.

Budget Budget preparation is tiresome and difficult, especially for the novice. And yet it is important because it shows whether the author really understands the practical requirements of the proposed project. Careless budget preparation may suggest that the applicant would be unable to support a needed operation in the later phases of the project.

Parts of the budget It is important at the outset to investigate the budget requirements of one's own institution and those of the granting agency. Explain in detail how estimates are determined. Do not pad and do not overlook overhead and other entitlements. Budget forms differ from one department to another, but they are likely to contain provision for the following expenditure categories:

1 *Personnel* Specify how total amounts were calculated. For example:

Consultant, statistical, ten days at $100 a day	$1000
Asst. Project Director, Two years half-time at	
$10,000 per year plus $550 annual increment	$10,275
Secretary, four months at $500 per month	$2000

Note that U.S. Office of Education does not ordinarily approve amounts greater than $100 a day for consultants unless the organization requesting funds customarily pays more or unless there is a special reason for a higher fee.

2 *Benefits* The grantee may elect to pay benefits. Otherwise do not forget these categories: retirement, social security, health benefits. The business office in your organization or the state accounting office can provide the percentage to be used for estimation of professional and nonprofessional retirement, social security, and health benefits.

3 *Travel* There has been a general tightening up on travel allowances in the past few years. However, it is still reasonable to ask for money to make reports at one or two important conferences, to travel to visit consultants and other projects of a similar nature, to pay for consultant travel and for local travel of project personnel on official business. The rate for the latter should be at the level of the organization sponsoring the proposal; for example, 12 cents per mile.

4 *Supplies* It takes paper to run the project. There are reports, correspondence, memorandums, etc., for which supplies will be needed. Film, audio tapes, and other materials of this type will be needed if students are to be instructed through the project.

5 *Equipment* Some agencies will permit the purchase of research equipment; others will not. Some will buy 20 percent the first year, 20 percent of the remaining costs the second year, and so forth. In general, the purchase of office equipment is not encouraged, although it is not unusual to allow rental of typewriters or other office equipment.

6 *Communications* Telephone costs to be included are the regular trunk costs plus long distance calls. This category also includes the cost of postage.

7 *Services* These include items such as the development of film, computer rental, data processing, etc.

8 *Rental* Rental of office space may be budgeted, but it will normally be charged to overhead. Find out the cost per square foot of renting space in your area, estimate the number of square feet needed, and figure a total. Utilities and custodial service charges will increase if more space is required. Some of these costs may be paid out of local money in order to make the local contribution a real one.

9 *Indirect costs* The allowance varies from one agency to another and the policy varies from one year to the next. Some large organizations, such as universities, have determined a flat percentage charge for overhead, based on estimates obtained by their auditors. Smaller organizations may have to negotiate the overhead percentage or budget separate items as direct cost expenditures. Some agencies allow a flat percentage; others allow no overhead at all.

The overhead is an estimate of the additional expense an institution will incur if it supports a grant project. Project administration adds many hours of time and many headaches to administrators who are not on the project budget. The business office has bills to pay and the superintendent has phone calls and visits to make in connection with the project. One method of arriving at an estimate of overhead is to obtain the total budget figure for the administration of a district and take a fixed percentage of it.

Local contribution Some vocational education projects require the local district to make a 50 percent contribution to costs of the project on the premise that the government should not be the only agency willing to support projects at the local level. Typical local contributions are for secretarial help, travel, consultation, employee benefits, office materials, telephone, postage, rental, utilities, and estimated administrative overhead not reimbursed by the government.

Deviations from budget It is unlikely that anyone will stay exactly on the budget to the last dollar. A common rule of thumb is that deviations from the line item expenditure estimates may be made to the extent of 15 percent, except for sensitive items such as travel and equipment. In other words, transfer from one item to another may be made without notifying the agency if the amounts do not exceed 10 percent of the budget item from which the transfer is to be made. Each agency should be consulted about its policy.

Evaluation of Proposals

After the proposal is received by the funding agency, it is usually circulated to reviewers who are experts in the field under investigation. Reviewers normally employ about four basic criteria or questions in judging the worth of a proposal:

1 Is the problem educationally significant, as measured by

(a) the importance of the problem

(b) a sound theoretical basis for the problem

(c) the extent to which results can be generalized

(d) the relationship to similar known research

2 Are personnel and facilities adequate, as measured by

(a) professional competence and experience of the investigator

(b) necessary space, personnel, and equipment for performing the work

3 Is the research design sound, as measured by

(a) clear and logical statements and relationships among the problem, objectives, and procedures

(b) information in the statement of procedures including, where applicable, sampling techniques, controls, data to be gathered, instruments to be used, and statistical and other analyses to be made

4 Is the proposal economically efficient, as measured by a favorable relationship between the probable outcome of the project and the total effort expended

The following inadequacies may be identified (12) as among the most frequent and serious that occur in research proposals:

1 *The problem is trivial.*

2 *The problem is not delimited.*

3 *The objectives, hypotheses, or questions are stated too broadly.*

4 *The procedures are lacking in detail.*

5 *The design is not appropriate for the problem; that is, a simple design is frequently used to investigate a complex problem.*

6 *Relevant variables are not considered or are lightly dismissed.*

Examples of
Vocational Education Research

Research relating to vocational education is in its formative stages, as a majority of the research activities have taken place since the funding of the Vocational Education Act of 1963. The purpose of this section is to illustrate the nature and scope of research in vocational and technical education. No attempt is made to cover the research already performed or underway in the various specialized fields of vocational education. Research projects cited in other sections of the book are not repeated in this chapter.

Career Education

A series of USOE-funded projects concerned with the development and validation of career education curriculum guides in each of the 15 occupational clusters are underway or have been completed. The objectives of the business and office education project are typical of those for each cluster: (a) to develop and disseminate career education curriculum guides and instructional materials for teacher use in the business and office occupations area, grades K–14; (b) to devise renewal and validation processes that may be used for future updating of curricula and materials; (c) to revitalize the thinking of business and office education in relation to its own development, its relationship to career education, and its interaction with business and industry; (d) to use a systems approach to curriculum development in the business and office education field; (e) to upgrade business and office education teacher performance with materials and methods involving career education. The principal outcome of this project will be a series of career education guides, with supporting instructional modules, comprising an instructional system for teacher use in the business and office education curriculum.

Curriculum Organization

Research seems to indicate that a broadly prepared individual, with both skills and cognitive background for a cluster of occupations, is likely to be better prepared to adjust to technological developments in his or her own field. Maley's study at the University of Maryland (13) is an example of an investigation into the cluster concept of vocational education at the secondary level.

Competency-Based Education

Several studies have been completed or are in process that focus on the competency approach to curriculum construction. An example is Crawford's study (14) in distributive education, which entailed (a) a validated list of basic beliefs about distributive education, (b) an identification of the critical tasks of the distributive teacher-coordinator, and (c) the know-how for the performance of these tasks and for the implementation of the basic beliefs.

Curriculum Modification

The SCOPE project (Study of Curriculums for Occupational Preparation and Education) at Rutgers University (15) was initiated to coordinate and contribute to national curriculum development efforts at the secondary level. It was aimed at increasing the relevance of high school education for the large majority of the nation's youth, who must seek employment or further job training following graduation. An initial task of the project was to assist 15 state-supported vocational curriculum development centers to establish better communication and cooperation among themselves and to provide information concerning present trends in the production of curriculum materials.

Curriculum Evaluation

Hemp et al (16) evaluated pilot programs in Illinois that had as their main focus innovations in educational programs for high school students who were preparing for employment in both farm and nonfarm occupations. The report of this two-year study included a comprehensive list of guidelines and suggestions for planning and conducting programs in agricultural occupations for high school youth.

Curriculum Revision

The NOBELS study (New Office and Business Education Learning Systems) was a major research study involving the coordinated efforts of five educational institutions located throughout the United States—Lanham, Michigan; Tonne, New York; Calhoun, Georgia; Price, Minnesota; Erickson, California. The primary purpose of the study was the development of an inventory of educational specifications in behavioral terms that represent basic tasks performed by office workers in the 16–24 age group. Based on empirical data collected by interview from 1232 office employees and their supervisors from four regions of the United States, the educational specifications were drawn from 4548 basic tasks and 32,447 steps of task performance. Analysis of the resulting data suggests clues for curriculum renewal.

At least two precedents were established for business education by the NOBELS study that have implications for other vocational fields: 1. For the first time, a profession-wide group of business educators cooperatively planned and implemented a research effort designed to bring the field abreast of changes in business and industry. The involvement of all segments of the profession produced a research product with maximum potential impact. 2. This research pointed the way toward meaningful revisions of business curricula through the systems approach.

Curriculum Consortium

In an effort to coordinate vocational education curriculum development and management at the national level, the U.S. Office of Education funded the formation of a national network of seven curriculum centers, located in California, Illinois, Kentucky, Mississippi, New Jersey, Oklahoma, and Washington. Five purposes were identified for the network and the affiliated states: (a) to provide a mechanism for the sharing of information on curriculum materials available and under development; (b) to develop guidelines for curriculum development, with the ultimate goal of increasing the effectiveness of curriculum materials and enhancing their transportability; (c) to establish a system for determining curriculum needs in vocational-technical education and for reporting conclusions to the field; (d) to coordinate activities in curriculum development, dissemination, and utilization, with the aim of avoiding unwarranted duplication, enhancing quality of effort, and improving the acceptance and use of curriculum materials; and (e) to report these curriculum coordination efforts to the field. Abstracts of curriculum developments are also included in a special section of AIM, *Abstracts of Instructional Materials in Vocational and Technical Education.*

The following may be identified as advantages to an individual state as a result of this consortium membership:

1 a survey of incumbent workers and, thus, knowledge of what is being done in the field

2 a core of people who can analyze occupational data and convert those data into meaningful performance objectives that are linked to the actual job

3 a core of people who have expertise in writing performance objectives and criterion test items

4 a commonality study of tasks across domain areas for purposes of developing a core curriculum

5 a framework for curriculum development

6 articulation across levels of instruction by labeling the tasks in a sequential manner

7 knowledge of a systems approach to curriculum

8 information about placement that can have monumental implications for vocational counseling and guidance

9 the opportunity to share in-service activity plans with other states

10 a series of catalogs of performance objectives and criterion-referenced measures in many domain areas

11 a network of instructors throughout the state who are trained to provide relevant instruction through the use of valid and reliable objectives and test items

12 a boon to individualized instruction

13 a move toward educational accountability

Vocational, General, College Preparatory Programs

Kaufman and others (17) examined the role of the secondary school in occupational preparation of its graduates by reviewing vocational, general, and college preparation programs in large, medium, and small cities. The results of this regional study generally supported the notion that vocational education has an unrealized and underused potential for education. In general the results of the program evaluations presented a picture of sins of omission rather than sins of commission. What the schools were doing, they were doing adequately. Their weaknesses reflected those things they should have been doing but were not. Most prominent among these omissions was the failure to develop programs for those students who could not profit from present offerings. The proportion of students enrolled in the vocational curriculum compared to the proportion of those who obtained jobs upon leaving school attests to the need for new approaches. Other significant weaknesses were the poor guidance programs and the insufficient use of advisory committees.

Occupational Analyses

Occupational analyses have been applied to almost every area of vocational education. Huffman and Gust (18) attempted to identify high-priority abilities needed for new office occupations. Brandon (19) explored the understandings needed by technicians, whereas Loreen (20), and Drake and Tom (21) investigated nonfarm agricultural jobs. Ertel (22) identified the major tasks performed by merchandising employees.

Research has made great contributions to the advancement of all segments of our society. Education has, however, benefited less than other areas such as agriculture, industry, and medicine. Several changes are necessary for improvement of research in vocational education: More funds must be allocated for research; persons sponsoring research must be active, competent researchers; the primary purpose for research should be to gain new knowledge, not to achieve status by getting a degree; efforts of independent researchers should be coordinated to maximize research output; there should be uniformity in preparation of studies to facilitate summarization; and mistakes of the past should be recognized by individuals striving to attain higher levels of objective research.

Summary

Research in vocational education has not kept pace with such activity in other education fields or in business and industry because of the field's service orientation and the lack of systematic federal funding before 1963.

Four types of research activities may be identified in vocational education: basic research, applied research, research and development, and action research. Certain well-defined competencies are necessary for the vocational educator who engages in such research, whether he or she is a teacher, supervisor, or teacher educator. These competencies emphasize research-mindedness and the ability to plan, execute, and evaluate the findings of research.

The ERIC Clearinghouse for Vocational and Career Education (its publication, *Research in Education*) and the Center for Vocational Education (AIM/ARM documents) have been highly effective in disseminating the results of research and development in vocational and technical education. Research centers, such as those at The Ohio State University, North Carolina State University, and the University of Wisconsin, have been active in promoting and conducting a wide variety of research in this field.

Examples of problem areas that need investigation include the building of curricula for the disadvantaged, the preparation of professional personnel, identification of competencies needed by beginning and experienced workers, clarification of objectives, and prediction of student success.

A key factor in the improvement of education is the amount and quality of research that is undertaken. Despite the long-range increase in the level of financial support by all agencies for educational research and development, the total remains low. Experts recommend that support should be increased until at least 1 percent of the national expenditure for education is devoted to research and development.

The newest federal research agency is the National Institute of Education. Created in 1972 as a vehicle for supporting research and development in education, NIE adopted priorities related to basic research into the learning process, problems of education for the disadvantaged, educational financing, improving the education of educators, linkage between research and development institutions and schools and universities, and emerging approaches to education.

The primary vehicle for contract and grant support to research in vocational education is the Bureau of Occupational and Adult Education. Under Part C of the Vocational Education Act, the bureau carries out a wide variety of research and training projects.

It is important for the vocational educator to develop a degree of competence in the preparation of research and development proposals. The components of such proposals normally include the rationale and statement of the problem, review of the literature, objectives, hypotheses (if applicable), the design, procedures, evaluation, dissemination, facilities, personnel, and budget. Detailed suggestions are provided in this chapter in relation to the preparation of each of these components. The four basic criteria that are usually applied to the evaluation of proposals include educational significance, economic efficiency, soundness of the research design, and adequacy of personnel and facilities.

Activities

For review

1 What is the function of the ERIC Clearinghouse?

2 Identify at least three functions of educational research.

3 What positions are taken by practitioners, professional researchers, and proponents of interdisciplinary research regarding the focus of research?

4 Why is there a lag between the completion of vocational research and its use in the classroom?

5 Explain the research function of the Bureau of Occupational and Adult Education with regard to the Vocational Education Act of 1963, as amended.

6 What are the usual components of a research proposal?

7 Why is a review of literature needed in a research proposal?

8 What are the criteria used by reviewers to evaluate research proposals?

9 How might vocational education research be improved?

10 Identify at least four weaknesses of research proposals.

For discussion

1 Do you agree with the list of competencies suggested for vocational teachers? Are there others that you would add to the list? Would a teacher with a four-year degree possess these qualifications? Should more emphasis be placed in the undergraduate and graduate programs on developing research consumers?

2 What are some of the means that could be used to make research findings in vocational education more readily available to the consumer?

3 Cite some examples of changes in vocational education that are the result of research.

4 How may local school systems work with colleges and universities in conducting and/or implementing vocational research?

5 Identify some problem areas that, in your opinion, need to be researched in vocational education.

6 What research studies have made the greatest impact on your vocational field?

7 What sources are available in your campus library that include summaries or abstracts of vocational research?

8 Explain how research can help a teacher to change classroom practices.

For exploration

1 Compare your research competencies with those suggested for a person in your position (teacher, supervisor, teacher educator). Identify areas of weakness that you need to strengthen.

2 Bring to class one example of each of four types of research. Explain the basis on which you classified each.

3 Interview one vocational teacher, supervisor, and teacher educator. Ask each one to read the list of recommended research competencies and to make suggestions for revision.

4 Evaluate a research study, using the criteria suggested in this chapter or a comparable reference. Write up your review and report it to the class.

5 Select an area of concern and survey the research literature for solutions.

6 Examine the guidelines for proposal preparation provided by the U.S. Office of Education or other funding agency. How do they differ from the guidelines suggested in this chapter?

7 Invite a vocational supervisor, state department representative, or USOE representative to discuss the outlook for funded research.

8 Invite a publishing company representative to discuss how research findings are used in textbooks and supplementary materials.

9 Outline a research study that you could implement on your job.

10 Select an area of interest or concern to you. What research is reported in *Research in Education* (ERIC) or in AIM/ARM that is related to the topic? Examine the *Review and Synthesis of Research* series in various vocational fields for further information.

References

1 George L. Brandon, "Vocational and Technical Education," in *Encyclopedia of Educational Research*, Fourth Edition, ed. Robert L. Ebel (New York: The Macmillan Company, 1969), p. 1511. (Reproduced by permission)

2 Geraldine M. Farmer, "Research Competencies of the Business Educator," in *Contributions of Research to Business Education*, eds. Calfrey C. Calhoun and Mildred Hillestad (Washington, D.C.: National Business Education Association, 1971), pp. 353–354. (Reproduced by permission)

3 Ibid, pp. 355–356. (Reproduced by permission)

4 Ibid, pp. 356–358. (Reproduced by permission)

5 George L. Brandon. See Ref. 1, p. 1519.

6 Ralph W. Tyler, "The Field of Educational Research," in *The Training and Nurture of Educational Researchers*, eds. E. Guba and S. Elam (Bloomington, Indiana: Phi Delta Kappa, 1965), pp. 8–9.

7 Carl J. Schaefer and Gordon F. Law, "Research on Teaching Vocational Skills," in *Second Handbook of Research on Teaching*, ed. Robert W. Travers (Chicago: Rand McNally College Publishing Company, 1973), p. 1304.

8 Kenneth R. Harvey and John M. Kean, "The Teacher as a Consumer of Research and Developmental Products," in *Research, Development, and the Classroom Teacher Producer/Consumer*, ed. M. Vere de Vault (Washington, D.C.: The Association of Childhood Education International, 1970), pp. 29–30. (Reproduced by permission)

9 *Digest of Educational Statistics*, 1968 (Washington: U.S. Government Printing Office, 1968), p. 17.

10 Francis S. Chase, "Research and Development in the Remodeling of Education," in *Phi Delta Kappan*, 1970, pp. 299–304.

11 House of Representatives, 92nd Congress, First Session, Report No. 92–554, October 8, 1971, pp. 65–66.

12 Gerald R. Smith, "A Critique of Proposals Submitted to the Cooperative Research Program," in *Educational Research: New Perspectives*, eds. Jack A. Culbertson and Stephen P. Hensley (Danville, Illinois: Interstate Printers and Publishers, Inc., 1963), pp. 281–285.

13 Donald Maley et al, *An Investigation and Development of the Cluster Concept as a Program in Vocational Education at the Secondary Level* (College Park: University of Maryland, 1965).

14 Lucy C. Crawford, *A Competency Pattern Approach to Curriculum Construction in Distributive Education* (Blacksburg: Virginia Polytechnic Institute, 1967).

15 Bruce W. Tuckman, *A Study of Curriculums for Occupational Preparation and Education* (New Brunswick, N.J.: Rutgers University, 1968).

16 Paul E. Hemp, Lloyd J. Phipps, Robert Warmsbrod, Norman Ehresman, and Martin McMillion, *Illinois Agricultural Education Curriculum Project: Pilot Programs in Agricultural Education* (Urbana, Illinois: Vocational and Technical Education Department, University of Illinois, 1966).

17 J. J. Kaufman, C. J. Schaefer, M. V. Lewis, D. W. Stevens, and E. W. House, *The Role of the Secondary Schools in the Preparation of Youth for Employment* (University Park, Pa.: The Pennsylvania State University Institute for Research on Human Resources, 1967).

18 Harry Huffman and D. D. Gust, *Business Education for the Emergent Office* (Columbus: Center for Vocational and Technical Education, The Ohio State University, 1970).

19 George L. Brandon, director, *Explorations in Research Design: Curricula for Technicians* (East Lansing: Michigan State University, 1960).

20 C. O. Loreen, *Occupational Opportunities and Training Needs for Youth for Non-Farm Agricultural Jobs in Washington State* (Pullman: Washington State University, 1967).

21 W. E. Drake and F. K. Tom, *Entry Occupations in Off-Farm Agriculture —A Survey and Task Analysis of Entry Level Off-Farm Agricultural Occupations in New York State* (Ithaca, New York: Cornell University, 1968).

22 K. H. Ertel, *Identification of Major Tasks Performed by Merchandising Employees Working in Standard Industrial Classifications of Retail Establishments* (Moscow, Idaho: University of Idaho, 1966).

Chapter 12

State and Federal

Support

for

Vocational Education

Introduction

This chapter deals with the sources of funding for vocational education —federal, state, and local—and reviews the purposes of funding, requirements and allowances, amounts available, and eligibility criteria. Attention is also given to research related to the financing of vocational education and the organization of research agencies. Vocational education as an economic asset is treated in Chapter 1.

In the long run, educating young people for employment costs society less than educating them for college, which they may never reach, and then providing remedial training thereafter. But the federal government invests nearly four dollars in remedial labor programs for each one dollar it invests in preventive vocational programs. And in the short-run budget of a school district, because it costs more in equipment and facilities to prepare a student for a job than to prepare him or her for college, vocational education usually receives less than adequate support.

As a result, it is at the state level that vocational education receives most support. Each state is responsible for guaranteeing that all its citizens are provided with opportunities for quality education and that the resources of the state are allocated in such a way as to maximize educational development and economic efficiency. Recognition of such responsibility by state education leadership appears to be a major factor leading toward state-increased coordination, control, and financial support of new efforts in vocational-technical education.

The scope of federal, state, and local support for vocational education in all states in 1973 is shown in Table 12.1.

Table 12.1 Expenditures of Federal, State, and Local
Funds for Vocational Education, by State: Fiscal Year 1973

State	Total	Federal expenditure	State & local expenditure
United States and outlying areas	$3,033,657,510	$482,390,800	$2,551,266,710
Alabama	37,905,610	10,288,550	27,617,060
Alaska	6,256,855	948,096	5,308,759
Arizona	21,772,726	4,792,931	16,979,795
Arkansas	16,960,997	5,212,592	11,748,405
California	276,170,235	37,602,746	238,567,489
Colorado	33,634,197	5,578,225	28,055,972
Connecticut	43,465,826	5,822,344	37,643,482
Delaware	9,812,230	1,461,600	8,350,630
District of Columbia	4,629,553	2,091,317	2,538,236
Florida	128,935,304	14,748,673	114,186,631
Georgia	48,025,369	12,447,116	35,578,253
Hawaii	8,084,800	2,100,192	5,984,608
Idaho	7,897,530	2,243,115	5,654,415
Illinois	209,710,964	20,579,761	189,131,203
Indiana	34,928,486	11,051,904	23,876,582
Iowa	43,673,732	7,476,727	36,197,005
Kansas	21,341,282	5,261,198	16,080,084
Kentucky	32,738,400	8,872,347	23,866,053
Louisiana	38,347,498	11,195,197	27,152,301
Maine	17,107,374	3,078,641	14,030,733
Maryland	73,090,639	8,652,929	64,437,710
Massachusetts	145,390,052	12,585,935	132,804,117
Michigan	75,235,895	19,905,196	55,330,699
Minnesota	84,786,679	8,572,956	76,213,723
Mississippi	26,662,487	6,161,837	20,500,650
Missouri	48,176,784	11,951,317	36,225,467
Montana	8,764,902	2,137,083	6,627,819
Nebraska	15,000,732	3,926,634	11,074,098
Nevada	4,514,565	1,269,004	3,245,561
New Hampshire	8,628,923	2,362,788	6,266,135
New Jersey	62,272,762	12,470,835	49,801,927
New Mexico	15,311,082	3,020,938	12,290,144
New York	376,328,709	33,610,057	342,718,652
North Carolina	113,315,533	16,170,875	97,144,658
North Dakota	6,644,531	2,004,581	4,639,950
Ohio	148,708,188	23,521,379	125,186,809
Oklahoma	29,502,464	6,666,648	22,835,816
Oregon	53,436,358	4,673,706	48,762,652
Pennsylvania	169,146,304	24,144,755	145,001,549
Rhode Island	10,140,959	2,774,583	7,366,376

Table 12.1   (Continued)

State	Total	Federal expenditure	State & local expenditure
South Carolina	24,089,234	8,072,510	16,016,724
South Dakota	5,969,020	1,955,775	4,013,245
Tennessee	45,867,096	10,904,436	34,962,660
Texas	150,657,652	33,487,600	117,170,052
Utah	21,620,186	3,038,982	18,581,204
Vermont	9,167,899	1,364,740	7,803,159
Virginia	50,802,695	11,505,591	39,297,104
Washington	68,678,333	7,324,609	61,353,724
West Virginia	17,678,782	5,323,288	12,355,494
Wisconsin	84,686,470	10,205,479	74,480,991
Wyoming	5,189,028	1,155,718	4,033,310
American Samoa	0*	0*	0*
Guam	1,471,815	295,988	1,175,827
Puerto Rico	29,602,834	8,068,502	21,534,332
Trust Territory of Pacific	1,716,950	250,274	1,466,676
Virgin Islands	0*	0*	0*

Figures unavailable.
Source: *U.S. Department of Health, Education and Welfare, Office of Education,* Vocational and Technical Education, Annual Report, *Fiscal Year 1973.*

State and Local
Tax Support for Schools

Public education is a state responsibility that is supported by local, state, and federal resources. State and local taxes provide 92 cents of every school dollar; the remaining eight cents comes from federal sources. Local school districts use their tax funds to pay salaries of teachers, administrators, and support personnel; maintain and operate school plants; purchase goods and services necessary for school operation; and pay interest on school debts. Capital improvement and new construction expenses normally come from the sale of bonds issued by the school board with approval of the district voters. Recent court decisions at both state and federal levels have shown the nation is headed toward major changes in the pattern of support of public elementary and secondary education. But it is not clear, at this point, just what the direction will be.

State laws generally provide for school support through public taxation. State school funds come from a wide range of tax sources, including personal income taxes, sales taxes, use and occupation taxes, franchise and license fees, inheritance and gift taxes. Some states designate certain taxes for education; others draw on the general tax funds to meet their obligations to local districts. The states vary considerably in the machinery used to channel state tax funds to local districts.

Two funding devices that are commonly used by states are the flat grant and the equalization grant. The state flat grants generally go to districts on the basis of average daily attendance during the *previous* school year. Some states provide for adjustments of attendance bases during the current year to account for rapid increases in school enrollments. The grants, computed on district reports, are paid to the local school units periodically during the fiscal year.

Equalization support is a method used by some states to bring a degree of equality to district school funding. With the nation's increased urbanization has come a polarization of schools into rich and poor districts. The richer districts have been able to offer their children substantially more educational resources than the poor districts have. As a result, those states with an equalization plan apportion funds to local districts by statutory formulas, which involve district property valuation, local tax rate for education, and the number of pupils. Under such plans, state funds are allocated on the basis of local need. Achievement of equality of educational opportunity in a given state depends on the effectiveness of the tax-allocation system among the school districts. Although the constitutional provisions for school finance vary widely, the need for such revised plans for school support is evident.

The state may encourage local taxation for education by setting minimum tax rates to qualify the district for state support. These qualifying tax rates are expressed either in mills (tenth of a cent) per dollar, or in cents per $100 of assessed valuation. State law or state constitutions may also set upper limits on local school taxes; if the district's tax rate is below that limit, the voters of the district may authorize an additional amount to be levied on all taxable property. But many local districts are near their upper limits of taxation and so face severe school-finance problems.

Local taxes are imposed under taxing power granted to the district by the state legislature. Whenever the state laws grant local school districts the power to tax, the statute will be construed strictly. Generally the districts' tax objects are real and personal property, although some states extend local school taxes to other objects and sources. Computation of local school taxes is done by simple formula: the school tax rate (expressed in mills or cents) times the assessed valuation of taxable property equals the school tax. Assessed valuation may not be the market value of property but rather some fraction of its market value. In some states assessed valuation may be less than one-half the market value; in other states it may be nearer the market value.

Subject to constitutional or statutory limitations, the local school board determines its budget in advance of the fiscal year, estimates the assessed valuation of the district's taxable property, and computes the rate necessary to raise the needed revenue. The board may be fiscally dependent or independent; if dependent, the board must seek budget approval from some other public body, such as the city, county, or intermediate governing body. Fiscally independent boards determine their own budgets and tax rates. The law generally provides opportunity for the public to inspect the school budget and to make objections and suggestions at a public hearing.

The school tax may be coupled with other governmental units and a single tax bill prepared for property owners. In some states the tax-assessment and tax-collection functions are performed by different public officials. Regardless of the scheme, the local school districts ultimately receive local tax funds for school use. The payments may come to the district in periodic installments, and the local board may then have the power to invest excess operating funds in certain types of securities until the funds are needed. However, state laws generally restrict the board's power to invest school funds in order to safeguard the public against the board's speculation and possible reduction or loss of tax monies. The management of school-tax funds is a technical matter, and reference to specific state laws is necessary for an accurate understanding of the procedures and limitations.

Most states provide for public participation in decisions about school taxes. The upper limits of school taxation may be determined by statute; periodic referenda to registered voters in the district are common forms of public participation. Tax increases are presented to voters in the form of referenda, which are conducted under statutory authority and specified procedures. If a referendum fails, the board must adjust projected expenditures downward to stay within its school income. Borrowing against future tax income, however, is permitted in many states. Whenever the board cannot meet its fiscal needs from current tax income, the evidence of future tax receipts may be "sold" to lending institutions and the receipts used for current school expenses. By trimming future expenses or by receiving increased tax income, the school board repays "borrowed" funds in subsequent fiscal years.

It should be noted that the board cannot depend on receiving all taxes that are due. In a given year, a portion of anticipated taxes are not paid, and the board must await the collection of such delinquent taxes. The board's failure to anticipate delinquent taxes in its accounting can cause financial embarrassment to the district.

Tax funds generally must be used for current operating expenses, that is, for expenses incurred during a given fiscal year, such as for salaries, supplies, materials, utilities, and maintenance costs. Accumulation of excess operating funds is generally limited by statute. The purpose of this limitation is to hold school-tax income to a level near to school needs and minimize "overtaxation" for school purposes.

Funds for capital expenditures for major school plant improvement and new construction generally come from the sale of bonds. The board's authority to issue bonds must be granted by state law; such authority will not be implied. Bonds are certificates evidencing a debt by the school district and generally must be approved by the voters in a special election. On approval by the voters, the school district sells the bonds and uses the proceeds for the purpose specified in the bond referendum.

Table 12.2   Major Federal Legislation Affecting Vocational Education

Legislation	Date of enactment
Morrill Land-Grant Act	1862
Hatch Act	1887
Second Morrill Act	1890
Smith-Hughes Act	1917
* George-Reed Act	1929
George-Ellzey Act	1935
George-Deen Act	1937
Fitzgerald Act	1937
Servicemen's Readjustment Act	1944
George-Barden Act	1946
Cooperative Research Act	1954
National Defense Education Act	1958
Mutual Educational and Cultural Exchange Act	1961
Area Redevelopment Act	1962
Manpower Development and Training Act	1962
Manpower Development and Training Amendments	1965, 1968
Higher Education Facilities Act	1963
Vocational Education Act	1963
Vocational Education Amendments	1968
Economic Opportunity Act	1964
National Vocational Student Loan Insurance Act	1965
Public Works and Economic Development Act	1965
Appalachian Regional Development Act	1965
Elementary and Secondary Education Act	1965
Education Professions Development Act	1972
Vocational Education Act (extension only)	1972
Comprehensive Employment and Training Act	1973
Education Amendments Act	1974

* Indentation indicates amendment of previous legislation.

Now that we have set the stage with a general discussion of the features of state and local tax support of education, let us turn to a more direct discussion of federal aid to vocational education.

Federal Aid for Vocational Education

Federal land grants provided under the Northwest Ordinance of 1787 represent the first instance of the U.S. government's financial assistance of education. With this enactment, the federal government embarked on a program of educational support that was unique in its commitment to state and local autonomy and in the responsibility it assumed for a public function of national interest.

The federal government supports educational activities in a variety of ways, including financial grants and loans, allocation of surplus commodities and federally owned property, operation of special programs and institutions, and reimbursement of the cost of services or contracts. This highly complex federal educational involvement affects, directly or indirectly, every person in the country as well as many foreign nationals attending American schools. Programs may be for the purchase of research and training services in educational institutions; for support of individuals for whom there is a special federal responsibility; for support of schools in areas where federal activities would result in undue burdens on school services without such support; for support of vocational education, foreign language study, and similar special programs; or for numerous other purposes.

The historical development of federal support for vocational education is traced in Table 12.2.

The following list of selected federal educational legislation, each of which contained support for vocational services, provides a capsule view of the history of federal legislation.

Year	Program
1787	Northwest Ordinance—authorized land grants for the establishment of educational institutions.
1862	First Morrill Act—authorized public land grants to the states for the establishment and maintenance of agricultural and mechanical colleges.
1890	Second Morrill Act—provided for money grants for support of instruction in the agricultural and mechanical colleges.
1917	Smith-Hughes Act—provided for grants to states for support of vocational education.
1918	Vocational Rehabilitation Act—authorized funds for rehabilitation of World War I veterans.
1920	Smith-Bankhead Act—authorized grants to states for vocational rehabilitation programs.
1935	Bankhead-Jones Act—made grants to states for agricultural experiment stations.
1943	Vocational Rehabilitation Act—provided assistance to disabled veterans.
1944	Servicemen's Readjustment Act—provided assistance for the education of veterans.
1946	George-Barden Act—expanded federal support for vocational education.
1954	Cooperative Research Act—authorized cooperative arrangements with universities, colleges, and state education agencies for educational research.
1957	Practical Nurse Training Act—provided grants to states for practical nurse training.
1958	National Defense Education Act—provided assistance to state and local school systems for strengthening instruction in science, mathematics, foreign languages, and other critical subjects; improvement of state statistical services; guidance, counseling, and testing services and training institutes; higher edu-

Year	Program

cation student loans and fellowships; experimentation and dissemination of information on more effective use of television, motion picture, and related media for educational purposes; and vocational education for technical occupations, such as data processing, necessary to the national defense.

Public Law 89–926—federal assistance for training teachers of the handicapped, was authorized.

1961   Area Redevelopment Act—included provisions for training or retraining of persons in redevelopment areas.

1962   Manpower Development and Training Act—provided training in new and improved skills for the unemployed and underemployed.

1963   Vocational Education Act of 1963—increased federal support of vocational education, including support of residential vocational schools, vocational work-study programs, and research, training, and demonstrations in vocational education.

Health Professions Educational Assistance Act—provided funds to expand teaching facilities and for loans to students in the health professions.

Higher Education Facilities Act—authorized grants and loans for classrooms and laboratories in public community colleges and technical institutes as well as for undergraduate and graduate facilities in other institutions of higher education.

1964   Economic Opportunity Act—authorized grants for college work-study programs for students of low-income families; established a Job Corps program and authorized support for work-training programs to provide education and vocational training and work experience for unemployed youth; provided training and work experience opportunities in welfare programs; authorized support of education and training activities and of community action programs including Head Start, Follow Through, Upward Bound; authorized the establishment of the Volunteers in Service to America (VISTA).

1965   Elementary and Secondary Education Act—authorized grants for elementary and secondary school programs for children of low-income families; school library resources, textbooks, and other instructional materials for school children; supplementary educational centers and services; strengthening state education agencies; and educational research and development training.

Health Professions Educational Assistance Amendments—authorized scholarships to aid needy students in the health professions and grants to improve the quality of teaching in schools of medicine, dentistry, osteopathy, optometry, and podiatry.

Higher Education Act—provided grants for university community service programs, college library assistance, library training and research, strengthening developing institutions, and educational opportunity; insured student loans; teacher training programs; and undergraduate instructional equipment. Established a National Teacher Corps and provided for graduate teacher training fellowships.

Medical Library Assistance Act—provided assistance for construction and improvement of health sciences libraries.

National Vocational Student Loan Insurance Act—encouraged state and nonprofit private institutions and organizations to establish adequate loan insurance programs to assist students to attend postsecondary business, trade, technical, and other vocational schools.

Year	Program
1966	International Education Act—provided grants to institutions of higher education for the establishment, strengthening, and operation of centers for research and training in international studies and the international aspects of professional and other fields of study.
	Adult Education Act—authorized grants to states for the encouragement and expansion of educational programs for adults, including training of teachers of adults and demonstrations in adult education (previously part of the Economic Opportunity Act of 1964).
1967	Education Professions Development Act—amended the Higher Education Act of 1965 for the purpose of improving the quality of teaching and to help meet critical shortages of adequately trained educational personnel by authorizing support for the development of information on needs for educational personnel, training and retraining opportunities responsive to changing labor needs; attracting persons who can stimulate creativity in the arts and other skills to undertake short-term and long-term assignments in education; and helping to make educator training more responsive to the needs of schools and colleges.
1968	Vocational Education Amendments—changed the basic formula for allotting funds; provided for a National Advisory Council on Vocational Education; expansion of vocational education services to meet the needs of the disadvantaged; and the collection and dissemination of information on programs administered by the Commissioner of Education.
1971	Comprehensive Health Manpower Training Act—increased and expanded provisions for nurse training facilities.
1972	Education Amendments—established a National Institute of Education; general aid for institutions of higher education; federal matching grants for state student incentive grants; a National Commission on Financing Postsecondary Education; State Advisory Councils on Community Colleges; a Bureau of Occupational and Adult Education; and state grants for the design, establishment, and conduct of postsecondary occupational education; and a bureau-level Office of Indian Education.
1973	Comprehensive Employment and Training Act—consolidated previous labor and public service programs; funds for employment counseling, supportive services, classroom training, training on the job, work experience, and public service employment; incorporates essential principles of revenue sharing, giving state and local governments more control over use of funds and determination of programs.
1974	Education Amendments—established the National Center for Educational Statistics; continued research activities under the Education for the Handicapped Act.

The funding provisions and effects of key federal legislation on vocational education are treated in the following section.

Vocational Education Acts

The Morrill Act of 1862, which established the colleges of agriculture and mechanic arts, is often cited as the beginning of the federal relationship to vocational education. With the growing need for trained workers over the years, the federal government has frequently stepped in to provide support for programs relating to vocational education.

Because constitutional provisions place the control of education with the states rather than with the federal government, all of the federal legislation includes certain features that respect this relationship. Federal legislation over the years has not only helped to finance vocational education, but it has also established priorities and standards of service that have shaped the nature of state and local programs in important ways. Federal legislation continues to exert a strong influence on vocational education, and this makes it necessary that those who plan and conduct programs of vocational education be acquainted with the purposes and provisions of the major laws.

Smith-Hughes Act

This pioneering piece of legislation, passed in 1917, provided the first major federal stimulus for vocational education. It did so (a) by granting federal funds to the states in order that they might encourage local programs and (b) by setting goals and standards. Three major occupational areas were recognized and supported in the law: agriculture, trade and industry, and home economics. Minimum requirements for students, teachers, instructional time allocations, and the administration of programs were included. Funds for the preparation of teachers and for conducting studies and research were authorized. Funds appropriated for the salaries of teachers, supervisors, and directors of agricultural subjects were allotted to each state in the proportion its rural population bore to the rural population of the nation. For the salaries of teachers of trade, industrial, and home economics subjects, funds were allocated on the basis of the state-federal urban population ratio. The matching of federal funds with state and local funds was a requirement of the law in order that all three levels of support would be involved.

The Smith-Hughes Act was unique in a number of important respects: 1. It provided funds for vocational education but earmarked them for specific purposes. Prior educational efforts had allowed wide latitude in state use of funds. 2. It included a $7.2 million permanent appropriation so that vocational educators did not have to appeal to Congress each year for funds. 3. It placed the federal government squarely on record as favoring a more active role in the extension of vocational education.

Amendments to George-
Barden and Smith-Hughes Acts

The success of the Smith-Hughes Act led to the enactment of other laws supporting vocational education, as identified in Table 12.2. Most of these laws increased the appropriation for various specific services. The original Smith-Hughes Act provided funds for agriculture, home economics, trade and industrial education, and teacher education. The George-Reed Act (in effect 1930–34) was a temporary measure with an inclusive authorization of $1.5 million to expand vocational education in agriculture and home economics beyond the amount appropriated in the Smith-Hughes law. The George-Ellzey Act (in effect 1935–37) replaced the George-Reed Act with an inclusive authorization of $3 million to be appropriated equally in agriculture, home economics, and trade and industries. The George-Deen Act (in effect 1937–47) replaced the George-Ellzey Act with a continuous authorization for vocational education. Over $14 million was authorized: $4 million each to agriculture, home economics, and trade and industries; $1 million to teacher education; and $1.3 million for the distributive occupations, for the first time. The George-Barden Act (in effect 1947–68) replaced the George-Deen Act, authorizing appropriations for vocational education at $29 million annually. One interesting feature of this act was the provision for greater flexibility in the use of funds. No specific funds were allocated for teacher training or for guidance, although states could write such items into their state plans if they desired. A further amendment to the George-Barden Act, passed in 1956 as the Health Amendments Act, authorized funds to be distributed to the states for the training of practical nurses and other health workers.

In each of these acts, the disbursement of monies to the states generally followed the pattern of: agriculture, the ratio of state farm population to national farm population; home economics, the ratio of state to national rural population; trade and industrial, the ratio of state-national nonfarm population; distributive education, the ratio of state-national total population; and teacher education, the state-national total population ratio.

In interpreting the vocational education acts, one must distinguish between *authorizations* and *appropriations.* In the legislative process, two congressional steps are usually required for funding. First is the act of authorizing, which specifies the maximum amount of funds that can be appropriated. In the second step the funds are actually appropriated, usually at an amount somewhat lower than the maximum. In the Smith-Hughes Act, the authorization and appropriation were together in the original law, meaning that vocational educators did not have to appeal to Congress each year. This is the only example of an education bill that has passed Congress with such construction.

Vocational Education Act of 1963

The 1963 Act was in many ways a landmark piece of federal vocational legislation. It retained the federal-state relationship established by the Smith-Hughes Act and added a requirement that a state must submit a state plan in order to qualify for financial grants. In many other ways, however, this Act departed from the approach of the Smith-Hughes Act. The law authorized federal grants, construction of area vocational schools, research and experimentation, and work-study programs in residential vocational schools. It also amended the Smith-Hughes, George-Barden, and National Defense Education Acts, and allowed states to transfer funds among categories and between the various acts.

In the Vocational Education Act of 1963, Congress recognized that it was no longer wise or possible to specify legislatively the particular occupations to be included in the vocational education acts—this recognition represented a departure from all previous vocational legislation. The law thus permitted funds to be used to prepare persons for any recognized occupation, excluding only those occupations considered to be professional or requiring a bachelor's or higher degree. It approved courses at the secondary and postsecondary levels and specifically included courses in community or junior colleges, area vocational schools, and comprehensive high schools. It permitted the use of grant funds for the construction of buildings and the purchase of equipment, when matched with state or local funds. It required states and localities to develop cooperative arrangements with the public employment agency in deciding the occupations for which training was to be given and in providing vocational guidance and counseling.

The 1963 Act centered on people in need of vocational education rather than on areas of occupational life. It stated that among those to be served were persons attending high school, persons who had completed high school, persons already at work, and persons with academic, socioeconomic, or other handicaps that prevented their succeeding in regular programs of vocational education. Funds were also provided for teacher education, curriculum development, and program evaluation. A most important provision of the law was the allocation of significant sums of money for research and for pilot programs aimed at improving the scope and quality of vocational education services. The Act required that state and local programs be subjected to periodic evaluations for relevance and quality and that a national evaluation of the program be conducted by a special ad hoc commission at five-year intervals. Another section of the law, which was of special interest to local educators, was the provision of funds to compensate students for part-time work activity when students required some income in order to enroll or remain in an approved vocational program.

The authorization for fiscal year 1964 was set at $60 million; it increased each year to a maximum of $225 million for fiscal 1967 and thereafter. Of these sums, 90 percent were for extension and development programs and were distributed to the states by a formula based on population ratios and per capita income. The remaining 10 percent of the annual appropriation was to be used for research and for experimental and pilot programs.

Funds appropriated for fiscal year 1964 and thereafter were to be matched on a dollar-for-dollar basis by state and local funds. One-third of the individual state's annual allotment prior to 1968, and 25 percent thereafter, was used for youth who had left school and/or for the construction of area schools. Special consideration in making grants was given to areas having substantial school dropouts and unemployment.

Vocational Education
Amendments of 1968

The Vocational Education Act of 1963 was amended in 1968; the amendments were, essentially, a rewrite of the 1963 Act. The major purpose of the 1968 Amendments was to provide ready access for all citizens to suitable training or retraining. Under the provisions of the Act funds were authorized on a dollar-for-dollar matching basis to the states to maintain, extend, and improve vocational education. In 1969, $355 million was authorized; in 1970, $565 million; in 1971 and 1972, $675 million each; and $565 million thereafter.

In addition to provisions for on-going general programs and research, the Act authorized several short-term programs requiring little or no matching funds from the states: exemplary programs, cooperative training programs, demonstration residential school, dormitory loans, curriculum development, professional development, and disadvantaged required no matching funds; work-study programs, 8–20 matching plan (80 percent federal, 20 percent state/local); state grants for residential schools, 90–10 matching plan; and homemaking, 50–50 matching plan.

In all cases, however, from 1969–1973, the states overmatched the federal expenditures. The average state expenditure for each federal dollar and the state expenditure of the ten highest states and ten lowest states are shown in the following illustrations.

State/Local Expenditures per Dollar of Federal Funds					
	1973	1972	1971	1970	1969
For all programs	$5.29	$4.71	$4.92	$5.14	$4.37

By states

Ten high states		Ten low states	
Massachusetts	$10.55	District of Columbia	$1.21
Oregon	10.43	South Carolina	1.98
New York	10.20	South Dakota	2.05
Illinois	9.19	Indiana	2.16
Minnesota	8.89	Arkansas	2.25
Washington	8.38	North Dakota	2.31
Florida	7.74	West Virginia	2.32
Maryland	7.45	Louisiana	2.43
Wisconsin	7.30	Idaho	2.52
Connecticut	6.47	Nevada	2.56

Two additional provisions of the 1968 Amendments were the creation of a National Advisory Council and the requirement of state plans from all states participating in the vocational education programs. Other important features of the Act include the repeal of the amendments to the Smith-Hughes Act, the repeal of the George-Barden Act, the reduction of age requirements of the Adult Basic Education Act of 1965 from 18 to 16 years and an amendment to the Higher Education Act of 1965 to authorize training and developmental programs for vocational personnel.

National Advisory
Council on Vocational Education

This advisory council was created by Congress through the Vocational Education Amendments of 1968. It is composed of 21 persons, appointed by the President, from diverse backgrounds in labor, management, and education. It is charged by law to advise the Commissioner of Education concerning the operation of vocational education programs, to make recommendations concerning such programs, and to make annual reports to the Secretary of Health, Education and Welfare for transmittal to Congress. In a transmittal letter accompanying the council's *Fourth Annual Report*, the chairman dealt with the problems of financing vocational education (1):

☐ *We have allowed to develop in this country a system of financing vocational education which precludes the creation of imaginative career education programs in the public schools. Many of the complaints so frequently heard about the quality of vocational education courses, facilities, and faculties can be traced to a funding system which so narrowly defines what can be funded as vocational education that it excludes new and often needed forms of career education.*

The steadily increasing support of vocational education at all levels is reflected in the summary of expenditures from 1920–1972, as reported in Table 12.3.

Comprehensive
Employment and Training Act

On December 28, 1973, President Nixon signed into law the Comprehensive Employment and Training Act, carrying an initial annual authorization of $250 million. This Act made federal monies available to state and local governments for their use in providing a wide array of labor services, and it consolidated the patchwork system of individual categorical programs begun in the early 1960s.

Labor services that state and local governments could provide under this legislation included employment counseling, supportive services, classroom, educational and occupational skills training, training on the job, work experience, and transitional public service employment. These services were not new ones; what was new, however, was that funds

Table 12.3   Federal, State, and Local Expenditures
for Vocational Education: 1920–1972 (in thousands)

Fiscal year	Total	Federal	State	Local
1	2	3	4	5
1920	$8,535	$2,477	$2,670	$3,388
1930	29,909	7,404	8,233	14,272
1940	55,081	20,004	11,737	23,340
1942	59,023	20,758	14,045	24,220
1944	64,299	19,958	15,016	29,325
1946	72,807	20,628	18,538	33,641
1948	103,339	26,200	25,834	51,305
1950	128,717	26,623	40,534	61,561
1952	146,466	25,863	47,818	72,784
1954	151,289	25,419	54,550	71,320
1956	175,886	33,180	61,821	80,884
1958	209,748	38,733	72,305	98,710
1960	238,812	45,313	82,466	111,033
1962	283,948	51,438	104,264	128,246
1964	332,785	55,027	124,975	152,784
1966	799,895	233,794	216,583	349,518
1968	1,192,863	262,384	400,362	530,117
1970	1,841,846	300,046	(1)	[1]1,541,801
1971	2,347,353	396,378	(1)	[1]1,950,975
1972	2,660,759	466,029	(1)	[1]2,194,730

[1] State funds are included with local funds in column 5.

NOTE.—Because of rounding, detail may not add to totals.

SOURCES: U.S. Department of Health, Education, and Welfare, Office of Education, annual reports on *Vocational and Technical Education*; and unpublished data.

would be available, for the first time, without any federal strings attached as to the kind and amount of services to be provided. The Comprehensive Employment and Training Act represented a significant shift in inter-government responsibilities in that it allowed state and local governments to become more involved as decision makers. In this way the bill incorporated the essential principles of revenue sharing.

This employment and training program was a vital part of the national effort to conserve and develop human resources and to help individuals adjust to changing economic conditions—including temporary dislocations from the energy shortage or from unemployment. Additional funds could also be used by state and local governments to provide transitional public service jobs in times of high unemployment.

No single total of federal funds for education that could be cited would be meaningful for all purposes, but there are many totals that may be constructed to serve particular needs. This multiplicity is a result of the many kinds of assistance provided, the differences in the manner of distributing assistance, the varying descriptions of program beneficiaries depending on the special purpose for which each program was legislatively tailored and, of course, the purposes of the data user. However, Table 12.4, Part I, "Federal Funds for Education and Related Activities," presents

Table 12.4 Part I Federal Funds for Education and Related Activities: Obligations for Fiscal Years 1962–1967 and Outlay for Fiscal Years 1968–1974 (in thousands)

Type of support, level, and program area	New obligational authority						Outlay						
	1962	1963	1964	1965	1966	1967	1968	1969	1970	1971	1972	1973 (estimated)	1974 (estimated)
1	2	3	4	5	6	7	8	9	10	11	12	13	14
Total grants and loans	$2,173,700	$2,507,600	$2,749,300	$3,908,700	$6,779,578	$8,352,866	$7,804,454	$8,055,396	$9,222,139	$10,927,646	$11,901,721	$13,070,635	$12,868,823
Grants, total	1,853,200	2,111,700	2,350,500	3,379,600	6,167,878	7,611,283	7,201,173	7,523,169	8,615,843	10,442,808	11,325,086	12,440,088	12,462,906
Elementary-secondary education	555,100	600,400	666,300	942,900	2,480,078	3,037,637	2,967,004	2,838,439	3,212,418	3,724,363	3,856,527	4,088,258	4,062,779
PART I. Federal funds supporting education in educational institutions													
School assistance in federally affected areas[1]	304,900	330,300	323,100	407,600	433,900	469,137	506,372	397,581	656,372	527,043	648,608	467,452	130,910
Economic opportunity programs[1]	53,000	60,900	67,000	123,500	404,300	721,257	628,533	552,434	534,482	664,355	473,307	764,701	683,936
National Defense Education Act—equipment[2]	59,300	58,700	92,900	90,900	104,400	109,009	109,000	74,316	58,547	44,647	42,629	38,260	11,764
Supporting services[3]	4,300	4,700	5,200	6,500	173,100	273,551	280,481	290,107	237,532	215,252	267,749	346,111	186,020
Assistance for educationally deprived children[4]					959,000	1,057,455	1,056,983	1,096,106	1,207,894	1,575,282	1,613,847	1,564,700	455,029
Teacher Corps	4,000	6,800	5,100		6,500	11,324	16,019	19,358	18,191	28,761	23,887	40,613	37,565
Vocational education	26,400	26,300	24,900	127,700	184,678	194,636	185,224	152,441	181,379	241,481	282,545	294,876	153,536
Dependents' schools abroad[2]	40,500	45,300	61,500	80,500	86,100	87,533	68,220	108,589	137,138	146,615	168,908	191,621	211,102
Public lands revenue for schools	43,500	44,600	48,600	51,500	54,100	50,173	52,294	66,112	82,376	78,893	73,285	89,377	98,634
Assistance in special areas[5]	14,800	17,700	32,600	50,200	68,800	56,969	58,286	71,118	78,992	120,719	156,757	170,988	162,400
Veterans' education						1,294	3,200	4,924	6,233	13,763	16,674	37,708	36,378
Emergency school assistance										51,239	68,816	54,364	175,012
Education revenue sharing													1,692,699
Other[6]	4,400	5,100	5,400	4,500	5,200	5,108	2,383	5,353	13,282	16,313	19,515	27,487	27,794
Higher education	1,210,300	1,397,800	1,480,400	2,052,600	2,830,400	3,634,494	3,262,988	3,318,177	3,814,332	4,745,192	4,963,464	5,760,253	5,937,467
Basic research in U.S. educational institutions proper[7]	602,900	691,600	698,600	784,900	940,300	1,032,823	1,061,818	1,020,905	985,784	1,054,385	1,199,980	1,325,335	1,350,000
Research facilities[7]	121,800	157,900	133,500	191,700	194,000	250,568	199,790	238,516	225,130	227,908	186,864	213,601	218,000
Training grants	196,000	234,600	261,200	282,400	365,500	363,608	381,116	404,990	704,689	769,295	982,008	1,143,343	1,010,851
Fellowships and traineeships	103,900	143,000	181,800	196,900	264,900	350,162	320,303	247,840	191,271	267,907	400,147	263,201	254,260
Facilities and equipment	37,100	41,000	56,100	384,100	668,900	822,203	549,382	482,387	513,162	518,944	292,291	352,474	350,441
Other institutional support	33,000	43,400	69,500	93,400	163,800	169,925	139,637	173,066	178,156	266,090			
Other student assistance	103,900	69,900	62,300	100,400	214,200	590,586	608,883	740,498	1,003,594	1,631,185	1,902,174	2,462,299	2,753,915
Other higher education assistance	11,700	16,400	17,400	18,800	18,800	54,619	2,059	9,975	12,546	9,478	9,478		
Vocational-technical and continuing education (not classifiable by level)	87,800	113,500	203,800	384,100	857,400	939,152	971,181	1,366,553	1,589,093	1,973,253	2,505,095	2,591,577	2,462,660
Vocational, technical, and work training[9]	34,600	82,700	171,000	364,300	817,900	827,303	851,683	1,163,444	1,269,254	1,515,741	1,941,281	1,895,683	1,768,225
Veterans' education	49,900	29,000	25,100	10,300	6,300	54,000	79,645	123,970	244,634	357,414	429,229	534,889	555,364
General continuing education[10]	400	400	1,900	1,500	19,200	29,200	28,701	60,364	65,855	88,305	125,715	147,087	122,244
Training State and local personnel	2,900	1,400	5,800	8,000	14,000	28,649	11,152	18,775	9,350	11,793	8,870	13,918	16,827
Loans, total (higher education)	320,500	395,900	398,800	529,100	611,700	741,583	603,281	532,227	606,296	484,837	576,635	630,547	405,917
Student loan program, National Defense Education Act[11]	74,600	90,700	111,300	160,100	235,900	237,954	226,303	269,641	295,173	382,102	515,072	595,400	380,341
College facilities loans[12]	245,900	305,200	287,500	369,000	375,800	503,629	376,978	272,586	311,123	102,735	61,563	35,147	25,576

Part II Other Federal Funds for Education and Related Activities

	$2,777,364	$2,935,341	$3,239,851	$3,717,232	$3,903,.9	$3,930,053	$3,606,629	$3,339,667	$3,428,724	$4,011,245	$4,563,964	$5,124,563	$5,037,412
Total													
Applied research and development[7]	754,700	805,700	906,300	952,300	1,026,600	1,088,150	1,142,350	1,237,499	1,236,749	1,318,963	1,497,999	1,618,718	1,649,000
School lunch and milk programs	366,800	379,300	411,700	507,500	421,900	448,005	543,845	597,700	676,196	928,186	1,213,075	1,472,890	1,273,263
Training of Federal personnel	1,177,500	1,279,600	1,370,400	1,577,900	1,706,700	1,537,399	1,138,333	639,853	691,694	854,930	961,215	1,045,679	1,115,027
U.S. academies	59,416	59,099	119,796	130,971	154,593	133,002	141,599	170,468	184,262	218,869	232,047	233,288	232,340
Professional training, military	1,086,584	1,188,601	1,202,604	1,373,229	1,470,507	1,309,948	923,470	375,105	492,040	614,099	718,180	800,018	867,637
Civilian education and training in non-Federal facilities	31,500	31,900	48,000	73,700	81,600	94,449	73,264	94,280	15,392	21,962	10,988	12,373	15,050
Library services	22,200	23,900	25,300	82,900	86,300	141,381	136,099	186,124	170,135	186,338	165,096	174,657	150,744
Grants to public libraries	6,900	7,400	7,500	54,900	55,000	76,000	62,017	62,794	50,235	52,975	56,246	50,873	17,904
National library services[1,3]	15,300	16,500	17,800	28,000	31,300	65,381	74,082	123,330	119,900	133,363	108,850	123,784	132,840
International education	109,100	116,100	130,000	178,700	232,658	326,742	272,008	278,135	193,464	180,668	122,740	136,335	139,098
Educational exchange program	28,100	35,600	38,000	37,400	53,500	44,712	41,670	38,172	30,850	36,101	37,837	42,442	47,711
Agency for International Development projects	81,000	80,500	84,600	87,800	111,800	203,270	140,000	170,000	111,325	105,608	55,612	65,862	64,889
Action (previously Peace Corps)	.....	.....	.....	44,300	57,175	41,944	43,641	44,095	28,150	25,026	19,819	20,983	18,925
Other international education and training	.....	.....	7,400	9,200	10,183	36,816	46,697	25,868	23,139	13,933	9,472	7,048	7,573
Other	346,964	330,741	396,151	417,932	429,701	388,376	372,994	400,356	460,486	542,160	593,839	676,304	710,280
Agricultural extension service	59,300	63,000	79,400	85,400	90,700	92,824	90,030	97,273	124,526	154,672	169,811	191,698	197,198
Educational television facilities	.....	.....	5,200	5,100	15,200	3,304	6,737	8,756	19,163	28,580	8,000	8,000	11,000
Education in Federal correctional institutions	2,100	2,500	2,900	3,500	3,600	6,341	3,662	3,816	5,007	6,333	9,066	9,551	9,945
Value of surplus property transferred:													
Acquisition cost of personal property	244,900	223,800	268,700	277,300	266,400	215,509	199,383	223,503	246,330	255,668	299,805	329,788	362,767
Fair value of real property	21,000	21,100	15,100	17,900	15,100	16,684	26,276	13,254	12,468	25,718	12,200	23,000	20,000
Other[14]	19,664	20,341	24,851	28,732	38,701	53,714	46,906	53,754	52,992	71,189	94,957	114,267	109,370

1 Includes Office of Economic Opportunity, Indian education, Appalachian Regional Development, Department of Labor, NYC in-school work support, and Head Start Preschool.

2 Includes small amounts for National Defense Education Act loans to private elementary-secondary schools.

3 Includes supplemental centers, school library materials, strengthening State education agencies, American Printing House for the deaf, dissemination of information, school counseling and testing, planning and evaluation.

4 Includes Elementary and Secondary Education Act, Title I, handicapped children, Dropout prevention, bilingual education, Kendall School for the Deaf, and Model School for the Deaf.

5 Includes District of Columbia, Canal Zone, territories and dependencies, Cuban refugees, and payments in lieu of taxes by the Atomic Energy Commission and the Tennessee Valley Authority.

6 Includes elementary-secondary programs of the National Science Foundation, National Foundation on the Arts and the Humanities, Department of Defense, Junior ROTC, and National Aeronautics and Space Administration; also, Office of Child Development programs not included elsewhere, and Office of Education programs and expenditures not otherwise included.

7 Data are from Federal Funds for Research, Development, and Other Scientific Activities, annual publication, National Science Foundation. Includes university-operated research centers.

8 1974 amounts are estimated by the Office of Education at 1.9 percent increase over 1973 level.

9 Includes adult vocational education and manpower training programs.

10 Includes Office of Education, Action, Social and Rehabilitation Service, Department of Housing and Urban Development, Office of Economic Development, and additional programs for continuing education.

11 Includes National Defense Education Act and insured student loans.

12 Includes Department of Housing and Urban Development college housing loans and Office of Education college facilities loans.

13 Includes Library of Congress, Smithsonian Institution, General Services Administration, National Archives and Records Service, National Agricultural Library, National Library of Medicine, and Government Printing Office depository library and catalog and index activities.

14 Includes Office of Education and education programs and administration expenditures not otherwise included.

NOTE.—Because of the exclusion of some programs and because data are based on Federal disbursement rather than on the authority to spend, the figures since 1968 are not strictly comparable with those for earlier years.

SOURCE: Compiled by the National Center for Educational Statistics, Office of Education, U.S. Department of Health, Education, and Welfare, from information collected by the Office of Management and Budget for its report Special Analyses, Budget of the United States, Fiscal year 1974. Research data are from Federal Funds for Research, Development, and Other Scientific Activities, Vol. XXI, National Science Foundation.

Table 12.5 Office of Education Expenditures, by Legislative Program: Fiscal Years 1960-1974 (in thousands)

Legislative program	1960	1962	1964	1966	1968	1970	1971	1972	1973[1]	1974[1]
1	2	3	4	5	6	7	8	9	10	11
Total	$459,965	$547,408	$673,005	$2,024,428	$3,613,476	$4,111,598	$4,543,641	$4,903,711	$4,868,661	$4,975,084
Elementary and Secondary Education Act[2]	811	1,247	1,648	816,982	1,327,723	1,412,949	1,743,115	1,835,564	1,798,028	613,669
Title I. Educationally deprived children				746,904	1,049,116	[3]1,170,355	1,516,210	1,570,388	1,500,004	411,000
Title II. Library resources				47,871	91,054	44,670	59,253	74,648	76,800	59,963
Title III. Supplementary education centers				10,938	161,256	158,781	112,071	122,527	142,270	83,191
Title V. Strengthening State departments of education[4]	811	1,247	1,648	11,269	26,297	29,247	28,545	32,879	33,336	10,862
Title VII. Bilingual education						6,192	20,876	26,010	35,708	40,056
Title VIII. Dropout prevention						3,704	6,160	9,112	9,910	8,597
School assistance in federally affected areas	258,198	282,909	334,289	409,593	506,372	656,372	527,043	648,608	467,452	130,910
Maintenance and operation	174,850	226,419	283,688	353,851	470,887	620,463	506,851	628,305	442,248	106,235
Construction	83,348	56,490	50,601	55,742	35,485	35,909	20,192	20,303	25,204	24,675
Higher Education Act				35,232	365,884	531,090	653,307	772,707	943,042	1,451,307
Title I. University community services				3,926	9,897	10,669	10,963	9,518	5,894	
Title II. Library programs:[5]										
College library resources					48,906	34,063	5,596	3,913	10,973	8,298
Library training					11,381	7,005	4,769	2,469	2,678	3,597
Acquisition and cataloging by Library of Congress				300	5,478	5,721	7,079			
Title III. Strengthening developing institutions					22,428	27,731	35,894	35,766	50,000	77,577
Title IV. Student assistance:										
Equal opportunity grants					103,104	142,577	160,676	167,600	218,267	[6]634,704
Work-study program and cooperative education				30,634	111,812	172,075	191,665	251,997	258,513	263,535
Insured loans					28,947	98,330	150,396	201,321	246,945	294,710
Student loans insurance fund						2,323	11,035	26,589	46,167	57,000
Title V. Teacher Corps				362	16,019	18,191	28,761	23,887	40,613	37,565
Title VI. Undergraduate instructional assistance:										
Television and other equipment					5,415	4,968	2,258	5,684	10,258	3,990
Special programs for disadvantaged—Talent Search, Special Services, Upward Bound				10	2,497	7,437	44,215	43,963	52,734	70,331
Higher Education Facilities Act				105,526	461,965	437,387	340,033	212,628	134,545	109,838
Title I. Public community colleges and technical institutes and other undergraduate facilities				48,739	317,063	317,227	277,690	180,700	106,634	71,362
State administration and planning				1,675	5,066	5,961	5,540	7,221	3,550	2,900
Major disaster areas					147			200		
Title II. Graduate facilities				4,220	37,970					
Title III. College construction loans				50,892	101,719	114,199	56,802	24,468	14,361	15,576
Construction loans interest subsidization							1	39	10,000	20,000
Vocational education[7]	45,179	51,762	54,503	128,468	255,224	285,568	370,954	430,722	453,265	251,612
George-Barden and supplemental acts	45,179	51,762	54,503	118,396	250,197	271,282	328,087	370,619	384,910	202,619
Smith-Hughes Act				10,072	5,027	5,322	16,011	24,256	25,110	16,291
Work-study program and cooperative education						1,593	8,801	13,777	16,958	16,692
Innovative programs in vocational education and research						94	271	321	324	69
National advisory councils						2,218	2,474	2,658	2,690	93
State advisory councils										
Consumer and homemaking education						5,059	15,310	19,091	23,273	15,848

Legislative program	1960	1962	1964	1966	1968	1970	1971	1972	1973[1]	1974[1]
1	2	3	4	5	6	7	8	9	10	11
Education professions development	8,683	13,893	13,969	42,147	60,271	104,671	93,541	93,117	98,123	77,125
Elementary and secondary teacher training programs[8]	8,683	13,893	13,969	42,147	58,387	72,924	63,078	69,641	79,195	66,587
Preschool, elementary, and secondary training grants to States					1,884	21,500	22,525	13,552	7,837	2,351
Higher education training programs						10,247	7,938	9,924	11,091	8,187
Public Library Services and Construction Act	6,066	6,932	7,443	40,915	62,017	52,687	52,270	54,066	48,367	14,631
Public library services	6,066	6,932	7,443	25,000	34,306	33,489	37,637	44,284	35,681	9,329
Construction				15,915	26,615	17,527	12,788	7,184	10,068	4,685
Interlibrary cooperation					1,096	1,671	1,845	2,618	2,618	617
Educational improvement for the handicapped	380	1,191	4,982	15,366	40,955	79,065	85,146	93,138	113,500	89,760
Education for the handicapped					7,867	31,073	29,280	32,657	36,844	10,780
Teacher education and recruitment	308	943	2,466	10,448	24,162	31,219	27,366	25,205	35,273	29,970
Research and innovation (includes deaf-blind and resource centers)			1,016	3,227	8,277	12,515	20,667	16,883	22,476	25,970
Captioned films and media services	72	248	1,500	1,691	649	4,258	5,079	11,706	11,446	12,255
Early childhood education							2,754	6,687	7,461	10,785
National Defense Education Act	117,965	158,801	216,338	320,172	370,034	332,898	330,783	392,233	389,902	62,683
Title II. Student loans and cancellations	40,326	74,532	111,729	177,394	182,825	194,520	231,706	287,163	305,906	28,631
Title III. Instructional assistance:										
Grants and loans[9]	49,848	39,510	56,131	76,175	85,916	58,547	44,647	42,629	38,260	11,764
Title IV. College teacher fellowships	4,620	17,313	19,680	31,974	60,650	63,518	40,884	53,782	1027,500	1020,228
Title V. Guidance, counseling, and testing	12,870	14,064	13,710	22,017	23,093					
Title VI. Language development:[11]										
Language and area centers, fellowships, and research	10,301	13,382	15,088	12,612	17,550	16,313	13,546	8,659	18,234	2,060
Research and development	6,004	7,461	12,712	31,245	79,955	87,823	114,905	12102,235	12106,972	1269,762
Training and research					4,832	6,736	6,929	4,844	2,483	662
Construction					333	1,917	3,582	13,065	8,505	3,185
Research and development and educational media research and dissemination (includes amounts for research in education renewal proposal)[13]	6,004	7,461	12,712	31,245	74,790	79,170	104,394	1484,306	1495,884	1466,915
Adult basic education[15]				33,616	28,701	43,464	57,018	55,971	61,472	27,245
Civil rights activities				5,291	7,437	10,608	19,132	22,315	17,791	16,096
Land-grant colleges	5,052	10,744	14,500	14,500	14,500	21,961	12,680	12,600	8,700	2,700
Education revenue sharing										1,692,699
Drug Abuse								6,916	11,172	9,968
Special foreign currency program–training, research and study (grants to American institutions overseas)			138	500	857	774	1,749	2,279	2,736	3,257
Educational broadcasting facilities[16]		6				4,163	5,580	12,182	12,845	11,818
Follow Through								2,024	43,810	52,298
Emergency school assistance							51,239	69,899	54,443	180,157
Office of Education salaries and expenses including technical services and planning and evaluation	11,608	12,664	14,251	26,901	40,906	47,714	68,170	73,845	98,293	100,737
Miscellaneous expired accounts	+29	-202	-1,768	-1,026	-9,325	+2,404	17,745	11,049	4,203	6,612
Consolidated Working Fund–net advances and reimbursements							-207	-769		

Table 12.5 (Continued)

Legislative program	1960	1962	1964	1966	1968	1970	1971	1972	1973[1]	1974[1]
1	2	3	4	5	6	7	8	9	10	11
Expenditures from funds transferred to the Office of Education by other Federal agencies:[17]										
Manpower Development and Training Act[18]	……	……	64,777	75,532	99,451	121,451	141,529	126,500	……	……
Educational television facilities	……	……	1,962	4,663	6,737	0	……	……	……	……
Mutual exchange activities (foreign currency)[19]	……	……	……	1,592	1,434	930	944	873	……	……
Appalachian Regional Development and Training Act[20]	……	……	……	……	21,753	27,128	37,906	36,640[21]	……	……
Cuban Refugee Program	……	5,196	9,603	9,302	16,990	19,488	19,851	18,110	……	……
Office of Economic Opportunity[22]	……	……	……	54,681	686	38,234	47,280	78,096	……	……
Consolidated Working Fund–gross outlay	62	3,068	2,250	10,515	11,395	6,165	56,000	3,377	……	……

1 Estimated.
2 Title VI for education of the handicapped is not included here but is included under "Educational improvement" for the handicapped." "Nutrition and Health" included in "Research and Development."
3 Includes some elementary-secondary school expenditures from expired accounts.
4 Includes Title X, National Defense Education Act (NDEA).
5 Amounts for college library improvement are included under research and development.
6 Includes Basic Educational Opportunity Grants.
7 Amounts for vocational research are included under research and development.
8 Includes funds for teacher training institutes (after 1969) provided under the National Foundation on the Arts and the Humanities Act and NDEA.
9 Includes assistance under the National Foundation on the Arts and the Humanities Act.
10 Includes "Ellender" fellowships.
11 Includes Fulbright-Hays Act.
12 Includes transfers to the National Institute of Education.
13 Includes amounts for college library improvement and vocational research in addition to other R. & D. funds.
14 Includes "Nutrition and Health."
15 Includes amounts for adult vocational education and adult vocational-education teacher training.
16 Amounts for this activity supported with transferred funds prior to 1969.
17 Amounts listed below are not included in the Office of Education expenditure totals.
18 Includes amounts for Area Redevelopment Act.
19 Includes Educational Exchange.
20 Funds transferred prior to 1967 are included in the Consolidated Working Fund.
21 Also includes Development Facilities, Economic Development Assistance, Department of Commerce ($1,981 thousand): Regional Development Programs, Regional Action, Planning Commission ($3,319 thousand); and Military Construction, Army ($470 thousand).
22 Some OEO transfers also included in the Consolidated Working Fund.

SOURCE: Compiled by the National Center for Educational Statistics and the Office of Administration, Office of Education, U.S. Department of Health, Education, and Welfare.

an extensive summary that the Office of Education has found useful. Part I includes those programs more frequently considered in the general category of federal aid to education. Grants and loans are separated because of the obvious fact that loans require repayment but grants do not. Part II includes data for other programs that may also be considered in determining federal funds for education.

A summary of U.S. Office of Education disbursements for the years from 1960 to 1974, by legislative program, is presented in Table 12.5. This table reveals the support pattern for the Office of Education by showing changes in levels of support for different educational activities and the appearance of new activities.

Research Related to
Financing Vocational Education

The role of the federal government in financing public vocational education was studied by Penn (2) in 1968. He found that (a) the primary impetus behind initial federal financial aid to public vocational education was a mandate by the American people for a more practical educational system; (b) cordial and effective relationships existed between federal, state, and local agencies responsible for the administration of programs under provisions of federal vocational acts; and (c) the states showed a high degree of individuality in their spending patterns and trends relative to public vocational education programs.

In 1966, Davie and Patterson (3) investigated intergovernmental fiscal relations as they pertain to vocational education. They attempted to answer two basic questions: 1. Can the procedures used to allot federal vocational education funds among the states be improved? 2. Has federal aid stimulated state-local expenditures for vocational education? In answer to the first question, the investigators felt that significant changes in allotment procedures could be made that would better meet national education objectives; the inclusion of an equalization provision in the allotment procedures, as required by the Vocational Education Act of 1963, was seen as a major innovation. The answer to the second question was a qualified negative; the study indicated that no significant relationship existed between changes in federal expenditures for vocational education and changes in state-local expenditures.

It is generally recognized that the cost of most vocational and technical education programs is higher than the cost of most academic programs. This cost differential has been frequently used to justify special financial support for vocational education. Anderson (4) did a study of the relationship of the unit costs of special vocational and technical curricula to the unit costs of liberal arts and transfer curricula. He found that the majority of the vocational and technical curricula cost more per student than the transfer curricula in the same institution. The average cost ratios Anderson reported for eight types of vocational and technical curricula are as follows:

applied arts 1.76
engineering technologies 1.95
business and office occupations .... .95
health and medical occupations 1.49
industrial technical occupations 1.52
dietetics and home economics occupations 1.21
public service occupations .... .96
(average cost of transfer curricula .... 1.00)

This study included only comprehensive junior colleges that had been in operation for a minimum of five years and, therefore, does not reflect the "start up" costs of initiating and developing vocational and technical programs.

An analysis of expenditures for vocational-technical programs has been done as a part of Swanson's 1967 *Nationwide Study of the Administration of Vocational-Technical Education at the State Level* (5). Considerable evidence was found that a very large percentage of all funds expended for vocational and technical education was used at the point of operation, the local program. This was particularly true of federal funds, where 92 percent was used either for school construction, program equipment, or program operation.

Henderson (6) suggested that new opportunities in continuing education for adults would come from the impetus provided by expanded federal legislation. The enactment of the Vocational Education Act of 1963 and the subsequent Amendments of 1968 provided a new philosophy of and major financial support for vocational education, resulting in a major redirection of occupational education in every state. Other national legislation, such as the Adult Basic Education Act, the Comprehensive Employment and Training Act, the Economic Opportunity Act, and the National Defense Education Act have stimulated innovative and creative means to meet adult occupational needs, especially in the impacted areas of the nation.

Expenditures for Vocational Education

The vocational education program under the Vocational Education Amendments of 1968 is conducted in each state in accordance with an approved state plan. All states and outlying areas of the United States participate in the program. The tables and figure in this section indicate that vocational education has experienced significant growth, particularly after the Vocational Education Amendments of 1968. The full impact of this Act was not apparent until fiscal year 1971, because funds were not available until late in the 1970 fiscal year. In addition to expansion in enrollments and increased expenditures, positive changes have occurred in the quality and scope of vocational programs.

The following highlights illustrate the kinds of information related to expenditures revealed in the tables and figure:

■ Over $3 billion from federal, state, and local sources were expended for vocational education during fiscal year 1973, an increase of 12.8 percent, with 15.9 percent of the total being federal and 84.1 percent being state and local funds.

■ For each dollar of federal funds expended, the states expended $5.29, with a range among the states of $1.21 to $10.55.

■ Of the total expenditure of Part B funds, 23.5 percent was allocated to postsecondary programs, 17.1 percent to programs for the disadvantaged, and 11.2 percent to programs for the handicapped.

As shown in Figure 12.1, the federal funding available for vocational education increased significantly, with federal allotments rising from $157 million in 1965 to $482 million in 1973.

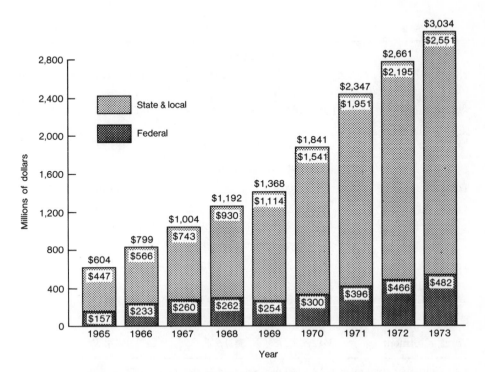

Figure 12.1 Expenditures for vocational education, by source of funds: 1965–1973 (in millions). Source: Annual Reports, Division of Vocational and Technical Education, U.S. Office of Education, 1965–1973.

Table 12.6 shows that state and local expenditures greatly overmatch the federal dollar ($5.29: $1.00 in 1973). State and local expenditures accounted for more than 80 percent of the total expenditures, and between 1972 and 1973 they increased at a rate four times greater than the federal expenditures, 16.2 percent state/local to 3.5 percent federal.

It should be noted that the federal funds expended each year prior to 1973 were less than the allotment available. The lateness of appropriations, particularly in 1970, created a backlog in funds, which was carried forward to the next fiscal year. The lag was finally overcome in 1973. However, the amount of 1973 funds carried over to 1974 approximated $86 million.

Table 12.7 illustrates total expenditures and percentage distribution for vocational education, by function. The proportion spent for instructional salaries is about 68 percent of the total expenditures. Expenditures for other instructional costs, administration and supervision, and instructional equipment rank next, with 12 percent, 8.3 percent, and 5.9 percent respectively. Other instructional costs include student transportation,

Table 12.6 Total Expenditures for Vocational Education, by Source of Funds: Fiscal Years 1971–1978

	1971	1972	1973	1978 (Projected)
		Amount		
Total	$2,347,353,175	$2,660,758,658	$3,033,657,510	$6,310,000,000
Federal	396,378,405	466,029,820	482,390,800	972,000,000
State/Local	1,950,974,770	2,194,728,838	2,551,266,710	5,338,000,000
Ratio: State/Local to Federal	$4.92	$4.71	$5.29	$5.50
		Percentage distribution		
Total	100.0	100.0	100.0	100.0
Federal	16.9	17.5	15.9	15.4
State/Local	83.1	82.5	84.1	84.6
		Percentage change from previous year		
Total	27.4	13.4	14.0	—
Federal	32.1	17.6	3.5	—
State/Local	26.5	12.5	16.2	—
		Federal allotment		
Total allotment	$412,812,093	$471,968,455	$471,968,455*	

* An additional amount of $77,119,000 was released in fiscal year 1974.

Source: Bureau of Occupational and Adult Education, Office of Education, U.S. Department of Health, Education, and welfare, Trends in Vocational Education, Fiscal Year 1973.

space rental, insurance, teacher travel, and utilities. The 1978 projected percentage distribution of expenditures shows increases over 1973 in these areas: salaries, from 67.1 percent to 75 percent; guidance from 3.7 to 3.9 percent; research from 0.6 to 1.5 percent; and curriculum development from 0.3 to 0.6 percent.

Table 12.8 contains the allocation of federal funds expended for various purposes outlined in the 1968 Act. Of significance is the percentage increase in expenditures for secondary programs (33.1 percent in 1973). Other purposes showing increasing percentages of the total are disadvantaged, handicapped, ancillary services, and guidance and counseling. Postsecondary expenditures remain rather stable at about 23 percent, which is well above the 15 percent required by the legislation. Similarly, expenditures for the disadvantaged exceed the 15 percent minimum but to a lesser degree. Expenditures for the handicapped are only slightly above the 10 percent minimum. Expenditures for construction of area vocational schools decline to about 9 percent. Only a small amount of funds are expended under the contracting of instruction provision.

Table 12.7 Total Expenditures for Vocational Education, by Function*: Fiscal Years 1971–1978 (in thousands)

	1971	1972	1973	1978 (Projected)
	Amount			
Total	$2,075,881	$2,410,086	$2,801,553	$6,051,000
instructional salaries	1,426,330	1,585,709	1,879,306	4,540,000
instructional equipment	141,401	147,908	166,351	200,000
other instructional costs	251,114	333,964	364,258	556,000
vocational guidance	66,609	89,778	103,754	235,000
administration and supervision	142,813	193,900	232,128	350,000
teacher education	26,879	31,065	30,580	45,000
research	12,260	18,462	15,710	90,000
curriculum development	8,475	9,300	9,466	35,000
	Percentage distribution			
Total	100.0	100.0	100.0	100.0
instructional salaries	68.7	65.8	67.1	75.0
instructional equipment	6.8	6.1	5.9	3.3
other instructional costs	12.1	13.9	13.0	9.2
vocational guidance	3.2	3.7	3.7	3.9
administration and supervision	6.8	8.0	8.3	5.8
teacher education	1.3	1.3	1.1	0.7
research	0.7	0.8	0.6	1.5
curriculum development	0.4	0.4	0.3	0.6

* *Excludes construction and work-study.*

Source: *Bureau of Occupational and Adult Education, Office of Education, U.S. Department of Health, Education, and Welfare,* Trends in Vocational Education, *Fiscal Year 1973.*

Table 12.8 Expenditures from Vocational Education Act of 1963, as Amended, by Purpose: Fiscal Years 1971–1973

	1971		1972		1973	
	Amount	Percentage of total	Amount	Percentage of total	Amount	Percentage of total
Total	$317,083,369*	100.0	$370,132,642*	100.0	$387,664,484*	100.0
secondary	88,362,942	27.9	109,045,448	29.5	126,531,324	33.1
postsecondary	72,107,104	22.8	82,229,785	22.2	91,190,849	23.9
adult	15,983,122	5.1	21,481,578	5.8	19,103,967	5.0
disadvantaged	51,819,442	16.3	63,565,259	17.2	66,314,918	17.4
handicapped	33,871,902	10.7	37,899,822	10.2	43,234,940	11.3
construction	51,477,906	16.2	55,701,484	15.0	35,422,931	9.3
ancillary services	(40,072,020)†	(12.8)	(50,178,827)	(13.6)	(63,073,834)	(16.3)
guidance and counseling	(7,333,812)	(2.3)	(10,141,102)	(2.7)	(11,770,598)	(3.0)
contracted instruction	(1,488,325)	(0.5)	(506,951)	(0.1)	(1,348,467)	(0.3)

* Total not sum of purposes because of variances among states in allocation of ancillary services.
† Amounts in parentheses are expended by level or target group.

Source: Bureau of Occupational and Adult Education, Office of Education, U.S. Department of Health, Education, and Welfare, Trends in Vocational Education, Fiscal Year 1973.

Table 12.9 Expenditures for Vocational Education, by
Level and Source: Fiscal Years 1971–1978 (in thousands)

	1971	1972	1973	1978 (Projected)
Secondary	$1,560,889	$1,752,449	$1,998,732	$4,377,000
Federal	250,328	296,347	310,292	680,000
State/Local	1,310,561	1,456,102	1,688,440	3,697,000
Postsecondary	566,978	707,163	843,402	1,538,000
Federal	110,046	123,567	130,597	240,000
State/Local	455,932	583,596	712,805	1,298,000
Adult	218,194	196,514	191,528	395,000
Federal	33,719	44,092	41,373	84,000
State/Local	184,475	152,422	150,155	311,000

Source: Bureau of Occupational and Adult Education, Office of Education, U.S. Department
of Health, Education, and Welfare, Trends in Vocational Education, Fiscal Year 1973.

Table 12.10 Total Expenditures for Vocational Education, by
Target Group and Level: Fiscal Years 1971–1978 (in thousands)

	1971	1972	1973	1978 (Projected)
Disadvantaged	$ 219,127	$ 290,074	$ 312,135	$ 900,000
Secondary	147,792	214,190	239,425	690,000
Postsecondary	31,460	37,768	43,725	126,000
Adult	39,875	38,116	28,985	84,000
Handicapped	62,983	67,467	94,074	205,000
Secondary	46,353	54,731	76,617	167,000
Postsecondary	9,618	8,022	12,629	27,000
Adult	7,012	4,714	4,828	11,000
Regular	2,063,959	2,298,585	2,627,453	5,205,000
Secondary	1,366,744	1,483,527	1,682,690	3,331,000
Postsecondary	525,908	661,374	787,048	1,562,000
Adult	171,307	153,684	157,715	312,000

Source: Bureau of Occupational and Adult Education, Office of Education, U.S. Department
of Health, Education, and Welfare, Trends in Vocational Education, Fiscal Year 1973.

Table 12.11   Number of Area Vocational Schools and Expenditures
for Construction of Facilities: Fiscal Years 1971–1973 (in thousands)

	1971	1972	1973
Number of approved area vocational schools	1,676	1,889	2,148
Number of construction projects	400	436	368
Expenditures: total	$317,569	$265,158	$228,186

Source: Bureau of Occupational and Adult Education, Office of Education, U.S. Department
of Health, Education, and Welfare, Trends in Vocational Education, Fiscal Year 1973.

Table 12.12   Expenditures for Vocational Work-
Study Programs: Fiscal Years 1971–1973

	1971	1972	1973
Total	$9,042,766	$11,409,966	$9,777,319
Federal	5,783,711	6,289,386	6,163,959
State/Local	3,259,055	5,120,580	3,613,360

Source: Bureau of Occupational and Adult Education, Office of Education, U.S. Department
of Health, Education, and Welfare, Trends in Vocational Education, Fiscal Year 1973.

Table 12.13   Expenditures for Cooperative Education
Programs Under Part G: Fiscal Years 1971–1973

	1971	1972	1973
Total	$28,025,961	$32,797,274	$48,822,802
Federal	17,585,628	19,948,690	21,709,942
State/Local	10,440,333	12,848,584	27,112,860

Source: Bureau of Occupational and Adult Education, Office of Education, U.S. Department
of Health, Education, and Welfare, Trends in Vocational Education, Fiscal Year 1973.

Table 12.9 indicates total expenditures, by level and source, allocated
to secondary, postsecondary, and adult levels of education. In 1973, 65.9
percent of the expenditures were for secondary, 27.8 percent for postsecondary, and 6.3 percent for adult, as compared to 66.5, 24.2, and 9.3
respectively in 1971. It can be noted that the ratio of federal funds to state
and local funds was somewhat higher for adult than for the other levels,
21.6 percent federal funds for adult compared with 15.5 percent federal
funds for secondary and postsecondary.

Table 12.10 indicates total expenditures for all programs, allocated by target population and by level. In 1973, 10.3 percent of the total expenditure was for the disadvantaged, up from 9.3 percent in 1971; and 3.1 percent was for the handicapped, up from 2.7 percent in 1971. Although there were decreases in expenditures for *adult* programs from 1971–73, there were increases in funds for all three target groups (disadvantaged, handicapped and regular) at both the *secondary* and *postsecondary* levels.

Table 12.11 shows a decline in the expenditures for area vocational school construction. Apparently the need for additional facilities has been met in many states; in other states construction is entirely financed with state and local funds. The number of institutions designated as approved area vocational schools, however, continues to increase, and in 1973 there were 2148 such schools.

Table 12.12 reveals a rather stable expenditure for work-study programs, the result of a constant level of appropriations for this purpose. Table 12.13 shows that the expenditures for cooperative programs under Part G of the Act have almost doubled from 1971 to 1973. Even though no matching of Part G funds, cooperative programs, is required, states in 1973 expended more of their own funds than federal funds.

Summary

Public education is a state responsibility supported by local, state, and federal resources. Only about eight cents out of every school dollar, however, has come from federal sources. Nevertheless, a continually escalating level of federal "seed money" and the "matching funds principle" in vocational education have encouraged the states and school districts to provide additional financial effort.

State laws provide for school support through public taxation from a wide range of sources, including income taxes, sales taxes, use and occupations taxes, franchise and license fees, inheritance and gift taxes, and so on. As urbanization has continued, school districts have increasingly become polarized in terms of income, creating thorny issues of equalization for school boards and the courts. Equalization formulas, such as those used in the Vocational Education Act, have served to alleviate some of the inequities among school communities throughout the nation.

Federal aid to vocational education dates from 1787, with an allocation of federal property to the states. A variety of educational procedures have followed, including financial grants, loans, operation of special programs and institutions, and funding of services through contracts with the federal government. Landmark federal legislation affecting vocational education includes the Morrill Land-Grant Acts, Smith-Hughes Act, George-Barden Act, Vocational Education Act of 1963, Vocational Education Amendments of 1968, and the Comprehensive Employment and Training Act of 1973. Each of these acts has infused increasingly larger sums of money into vocational education programs. The National Advisory

Council on Vocational Education drew attention in its *Fourth Annual Report* to some of the current and unique problems of financing and planning vocational and technical education.

It is generally recognized that the cost of most vocational and technical education programs is higher than the cost of most academic programs. One justification for special financial support for vocational education has been this differential in cost.

Activities

For review

1 What proportion of the school dollar is furnished by the federal government for education purposes?

2 What is an "equalization formula" and how does it work in school finance?

3 Why are equalization formulas needed in vocational education?

4 What is the formula for computing local school taxes?

5 Distinguish between the terms "authorization" and "appropriation" as used in legislative funding.

6 How did the Comprehensive Employment and Training Act of 1973 affect existing labor training programs?

7 Has federal aid stimulated state-local expenditures for vocational education? Explain.

8 What was the ratio of (a) federal, and (b) state, vocational education expenditures to total expenditures for vocational education in the United States in 1973, as shown in Table 12.1?

9 What is a tax referendum?

For discussion

1 What is meant by the "matching principle" in vocational education legislation? What is its purpose?

2 Why is the cost of vocational-technical education usually greater than that for academic education?

3 Why do members of Congress frequently express misgivings about monies that are earmarked for educational research and development?

4 Do you feel that there should continue to be expanded federal acts supporting: (a) vocational education and other specialized programs separately, or (b) all education without respect to type? Explain your position.

5 What reasons can you give for the difference between the amount of funds *authorized* and the amount *appropriated* for the various vocational education acts?

For exploration

1 In what ways has the use of federal funds for vocational education changed since the passage of the Smith-Hughes Act? Cite major differences, for example, between the funding provisions of the Smith-Hughes Act and the Vocational Education Act of 1963.

2 The Vocational Education Act of 1963 largely abandoned the use of categorical aid, that is, the earmarking of funds for specific vocational education fields. What was the reasoning behind this action by Congress?

3 What financial problems did the 1968 National Advisory Council on Vocational Education identify? What solutions did it propose?

4 What changes do you foresee in the pattern of federal funding for vocational education in the future? Explain your ideas.

5 Examine the equalization provisions in the allotment procedures of the Vocational Education Act of 1963. What were these provisions?

6 Conduct a survey of (a) the literature, or (b) a few people in business, to determine what percentage of the company budget should be spent in research and development of new products or services. How does the amount actually spent in firms compare with the amount spent nationally for educational research and development? How did the amount of educational research and development funds compare, as a percentage of the gross national product, in 1972?

References

1 Hugh Calkins, chairman, National Advisory Council on Vocational Education, excerpt from letter to Elliot W. Richardson, Secretary, Department of Health, Education and Welfare, dated January 16, 1974.

2 Thomas L. Penn, "A Study of Federal Financial Aid to Public Vocational Education (Doctoral Dissertation, The American University; Ann Arbor, Michigan: University Microfilms, 1968), p. 41.

3 Bruce F. Davie and Philip D. Patterson, Jr., *Vocational Education and Inter-Governmental Fiscal Relations in the Post War Period* (Washington, D.C.: Georgetown University, 1966), p. 41.

4 Ernest F. Anderson, "Differentiated Costs in Comprehensive Junior Colleges," (Doctoral Dissertation, University of Illinois; Ann Arbor, Michigan: University Microfilms, 1966), p. 42.

5 J. Chester Swanson, *A Nationwide Study of the Administration of Vocational Education at the State Level*, Vol. 2, Final Report (Berkeley, California: School of Education, 1967) University of California, pp. 10, 42, 44.

6 Lee Henderson, "Financial Resources—Federal, State, Local," in *Excellence in Continuing Education*, proceedings of the Sixth Annual Junior College Administrative Teams Institute (Gainesville, Florida: University of Florida, August 7–9, 1966), p. 43.

Chapter 13

Public Relations

for

Vocational-Technical

Education

Introduction

American schools have extended their mission and services until they touch more lives than ever before. But, paradoxically, many of the "whys" of education have, to an increasing extent, eluded the public grasp. Schools appear to move from one crisis to another, sometimes following and sometimes leading in the race to keep abreast of change. Education must deal with many problems, but its most fundamental challenge is to justify itself in the minds of those who finance it.

The schools have suffered from a failure to understand the community and to develop an understanding by the community of the school, its services, objectives, problems, and successes. In too many instances, the school has failed to create a climate conducive to an exchange of views between the school and its publics. Administrators and teachers have been too fully absorbed in the immediate problems at hand to give adequate attention to the problems of informing the public and enlisting its cooperation. Too frequently, school administrators, including vocational administrators, have assumed that "if we run a good school," the public must necessarily approve, despite the fact that conceptions may vary widely as to what constitutes a "good school."

The 1960s were years of rapid change and shifting social patterns, years in which the nation's schools were caught up in a web of difficult relationships. News of public education and its problems moved to the front pages of newspapers, with headlines reporting teacher strikes, school bond defeats, parental opposition to busing, and student riots. Growth in news coverage of education in part reflected the public's increased awareness of schools and their impact on society. The events and circumstances of the Sixties—the civil rights movement, protests in the streets, discovery of the poor, acceleration of industrial technology, and swiftly changing social patterns—all served to establish firmly in the public mind the social urgency of public education.

The 1970s have seen public demands for accountability and a reluctance, in the face of declining student enrollments, to raise levels of financial support. In combination with the poor economic conditions of the mid-1970s, these pressures have resulted in a retrenchment in education and a demand that the need for and quality of existing and proposed programs be reviewed. These developments have led to significant changes in the structure of educational programs and an increasing sensitivity to the role of the school as a cooperative agency in the educational enterprise.

Vocational education must continue to adapt to the processes of change and progress. It is the consensus of many educators that the public schools will make progress about as rapidly as the general public will support change. Thus public relations becomes an essential facilitator of change.

□ *Changes in regard to purpose, content and teaching method, along with the increasing size and costs of schools have tended to confuse the general public and leave them without adequate information. Today's complex and urbanized society demands that public school pupils be provided educational experiences quite different from many of those which present-day parents themselves received in school.* (1)

For this reason, it is more important than ever that the public be intelligently informed as to what schools are attempting to do. The public will continue its support of the best in education only when it is kept well informed of the progress of its schools.

Public opinion—the state of the public's education on a given subject—is not stable. Changes are especially marked in a highly competitive society. The instability of public opinion is manifested on such diverse subjects as the actions of particular foreign countries, conservation of natural and human resources, or the varying uses of the tax dollar. This particular feature of public opinion is the reason why a good public relations program must be continuous and consistent.

During recent years there has been a general awakening to the importance and possibilities of an intelligent school public relations program. However, there has been a tendency to give this information to the public only when a new bond issue was to be passed or other financial assistance was to be secured. Thus the program assumed a somewhat selfish aspect and was not inclined to add to the confidence of the general public.

Educators are gradually coming to understand that every person who is in any way connected with the educational program is a public relations agent, whether or not that person is aware of the fact. Students, by virtue of their role as the most direct beneficiaries of educational programs, become the schools' most important public relations agents; the impressions they transmit to their parents are frequently accepted without question. Therefore, public relations must take on an in-school as well as an out-of-school emphasis. Teachers undoubtedly are the most important official agents in school public relations, although all school personnel play a public relations role. It is important, too, that various community groups be made aware of the part they play in the important task of making good schools better.

That the American public has great faith in its schools is evidenced by their continuous support over the years. As long as the great majority of people believe in education, sporadic attacks in the press or from pressure groups will not defeat the schools. However, in some communities where programs have been developed without adequate explanation and without participation of the community, progress has been retarded, and ill-advised changes have been made because of opposition from uninformed groups.

The public school system receives its support from the people. Just as the stockholders in a business enterprise have a right to know the facts concerning the status of the business they own, so also the people of any community have a right to know what is going on in their schools, which belong to them and are operated for the benefit of their children and the community. Therefore, educators need to take the public into their confidence, providing them with the information they need to understand the total school program. Such information programs should not be deferred until a crisis arises.

Philosophy in the field of public relations is often more advanced than is practice. But it is generally believed that a sound curriculum is the basis on which a public relations program should be founded. The student's development and growth furnish the standard. For the school administrator, however, the question is how to proceed beyond this point. It is only natural that he or she should turn to private business, which has had such successful experience in public relations work.

American education has lagged far behind business and industry in the acceptance, development, and refinement of public relations techniques. But just because public relations cannot qualify as an exact science, its processes should not be rejected. Whatever is known, with reasonable sureness, about public relations should be studied by all who deal with and depend on the public. Because the schools have been created for service and not for profit, however, the methods should be adapted for use in education. It would be worse than a mistake for any public institution to adopt outright the methods that have been successful in private enterprise.

Public Relations in the Changing Educational Scene

Public relations has been defined (2) as "that field of action which concerns itself with the relations of an individual, an idea, an institution with the publics upon which it depends for its visibility." An earlier but still highly relevant description of school public relations was provided by Kindred (3), who stated the following in 1957:

□ *School public relations is a process of communication between the school and the community for the purpose of increasing citizen understanding of educational needs and practices, and encourages intelligent citizen interest and cooperation in the work of improving the school.*

A decade later, Jones (4) reaffirmed the two-way relationship between the school and the community when he stated that "public relations designates all the functions and relationships that pertain in exchange of ideas between school and community that establish the basis for joint understanding."

Because school public relations is a two-way process, it involves *listening* as well as talking, and it should not be confused with "publicity," a one-way process of information giving that does not necessarily ensure understanding. The question confronting educators is not whether or not they want public relations, but whether they want *planned* or *unplanned* public relations, favorable or unfavorable public relations.

Importance of
School Public Relations

The development of good public relations is impossible without good communication. In the absence of communication, there is no public relations, because relations with people are established only by communicating *with* them. Public relations, as a process, involves an interchange of facts, viewpoints, and ideas.

Basically a school or vocational department communication program should be organized on the basis of its internal and external publics. *Internal publics* may be described as those within the environs of the school; that is, students, teachers, administrators, guidance personnel, and nonteaching personnel. *External publics* include those beyond the environs of the school; that is, parents, alumni, merchants and people engaged in business, civic and service groups, the news media, feeder schools, postsecondary vocational schools, colleges, and universities. Both these types of publics represent persons with varied backgrounds, experiences, and interests. Consequently, the communication process must be tailored to fit the characteristics of each group. To think of "the public" as one massive assemblage is a common mistake, and efforts to communicate effectively with the "general public" are on the whole unsuccessful and ineffective.

Several principles may be identified as being fundamental to the establishment of effective two-way communication between the school and its publics:

1 There must be a genuine willingness to share information.

2 Communication should not be deliberately distorted or misleading, but should be factual, accurate, and temperate.

3 Information should be timely and messages transmitted quickly to avoid misunderstanding.

4 Repetition is essential. Information should be repeated in different terms and through different media to make it clearly understood.

5 Information should be communicated in small amounts for clear understanding.

The sole justification for any segment of the school system is to provide appropriate educational opportunities for all students, a process that is best achieved through the coordinated efforts of the school and its publics. The effectiveness of the school is conditioned by the amount of confidence it enjoys. Confidence is built on understanding, trust, and appreciation. To bring about better understanding between the school's internal and external publics, to meet attack and criticism, to understand the broader community so that the school can adapt its program to changing conditions, and to foster a more adequate program of financial support, a planned and systematic approach to public relations is essential. Although public relations is intangible, its efforts clearly contribute to the work of the school.

Need for Effective Public
Relations in Vocational Education

Because vocational education is an integral part of the educational continuum, vocational educators face the continuous and challenging task of interpreting the objectives and purposes of their field to publics both inside and outside the school. In addition, vocational educators are particularly concerned with relationships arising from existing or potential contact with employers in business, industry, and government, as an important facet of their educational program.

At least eight types of problems faced by vocational educators have strong implications for a public relations program:

1 the need to develop a strong liaison between vocational educators and members of Congress and state legislatures to maintain and extend federal and state support for vocational education

2 the need to define vocational education, to point out its relationship to academic and career education, to identify its objectives and goals

3 the need to define the standards to which vocational education ascribes

4 the need to interpret methods of designing, teaching, and evaluating vocational curricula

5 the need to change the stereotypes that have become so deeply rooted in the minds of some people about vocational education

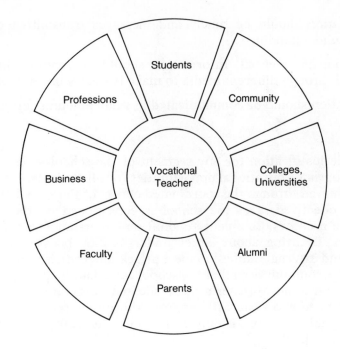

Figure 13.1 Public relations through cooperative endeavor: A two-way relationship.

6 the need to point out the accomplishments and the problems of vocational education

7 the need to interpret what is being done to improve the quality of vocational programs

8 the need to justify the role of vocational education as an essential component in the education of all students

A closer relationship is developing between the business and academic communities. Vocational educators are finding that many of the problems and techniques discussed in the classroom have reality in business, and they are looking more to business and industry for counsel and advice. On the other hand, business leaders are recognizing their responsibility to schools and colleges as sources of educated labor, scientific knowledge, a more favorable business climate, instructional materials, and on-the-job instruction.

The vocational educator is an important link between the school and the employer, as illustrated in Figure 13.1. The strength of that link will determine, in large measure, whether or not the school is keeping abreast of the needs of the community and whether the school is actually fitting its graduates to take their places in the world of work. In making a positive effort to know the needs of local business, such as by promoting cooperative vocational work experience programs, follow-up studies of graduates, field trips, and informal contacts with business employers, the school can adjust its curriculum to meet the needs of its employment community and of its graduates. These liaison-with-business activities of the vocational educator, if properly coordinated, will do much to bring into proper focus the school, the student, and the business and industrial community.

Because of this unique relationship between vocational educators and the community, vocational teachers should be leaders in the field of public relations. They should keep their perspective by remembering that there are weaknesses in every school system; they should not shut their eyes to these problems but rather should indicate a willingness to work on them. They should take the initiative in securing more meaningful cooperation of internal and external school publics.

The student represents the most significant and important force in the public evaluation of a school program because he or she is the focal point of the educational process. Experiences of the student after graduation reflect his or her former experiences within the school and thus serve to color the school's reputation. High school graduates who enroll in post-secondary institutions are representatives of their particular high schools. Likewise, students entering the labor market mold public attitudes toward the school by their dress, manner of speech, general conduct, and job performance.

Communication Needs
in Vocational Education

One of the dilemmas confronting vocational educators is how to satisfy the diversity of opinions and demands of the various groups constituting its publics. It becomes necessary for vocational educators to operate on the same principle that all other public institutions must operate on, that is, in accordance with the wishes of the majority. How can vocational educators know that their programs are being operated according to the wishes of the people? First, enlightened public opinion cannot be developed unless people have full access to the facts—they must know *what* vocational education is trying to accomplish, *how* it is going about achieving its objectives, *how well* it is succeeding, and the problems it is encountering. Merely dispensing the above information to the public does not ensure understanding. Second, through needs assessments, opinion polls, advisory committees, and other public relations activities, the people can make their opinions known and vocational educators can use the information to make more effective decisions.

Communication between the schools and local industry can be improved by (a) schools increasing their efforts to maintain close contact with business and industry to gauge training requirements; and (b) business and industry taking a greater interest in the schools, learning their capabilities, informing the institution of skills required today and of those needed in the future.

Advisory Committees
in Vocational Education

Advisory committees can be effectively used to establish closer contact between schools and business and industry. Such committees have been important to vocational education for many years, especially in job-training programs for young people and adults. Four groups appear to have particular relevance to programs of vocational education: school administrative personnel, labor and management segments of business and industry, labor organizations, and students.

Although the literature about industry-education cooperation recommends the use of advisory committees, it is concerned largely with the use of formally organized advisory committees to achieve the desired cooperative participation of industry. Unfortunately, only occasionally is there provision for the use of specially assigned school staff for industry- or community-liaison purposes.

In an effort to establish more meaningful relationships between business, industry, and the public schools, McGowan (5) surveyed nine major California employers in 1965 to gather data concerning entry-level jobs for which it was difficult to find employees. He concluded his report by making suggestions for improving vocational education through the involvement of business, industry, and the schools. He recommended that clearing houses for vocational information and materials be set up for use in both training and guidance programs. He further recommended that a vocational education council be established for each county, to consist of representatives from business, industry, and labor.

Consulting or advisory committees should be carefully selected. Among the more important characteristics of committee members are that

1 they are able, intelligent people

2 they are public-spirited people, willing to contribute to the betterment of the community

3 they possess outstanding personal qualities of responsibility, integrity, open-mindedness, cooperativeness and insight

4 they are representative of all elements of the community or special program interests they serve; consideration is given to sex, experience, age, religion, politics, and organizational affiliation

5 if they represent a special program area, they bring the needed expertise and interest to the committee; of special importance is the keen interest and insight into their specialty

The specialized committee for vocational-technical education has also been referred to as an occupational advisory committee. Some of its functions are to:

1 serve as a communications channel between colleges and community occupational groups

2 list the specific skills and suggest related and technical information for the course

3 recommend competent personnel from business and industry as potential instructors

4 help evaluate the program on instruction

5 assist in recruiting students, in providing work training stations, and in placing qualified graduates in appropriate jobs

6 keep the school informed about changes in the labor market, specific needs, and surpluses

7 provide means for the school to inform the community of occupational programs

8 assess program needs in terms of the entire community

9 suggest ways of improving the public relations program of the school

Principles of Public Relations   ✳ KNOW !!

The soundness, consistency, and defensibility of a school public relations program are dictated by the assumptions and principles underlying it. However, the development and acceptance of principles do not in themselves guarantee that a program will be effective. Principles must be translated into policies and plans for implementation.

The following assumptions underlie the development of a sound public relations program:

1 Good public relations are a necessary and desirable aim of public schools.

2 The activities or techniques employed in a school's public relations program are necessarily subordinate to and in line with the school's philosophy and objectives.

3 Public relations begin with certain types of activities.

4 Some activities and media are more effective as interpretive and communicative agents than others.

5 The positive identification of activities and practices that have public relations value contributes to a more successful school program.

6 Vocational education is only a part of the total school program; consequently, any formal public relations activity undertaken on behalf of vocational education must be coordinated with the overall school public relations program.

The place and role of public education in a democratic society dictate the principles that underlie an effective school public relations program. The following are examples of principles on which a good public relations program may be organized and operationalized:

1 The school as a social institution is inaugurated by the people for the achievement of their purposes and has no value apart from the purposes and wishes of the people.

2 The role of education is unchanged; however, the organization and implementation of formal education must be considered transitory.

3 The school as a democratic social institution rests on public confidence, which, in turn, depends on the honesty and sincerity of institutional functioning.

4 The school, as an impartial democratic agency, operates on the central tendency of public opinion.

5 The theory of democratic institutional authority limits the purpose and method of the school public relations activity because enlargement or contraction of institutional activity is recognized as being a function of the people. The interests of all the people are superior to those of the teaching profession or of any other minority interest group.

6 The public school exists as an agency for harmonizing cultural differences.

7 The cooperative partnership concept of public education is contingent on the active, intelligent participation of parents, citizens, business/community leaders, and other social agencies.

8 The legal responsibility for determining the school's public relations policy and approving methods of implementation rests with the board of education.

School public relations programs are characterized by standards generally agreed on by researchers and public relations specialists. These include dimensions of honesty, positiveness, comprehensiveness, and sensitivity to publics represented. Elements of repetitiveness, continuity, and follow-through are also important. The school public relations program should be well planned, staffed by competent personnel, adequately funded, well coordinated and continuous, and sensitive to the changing needs of its publics. In addition, the program should provide opportuni-

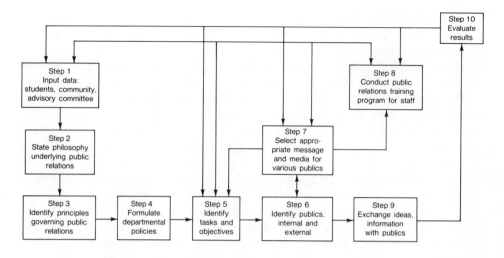

Figure 13.2 Vocational Education Public Relations Model.

ties for involvement by all publics, should communicate its ideas simply, and should be appraised continuously and improved through study, research, and experimentation.

The above characteristics of effective public relations programs show that vocational educators cannot depend on incidental, "hit-or-miss" efforts to ensure desired results. An effective public relations program for vocational education must be systematically planned, developed, implemented, and evaluated. Figure 13.2, A Vocational Education Public Relations Model, illustrates a systematic approach toward planning and implementing a public relations program.

Public Relations
Checklist for Vocational Education

What are the public relations activities, procedures, techniques, and media that have been used to promote vocational education? Who are the publics to be reached?

A number of internal or in-school publics exist through which better public relations for vocational education may be promoted. These publics include the following: school administrators; teachers; guidance personnel; clerical and secretarial personnel; custodial, maintenance, and service personnel; paraprofessional personnel; and students. There exists also an almost unlimited number of external publics, those beyond the environs of the school itself, including merchants and people engaged in business, parents, community organizations, professional education associations, middle and junior high schools, high schools, post-high school vocational-technical schools, junior colleges, and colleges and universities.

The Public Relations Checklist for Vocational Education, which appears on the following pages, is a modification of a doctoral research study completed by the author (6) at Ohio State University. It answers the primary question, What are the nature and scope of public relations practices used in vocational education as shown by research studies and the general literature? It classifies public relations activities and media into three principal categories: (a) those that may be used by the vocational educator to reach *external* school publics; (b) those that he or she may use to reach *internal* school publics; and (c) *school-sponsored* activities that, of themselves, may promote good public relations for vocational education.

Originally designed for high school vocational teachers, the checklist has been modified so that vocational educators at any level may use it to evaluate their own public relations activities against those that are recommended by researchers as being effective. A qualitative appraisal of the relative value of these activities and media would do much to increase the effectiveness of public relations efforts in the field. With a view toward facilitating such an evaluation, the categorized activities have been arranged into a checklist under a coded column headed "Value of Activity" (Limited = L; Average = A; and Excellent = E.) An additional column headed "Have Used" (Yes or No) is designed to determine whether or not the respondent has had experience with the activity or media under evaluation. A qualitative evaluation of the items by vocational educators would point up those activities believed to be most effective as public relations tools. To accomplish such a result, one could administer the instrument to one or more groups, assign a numerical value to each possible response on the checklist, then rank the items on a scale from most effective to least effective.

Public Relations
Checklist for Vocational Education

Directions Listed below are some activities and media that have been identified through research as having possibilities for promoting vocational education with its internal and external publics. The purpose of this appraisal sheet is to secure an evaluation of the worth of the following items as public relations instruments for vocational education.

In the first group of columns ("VALUE OF ACTIVITY"), please *circle one letter value* (L = Limited; A = Average; or E = Excellent) for each item. In the second group of columns ("HAVE USED"), indicate by *circling the appropriate letter* (Y = Yes; N = No) whether or not you have ever used this idea or technique in your vocational education program or have had any first-hand experience with it that would aid you in evaluating its effectiveness.

Activities	Value of Activity			Have Used	
	(Circle 1)			(Circle 1)	

Activities used by the vocational educator to reach external publics

A Public relations contacts of vocational educator with business and industry

Activities	Value of Activity			Have Used	
1 Career day activities	L	A	E	YES	NO
2 School Advisory committee(s)	L	A	E	YES	NO
3 Job analyses made by vocational teacher	L	A	E	YES	NO
4 Personal contacts with persons in business	L	A	E	YES	NO
5 Cooperative work experience program	L	A	E	YES	NO
6 Vocational teacher receives occupational training through summer business job	L	A	E	YES	NO
7 Vocational teacher provides local firms with publicity and information about the program	L	A	E	YES	NO
8 Vocational teacher patronage of local stores	L	A	E	YES	NO
9 Junior Achievement organization (local firm sponsors temporary student-operated business ventures for educational purposes)	L	A	E	YES	NO
10 Persons in business serve as resource people to the school (consultants, speakers, etc.)	L	A	E	YES	NO
11 Business surveys conducted by vocational teacher (job survey, equipment survey, or needs assessment)	L	A	E	YES	NO
12 Vocational teacher serves as consultant to business firms (employee training, systems and procedures)	L	A	E	YES	NO
13 Business-sponsored instructional materials	L	A	E	YES	NO
14 Business machines show staged in school	L	A	E	YES	NO
15 Adult vocational education program (short courses, workshops, training or retraining for vocational or avocational purposes)	L	A	E	YES	NO

Activities	Value of Activity			Have Used	
	(Circle 1)			(Circle 1)	
B Public relations contacts of vocational educator with community organizations					
1 Membership and active participation in business-related groups					
(a) Administrative Management Society	L	A	E	YES	NO
(b) Better Business Bureau	L	A	E	YES	NO
(c) Chamber of Commerce	L	A	E	YES	NO
(d) Community Improvement Association	L	A	E	YES	NO
(e) National Secretaries Association ..	L	A	E	YES	NO
(f) Retail Merchants Association	L	A	E	YES	NO
(g) Other (List) _____	L	A	E	YES	NO
2 Membership and participation in community councils, forums, and committees dealing with education and school planning	L	A	E	YES	NO
3 Membership and participation in Civic-service club activities (Civitan, Kiwanis, Lions, Rotary, etc.)	L	A	E	YES	NO
4 Membership and participation in church groups and activities	L	A	E	YES	NO
C Public relations contacts of vocational educator with parents					
1 Evaluation of students' work through report cards, letters, parent-teacher conferences	L	A	E	YES	NO
2 School open-house event	L	A	E	YES	NO
3 Bulletins and informational reports sent to parents concerning the school program	L	A	E	YES	NO
4 Personal contacts with parents outside the school	L	A	E	YES	NO
5 Invitations to parents to visit the school and vocational program	L	A	E	YES	NO
6 Reception of visitors at school	L	A	E	YES	NO
7 Back-to-school night (parents attend abbreviated sessions of their student's classes)	L	A	E	YES	NO
8 Parent-Teacher Association activities ..	L	A	E	YES	NO
9 Parental involvement in curriculum planning, evaluation, and determination of program needs and priorities	L	A	E	YES	NO

Activities	Value of Activity			Have Used	
	(Circle 1)			(Circle 1)	
D Public relations through vocational educator membership, attendance, and participation in professional groups					
1 National and state *education* associations	L	A	E	YES	NO
2 National and state *vocational education* associations	L	A	E	YES	NO
3 Local *education* associations	L	A	E	YES	NO
4 Local *vocational education* associations	L	A	E	YES	NO
E Public relations through vocational educator contacts with middle school/junior high schools					
1 Serving as speaker or consultant for career exploration classes	L	A	E	YES	NO
2 Providing instructional materials/media for career education program	L	A	E	YES	NO
3 Providing information to prospective students about the vocational program through interviews, conferences, or direct mail	L	A	E	YES	NO
4 Vocational teacher as assembly guest speaker	L	A	E	YES	NO
F Public relations contacts of vocational educators with area vocational-technical schools and junior colleges					
1 School open-house event	L	A	E	YES	NO
2 Joint programs (high school with vocational-technical school or junior college; junior college and vocational-technical school)	L	A	E	YES	NO
3 Shared services and facilities	L	A	E	YES	NO
G Public relations through vocational educator contacts with colleges and universities	L	A	E	YES	NO
1 Cooperation in guidance of student teachers assigned to vocational program for pre-service training	L	A	E	YES	NO
2 Cooperation in advanced research conducted by graduate students and colleges	L	A	E	YES	NO

Activities	Value of Activity			Have Used	
	(Circle 1)			(Circle 1)	
3 Attendance and participation in vocational education conferences, clinics, workshops, institutes, and staff development activities sponsored by the college	L	A	E	YES	NO
4 Attendance at summer schools	L	A	E	YES	NO
5 Attendance at campus and in-service classes	L	A	E	YES	NO
H Public relations contacts of vocational educator with alumni					
1 Surveys of alumni, requesting information, evaluation of experiences or of the vocational program	L	A	E	YES	NO
2 Providing placement services for school alumni	L	A	E	YES	NO
3 Furnishing departmental publications and reports to alumni (new personnel, equipment, curricula, etc.)	L	A	E	YES	NO
4 Alumni reunions sponsored by vocational education department	L	A	E	YES	NO
I Public relations contacts of vocational educator with the community					
1 Sharing instructional materials, tests, films, etc., with vocational programs of other schools	L	A	E	YES	NO
2 Contacts with newspaper and magazine editors through news stories about the vocational programs	L	A	E	YES	NO
3 Providing information regarding student qualification for jobs when requested by employment bureaus and employers	L	A	E	YES	NO

School-sponsored activities, practices, and media that promote good relations for vocational education

A School clubs enrolling vocational students

1 Distributive Education Clubs of America	L	A	E	YES	NO
2 Future Business Leaders of America, Phi Beta Lambda	L	A	E	YES	NO
3 Future Farmers of America	L	A	E	YES	NO
4 Future Homemakers of America	L	A	E	YES	NO
5 Future Secretaries Association	L	A	E	YES	NO

Activities	Value of Activity			Have Used	
	(Circle 1)			(Circle 1)	
6 Office Education Association	L	A	E	YES	NO
7 Vocational Industrial Clubs of America	L	A	E	YES	NO
B Student publications involving vocational students					
1 School newspaper (including news of vocational programs and students) ...	L	A	E	YES	NO
2 School news section of community newspaper (featuring copy on vocational programs and activities)	L	A	E	YES	NO
3 School yearbook (sales, advertising, and vocational education content handled by vocational students)	L	A	E	YES	NO
C School assemblies depicting vocational education					
1 Demonstrations by vocational students	L	A	E	YES	NO
2 Plays illustrating business situations ..	L	A	E	YES	NO
D School displays and exhibits featuring vocational education					
1 Class work displays on school bulletin boards	L	A	E	YES	NO
2 Exhibits of departmental work displayed in stores	L	A	E	YES	NO
3 Exhibits of departmental work displayed at fairs and festivals	L	A	E	YES	NO
	L	A	E	YES	NO
4 School-wide exhibits of materials and equipment used in classes	L	A	E	YES	NO
5 Photographic displays	L	A	E	YES	NO
E School celebration of special days and weeks					
1 Parent-Visitation Day	L	A	E	YES	NO
2 Business-Industry-Education Day	L	A	E	YES	NO
3 High School Day (students operate local firm for a day)	L	A	E	YES	NO
4 Vocational Education Week	L	A	E	YES	NO
5 Career Week (outside speakers discuss job opportunities and requirements with students)	L	A	E	YES	NO
F Special services by vocational students to teachers, administrators, and community					
1 Serving as information attendant and school guide to visitors	L	A	E	YES	NO

Activities	Value of Activity	Have Used
	(Circle 1)	(Circle 1)
2 Serving as office assistant to administration or school faculty	L A E	YES NO
3 Serving as host or hostess at school or departmental open house	L A E	YES NO
4 Student tutorial program (advanced students coach other students needing extra help)	L A E	YES NO
5 Volunteer community service work . . .	L A E	YES NO
6 Serving as guest speaker representing vocational education before community groups	L A E	YES NO

G Other activities that promote vocational education

Activities	Value of Activity	Have Used
1 Field trips to offices, stores, plants . . .	L A E	YES NO
2 Student-faculty speakers' bureau	L A E	YES NO
3 Student-operated school store	L A E	YES NO
4 Radio shows interpreting vocational education	L A E	YES NO
5 Television programs featuring vocational education	L A E	YES NO
6 Fashion shows involving vocational students	L A E	YES NO
7 Scholarship contests at state, district, or local level	L A E	YES NO
8 Subject-matter achievement contests .	L A E	YES NO

Activities used by vocational educators to reach internal (in-school) publics

A Effective public relations through vocational educator contacts with students

Activities	Value of Activity	Have Used
1 Cooperative teacher-student planning .	L A E	YES NO
2 Quality of the school instructional program	L A E	YES NO
3 Use of individualized, multimedia materials	L A E	YES NO
4 Teacher guidance of students (in program planning, choosing an occupation, with personal problems, etc.)	L A E	YES NO
5 Use of a simulated or open laboratory in vocational programs	L A E	YES NO
6 Recognized outstanding student achievement (through awards, commendation, news releases, honor roll, etc.)	L A E	YES NO

Activities	Value of Activity			Have Used	
	(Circle 1)			(Circle 1)	
7 Sponsoring and participating in student organizations and programs	L	A	E	YES	NO
8 Teacher visitation of students on co-operative part-time job (work under joint supervision of school and business employer)	L	A	E	YES	NO
9 Teacher follow-up of graduates (through job, evaluation, or placement follow-up)	L	A	E	YES	NO
10 Teacher provides in-service training and retraining for former graduates and employees	L	A	E	YES	NO

B Public relations contacts of vocational educators with school administrators and supervisors

Activities	Value of Activity			Have Used	
1 Keeping administrators informed through the annual report	L	A	E	YES	NO
2 Special reports of vocational education programs and activities	L	A	E	YES	NO
3 Reporting newspaper and magazine articles published by departmental staff	L	A	E	YES	NO
4 Departmental booklets and brochures describing the programs	L	A	E	YES	NO
5 Furnishing samples of outstanding work done by vocational students	L	A	E	YES	NO

C Vocational education relationships with school faculty

Activities	Value of Activity			Have Used	
1 Faculty meetings	L	A	E	YES	NO
2 Interdepartmental materials and methods conferences and committees	L	A	E	YES	NO
3 Exchange of professional literature and/or instructional materials	L	A	E	YES	NO
4 Sponsoring in-service courses for teachers	L	A	E	YES	NO
5 Maintaining a service pool from which teachers may requisition student services	L	A	E	YES	NO
6 Participating in school and/or department staff development activities	L	A	E	YES	NO

Activities	Value of Activity			Have Used	

D Vocational educator contacts with school guidance personnel

1 Cooperating in instructional and job placement of students	L	A	E	YES	NO
2 Cooperating in administering and analyzing tests for students (aptitude, achievement, etc.)	L	A	E	YES	NO
3 Keeping counseling staff informed of latest developments in vocational fields	L	A	E	YES	NO
4 Cooperating in preparation and maintenance of literature dealing with job opportunities and requirements in vocational fields	L	A	E	YES	NO

E Vocational educator contacts with clerical, secretarial, and administrative staff workers of the school

1 Serving as consultant on systems and layout	L	A	E	YES	NO
2 Using school offices as training stations	L	A	E	YES	NO
3 Providing current information about courses and curricula to staff	L	A	E	YES	NO

F Vocational educator contacts with school maintenance, custodial, and service personnel

1 Voluntary assistance to school service personnel	L	A	E	YES	NO
2 Invitations to visit the department during open house, displays, exhibits, and other special events	L	A	E	YES	NO

G Vocational educator relationships with the school as a whole

1 Informal conversations with school personnel	L	A	E	YES	NO
2 Invitations to participate in department events	L	A	E	YES	NO
3 Making department equipment, facilities available	L	A	E	YES	NO
4 Intraschool communications	L	A	E	YES	NO
5 Voluntary services by the vocational staff	L	A	E	YES	NO

This Public Relations Checklist for Vocational Education identifies a broad scope of public relations practices and media. Such a checklist, developed from the general literature and from research studies, provides the basis for an effective evaluation of a comprehensive cross section of techniques used for public relations purposes in the area of vocational education.

To evaluate the theoretical worth of these activities and media, the checklist might be adapted to a local situation and administered to a jury of persons who are especially competent in public relations practice. Such a jury might be divided into three groups: public relations directors or consultants in business, school public relations directors, and vocational education authorities.

To test the practical value of the activities and media that the jury has judged effective, it is further suggested that the opinions of a sample of outstanding vocational teachers be surveyed. The ratings assigned to individual activities, by both the jury and the teachers, could then be assigned arithmetic weights and the items ranked from high to low. The lower-value items might then be dropped from the checklist.

A final step might involve an on-the-spot examination of a number of schools that have excellent vocational education programs. A study could be made to determine whether or not the checklist activities are used in these schools and, if so, to what extent they are felt to be effective. A definite tendency among the schools surveyed toward the effective use of the checklist activities and media would serve to validate the items.

The checklist and the flowchart (Figure 13.2) presented earlier in the chapter suggest how schools may go about developing, implementing, and evaluating a program of public relations. The ultimate objective is, of course, the improvement of vocational education through the cultivation of a pattern of highly recommended activities and media, designed to increase public confidence and support for the program. Such activities should result in better performance of vocational teachers by improving cooperation between the various vocational programs and their internal and external publics.

Summary

This chapter has considered the fundamentals of public relations as they affect the development of positive relationships with internal and external school publics. Principles, problems, techniques, and media affecting public relations have been examined as they apply to the implementation of school programs, including vocational education. Public relations has been viewed as a two-way process, a cooperative effort for mutual understanding and effective teamwork between the community and the school. Emphasis was placed on developing a continuous program of interpretation, involvement, and cooperation as the school seeks to serve the individual and vocational needs of its publics.

The effective school public relations program should be well planned, staffed by competent personnel, adequately funded, coordinated, continuous, and sensitive to the changing needs of its publics. It should provide opportunities for involvement by all publics, communicate its ideas simply, and it should be appraised continuously.

A vocational education public relations model involves the following components: (a) collecting input data from students, community, and advisory committee; (b) formulating philosophy underlying public relations program; (c) identifying principles governing public relations; (d) formulating departmental policies; (e) identifying public relations tasks and objectives; (f) identifying appropriate internal and external publics; (g) selecting appropriate message and media for various publics; (h) conducting public relations training program for staff; (i) exchanging ideas and information with publics; and (j) evaluating results.

A checklist for vocational education identifies a wide range of public relations activities and media and classifies them into three principal categories: (a) those that may be used by the vocational educator to reach external school publics; (b) those that he or she may use to reach internal school publics; and (c) school-sponsored activities that promote good public relations for vocational education. The checklist is arranged so that vocational educators may evaluate their public relations efforts against those recommended by the literature as being effective.

Activities

For review

1 Differentiate between "public relations" and "publicity."

2 Summarize the principles underlying effective communication between the school and its internal and external publics.

3 Identify specifically the internal and external publics that possess an interest in your own vocational field.

4 Discuss the role of the student in the public relations program of (a) the school and (b) the vocational education department.

For discussion

1 If a vocational department has no planned program of public relations, what responsibilities should the individual classroom teacher assume?

2 Numerous reasons are given in this chapter as to why a school or vocational department should be concerned about its public relations. What are five of the most important reasons for vocational educators to be concerned about their public relations program?

3 Explain the underlying philosophy that you think should support a public relations program in your vocational field.

4 How can state supervisors in the various vocational fields provide leadership for public relations programs?

5 What are some activities that teachers can use to improve their communication with parents?

6 It has been suggested that teachers are their own worst enemies in lowering the status of the group to which they belong. They do not keep professional business to themselves or within their own ranks, but rather they talk about their disputes and disagreements in the community. Do you agree or disagree? If you were a vocational department chairman, what steps would you take to prevent such an occurrence?

7 In planning the curriculum, should top priority be given to public opinion or to the professional opinion of the vocational educator?

For exploration

1 Review your local newspaper for several days. Summarize the articles that relate to (a) the total school system and (b) vocational education.

2 Interview one or two business or industrial leaders in the community. Find out how much they know about local vocational education programs; for example, objectives, courses, equipment, etc.

3 Report cards are one means of communicating with parents of students you teach. Evaluate the effectiveness of report cards you use or with which you are familiar. What changes would you recommend to improve the reporting system?

4 Using the checklist provided in this chapter, evaluate the public relations program in your department. Invite other vocational educators to evaluate their own programs.

5 Select one list of principles reported in the chapter and write one objective for each, showing how the vocational education public relations effort can realize each principle.

References

1 James J. Jones, *School Public Relations* (New York: Center for Applied Research in Education, Inc., 1966), pp. 2–3.

2 Edward L. Bernays, "Parity for Public Relations in Higher Education," in *College and University Journal*, Vol. 11, No. 4, September 1972, p. 7.

3 Leslie W. Kindred, *School Public Relations* (Englewood Cliffs, N.J.: Prentice-Hall, Inc., 1957), p. 16.

4 James J. Jones. See Ref. 1, p. 2.

5 William McGowan, *Vocational Education, A Message from Business* (Sacramento, California: California Association of Secondary School Administrators, 1965) (ED 016789), p. 50.

6 Calfrey C. Calhoun, "The Identification, Classification and Evaluation of Public Relations Activities and Practices in Secondary School Business Education" (Doctoral dissertation, The Ohio State University, Columbus, 1960), pp. 316–319.

Chapter 14

Evaluation

in

Vocational-Technical

Education

Introduction

The need for assessment is present in every important aspect of vocational education. How may the effectiveness of instructional programs be increased? How accurately has the occupational competency of students been determined? How appropriately do the materials and methods of instruction reflect the abilities and needs of students? How do students perceive themselves, their teachers, and the educational process? These kinds of questions provide direction to those involved in measuring the success of vocational education.

Evaluation is in a period of crisis and change. Parents, teachers, administrators of public schools and technical institutes, college and university personnel, and the critics of education in general are questioning the validity of time-honored evaluation procedures. What is the impact of an evaluation program on those whom it is designed to serve? Do evaluation measures illuminate and guide, or do they obscure and confuse? It is difficult to conceive of effective vocational teaching without procedures for determining students' interim and terminal skills and the degree to which their educational progress parallels that of their peers.

Planning for the evaluation of vocational programs takes place at all levels of the educational system and is tailored to the objectives defined for each level. Such an approach yields an evaluation system that is built on an individual student record system and that makes possible the measurement of program effectiveness in terms of the individual's ultimate employment, taking into consideration continued education beyond the job-entry level. Program evaluation also involves consideration of resource-allocation and cost-effectiveness factors.

This chapter outlines some of the guiding principles on which an effective evaluation of vocational education is built. Benefits of evaluation are discussed in terms of individual student growth, program operations, credibility, cost effectiveness, and other uses. Three evaluation models are presented and their characteristics explained. Attention is given to overall program evaluation in relation to vocational curricula, personnel, and facilities evaluation. A special section is provided on measurement and data collection, including criterion-referenced and norm-referenced tests, informal evaluation measures, questionnaires, and needs assessment. A discussion of the cognitive, affective, and psychomotor classification of behaviors as a basis for evaluation is summarized. Finally, a few of the more important issues involved in the evaluation of vocational education are summarized. The chapter concludes with a discussion of the consultative role that accrediting agencies perform in the evaluation process.

Guiding Philosophy of Evaluation

A realistic conception of evaluation is based on well-defined principles. This section defines evaluation and presents some of the basic principles that give direction to evaluation in vocational education and other fields.

Definition and Scope

The necessity for evaluation of vocational programs is generally accepted in principle. However, the method of evaluation is a difficult and complex process for several reasons. First, vocational education programs are widely divergent in nature. Second, the present state of the methodology of evaluation is inadequate to serve as the basis for determining program effectiveness. In essence, evaluation is the process of securing value judgments concerning a condition or a process. Such value judgments should be based on a critical consideration of the best evidence available concerning the given condition or process.

Bloom, Hastings, and Madaus (1) view evaluation of learning as "the systematic collection of evidence to determine whether in fact certain changes are taking place in the learners as well as to determine the amount or degree of change in individual students."

A management-oriented view of curriculum evaluation is expressed in the following statement by Taylor and Maguire (2):

□ *Curriculum evaluation can be viewed as a process of collecting and processing data pertaining to an educational program, on the basis of which decisions can be made about that program. The data are of two kinds: (a) objective description of goals, environments, personnel, methods and content, and immediate and long-range outcomes; and (b) recorded personal judgments of the quality and appropriateness of goals, inputs, and outcomes. The data—in both raw and analyzed forms—can be used either to delineate and resolve problems in educational programs being developed or to answer absolute and comparative questions about established programs.*

Ammons (3) sees evaluation as the description of student progress toward educational objectives. She notes that, in contrast to testing, evaluation is directed more to individuals than to groups; it seeks to describe the progress of the individual student toward certain school-defined objectives.

Evaluation is viewed by Harris (4) as

☐ *the systematic process of judging the worth, desirability, effectiveness, or adequacy of something according to definite criteria and purposes. The judgment is based upon a careful comparison of observation data with criteria standards. Precise definitions of what is to be appraised, clearly stated purposes, specific standards for the criteria traits, accurate observations, and measurements, and logical conclusions are hallmarks of valid evaluation.*

Guba (5) views evaluation as the "process of . . . obtaining and . . . providing . . . useful . . . information for making . . . educational decisions." Tyler (6) presents evaluation as related to instruction, seeing it as a ". . . process for finding out how far the learning experiences as developed and organized are actually producing the desired results."

A similar definition that reflects the changing role and purpose of evaluation has been formulated by the Phi Delta Kappa National Study Committee on Evaluation (7) as follows: "Educational evaluation is the process of delineating, obtaining, and providing useful information for judging decision alternatives."

In summary, evaluation may be viewed as a systematic process of obtaining information for judging the effectiveness of vocational programs in relation to acceptable criteria or objectives.

Principles of Evaluation

An effective approach toward evaluation is based on principles that reflect a clear sense of direction, a flexibility to change, and an honest desire to improve and upgrade all persons, programs, and processes involved in vocational education. The following principles and characteristics illustrate fundamental considerations that are involved in implementing an evaluation process.

1 Evaluations must have a *definite frame of reference;* that is, evaluations are to be made in terms of specific values, goals, or objectives if such evaluations are to be meaningful. Evaluative procedures that fail to take into account the self-determined goals of the individual or institution are not only worthless, but may actually be harmful in their distorting or coercive effects.

2 Evaluations should be *continuous and cumulative.* Any evaluation as of a given moment is likely to be erroneous or incomplete in certain particulars. Furthermore, because goals change as conditions change, it is necessary for sound evaluative procedures to take such changes into account. The predictive significance of a given evidence of excellence may vary in such a way as to make that evidence of greatly unequal value on different occasions. Thus evaluations should be made regularly over a period of time.

3 Evaluations should be *comprehensive and conclusive*. Because in any given situation multiple goals are usually being sought, it is necessary to find out the extent to which each of the goals is being attained. It is clear that, in certain instances, success in achieving certain goals may be offset by losses with respect to other goals. Whereas individuals or institutions should be evaluated on the basis of a "total pattern" of characteristics, it should be recognized that superiority in some characteristics may be regarded as compensating, to some extent, for deficiencies in others.

4 The primary purpose of all evaluative procedures is that of *encouraging and promoting improvement* with respect to the condition or activity being evaluated. Consequently, all evaluative procedures should provide for specific, constructive suggestions for improvement. In general, effective evaluation will make slight and incidental, if any, use of inter-individual or inter-institutional comparisons; rather it will compare the record of the given individual or institution at successive time intervals and always in the light of its own unique needs and purposes.

5 In view of the essential nature of evaluation (making value judgments of the progress being made toward specific objectives) and of the basic purpose of evaluation (improvement of a condition or a process), it is clear that sound evaluative procedures will involve the *actual participation* of the person or institution concerned; that is, effective evaluation will emphasize self-appraisal activities. However, this statement does not exclude the use of outside persons or agencies who, on invitation, may be prepared to serve in a resource or consultant capacity on various technical aspects of the evaluation program.

6 All evaluations should involve *three fundamental processes:*
(a) the formulation and acceptance of specific values or goals
(b) the securing of specific evidence relative to the existence, quantity, and quality of a condition or a process
(c) the act of making a judgment, in the light of the available evidence, concerning the extent to which the desired values or goals have been attained

It is obvious that evaluative techniques will be sound and effective in proportion to the accuracy and precision with which each of these three processes is carried out. For example, evaluations may be imperfect because of an inadequate formulation and analysis of objectives; that is, objectives may be stated in such value-laden or general terms that it is difficult or impossible to secure appropriate evidence concerning their realization. Because all evaluations are based on evidence of some sort, it is clear that evaluations will tend to be successful in proportion to the quantity and quality of the evidence available. In the same way, the worth or soundness of an evaluation will depend on the extent to which critical, reflective thinking has been employed in relating the obtained evidence to the objectives sought.

Among the criteria that Swanson (8) applies to vocational education are the following. If evaluation is to be meaningful, it must be considered in the context of principles such as these.

1 *Vocational education programs must develop and maintain input standards.*
(*a*) *The student must have the aptitude, the ability and motivation necessary to succeed in the program to which he is assigned.*
(*b*) *The teacher must have extensive training and experience in the occupation or technology which he teaches.*
(*c*) *The equipment and supplies must be similar to the equipment and supplies used by the student when he is employed.*
(*d*) *Instruction materials must be organized in a manner to give an adequate curriculum for the specific program of instruction.*

2 *Vocational education must develop and maintain output standards.*

3 *The content of vocational programs must be realistically related to the requirements of the labor market.*

4 *The number of persons in training must be related to the number of persons who will be needed by business, industry, commerce, and government.*

5 *Vocational education must involve business, labor, industry, and government as well as schools.*

Benefits of Evaluation

The benefits of evaluation may be applied to the overall vocational education program, to individual curricula, to single courses, or to experiences and activities within individual courses.

The Center for Vocational Education developed the *Innovations Evaluation Guide* (9), which provides criteria to aid educators in evaluating innovations. The format of this guide allows the evaluator to do a step-by-step analysis of benefits and costs. Potential users include classroom teachers, school administrators, state supervisors, local education agency project directors, state department personnel, teacher educators, and research and development personnel. By providing information for the applicable characteristics, the evaluator can gain support and approval from those who are affected by his or her decision.

The following checklist from the guide (9) summarizes benefits as they relate to innovations affecting individual pupil growth, program operations, cost effectiveness, and so on.

Individual student growth

1 *What effect will the innovation have on the rate of student learning?*

2 *How does the innovation affect the number and type of learning experiences and/or skills to which the students will be exposed?*

3 *What effect on attitudes can be attributed to the innovation? Are there experiences that assist students in the development of their self-concepts and their abilities to relate to other individuals?*

Program operations

1 *What information is available that will allow a cost benefit analysis of the innovation? How does this analysis compare to the present status of other alternatives?*

2 *What evidence indicates the innovation can achieve the required objectives to our satisfaction?*

Society and the economy

1 *What effect does the innovation have on increasing the opportunities to acquire job-entry skills?*

2 *What effect will the innovation have on productivity and costs to society in relation to such items as wages, occupational mobility, and school drop-out rates?*

3 *What attempts will be made to create an awareness of society through the teaching of concepts concerning institutions, laws, cultures, and social problems?*

4 *What benefits will accrue to the school and community after installing the innovation? What effect will the innovation have on school and community relations and the public image of the school?*

Credibility

1 *What evidence indicates that the innovation can achieve its objectives?*

2 *Where has the innovation been tested previously? How similar are these settings to our situation?*

Costs

1 *What is the cost per unit over time? Will the innovation involve a savings?*

2 *How can the innovation be funded? Must the cost be borne locally, or is assistance available wholly or in part from state, federal, or public* *sources such as foundations? What are the possibilities of reallocating present budget items to accommodate installation?*

3 *What processes and/or procedures must be followed to acquire the necessary funding? Is the local educational agency in a position to expend its own money and be reimbursed later, or are funds from other sources available prior to expenditure?*

4 *In what proportion are funds available from other sources? Do matching funds have to be local funds?*

5 *What limitations are placed on the use of other funds? Can funds be used for instruction only, equipment and instruction, or equipment, supplies, and instruction? Can funds be used for items such as construction, food, transportation, or consultants?*

Time considerations

1 *How much time does it take to get the innovation working?*

2 *What deadlines are placed on activities prior to the operating date? How much time is necessary to order and receive items such as texts and materials? How much time is needed to order, receive, and install equipment? Will the innovation require teacher orientation or advanced teacher planning time?*

3 *How much time must be devoted to planning by a teacher, coordinator, or administrator during each week?*

4 *What amount of time is required by the innovation in daily preparation, classroom activities, meetings, etc.?*

5 *What characteristics of the innovation dictate that it be installed at a particular time during the calendar or academic year?*

Installation considerations

1 *What barriers can be anticipated from the community, school personnel, or students concerning the installation of the innovation?*

2 *What is the extent of involvement necessary to install the innovation? How many staff members, students, schedules, classrooms, laboratories, or schools are involved?*

3 *What are the requirements concerning extent of installation? Can it be trial tested by the adopting unit before complete installation of the total product?*

4 *What changes in policy on the state and local level are necessary in order for the innovation to be successful?*

5 *Is the innovation in an installable form or does it require more development? Are additional materials or training activities necessary?*

6 *What evidence is there to indicate that the innovation will work in our situation?*

7 *What adjustments can be made to meet local conditions without damaging the authenticity of the innovation?*

Organizational change

1 *What interruption of routine is required by the innovation due to rescheduling of classes, retraining of teachers, sharing of facilities, etc.?*

2 *What effect will the innovation have on the present school or department structure? Does it create a need for a separate division or department?*

3 *What changes in duties and/or responsibilities are necessary for successful operation of the innovation?*

4 *What new kinds of relationships among departments or grade levels will be necessary for successful operation of the innovation?*

Personnel needs

1 *What additions to the staff are required? How many part-time or full-time people per unit are needed?*

2 *What staff experiences are necessary for successful operation of the innovation? Do leaders need to have a knowledge of the community?*

3 *What requirements are necessary for the development of certain role, attitudes, skills, and competencies not presently possessed by personnel? Is the present staff capable of, and willing to handle, the personnel development necessary for the success of the innovation? Are consultants available?*

Space requirements

1 *Are present facilities sufficient? If not, what physical facilities are necessary to house the innovation?*

2 *What acreage is necessary for installing the innovation?*

3 *Does the success of the innovation require close proximity to ongoing programs or present facilities? On the other hand, is a separate location desirable?*

4 *What are the options to acquiring needed space for the innovation?*

Equipment requirements

1 *What are the major items of equipment or their components necessary for the operation and success of the innovation?*

2 *What supplies are necessary for the operation of the innovation?*

Evaluation Systems and Models

Characteristic of the 1970s is the increased interest in evaluation by lay persons, legislators, and government agencies, as well as by school districts. The days of free spending and almost unlimited resources of tax dollars are coming to an end. Taxpayers and legislators are asking educators and other public agencies for justification of both proposed and existing expenditures. The increased use of systems in various facets of the educational process, such as curriculum construction and development of instructional materials, focuses additional attention on evaluation because it is built into systems models.

In view of the current interest in evaluation, various models have been introduced throughout the country. Three representative evaluation models will be considered briefly; each of these could be helpful in evaluating vocational programs or in the development of other models. Before each model is discussed, however, an examination of the systems approach and its application to evaluation is in order.

Systems are made up of sets of interrelated components that function together. A systems approach, then, is a way of thinking about the overall system and its components. Systems analysis includes the evaluation of alternative means to accomplish a particular objective. Mushkin and Pollak (10) refer to systems analysis as a "process of comparing and assessing costs and benefits of competing programs to support choice."

Characteristics of Evaluation Systems

McCaslin (11) describes six desirable characteristics that an evaluation plan in vocational education or any other field should possess if it is to be useful and effective.

□ *The first desirable characteristic of an evaluation system is that* realistic objectives *should be* formulated. *The formulation of these objectives should be realistic and involve both program and evaluation personnel. If there is basic agreement on these objectives, many misunderstandings can be avoided at a later time. However, it should be noted that mutual objective setting is not a panacea for avoiding conflict. In a practical sense, people operating programs have to believe in what they are doing; evaluation personnel, on the other hand, have to question what vocational education programs are doing. Both of these points must be reconciled in conducting the evaluation.*

Secondly, a sound basis for measuring *these objectives must be* established. *In some cases, appropriate measurement techniques may already exist. In other cases, these techniques may require modification. In still other cases, development of new measurement techniques may be required. A caveat is necessary; there is often a tendency to measure those items that are easy and to ignore the most difficult ones. For example, information on the number of students completing a program may be collected when information on the students' job performance (after completing the program) should be included. The objective to be measured should dictate the type of information to be collected.*

A third desirable characteristic of an evaluation system is that of clear and immediate feedback. *Feedback, in this instance, is considered a two-step process. First the administrator needs to inform the evaluator and/or program personnel of the adequacy of the evaluation results to meet his decision-making needs. Secondly, the evaluation and program personnel need to provide information to those programs from which the data were collected. All too often, evaluation has been a one-way, upward flow of information. People at all levels of the education community resist filling out forms and providing data. Some procedures must be provided to insure that those who complete the forms understand the reasons for the collection of and use of the information. For example, local schools should have a summary of the information they submitted returned to them. Perhaps a comparison of the results with the comparable state figure would be helpful. It is also important that the information should be summarized in a manner easily understood and as brief as possible. If the evaluation feedback is voluminous, chances are it will be ignored. Certainly, all of the information needed by a state will not be the same type of information needed by a local educational agency. Whenever possible, these requirements should supplement one another.*

A fourth characteristic is that the information collected by an evaluation system should reflect the original purpose(s) *of the evaluation. In this regard, planning and budgetary information should be future-oriented. Information on performance factors and motivation can be present and/or past oriented. The major problem has been that the administrator did not develop clear purposes for the evaluation initially. This results in information that is not relevant to the administrator's decision-making requirements. Given that the evaluation results are relevant, evaluation reports should include the negative as well as the positive effects of the programs. Evaluation results should also include suggestions for potential alternative courses of action for decision-makers. Additionally, both the advantages and disadvantages of each alternative would be specified by the evaluator. The administrator must realize that both the alternatives and advantages and disadvantages will undoubtedly reflect the biases of the evaluator. Therefore, these must be interpreted in that regard.*

A fifth characteristic of a desirable evaluation system is involvement of personnel interested in, and affected by, the program to be evaluated. *Many evaluations have encountered problems due to apparent misunderstandings that have arisen due to the noninvolvement of personnel. It is important that program evaluation reflect a consensus of these personnel on a number of issues, including (a) the goals of the program; (b) the nature of the program services; (c) measures that indicate the effectiveness of the program in meeting goals; (d) methods of selection of participants and controls; (e) allocation of responsibilities for participant selection, data collection, descriptions of program input, etc.; and (f) the decisional purposes that evaluation is expected to serve. Although total agreement on each of these points will not remove all the problems, it is likely to minimize them.*

A sixth, and final, characteristic to be discussed is that an effective evaluation system must be reasonable in cost. *Administrators need to be aware of ongoing evaluation efforts and their cost in order that realistic budgets can be prepared. Typically, evaluation studies range from approximately 5–10 percent of the program budgets. As a general rule, the larger the program budget, the smaller will be that required for evaluation. It has not been uncommon for some personnel to think that evaluation can be conducted for as little as one percent or less of total budgets. Personnel costs alone make it extremely difficult to conduct meaningful evaluations for most programs at this rate of funding. Again, anything less than a total effort is a waste of resources.*

Burnham (12) suggests five steps that are common to any systems approach to evaluation. The emphasis given to each step varies among the models and the headings differ, but the procedures are basically the same. The common steps are the following:

1 State the system objective *This refers to the outcomes of the system or subsystem being evaluated.*

2 Establish a criterion measure *The objective should be measureable or quantifiable to some extent. The more specific the objective, the better the measure, and the more rigorous the evaluation.*

3 Define the relevant variables *These are usually categorized as uncontrollable and controllable variables.*

4 Explicate the interactions between variables *How are the variables (men, material, money, tasks, time) interrelated?*

5 Analyze the interrelated variables in some technical model and enter the values each variable can assume *This involves input-output ratios, the extent of goal attainment, or simply the logic of the flow chart through the use of some decision rule.*

The final task of the evaluator, in any model, is to evaluate the evaluation. The criteria recommended by Stufflebeam (13) are closely related to those used to assess research:

Scientific Criteria	Practical Criteria	Prudential Criterion
Internal validity	*Relevance*	*Efficiency*
External validity	*Importance*	
Reliability	*Scope*	
Objectivity	*Credibility*	
	Timeliness	
	Pervasiveness	

In selecting an evaluation model, there are at least two questions that the vocational educator should consider: 1. Is the model appropriate for the situation to be evaluated? 2. Are the evaluators capable of handling the complexities of the model? Evaluation models vary considerably in the complexity of design and intent. Some of the more complex models are not appropriate for use by persons who are untrained in evaluation.

Kentucky Vocational Education Evaluation Program Model

The model illustrated in Figure 14.1 is a straightforward, relatively simple, yet effective system that was employed by the Kentucky Research Coordinating Unit in its Vocational Education Evaluation Project (VEEP) (14). It incorporates eight steps, ranging from assessment of needs to decision making.

The first step (*assess needs*) involves the collection of valid data to compare "where we are" with "where we want to be." The second step (*develop philosophy*) calls for the development of a basic underlying philosophy to guide the program. The third step (*write objectives*) is the

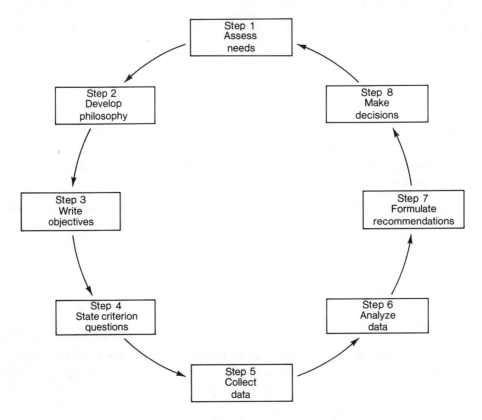

Figure 14.1   Kentucky Vocational Education Evaluation Program Model.

preparation of objectives that specify written outcomes as well as input. In step four (*state criterion questions*), specific criterion questions that reflect objectives are identified to give direction to data collection. In step five (*collect data*), many types of data, both process and product, are collected, using a variety of methods to answer the criterion questions. In step six (*analyze data*), the data are analyzed, using appropriate statistical techniques; the analysis report is presented in a clear, easy-to-read manner. The seventh step (*formulate recommendations*) involves the development of recommendations that are suggested by the data. The eighth and final step (*make decisions*) involves making appropriate decisions based on the information from the preceding steps. The decision-making component of the VEEP Model reflects the contemporary definitions of evaluation that stress the relationship of evaluation to decision making.

CIPP Evaluation Model

The Context-Input-Process-Product Evaluation Model (CIPP), developed by Stufflebeam, is a more complex model built on the theory that educational decisions may be classified into four categories: planning, programming, implementing, and recycling—and that for each there is an evaluation procedure (15).

☐ *Planning decisions are those which focus needed improvements by specifying the domain, major goals, and specific objectives to be served. Programming decisions specify procedures, personnel, facilities, budgets, and time requirements for implementing planned activities. Recycling decisions include terminating, continuing, evolving, or drastically modifying activities.*

Table 14.1 summarizes the four kinds of evaluation—context, input, process, product—recommended to assess educational decisions and the relation of each to decision making.

Stufflebeam (16) suggests that the structure of evaluation design is the same for all types of evaluation. He outlines six major components that compose the logical structure of a design.

1 *Focusing the evaluation*
  (*a*) *Identify the major level(s) of decision-making to be served, e.g., local, state, or national.*
  (*b*) *For each level of decision-making, project the decision situations to be served and describe each one in terms of its locus, focus, timing and composition of alternatives.*
  (*c*) *Define criteria for each decision situation by specifying variables for measurement and standards for use in the judgment of alternatives.*
  (*d*) *Define policies within which the evaluation must operate.*

Table 14.1   The CIPP Evaluation Model: Strategies for Evaluating Educational Change (15)

	Context evaluation	Input evaluation	Process evaluation	Product evaluation
objective	to define the operation context, to identify and assess needs in the context, and to identify and delineate problems underlying the needs	to identify and assess system capabilities, available input strategies, and designs for implementing the strategies	to identify or predict, in process, defects in the procedural design or its implementation, and to maintain a record of procedural events and activities.	to relate outcome information to objectives and to context, input, and process information.
method	by describing individually and in relevant perspectives the major subsystems of the context; by comparing actual and intended inputs and outputs of the subsystems; and by analyzing possible causes of discrepancies between actualities and intentions	by describing and analyzing available human and material resources, solution strategies, and procedural designs for relevance, feasibility, and economy in the course of action to be taken	by monitoring the activity's potential procedural barriers and remaining alert to unanticipated ones	by defining operationally and measuring criteria associated with the objectives, by comparing these measurements with predetermined standards or comparative bases, and by interpreting the outcome in terms of recorded input and process information
relation to decision-making in the change process	for deciding on the setting to be served, the goals associated with meeting needs, and the objectives associated with solving problems, i.e., for planning needed changes	for selecting sources of support, solution strategies, and procedural designs, i.e., for programming change activities	for implementing and refining the program design and procedure, i.e., for effecting process control	for deciding to continue, terminate, modify, or refocus a change activity, and for linking the activity to other major phases of the change process, i.e., for evolving change activities

2 *Collection of information*
(a) *Specify the source of the information to be collected.*
(b) *Specify the instruments and methods for collecting the needed information.*
(c) *Specify the sampling procedure to be employed.*
(d) *Specify the conditions and schedule for information collection.*

3 *Organization of information*
(a) *Specify a format for the information which is to be collected.*
(b) *Specify a means for coding, organizing, storing, and retrieving information.*

4 *Analysis of information*
(a) *Specify the analytical procedures to be employed.*
(b) *Specify a means for performing the analysis.*

5 *Reporting of information*
(a) *Define the audiences for the evaluation reports.*
(b) *Specify means for providing information to the audiences.*
(c) *Specify the format for evaluation reports and/or reporting sessions.*
(d) *Schedule the reporting of information.*

6 *Administration of the evaluation*
(a) *Summarize the evaluation schedule.*
(b) *Define staff and resource requirements and plans for meeting these requirements.*
(c) *Specify means for meeting policy requirements for conduct of the evaluation.*
(d) *Evaluate the potential of the evaluation design for providing information which is valid, reliable, credible, timely, and pervasive.*
(e) *Specify and schedule means for periodic updating of the evaluation design.*
(f) *Provide a budget for the total evaluation program.*

Phi Delta Kappa Model

The Phi Delta Kappa National Study Committee on Evaluation proposed an evaluation process that comprises three major aspects—delineating information needs, obtaining information, and providing information—as illustrated in Figure 14.2.

Implementing this approach to evaluation calls for a logical series of steps, including (17):

1 *the determination of what is to be evaluated: for what kinds of decisions are evaluative data needed?*

2 *the kinds of data needed in making these decisions*

3 *the collection of the data*

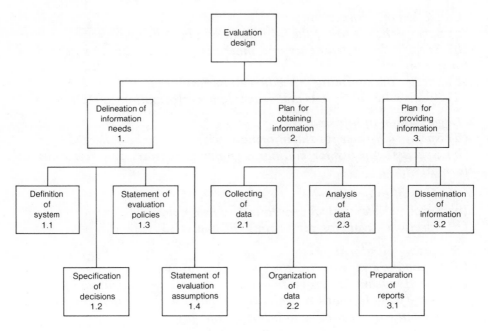

Figure 14.2   Phi Delta Kappa Evaluation Model (18).

4 *defining criteria for determining the quality of the matter being evaluated*

5 *analysis of the data in terms of these criteria*

6 *providing information for decision makers*

Unlike the VEEP Model, the Phi Delta Kappa evaluation design (Figure 14.2) does not include decision making as a component of the model itself, but rather stops at the point of providing information needed to make decisions. The designers of this model do not view decision making as a part of the evaluation process. There are others, however, who see decision making as an integral part of the evaluation process and as an obligation of the evaluator.

Program Evaluation

In this section we will discuss the elements involved in evaluating the curriculum, facilities, personnel, and teaching. Special consideration will be given to the use of needs assessment as a technique for getting at formative and summative evaluation of vocational education programs.

Formative-Summative Evaluation

An evaluation may be described as formative or summative, that is, process- or product-oriented. Summative (product) evaluation is concerned with judging the effectiveness of a curriculum, grading students, or assessing the effectiveness of personnel. Because it takes place at the culmination of a unit, course, or semester, it is frequently administered too late to provide remedial help for a particular person or program. Such data are valuable as assessments of overall effectiveness and as a basis for change in program elements. The most valuable summative-type evaluation would be in the form of periodic follow-ups of the effectiveness of graduates in their jobs. Needless to say, such longitudinal studies are time consuming and difficult to administer.

To be of value, however, evaluation must take place not only at the termination of a process but also during the formative stages, when the person or program is more susceptible to modification. Thus, formative (process) evaluation is concerned with collecting data to use as a basis for improving a program or process currently underway. Formative evaluation, as related to student assessment, for example, focuses on determining the degree of mastery of a given task, not on gathering data for grading the student. One of the basic objectives of formative evaluation is to provide feedback to students, informing them of both their accomplishments and their deficiencies. Such an evaluation provides clues to the teacher and student and allows them to better adjust the teaching-learning process.

Evaluation has two major purposes—accountability and program improvement. Accountability is an attempt to determine whether or not the results achieved can be equated to the resources expended. Evaluation for program improvement attempts to determine changes that will result in greater achievement of the objectives of the program. Obviously the objectives of these two types of evaluation are not mutually exclusive.

Evaluating the Curriculum

In evaluation for program improvement, criteria can be divided into two categories—those items that *cause* quality (process evaluation) and those items that *show* quality (product evaluation). There must be a demonstrated relationship between the two types of items.

It has been said that a primary defense against an undesirable reaction to the many good programs in vocational education is careful evaluation of results to ensure the elimination of defective programs. To accomplish this end, there must be a climate of mutual trust and concern between administrators, evaluators, and teachers. Supervisory personnel can find in individual program evaluations some very specific suggestions that, if used, can lead to program improvement.

Value judgment plays an important role in program evaluation. For example, selecting objectives and placing them in the order of priority involves the cooperative judgment of professionals and, to a certain degree, of parents, students, and community representatives. Judgments are involved at many different points during the completion of an evaluation study. However, the lack of completely objective measures should not hinder educators in their efforts to evaluate programs. Whenever pro-

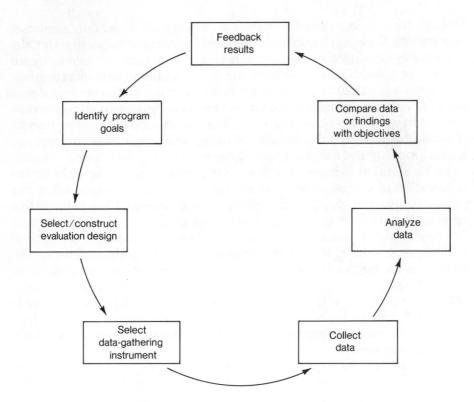

Figure 14.3   Model for curriculum evaluation.

grams are not evaluated, it becomes easy to lose sight of goals and to operate without change. Program evaluation requires the identification of program goals and a systematic, critical look to determine to what degree and in what ways the goals are being met. Figure 14.3 illustrates in more detail a typical model of curriculum evaluation.

There are several elements that should be considered in program evaluation. Plans for the evaluation itself should be made when the program is planned and begun. After goals are determined, these questions should be asked: 1. What means will be used to measure progress toward the goals? 2. What information will be needed to measure progress? 3. What data will be collected and maintained, and what steps taken, from the outset of the program, to assure adequate information at a later time?

All persons who participate in vocational education should be involved in its evaluation. Such evaluation should provide for assessment of all goals of the program, both quantitative and qualitative. Evaluation should include a heavy emphasis on progress being made; that is, *where we were* versus *where we are* versus *where we want to be*, as well as comparisons with other programs and norms. Finally, program evaluation should be concerned with both long-term and short-term goals.

There have been extensive changes in vocational education curricula over the years, changes that have resulted in increased course offerings, expanded program objectives, new teaching strategies, a variety of instructional materials and media, and an emphasis on individualization. Through such means, vocational educators are continuously seeking to find new ways to improve programs. Program changes, however, are sometimes judged by the wrong criteria. For instance, frequency of use is often confused with effectiveness. In other words, we tend to judge an innovation in terms of material, organization, and how many schools employ it rather than in terms of the effectiveness of the practice itself.

Some years ago, Dressel (19) recognized that at several points the evaluation process parallels the instructional process. He identified five such points:

1 *Evaluation is effective as it provides evidence of the extent of the changes in students.*

2 *Evaluation is most conducive to learning when it provides for and encourages self-evaluation.*

3 *Evaluation is conducive to good instruction when it reveals major types of inadequate behavior and the contributory causes.*

4 *Evaluation is most significant in learning when it permits and encourages the exercise of individual initiative.*

5 *Activities or exercises developed for the purposes of evaluating specified behavior are also useful for the teaching and learning of that behavior.*

As the emphasis on evaluation and accountability continues, evaluation instruments continue to be developed by vocational educators at national, state, and local levels, at colleges and universities, through funded projects, by individual researchers, and by accreditation agencies. Figure 14.4 provides some abbreviated examples of evaluation instruments that may be used to assess the organization of an individual classroom in vocational education.

Evaluating Student Progress

One measure of the effectiveness of the vocational curriculum or of institutional programs is the performance of students. The assessment of student mastery of skills and knowledge is also a measure of teacher effectiveness. Thus, student evaluation may be conducted for reasons other than those relating specifically to the student. At least three additional purposes for assessment of individual student progress may be identified. First, the individual student is evaluated to determine his or her readiness to pursue the next step of learning; this type of mastery test samples the concepts that are basic to the next step in the learning

Learner Characteristics	To high degree	To moderate degree	To slight degree	To no degree
Physiological				
• Are special sensory needs of learners met?				
• Are adequate safety measures carried out?				
• Do learners have sufficient opportunities for movement?				
Social				
• Is student-direction of learning situations encouraged?				
• Are students' group roles clearly defined?				
Affective				
• Is a reasonable opportunity for success insured?				
• Is stigmatization avoided?				
• Can the varied interests of students be met?				
Cognitive				
• Are the experience backgrounds of students utilized?				
• Can difference of learning rates be accommodated?				
Educational				
• Are planned experiences to meet specific skill needs possible?				
• Are sufficient opportunities provided for diagnosis?				

Figure 14.4 Checklist for evaluating classroom organization for vocational education instruction.

sequence. A second basic purpose for assessment is diagnosis, which is used either to place the student properly at the onset of instruction or to discover the underlying causes of deficiencies in student learning as instruction unfolds. A third purpose of assessment is to provide individual guidance; a problem the guidance person faces is to identify enough of the student's background to help him or her to take the next step.

Bloom et al (20) summarizes the function of diagnostic, formative, and summative evaluation of student learning as follows:

Diagnostic

1 *Placement: Determining the presence or absence of prerequisite skills. Determining the student's prior level of mastery.*

Instructional Goals

(This section would, of course, vary with the course objectives. Sample questions might include:

	Always	Usually	Sometimes	Never
• Are a variety of teaching-learning methods practiced?				
• Are opportunities available for students to practice what they have learned?				
Etc.)				

Implementation

Teacher Personnel
- Is teacher expertise maximally utilized?
- Are teacher preferences and interests considered?

Data Collection
- Can adequate samples of student behavior (as applied to content) be obtained?
- Can information regarding growth in specific skills be obtained?

Materials
- Can a variety of materials be employed?
- Are the requisite materials within the school's financial resources?

Figure 14.4   (*Continued*)

Classifying the student according to various characteristics known or thought to be related to alternative modes of instruction.

2 *Determination of underlying causes of repeated learning difficulties.*

Formative

1 *Feedback to student and teacher on student progress through a unit.*
2 *Location of errors in terms of the structure of a unit so that remedial alternative instruction techniques can be prescribed.*

Summative

1 *Certification or grading of students at the end of a unit, semester, or course.*

Current emphasis in student evaluation is focused on comparisons that are *intra-individual* rather than *inter-individual*. This emphasis represents a change from normative comparisons (that is, comparisons with other persons, such as through use of standardized tests) to absolute comparisons (comparison with absolute standards, as in a teacher-made criterion test). Intra-student evaluation is concerned with measuring *what* rather than *how much* the student has learned.

The increased emphasis on evaluation has resulted in an increased use of tests and, consequently, a need for good testing procedures. The first step in attempting to evaluate students enrolled in vocational-technical programs is to write a set of measurable objectives. Next, appropriate evaluation instruments must be selected or constructed. A variety of instruments are available, such as achievement tests, aptitude tests, criterion-referenced tests, interest inventories, attitude scales, checklists, teacher-made tests, and observation. The instrument that is used must measure the objectives previously determined and must be of the appropriate level of difficulty for the students being evaluated. Measurement instruments will be treated in more detail later in the chapter.

Evaluating Vocational Personnel

The increased emphasis on evaluation strongly suggests that vocational educators should develop appropriate systems for evaluating system personnel. To an extent, the design will depend on the purpose of the evaluation. Some of the more commonly recognized purposes of teacher evaluation have been identified by Bolton (21):

1 *to improve teaching, including out-of-classroom activities as well as classroom instruction*

2 *to supply information for modification of assignments*

3 *to reward superior performance*

4 *to protect individuals or the school system in legal matters*

5 *to validate the selection process*

6 *to provide a basis for career planning and individual growth and development of the teacher*

One of the key factors in the success of personnel evaluation is the involvement, from the beginning, of all staff to be evaluated. It is essential that all persons be aware of and understand the purposes of the evaluation. "Morale cannot be high if staff members are fearful or hostile." (22)

To be effective the personnel evaluation system should provide for continuous feedback, with an emphasis on improvement rather than on fault-finding. Figure 14.5 illustrates a typical personnel evaluation model that vocational educators may employ.

Several different methods are used for evaluating vocational personnel. Teacher effectiveness is often measured by the degree of skill exhibited by the student, such as his or her accuracy in blueprint drawing, com-

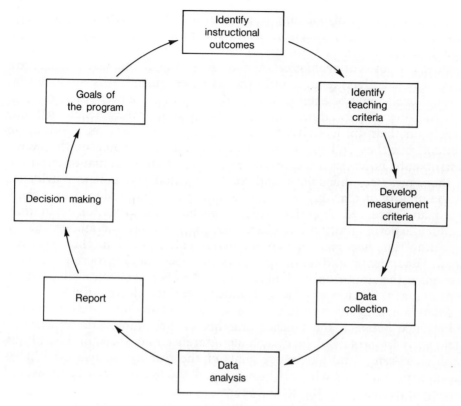

Figure 14.5   Personnel evaluation model (23).

petency in automotive body repair, or speed in transcribing dictation. A more recent approach to personnel evaluation is the use of a job-target approach, or management by objective, in which the evaluator and evaluatee jointly agree on the desired or target job performance, the kinds of evidence to be accepted, and the initial level of performance.

As a means of measuring personnel effectiveness, competency-based approaches are also being used and are receiving increasing attention (see Chapter 11, Research in Vocational Education). Vocational educators may be evaluated on the basis of competencies that generally fall into one of three categories: (a) in-classroom behavior of the teacher, (b) out-of-classroom behavior of the teacher, and (c) student accomplishment. Input into performance in these areas may come from peers, students, administrators, supervisors, paraprofessionals, and nonteaching personnel. Evaluative instruments for assessing the performance of teachers, department chairmen, supervisors, administrators, and aides have also been developed.

Evaluation of Teaching

Teacher evaluation serves a dual purpose: it provides a comprehensive guide for diagnosis and for constructive supervision, and it makes possible reliable ratings of teaching effectiveness. The collective judgment of administrators and supervisors as to the relative effectiveness of individual teachers must not be an end in itself, but rather must serve these broader purposes of evaluation. At the same time, if the best teachers are to be selected, given tenure, and otherwise recognized, it is obvious that a sound basis must be established for determining the best teachers.

Criticisms of procedures and devices used in rating teachers focus largely on their subjectivity. Most rating scales are not only limited in content, but they call for a record of opinion only. Some of the newer instruments, however, are constructed so as to require actual observation of those practices, behaviors, and conditions that give concrete evidence of the quality of teaching. Subjective opinion is thus reduced to a minimum, and observed objective evidence becomes the basis for evaluation.

Much experimentation has been done to determine the amount of observation time necessary for an adequate evaluation of teacher effectiveness. Supervisors and administrators of vocational programs should recognize the importance of observing a teacher systematically, over a representative period of time and under a variety of conditions.

Many school systems follow the practice of setting up a pre-supervisory conference between the teacher and his or her immediate supervisor. Held early in the school year, such a conference may focus on identifying both short-range and long-range goals of the teacher. It also establishes baseline data against which the progress of the teacher may be measured during or at the end of the school year.

Teacher evaluation, if it is to serve both a guidance and a merit-rating function, must be a cooperative process. Although the actual practices and conditions being observed and the learning content being presented will vary from teacher to teacher, instructors should be allowed to familiarize themselves with the evaluation scale. If formal observation and rating is conducted, composite evaluations by two or more competent persons will increase the reliability of results. Also, as a morale factor, teachers will more willingly accept the joint ratings of two or more persons.

At this time, research on classroom evaluation of teachers reveals little statistical relationship between teacher effectiveness (as measured by student behavioral change) and subjective classroom observation. However, the following sample items from *The Teaching Evaluation Record*, a teacher-rating scale developed by Dwight Beecher for Educators Publishing Company (24), illustrates evaluation of performance based on actual observed evidence.

1 The teacher is fair and impartial *The teacher's behavior is consistently unbiased.*

Sample evidence *Shows no favoritism or partiality; praise and criticism are based on fact; all criticism constructive; no pets; appraisal of students fair and reliable; no extensive criticism of individual students; maintains confidence of students.*

2 Teacher employs a variety of approaches in presenting new materials
Teacher shows adaptability and broad understanding of techniques in presentation of new methods.

Sample evidence *Teacher uses many illustrations; utilizes suggestions from pupils as to methods and procedures; changes method quickly when it is obvious that methods being used are not effective; encourages students to try out several solutions; teacher and students discuss the relative merits of the various solutions.*

Evaluating Facilities

In the evaluation of vocational education facilities, the total physical environment must be considered. The term *facilities* includes not only the building and its equipment and furnishings, but also its dimensions, types of surfaces (color of walls, type of floor, window coverings), amount of lighting, noise control and acoustical materials, air conditioning and ventilation. Human beings are greatly influenced by their environment whether it is the classroom, the athletic field, or an office. Such physical factors as lighting, acoustics, and the use of color have psychological implications and so should be planned carefully to provide an atmosphere that is conducive to learning.

Evaluation of facilities may take two forms: evaluation *for* facilities and evaluation *of* facilities. Evaluation *for* facilities includes a definition of the nature and extent of the educational program to be offered and the development of long-range plans to house the program; it might include labor surveys, follow-up studies, and review of needs by an advisory council. Evaluation *of* school facilities involves the congruence of a particular building, site, and type of equipment with the educational program that is operated in the facility; it would thus compare the existing facility with the needs of the program being operated, taking into consideration such factors as instructional needs, safety, and aesthetics.

An examination of evaluation instruments for vocational education developed by state departments of education, the American Vocational Association, accrediting agencies, and others reveals that facilities evaluation is included in the evaluation criteria. The following sources include extensive treatment of facilities evaluation:

Lane Ash, *National Study for Accreditation of Vocational-Technical Education* (Washington, D.C.: American Vocational Association, 1972).

Milton E. Larson and Duane L. Blake, *Planning Facilities and Equipment for Comprehensive Vocational Education Programs for the Future*, Final Report (Fort Collins: Colorado State University).

Richard F. Meckley et al., *A General Guide for Planning Facilities for Vocational-Technical Education*, Final Report (Columbus: The Center for Vocational and Technical Education, The Ohio State University, 1969).

Harris W. Reynolds et al., *Evaluative Criteria for Vocational-Technical Programs* (Harrisburg: Bureau of Curriculum Planning and School Evaluation, Pennsylvania State Department of Education, 1967).

Research Series No. 45, "A System for State Evaluation of Vocational Education," Interim Report (The Center for Vocational and Technical Education, The Ohio State University).

Evaluating
Through Needs Assessment

Needs assessment as a process in curriculum development was discussed in Chapter 10. A need was defined as the *discrepancy* that exists between what is desired and what exists. Discrepancies may be identified between the actual and the desired or between two groups in terms of a given variable (for example, home economics students versus business education students on a variable such as economic understanding).

Once educational needs have been specified in terms of discrepancies, then measurable objectives can be generated by stating goals or objectives as the reduction of needs over time. Needs assessments may also be used to study the effect of interventions that are planned to reduce such needs, because the needs assessment describes the state of affairs that exists initially. In other words, a needs assessment presents a diagnosis—identification of the needs and their interrelationships. The most effective assessment is therefore one that is detailed enough to suggest a prescription.

To effectively use needs assessment, vocational educators need to be familiar with measurement and the collection and interpretation of data.

Needs assessment as formative evaluation In some situations, the main difference between a formative and a summative evaluation is the purpose for which it will be used. The same is true of the needs assessment. During the formative stages of curriculum development, data from standardized tests, enrollment and attendance statistics, inventories of equipment, instructional materials, and library resources provide *validated* facts about the current conditions of the school.

Carefully constructed instruments (questionnaires, opinionnaires, interview schedules) are tools through which people (teachers, administrators, students, parents, community representatives) have a direct input into the curriculum construction process. Appendix A contains an example of an instrument that may be used to obtain *felt or perceived* needs. Because the instrument is concerned with obtaining data about a specific curriculum, it should be constructed to reflect the objectives, facilities, and instructional program of the particular school involved.

Needs assessment instruments do not need to be overly sophisticated, but they do need to be properly constructed to obtain the desired data.

Suppose, for example, you want several graduates to rate the assistance they received at school in various activities. The specific objectives or competencies may be identified as a basis for student rating, as in the example below:

Competency	Amount of Help from School		
	Great deal	Somewhat helpful	Little/no help
1. Getting a job			
2. Preparing for further education			
3. Understanding my abilities and interests			
4. Using my money wisely			

Data gained from such an instrument reflect the felt needs of students and provide valuable input into the instructional planning and evaluation process.

Needs assessment as summative evaluation To what extent do the people involved feel that the curriculum has been effective in realizing its objectives? Has a program designed, for example, to reduce absenteeism and the school drop out rate been successful? Is the achievement of students enrolled in an individualized instruction program equal to or superior to that of students enrolled in traditional programs? These are typical of the questions that might be raised at the end of a trial period for a revised curriculum or pilot program. The same, or similar instruments, that were used in formative evaluation now become instruments for summative evaluation.

Measurement and Data Collection

This section of the chapter focuses on some of the more common instruments used in evaluation, including standardized tests, criterion-referenced measures, performance (work-sample) tests, rating scales, and inquiry forms. Informal evaluation procedures are also covered.

Standardized Tests

Standardized tests are usually classified as norm-referenced, which means that an individual's performance is examined in relation to the performance of other persons. The test manual should explain the characteristics of the population used to establish the norm.

Before selecting a test, the following steps should be considered:

1 Determine the purpose for testing Because tests may be given for any number of reasons, the purpose for testing must be held clearly in mind so that an appropriate instrument may be selected.

2 Identify suitable tests Several tests may appear to be appropriate for the purpose identified. One of the most useful sources of assistance in locating and selecting suitable tests is the *Mental Measurement Yearbook*, edited by Oscar K. Buros (25). Available tests are listed and described, including such factors as cost, coverage, source, and a critical review.

3 Evaluate the test Before the final decision is made on a test, it should be carefully evaluated in terms of such factors as reliability, validity, economy, ease of administration, adequacy of the manual, relevance of norms, and appropriateness of content for students. One way to become familiar with a test is to take it yourself and then administer it to a few students. Specimen sets are available from publishers at a nominal cost.

Standardized tests possess several limitations that should be kept in mind:

1 Although a test may be standardized with regard to administration and scoring, it may be inappropriate for certain groups of individuals. Items may not be relevant or of the proper difficulty.

2 In an effort to develop a test that is brief, the test developer may sacrifice depth and breadth in sampling and may establish unrealistic time limits.

3 With certain students, group tests may not be the best measure of ability. Misread or misunderstood directions may result in incorrect responses to questions that these students may, in some other test format, answer correctly.

4 The format of the test limits the type of items used. For example, machine-scored tests are generally multiple choice, a format that does not adequately sample all behaviors.

Criterion-Referenced Measures

Recently there has been an increased emphasis on the use of criterion-referenced tests, which relate test performance to absolute standards that are usually stated in terms of behavioral objectives. These tests are especially valuable for assessing student mastery of specified objectives.

Otto (26) presents some contrasts between standardized achievement (norm-referenced) tests and criterion-referenced tests (absolute standards):

1 *Standardized tests have a low degree of overlap with the objectives of instruction at any given time and place. The overlap for criterion-refer-*

enced measures is absolute, for the objectives of instruction are *the referents.*

2 *Norm-referenced tests are not very useful as aids in planning instruction because of the low overlap just mentioned. Criterion-referenced measures can be used directly to assess the strengths and weaknesses of individuals with regard to instructional objectives.*

3 *Because of their nonspecificity, norm-referenced tests often require skills or aptitudes that may be influenced only to a limited extent by experiences in the classroom. This cannot be so for criterion-referenced measures because the referent for each test is also the referent for instruction.*

4 *Standardized tests do not indicate the extent to which individuals or groups of students have mastered the spectrum of instructional objectives. There is no such problem with criterion-referenced measures because they focus on the spectrum of instructional objectives in a given situation.*

The reader is cautioned that the above comparisons are not to be interpreted as implying that norm-referenced tests are of no value and that criterion-referenced tests are the solution to all testing problems. It is not usually a matter of choosing between the two types of tests. Instead, the two types of measurement should complement each other, with the appropriate type chosen according to the testing purpose.

There are limitations related to criterion-referenced testing that should be considered. The most obvious limitation relates to the appropriate selection of objectives reflecting goals in the three learning domains: affective, cognitive, and psychomotor. Too frequently, the hard-to-measure qualities are slighted. Objectives that focus on initial mastery may take precedence over those that focus on retention of skill and application to a new situation.

Specifying the universe of tasks to be dealt with is of extreme importance. In no type of testing situation will a good test compensate for poor objectives. Of special importance to vocational education is the task of determining proficiency standards. Should perfect, near-perfect, or less demanding performance be required? Should the same standards apply to all situations? to all students?

At the present time the number of criterion-referenced tests on the market within the field of vocational education is somewhat limited. Consequently, teachers are confronted with the task of devising their own criterion-referenced instruments.

Performance Tests

One of the more common types of evaluation in vocational education is the performance test, in which the student is asked to demonstrate a given activity. The product, then, is evaluated according to a predetermined standard. This *work-sample* test requires the student to perform a segment of an operation using tools, materials, and methods that are characteristic of the total task. In most instances, these tests might best be classified as simulated-condition examinations that are based on essential job activities, presented in such a manner as to approximate the real work situation.

Consideration must be given to whether the product of the activity, the process, or both are to be observed and measured. In some cases, the obvious procedure is to evaluate the activity in process. For example, the techniques employed by a typist, such as position, touch, and evenness of stroke, provide clues that assist the teacher in diagnosing difficulties and in prescribing improved work methods. In other types of activities, in which the product is all-important, the scoring or evaluating should focus on the output. When possible, the product should be measured against an objective standard, such as a micrometer, ruler, gauge, or pattern. Not all products, can be measured objectively. Sometimes more subjective measures such as check lists or rating scales are more appropriate.

Rating Scales

Earlier in the chapter it was noted that it is not always possible to use an objective means of evaluating a student's performance. In many cases, a number of separate tasks must be accomplished producing the finished product, so a number of variables must be considered in evaluating the student's performance. One technique that has proved useful under these conditions is the rating scale. Figure 14.6 presents a sample rating scale for evaluating student performance in woodworking.

The use of such a rating system does not guarantee reliability in judging individual differences in students' performance. Unreliability in such judgments may be the result of a number of factors. For example, evaluating a task on which students show only small individual differences makes it difficult to establish reliability. In addition, inadequate instructions to the rater, lack of training in using these particular rating instruments, and poorly designed instruments may also cause unreliability.

Rating scales constitute a form of evaluation that relies heavily on subjective judgment of amount, degree, or quality. Such rating devices are used on the assumption that better judgment can be obtained on the overall product by focusing attention on one aspect at a time. They are also based on the assumption that the general value of the product can be approximated by a summation of the values of the parts.

The rating scale has proved useful in evaluating teacher performance. Since subjective evaluation may be biased by a number of different types of error, a carefully developed rating scale usually results in higher reliability than subjective evaluations made without the use of such a scale. Such instruments are now in general use in many colleges. Their use by students allows an instructor to gain valuable insights into his or her

1. *Evidence of excessive glue under finish / Damage from glue*

1	2	3	4	5	6	7
Bubbles of glue under finish		Considerable discoloration		Slight discoloration		No evidence of glue

2. *Evidence of clamp damage*

1	2	3	4	5	6	7
Splitting		Deep Impressions		Marred surface		No evidence of clamps

3. *Evidence of inconsistent clamping pressure in assembly (squareness)*

1	2	3	4	5	6	7
Parts do not fit		Considerable warp		Some distortion		All parts square

4. *Evidence of lamination problems*

1	2	3	4	5	6	7
Splitting/ open joint		Buckling/ wide joint		Slight offset		Flat/tight joint

5. *Evidence of the improper use of fasteners (screws)*

1	2	3	4	5	6	7
Not holding/, head-stripped		Loose/head damage		Poor seating		Secure/no head damage

6. *Evidence of the improper use of fasteners (finish nails)*

1	2	3	4	5	6	7
Bent nail/ surface damage		Nail showing		Under or overfilled		Fill blends with surface

Figure 14.6 Evaluation form for a woodworking project (27). Source: *Handbook on Formative and Summative Evaluation of Student Learning* by Benjamin S. Bloom, J. Thomas Hastings, George F. Madaus. © 1971 by McGraw-Hill, Inc. Used with permission of McGraw-Hill Book Company.

teaching effectiveness as perceived by students—the chief beneficiaries of instruction. Likewise, they provide evidence of the teacher's effectiveness to the school administration. Such evidence may be used to document promotion, raises in salary, or the reverse as the case may be. The effectiveness of such instruments is further conditioned by their use, in good faith, by students, teachers, and administrators.

The College of Education at the University of Georgia has developed several student course evaluations as one means of improving course offerings, instruction, and course content. Such tabulated data also provide students with an objective measure of courses in which they are considering enrolling. Each instrument is accompanied by an IBM answer sheet for use in machine scoring. Results are made available to department heads, to the faculty member whose course is being evaluated, and to students. The course evaluation instrument development by the Graduate Student Council of the College of Education, University of Georgia, is contained in Appendix B.

Inquiry Forms

When data are collected from respondents in a written form, the instruments are referred to as inquiry forms. Examples include schedules, questionnaires, and opinionnaires. Although often misused, the questionnaire can be a useful data-gathering instrument to the vocational educator if it is properly constructed and administered. Through its use, information can be obtained from varied and scattered sources. The typical questionnaire contains three types of items: (a) identifying information, (b) factual census-type data, and (c) subject matter items. The subject matter may be geared to solicit opinions, information, advice, or explanations.

The inquiry form is especially useful in conducting needs assessment. A well-constructed instrument can be used to collect data from a large number of students, teachers, parents, and business or community leaders. The ratio of returns to the number of questionnaires sent out is important, as is the representative nature of the replies. Thus the sample selected for the survey may be representative, but the results may be biased if only a small fraction return the form.

Informal Procedures

In the process of evaluation, situations arise that call for data that are not readily available from existing school records or examinations. Informal procedures provide an appropriate technique in such cases. Examples of informal procedures include the following: 1. *Informal observation*—an effective technique used by skillful teachers and supervisors for gathering information about students and other school personnel; purposeful observation can provide real insight into the performance of the student or teacher. 2. *anecdotal records*—in their simplest form, a chronological collection of work samples and observation of happenings; these aid the teacher to keep in mind the developing characteristics of students. 3. *informal tests*—teacher-made nonstandardized tests and evaluations that accompany instructional materials; this is a widely used technique that provides a quick check of student progress. 4. *checklists*—generally in two categories: those completed by the student (such as questionnaires relating to work habits, inventories, and attitudes) and those completed by the teacher (such as assessments of the welding techniques used by a student).

Issues in Evaluation

Byram (28) has identified five issues that are of importance to those concerned with evaluation in vocational education. He defines an issue as a controversial question, the resolution of which contains more than one acceptable solution. The five issues relating to the purpose and process of evaluation are summarized as follows:

Issue 1 *The Purpose of Program Evaluation: Should it be to check on accountability or to develop a basis for program improvement?*

Position *The major reason for program evaluation is—or should be— to improve programs and program planning. Accountability should also be considered at all levels. The point of reference should be the extent of attainment of program objectives.*

Issue 2 *Who should determine the criteria on which evaluation of local and state programs of vocational education are based?*

Position *Criteria for evaluation of local and area programs should be determined by local and area administrators, teachers, and representatives of the public. Criteria to be used for evaluation of state programs likewise should be determined by staffs at that level and representatives of the public. Consultant help should be utilized at all levels in deciding on criteria.*

Issue 3 *Who should direct and be involved in local and area evaluation of programs?*

Position *Local and area program evaluations should be directed by personnel who are responsible for providing resources for the program at those levels and by those who are the beneficiaries of them. If this position is accepted, the one taken on the next issue follows logically.*

Issue 4 *What should be the role of state leaders in program evaluation?*

Position *State leaders should help to prepare local and area leaders for the task of directing evaluations and serve in a consultant capacity to them. This responsibility should be undertaken in addition to directing the evaluation of state programs and obtaining information to assist in program evaluation at the national level. Thus there is a dual role for persons in state leadership positions.*

Issue 5 *Should programs of vocational agriculture be evaluated separately or as part of a comprehensive evaluation of vocational-technical programs?*

Position *Programs of vocational agriculture, just as programs in any vocational field, should be considered as part of a comprehensive program of vocational-technical education. There is little to lose and much to gain through implementation of this concept. Teachers of vocational agriculture, because of their background and training, have much to offer in the conducting of an evaluation of a comprehensive program.*

The reader may wish to refer back to Chapter 6 for a discussion of other issues related to present and emerging programs of vocational-technical and career education.

Measuring Cognitive, Affective, and Psychomotor Outcomes

Because the goals of education are focused on the growth and development of the total individual, vocational educators must be concerned with cognitive, affective, and psychomotor behaviors. They must acquire an in-depth comprehension of students as thinking, feeling, moving beings. Without such comprehension, educators will continue to experience difficulty in selecting relevant learning experiences in the three learning domains.

Behavior may be conceptualized as falling into only one of the three learning domains, even though, in reality, an individual's behavior is usually observed as a combination of all three. When studying ways to bring about desirable behavior change, educators must isolate behavior into component parts; writing relevant behavioral objectives, educators in every curriculum focus on the primary concern and categorize objectives into these three classifications. The reader is referred to Chapter 3 for a previous discussion of the nature and characteristics of cognitive, affective, and psychomotor domains.

Cognitive Domain

Historically our educational institutions have placed high priority on cognitive outcomes. This emphasis may be attributed, in part, to the fact that our system of education, as Bloom et al (29) have stated, "is geared to producing people who can deal with words, concepts, and mathematical or scientific symbols so necessary for success in our technical society." Extensive research and development have produced the cognitive instructional strategies that are widely used in our schools. However, the pedagogic techniques used in cognitive development are not always appropriate to affective development.

Bloom et al (30) present Baldwin's modification of the original cognitive taxonomy, which they have found to be successful in working with industrial arts teachers. The modified system contains four levels—knowledge, understanding, application of knowledge, and application of understanding. *Evaluation of knowledge* requires assessing the student's recall of specific information or responses previously practiced in learning experiences. At the *understanding* level, behaviors such as interpretation, translation, summarization, analysis, detection of similarities and differences, which demonstrate understanding, as well as recall of knowledge are evaluated. *Application of knowledge* calls for evaluating the student's ability to apply previously learned knowledge to the solution of a known problem.

The most complex of the four levels is *application of understanding.* At least one element of the problem, either in the condition or in the solution required, must be new to the student; that is, it is expected that the student has not experienced this problem before.

It is evident from the brief description of measurement of the cognitive levels, both here and in Chapter 3, that evaluation strategies for the upper levels are more complex and sophisticated. It is logical to assume that more formative evaluation is also needed so that the student gains insight into the processes he or she uses or misuses in the effort to realize educational objectives.

Affective Domain

There is general agreement that it is more difficult to objectively measure the affective domain. In fact, how to evaluate affective objectives with validity, reliability, and objectivity may well be the number one research problem presented by the affective domain. Although an individual teacher may successfully evaluate changes in student behavior at the lower level of the taxonomy—receiving and responding—it becomes increasingly difficult to measure changes on the more complex levels. For instance, the teacher will probably not be able to maintain the same standards over a sufficient period of time to observe measurable changes in the student's more complex affective behaviors. This difficulty suggests that evaluation plans for measuring affective behavior should cover several years and should involve the cooperative efforts of several teachers. Such an approach would permit the collection of longitudinal data necessary to appraise the more complex behaviors, such as valuing, conceptualization, and organization.

Another problem related to the determination of affective objectives is the fact that it is not generally considered appropriate to assign a grade for attitudes, values, interests, and appreciations. Affective behaviors do not lend themselves as readily to paper-and-pencil measurement as do cognitive behaviors. There is also a greater possibility of "faking" desired responses, especially if the student believes that he or she is to be graded on them.

Formative evaluation is probably more appropriate than summative evaluation for assessing affective behavior. The diagnostic tools can provide feedback for students, indicating their progress toward predetermined goals. Both group and individual affective data are valuable. Group data, which make it possible for the individual to respond anonymously, provide evidence needed for curriculum decisions, whereas individual data are necessary for self-evaluation and guidance. Some of the more common tools used to measure affective behavior are the interview, open-ended questionnaire, closed-item questionnaire, semantic differential, and projective techniques.

Psychomotor Domain

In the psychomotor domain learning objectives emphasize muscular or motor skills, manipulation of materials and objects, or neuromuscular coordination. The psychomotor taxonomy of behaviors provides a framework for physical education, special education, fine arts, and vocational-technical education programs. In a sense, the psychomotor domain lends itself readily to the development and measurement of educational objectives because such behaviors are observable and so most of them can be objectively measured.

Research and study in the psychomotor domain has lagged behind that in the affective and cognitive domains. Psychologists have focused their research on motor behavior for which no specific training has been provided and which may thus be considered aptitude rather than achieve-

Content/skills	Mechanism	Complex overt response	Adaptation	Origination	Total test items
1. _____					
2. _____					
3. _____					
4. _____					
5. _____					
Total test items					

Figure 14.7 Matrix for developing test items in the psychomotor domain. Note that this matrix is based on Levels 4–7 of Simpson's taxonomy because these are the levels that are appropriate for vocational education evaluation. Levels 1–2, perception and set, are not readily observable behavior. Level 3, guided movement, may be classified as formative evaluation in the early stages of certain skills.

ment. Few, if any, of these tests are of value for measuring specific motor skills taught through vocational education programs.

The specification of educational objectives and, in turn, desired student behavior provides a framework for developing evaluation measures. Preparation of tables, in which the content or skill is listed on one axis and the taxonomical level on the other axis, helps the teacher to prepare or select measurement instruments that include the essential content in the desired proportion of its importance. Figure 14.7 provides an example.

An early model for classifying behaviors in the psychomotor domain was organized by Ragsdale (31), who categorized such behaviors as *object-motor activities* (manipulating objects), *language-motor activities* (recording, receiving, and communicating ideas), and *feeling-motor activities* (communication of attitudes, feelings, and emotions through the medium of movement).

Simpson's model (32), outlined in Chapter 3, contains seven hierarchical classification levels, each containing several subcategories. Simpson's model is useful when analyzing one particular movement skill that a student is attempting to master. The learner goes through the phase of interpreting the stimulus (*perception*); he or she then prepares for active response (*set*); because the skilled movement is new to him or her, the learner must first initiate what he or she perceives the task or movement to be. After some imitation (*guided response*), the learner practices the movement through trial-and-error learning. When the learner has acquired confidence in his or her performance of the movement; he or she is at the *mechanism* level; in other words, the movement pattern becomes habitual, progressing into a smooth *complex overt response*. When the learner has mastered the skilled movement, he or she is able to modify it (*adaptation*) and then to create movement patterns based on the acquired skilled movement (*origination*).

Harrow (33) provides a model complete with classification levels, subcategories, and divisions for classifying movement unique to the psychomotor domain. Level 1 is *reflex movements* (unconscious); Level 2 is categorized as *basic-fundamental movements* (inherent motor patterns based on reflexes); Level 3 lists *perceptual abilities* (cognitive-psychomotor; that is, data used by the brain centers for making response decisions); Level 4 comprises *physical abilities* (foundational to skill development and including strength, agility, endurance, etc.); Level 5 defines *skilled movements* (movements that are considered reasonably complex and that require learning—divided into beginning, intermediate, advanced, and highly skilled levels); Level 6 is *non-discursive communication* (style of movement that communicates feelings about one's objective self to the perceptive observer.) Table 14.2 summarizes these three models for classifying behaviors in the psychomotor domain.

Many of the psychomotor tasks in vocational education result in products that can be evaluated as evidence of degree of mastery of the psychomotor skill. Figure 14.6, an evaluation form for a woodworking project, is one such example. The evaluation of a typed letter would represent a means of assessing a student's mastery of the keyboard. Psychomotor tests designed to assess student performance of a specific skill may be more commonly known as work-sample or performance tests, a subject that was discussed earlier in the chapter. In objective measurement of the student's performance, the teacher may use an educational standard or an employment standard to which he or she compares the object or product being judged.

There are problems that are unique to psychomotor testing. In the majority of cognitive tests, the instructions are written and are the same for all students. In many situations involving psychomotor testing, however, the directions are given orally on an individual or small-group basis, which increases the chance of variation and so may produce differing results in student performance. Individual and small-group evaluation makes it more difficult to control environmental factors. It is also important that materials, tools, and equipment be comparable for all students.

A learner's intention to use a newly acquired skill makes the acquisition of that skill more personally important. A student learns to type in

Table 14.2   Three Models for Classifying Psychomotor Behaviors

Ragsdale Model	Simpson Model	Harrow Model
1 object-motor (manipulating or acting with direct reference to an object)	1 perception (interpreting)	1 reflex movements (segmental reflexes, intersegmental reflexes, suprasegmental reflexes)
2 language-motor (movements of speech, sight, handwriting)	2 set (preparing) 3 guided response (learning) 4 mechanism (automatizing)	2 basic-fundamental movements (locomotor movements, non-locomotor movements, manipulative movements) 3 perceptual abilities (kinesthetic discrimination, visual discrimination, auditory discrimination, tactile discrimination, coordinated abilities)
3 feeling-motor (movements communicating feelings and attitudes)	5 complex overt response (performing) 6 adaptation (modifying) 7 origination (creating)	4 physical abilities (endurance, strength, flexibility, agility) 5 skilled movements (simple adaptive skill, compound adaptive skill, complex adaptive skill) 6 non-discursive communication (expressive movement, interpretive movement)

order to facilitate work as a teacher aide or in the school office; a student may learn to work with engines in order to maintain his or her automobile. A learner converts opportunities into learning when he or she recognizes the personal values of the particular skill. Frequently, the skill (typing, engine repair, etc.) also involves income-producing aspects, which further enhance the learning potential.

If the primary concern of the vocational educator is to bring about manipulative or movement behavior change in the learner, the educational goal is in the psychomotor domain, and the teacher can prepare a relevant evaluation of the stated goal. It should be recognized, however, that many educational goals will have cognitive, psychomotor, and affective aspects; in such cases, each aspect of the stated educational goal must be evaluated.

Throughout this chapter we have emphasized the importance of the role of judgment as a factor in evaluation and decision making. The main emphasis of the "professional judgment" approach to evaluation is that of application of professional expertise to yield judgments about quality or effectiveness of programs. In the discussion of accreditation that follows, self-study and the maintenance of defined standards are formalized.

Evaluation for Accreditation

The accreditation movement among school administrators, which has become the most formalized of the "professional judgment" approaches to evaluation, arose during the 1920s and 1930s in the United States. In accreditation, standards for schools, colleges, and universities are generally arrived at through the collective judgments of persons possessing some expertise in the field of education. Institutions are asked to undergo an extensive self-study, based on a set of guidelines (evaluative criteria) provided by the accrediting agency. (The evaluative criteria are published by the National Study of School Evaluation, 2201 Wilson Boulevard, Arlington, Virginia 22201.) There are usually two sections of evaluative criteria, General and Subject Field, as follows:

General criteria

Section 1 Manual
2 School and Community
3 Philosophy and Objectives
4 Curriculum
5 Student Activities Program
6 Educational Media Services—Library and Audio-Visual
7 Guidance Services
8 School Facilities
9 School Staff and Administration
10 Individual Staff Member
11 Summary of Self-Evaluation

Subject-field criteria

Section 4-1   Agriculture
4-2   Art (including Crafts)
4-3   Business Education
4-4   Distributive Education
4-5   Driver and Traffic Safety
4-6   English
4-7   Foreign Languages
4-8   Health Education
4-9   Home Economics
4-10   Industrial Arts
4-11   Mathematics
4-12   Music
4-13   Physical Education
4-14   Religion
4-15   Science
4-16   Social Studies
4-17   Special Education
4-18   Trade, Technical, and Industrial Education

Experts conduct a site visit at regular intervals. Regional associations, such as the Southern Association of Colleges and Schools, reevaluate school programs once every ten years. (Separate commissions, within the association, are maintained for elementary schools, secondary schools, post-high school two-year vocational-technical schools, and colleges.) Using a set of criteria developed by the accrediting agency, the visiting team observes the operation of the institution, meets with officials, and talks with teachers, students, and others connected with the institution's operation. The visiting team deliberates on the quality of the program and writes a final report that is sent to the accrediting agency. Throughout its visit and in writing its recommendations, the visiting team takes a position of helpfulness. The agency then meets, deliberates, and takes any action that seems advisable. If deficiencies are found in the program, certification is withheld until the substandard conditions are corrected. Membership in the accreditation organization is entirely voluntary on the part of the schools, but schools do feel considerable pressure to join. (Both regional and state accrediting agencies are private organizations, and a modest fee is charged for membership services.)

The purpose of an accreditation agency is to stimulate the school to achieve and maintain a high level of professional competence. Colleges and state departments of education tend to place a premium on membership by high schools. Many colleges place restrictions on the admission of students from unaccredited high schools. Colleges, in turn, aspire to membership in state, regional, and specialized (for example, the National Council for the Accreditation of Teachers) accrediting associations as a symbol of professional excellence.

Accreditation is also available to private, proprietary schools through national, regional, and sometimes state organizations. For example, the national Association of Independent Schools of Business has done much to upgrade the quality of work done in the private schools of business.

Because of the leniency of laws in many states there are, unfortunately, flagrant violations by some organizations that establish schools for various purposes without adequate faculty, buildings, or facilities. Many of these schools advertise themselves as "universities" and offer graduate "degrees," sometimes through accelerated or correspondence-type courses or on the payment of a fee. Wherever such schools are found, it is the responsibility of the legislature and the state education department to investigate and take corrective action.

Summary

Evaluation in vocational education is a systematic process of obtaining information for judging the effectiveness of programs in relation to acceptable criteria or objectives. An effective approach is based on principles that reflect a clear sense of direction, flexibility to change, and a desire to improve and upgrade all persons, programs, and processes involved. The benefits of evaluation may be categorized in terms of individual student growth, program operations, society and the economy, credibility, costs, time and installation considerations, organizational change, personnel needs, and equipment requirements.

A systems approach to evaluation involves (a) stating what is to be evaluated; (b) establishing quantifiable criteria and data needed for making decisions; (c) collecting the data; (d) analyzing the data in terms of the criteria; and (e) evaluating the extent of goal attainment and providing information for decision makers. Such a systematic approach is employed in the Kentucky Vocational Education Evaluation Model (VEEP), the Context-Input-Process-Product Evaluation Model (CIPP), and the Phi Delta Kappa Evaluation Model.

Program evaluation requires the identification of program goals and a systematic, critical look to determine to what degree the goals are being met. Cooperative judgments are involved at many different points during the completion of an evaluation study. Among the major elements to be evaluated are the curriculum, the progress of individual students, vocational personnel, the instructional process, and facilities. Evaluation of these determinants involves both formative (process) and summative (product) forms of evaluation. Summative evaluation is concerned with judging the effectiveness of the curriculum, grading students, or assessing the effectiveness of personnel at key terminal points. The basic objective of formative evaluation is interim feedback to the student. Competency-based approaches are increasingly being applied to program evaluation; these call for the performance of predetermined competencies.

Measurement and data collection represent key steps in the evaluation process. Formal measures used in vocational education include standardized tests, criterion-referenced measures, performance tests, rating scales, and inquiry forms. Informal measures used most frequently include observation, anecdotal records, informal teacher-made tests, and checklists. The purpose of most classroom measurement devices is to evaluate the extent to which a student has attained the objectives of a course. Classroom tests, however, may be developed to motivate learning, determine class progress, isolate individual learning difficulties, provide guidance data, aid in supervision, serve in research studies, and certify student employability. Needs assessment is considered as a tool to establish collective involvement of those affected by the school program toward determining program needs. The needs assessment process may be viewed as both formative and summative in its purposes. As a formative evaluation technique, data are gathered from key school publics that provide input into the formation of the curriculum, facilities, and personnel. As a summative evaluation tool, data are collected at the end of a given period of time in order to determine how well the goals of a program have been achieved.

Behavior may be conceptualized as falling into one of three learning domains—cognitive, affective, or psychomotor—even though, in reality, an individual's behavior is usually observed as a combination of all three. Educators are more proficient in measuring cognitive behavior because our educational institutions place high priority on training persons to work with words, concepts, and symbols that are essential to success in our society. It is more difficult to assess affective behavior than cognitive or psychomotor behavior. Few instruments that are valid, reliable, and objective are available, and it is difficult to measure affective outcomes within a short period of time. Cooperative evaluation plans covering several years and involving the joint efforts of many people are needed. Commonly used instruments for measuring affective outcomes include interviews, questionnaires, semantic differential, and projective techniques. Many psychomotor tasks in vocational education result in products that can be evaluated as evidence of a degree of mastery of psychomotor skill. Performance tests, including work samples, provide a relatively objective measurement tool for appraising the student's output in relation to a standard. Such tests are used both as formative and as summative evaluation devices.

This chapter also examines the role of accrediting agencies in relation to the evaluation process. National, regional, state, and local agencies are viewed as primarily consultative, providing judgmental and other assistance needed by vocational educators to maintain improved programs.

It has been said that teachers and administrators do not want to be evaluated or to expose their programs to public scrutiny except in a most favorable light. The school administrator's preoccupation with avoidance of conflict has been preempted by a barrage of value conflicts, which show that the school is no longer "one happy family." The threat of awakened minorities, the organizing of teachers, and voter disenchantment with rising taxes, all have eroded public confidence in the school system. People now want proof of good education; and it is here that evaluation must play an increasingly important role.

It would be naive to suggest that adequate evaluation models exist. The efficient compliance with a master plan (attractive in the face of disunity) argues for a systems analysis type of evaluation. But such highly centralized evaluation plans do not always coincide with the talents of the people who must deal with them. Some contend that the techniques of systems analysis would make our schools more impersonal and inflexible than they are now. There is no one alternative. But grandiose evaluation schemes cannot substitute for negotiation, compromise, personal influence, and other manifestations of political rationality.

Various techniques exist for evaluating instruction, cutting costs, and determining public opinion. Evaluation can help one group to communicate with another, and it can help the administrator to justify his or her program. Under the separation of powers within the school system, teachers can possess considerable autonomy in how they operate. At the same time, the administrator is justified in seeking some evidence of good work —and so is the public from the administrator. Such evidence should be gathered in modest proportions.

Activities

For review

1 Compare a minimum of three definitions of evaluation, noting their differences and similarities. With which definition do you most nearly agree? Why?

2 Summarize at least four principles that should underlie an effective evaluation program.

3 What are two criteria that should be considered in selecting an evaluation model?

4 Differentiate between formative and summative evaluation and give an example of each.

5 What *informal* evaluation tool would a teacher use to note changes in a student's attitude?

6 How may a needs assessment be employed as a formative-type evaluation? As a summative-type evaluation?

7 What is a standardized test? What points should be considered in selecting such a test for use with students?

8 What advantages does the criterion-referenced vocational test have over the standardized test?

9 What is a work-sample and how is it used in vocational classes?

10 What types of instruments may be used for informal evaluation purposes?

11 Explain how accreditation is used in schools, colleges, or universities.

12 Briefly describe Bloom's cognitive taxonomy.

13 Identify some of the problems associated with measurement of the affective domain.

14 Describe at least one problem that is unique to psychomotor testing.

For discussion

1 Justify the inclusion of evaluation as a component of curriculum construction.

2 Compare the steps in the Kentucky VEEP Model with those in the scientific process of problem solving. How are they alike? How are they different?

3 Explain the relationship of evaluation to decision making as illustrated in the CIPP Model.

4 Justify the use of value judgment in evaluation.

5 Why should plans for evaluation be initiated in the early stages of vocational program planning?

6 What reasons can you cite both for and against the evaluation of teachers by their students?

7 Student accomplishment is an important measure of the performance of a teacher. What factors must be kept in mind when evaluating a teacher on the basis of student performance?

8 On what basis is it maintained that the classroom environment has sensory values?

9 Explain how a rating scale might be used in evaluating vocational student performance.

10 The role of the department head is crucial to evaluation of teaching. Explain.

11 Should vocational programs be evaluated separately (as agriculture education, business education, distributive education, etc.) or as an integral part of a comprehensive vocational education program? Why?

12 Cite a classroom situation for which teacher-made tests should be constructed even though published tests are available for the text being used in the course.

13 What caution should be observed by teachers in comparing classroom scores with national norms?

14 What are some of the tangible and intangible benefits to be derived from the evaluation of vocational programs?

15 To what extent may classroom examinations be regarded as *vocational* tests?

16 What are the chief strengths and weaknesses of accreditation-type evaluations?

17 Evaluate these statements. Do you agree or disagree with each of them? Give reasons for your answers.

(a) "Teachers and administrators do not want to be evaluated or to expose their programs to public scrutiny except in a most favorable light."

(b) "The techniques associated with a systems approach tend to dehumanize education."

(c) "It is naive to think that adequate evaluation models exist."

(d) "When a teacher tests, he or she is not teaching."

For exploration

1 What are the predominant issues facing vocational educators today? How are they related to evaluation?

2 Using the matrix in Figure 14.7, develop a test measuring psychomotor skill development for a short segment (one day to one week) for a vocational course taught in your school's curriculum.

3 Both state department of education personnel and accrediting organization personnel are concerned with standards. In what respect are such standards alike? In what respects are they different?

4 Read at least three magazine articles dealing with construction or use of performance tests. Prepare separate brief reports of the contents of each article, including a synopsis and the author's summary and conclusions. Give your own criticisms of each article.

5 Analyze and comment critically on two selected teacher-made objective examinations, preferably tests obtained from classroom teachers.

6 Work with two or three of your classmates or your own students to revise the sample course evaluation form printed in Appendix B. Administer the instrument to your classes at the end of a grading period and analyze the results.

7 Using the discussion in the chapter and the sample instrument in Appendix A, develop a needs assessment instrument for your own vocational program. Include items related to philosophy and objectives, equipment and facilities, teachers, course offerings, instructional materials, methods, committees and organizations, and community employment needs.

8 Administer a needs assessment instrument to a sample of students, faculty, administrators, parents, and community representatives, and prepare a summary of the results. Emphasize the changes in the program recommended by the respondents.

9 Using the Checklist for Evaluating Classroom Organization, Figure 14.4, evaluate (a) a vocational class that you teach, or (b) a class taught by someone else.

10 Select one course that you teach and prepare a master plan for student evaluation to include the following:
  (a) objectives of the plan
  (b) type evaluation to be used (diagnostic, formative, summative)
  (c) examples (standardized test, checklist, etc.)
  (d) time schedule

References

1 Benjamin S. Bloom, J. Thomas Hastings, George F. Madaus, *Handbook on Formative and Summative Evaluation of Student Learning* (New York: McGraw-Hill Book Company, 1971), p. 8. (Reproduced with permission)

2 P. A. Taylor and T. O. Maguire, "A Theoretical Evaluation Model," in *Manitoba Journal of Educational Research*, Vol. 1, 1966, pp. 12–17; in *Curriculum Evaluation*, ed. David A. Payne (Lexington, Mass.: D. C. Heath and Company, 1974), p. 11.

3 Margaret Ammons, "Evaluation: What Is It? Who Does It? When Should It Be Done?" in *Assessment Problems in Reading*, ed. Walter H. MacGinite (Newark, Delaware: International Reading Association, 1973), p. 69.

4 Wilbur Harris, "The Nature and Function of Educational Evaluation," in *Peabody Journal of Education*, September 1968, as quoted in N. L. McCaslin, "Program Evaluation: Problems, Prerequisites, Characteristics, and Implementation," in *Improving Administrative Programs of State Vocational Education Agencies* (Columbus: Center for Vocational and Technical Education, 1974), p. 91.

5 Egon Guba and Daniel L. Stufflebeam, *Evaluation: The Process of Stimulating, Aiding, and Abetting Insightful Action,* an address delivered at the Second National Symposium for Professors of Educational Research (Columbus: Evaluation Center, The Ohio State University, 1968).

6 Ralph W. Tyler, *Basic Principles of Curriculum and Instruction* (Chicago: University of Chicago Press, 1949), p. 105.

7 Phi Delta Kappa National Study Committee on Evaluation, David Stufflebeam, chairman, *Educational Evaluation and Decision Making* (Itasca, Illinois: F. E. Peacock Publishers, Inc., 1971), p. 40. (Reproduced with permission)

8 J. Chester Swanson, "Criteria for Effective Vocational Education," in *Contemporary Concepts in Vocational Education*, ed. Gordon F. Law (Washington, D.C.: American Vocational Association, 1971), pp. 23–24. (Reproduced with permission)

9 William L. Hull and Randall L. Wells, *Innovations Evaluation Guide* (Columbus: The Center for Vocational and Technical Education, The Ohio State University, 1972).

10 Selma J. Mushkin and William Pollak, "Analysis in a PPB Setting," in *Economic Factors Affecting the Financing of Education*, eds. R. L. Johns, I. J. Gaffman, Kern Alexander, D. H. Stollar (Gainesville, Florida: National Educational Finance Project, 1970), p. 329.

11 N. L. McCaslin, "Program Evaluation: Problems, Prerequisites, Characteristics, and Implementation," in *Improving Administrative Activities of State Vocational Education Agencies*, 6th Annual National Leadership Development Seminar for State Directors of Vocational Education, eds. Daniel E. Koble, Jr., and Robert U. Coker (Columbus: The Center for Vocational and Technical Education, The Ohio State University, 1974), pp. 94–96.

12 Robert A. Burnham, "Systems Evaluation and Goal Disagreement," in *School Evaluation, The Politics and Process*, ed. Ernest R. House (Berkeley, California: McCutchan Publishing Corporation, 1973), p. 245.

13 Phi Delta Kappa National Study Committee on Evaluation. See Ref. 7, pp. 27–30. (Reproduced with permission)

14 William T. Denton, *Program Evaluation in Vocational and Technical Education* (Columbus: The Center for Vocational and Technical Education, The Ohio State University, 1973), p. 12.

15 Daniel L. Stufflebeam, "Toward A Science of Educational Evaluation," in *Evaluation of Education* (Englewood Cliffs, N.J.: Educational Technology Publications, 1973), p. 22.

16 Ibid., p. 25.

17 J. Galen Saylor and William M. Alexander, *Planning Curriculum for Schools* (New York: Holt, Rinehart and Winston, Inc., 1974), pp. 302–303.

18 Phi Delta Kappa National Study Committee on Evaluation. See Ref. 7, p. 156.

19 P. L. Dressel, "Evaluation as Instruction," as quoted in *Curriculum Evaluation*, ed. David A. Payne (Lexington, Mass.: D. C. Heath and Company, 1974), p. 6.

20 Benjamin S. Bloom et al. See Ref. 1, p. 91. (Reproduced with permission)

21 Dale L. Bolton, *Teacher Evaluation* (Washington, D.C.: National Center for Educational Communication, 1971) as quoted in J. Marvin Robertson,

Personnel Evaluation (Columbus: The Center for Vocational and Technical Education, The Ohio State University, 1973), p. 3.

22 Ibid, p. 5.

23 Ibid, p. 2.

24 Dwight Beecher, *The Teaching Evaluation Record* (Educators Publishing Company, 1972).

25 Oscar K. Buros, ed., *The Sixth Mental Measurement Yearbook* (Highland Park, N.J.: Gryphon Press, 1965).

26 Wayne Otto, "Evaluating Instruments for Assessing Needs and Growth in Reading," in *Assessment Problems in Reading*, Walter H. MacGinitie, ed. (Newark, Delaware: International Reading Association, 1973). (Reprinted with permission of Wayne Otto and International Reading Association)

27 Benjamin S. Bloom et al. See Ref. 1, p. 885. (Reproduced with permission)

28 Harold M. Byram, "Five Issues in the Evaluation of Vocational Agriculture," in *American Vocational Journal*, Vol. 46, No. 2, February 1971, pp. 51–54. (Reproduced with permission)

29 Benjamin S. Bloom, et al. See Ref. 1, p. 225.

30 Ibid, p. 864.

31 C. E. Ragsdale, "How Children Learn Motor Types of Activities," in *Learning and Instruction*, Forty-ninth Yearbook of the National Society for the Study of Education (Chicago: University of Chicago Press, 1950), pp. 69–91.

32 Elizabeth J. Simpson, "The Classification of Educational Objectives: Psychomotor Domain," University of Illinois Research Project No. OE 5, 1966, pp. 85–104.

33 Anita J. Harrow, *A Taxonomy of the Psychomotor Domain* (New York: David McKay Company, 1972), pp. 96–97.

Appendices

Sample

Needs

Assessment

Instrument

The format and content of a needs assessment instrument should be adapted to the educational, social, and business-industrial needs of each community. Input from educators, students, parents, and lay people is solicited during the formative stages of program revision.

The following instrument is a sample modification of a needs assessment originally developed by Marilyn G. Butler of South Gwinnett High School, Snellville, Georgia.

Part 1 provides an overall evaluation of the current Business Education program. Part 2 includes a detailed assessment of actual and ideal program priorities. The instrument could be adapted for use with any vocational program.

Sample Needs Assessment for
Business Education Programs

Part 1

Directions Please evaluate the business education program at _____ _____ in each of the ten areas described below. Under each heading are two descriptive paragraphs headed "Inferior" and "Superior," and five blanks labeled "Inferior," "Below average," "Average," "Above average," and "Superior." Read each of the paragraphs. If the paragraph labeled "Inferior" describes current actual practices relating to business education, place an X in the first blank ("Inferior"). If the department meets all the criteria listed under the "Superior" heading, place an X in the last blank ("Superior"). If the department meets some, but not all, of the "Superior" statements, place an X in the most appropriate middle blank. Please list your recommendations for helping the department achieve a "Superior" rating.

A Instructional materials

Inferior Little supplementary material is available. Textbooks and other teaching materials are out of date and in poor condition. There is no centralized instructional materials center.

Superior Teachers regularly use such supplementary materials as books, magazines, newspapers, transparencies, filmstrips, films, tapes, and sound-slides. A multimedia center for the department provides a check-out and check-in system. Materials and equipment are up to date, maintained in good operating condition, and in frequent use. Money is allocated for rental of films.

Inferior	Below average	Average	Above average	Superior
_____	_____	_____	_____	_____

Action needed to close the gap:

B Library resources

Inferior Library is poorly stocked—no subscriptions to business periodicals; no references for economics, business law, or secretarial science. There are few audio-visual aids and very little encouragement to students and staff to use facilities.

Superior Library has comprehensive, extensive collections, including periodicals; national, state, and local newspapers; economics and law books; secretarial handbooks; file of pamphlets for use in business classes. Library is open before and after school as well as during school hours. Qualified librarians assist and encourage student and staff use. Audio-visual section has sufficient number of projectors of various types, recorders, record players, and cassette tape players, overhead projectors, and opaque projectors.

Inferior	Below average	Average	Above average	Superior
_____	_____	_____	_____	_____

Action needed to close the gap:

C Physical facilities and equipment

Inferior Classrooms are too small, with insufficient electrical outlets for multipurpose requirements. Environmental conditions of the classrooms are not conducive to concentration and efficient work.

Superior There are at least two multipurpose classrooms with sufficient electrical outlets for machines; two typewriting classrooms with provisions for electric typewriters; one general purpose classroom furnished with tables suitable for accounting instruction. Environmental conditions in all classrooms are conducive to business-like work.

Inferior	Below average	Average	Above average	Superior
_____	_____	_____	_____	_____

Action needed to close the gap:

D Staff

Inferior Less than 10% of the staff members possess master's degrees. Staff does not keep abreast of current trends and methods; shows little interest in teaching as a profession; little enthusiasm. Staff members do not possess practical work experience.

Superior At least 60% of the staff members possess master's degrees. All staff members are engaged in staff development activities for improving skills and keeping up to date with research and developments in business education. They are enthusiastic, active participants in professional organizations and growth activities, including work experience.

Inferior	Below average	Average	Above average	Superior
_____	_____	_____	_____	_____

Action needed to close the gap:

E Course offerings

Inferior The business education program offers basic instruction in typewriting, shorthand, accounting, business English, and business mathematics. No advanced classes are offered, and there are no courses in consumer economics or business organization and management, and no cooperative work-study program.

Superior A variety of courses are offered in the program. Courses are offered for vocational, job-entry skill development as well as for personal use. In addition to basic skill and career exploration courses, advanced classes and a cooperative vocational office training work-study program is provided.

Inferior	Below average	Average	Above average	Superior
_____	_____	_____	_____	_____

Action needed to close the gap:

F Instructional methods

Inferior Instruction is based on the lecture method, with all students working at the same speed.

Superior A variety of instructional strategies are used, fitting the method to the particular group and/or topic. There is recognition that students learn optimally at different rates and through different modes and provision is made for individualized instruction wherever possible. Students are involved in determining goals and self-evaluation. Instruction is well planned and provides immediate feedback to students concerning progress.

Inferior	Below average	Average	Above average	Superior
_____	_____	_____	_____	_____

Action needed to close the gap:

G Community employment needs

Inferior Students are given little or no employment information about job opportunities in the area and no preparation for job interviews. Course offerings are not adapted to changing job requirements or varying needs of the students in achieving job success.

Superior Job and career information is integrated into the classes wherever appropriate. A career information center is provided by the counseling department. Instruction in interview and job application techniques is given. As job requirements and employment needs change, attention is given to the feasibility of adaptation of course offerings and instruction.

Inferior	Below average	Average	Above average	Superior
_____	_____	_____	_____	_____

Action needed to close the gap:

H Equipment used in business and industry

Inferior Equipment in the business education program is obsolete. Typewriters, transcribing machines, calculators, and data processing equipment are out of date. No provisions are made for replacement on a regular basis.

Superior Equipment is replaced on a regular basis (3–5 years). Demonstration of equipment by office suppliers and field trips to companies enable students to learn about modern equipment that cannot be purchased by the school. Equipment used for instruction is representative of that used in the employment community.

Inferior	Below average	Average	Above average	Superior
_____	_____	_____	_____	_____

Action needed to close the gap:

I Advisory committee

Inferior An advisory committee does not exist, or it functions in name only. No opportunities are provided for the committee to make suggestions to the school or to be involved in curriculum planning and evaluation.

Superior An advisory committee is actively involved in a consultative role, advising the business education teachers about office-job requirements, job opportunities for graduates, and appraisal of the effectiveness of the job preparation of students.

Inferior	Below average	Average	Above average	Superior
_____	_____	_____	_____	_____

Action needed to close the gap:

J Youth organizations

Inferior A youth organization exists (Future Business Leaders of America, Office Education Association, Pi Omega Pi, etc.), but there is little student interest and little encouragement of student participation.

Superior Students actively participate in the business youth organization. They are provided opportunities to deal with actual problems. Membership is voluntary, and activities are conducted during school and after school. The club is highly visible to the community.

Inferior	Below average	Average	Above average	Superior
_____	_____	_____	_____	_____

Action needed to close the gap:

Part 2

Directions Read each of the following statements describing a specific practice or principle relating to business education. Under the column headed "Actual," place an X in the appropriate blank to indicate your agreement or disagreement with this practice or principle as it is presently carried out in the school. Under the column headed "Ideal," place an X in the appropriate blank to indicate a recommended view of the principle or practice.

Actual			Philosophy and objectives	Ideal		
Yes	No	No opinion		Yes	No	No opinion
—	—	————	**1** The basic purpose of business education is job preparation.	—	—	————
—	—	————	**2** Business education has two objectives: personal use and job preparation.	—	—	————
—	—	————	**3** A major objective of business education is to prepare students to be intelligent consumers.	—	—	————
—	—	————	**4** Business students try to specialize in one field, such as clerical, secretarial, management, or data processing.	—	—	————
—	—	————	**5** Business education objectives are developed by the faculty.	—	—	————

Equipment and facilities

Actual				Ideal		
—	—	————	**6** Electric typewriters are provided in all typewriting classes.	—	—	————
—	—	————	**7** An office training classroom is set up like a modern business office.	—	—	————
—	—	————	**8** A variety of name-brand business machines are provided.	—	—	————
—	—	————	**9** The business program uses modern equipment similar to that in an up-to-date business office.	—	—	————
—	—	————	**10** All business education rooms are adjoining.	—	—	————

Actual			Equipment and facilities (continued)	Ideal		
Yes	No	No opinion		Yes	No	No opinion
—	—	———	11 The business education department is air conditioned.	—	—	———
—	—	———	12 The business education department operates a center containing audio-visual materials and equipment and other resources.	—	—	———
—	—	———	13 Each business education lab is equipped with adequate storage space, filing cabinets, and counter space.	—	—	———
—	—	———	14 Selection of equipment is made by business education teachers.	—	—	———
—	—	———	15 Instruction is offered in the use of the full-key adding machine.	—	—	———
—	—	———	16 Instruction is offered in the use of the electronic calculator.	—	—	———
—	—	———	17 Instruction is offered in the use of the IBM Selectric typewriter.	—	—	———
—	—	———	18 Instruction is offered in the use of transcribing equipment.	—	—	———
—	—	———	19 Instruction is offered in the use of key-punch equipment.	—	—	———
—	—	———	20 Instruction is offered in the use of unit record equipment.	—	No	———
—	—	———	21 Instruction is offered in the use of computer terminals.	—	—	———

Business teachers

Actual				Ideal		
—	—	———	22 Business education teachers have a baccalaureate degree.	—	—	———

Actual			Business teachers (continued)	Ideal		
Yes	No	No opinion		Yes	No	No opinion
—	—	————	**23** Business teachers are employed on a twelve-month contract.	—	—	————
—	—	————	**24** Business teachers are highly proficient in the skills they teach.	—	—	————
—	—	————	**25** Business teachers are broadly trained in the field.	—	—	————
—	—	————	**26** Business teachers are required to update methods through in-service or college courses.	—	—	————
—	—	————	**27** Business teachers are required to have one year of work experience.	—	—	————
—	—	————	**28** Business teachers acquire practical work experience by working in an office for three months every five years.	—	—	————
—	—	————	**29** Business teachers are specialists in the use of audio-visual equipment.	—	—	————
—	—	————	**30** Business teachers are trained in specialized areas such as data processing, accounting, and shorthand.	—	—	————
—	—	————	**31** Business teachers make frequent surveys of business education programs in other schools for comparison and suggestions.	—	—	————

Course offerings

Actual				Ideal		
—	—	————	**32** Typewriting is offered at the eighth-grade level.	—	—	————
—	—	————	**33** Typewriting is required of all high school students.	—	—	————

Actual			Course offerings (continued)	Ideal		
Yes	No	No opinion		Yes	No	No opinion
—	—	————	**34** Consumer education courses are offered by the business program.	—	—	————
—	—	————	**35** Shorthand is offered even though there is widespread use of transcribing equipment in business.	—	—	————
—	—	————	**36** A course in data processing is offered to high school students.	—	—	————
—	—	————	**37** Instruction in the use of modern duplicating equipment is required of all vocationally-oriented students.	—	—	————
—	—	————	**38** Quarter hours of credit are given according to the percentage of work completed rather than on a pass-fail basis.	—	—	————
—	—	————	**39** The business math course is limited to students interested in a business career.	—	—	————
—	—	————	**40** An introductory course exploring business careers is offered at the ninth-grade level.	—	—	————
—	—	————	**41** A suggested program of study is available for students who are interested in pursuing a business career.	—	—	————
—	—	————	**42** A work-study program is provided for vocationally oriented students.	—	—	————
—	—	————	**43** Business education courses are provided in one-hour periods.	—	—	————
—	—	————	**44** Business education courses are taught on a flexible schedule.	—	—	————

Actual			Course offerings (continued)	Ideal		
Yes	No	No opinion		Yes	No	No opinion

45 Advanced business education skill courses are taught in a block (two or more periods).

Instructional methods and materials

46 Students are allowed to work at their own rate.

47 Students are able to contract for grades according to the amount of work completed.

48 Evaluation in advanced skills courses is based on accepted business practices.

49 Students are able to choose units of work according to vocational interests.

50 Instruction includes a variety of resources, including community personnel as speakers, field trips, etc.

51 Instruction in office skills includes simulated job activities.

52 Students are allowed to evaluate teachers.

53 Students are involved in cooperative evaluation of their work.

Community employment needs

54 Students are given information about job opportunities in the employment community.

55 Periodic follow-up studies are conducted to determine the relation-

	Actual		Community employment needs (continued)		Ideal	
Yes	No	No opinion		Yes	No	No opinion
			ship between course offerings and occupational roles.			
—	—	————		—	—	————
			56 Counseling and placement services are provided.			
—	—	————		—	—	————
			57 Frequent surveys are made to determine the type of office machines used in the business community.			
—	—	————		—	—	————

Committees and organizations

	Actual				Ideal	
			58 An advisory committee is used in a consultative role.			
—	—	————		—	—	————
			59 Former students serve on advisory committees.			
—	—	————		—	—	————
			60 People in business are included on the advisory committee.			
—	—	————		—	—	————
			61 Each school committee involved in the administration of business education includes student representatives.			
—	—	————		—	—	————
			62 Business education club activities are held after school hours.			
—	—	————		—	—	————
			63 Membership in the business club is voluntary.			
—	—	————		—	—	————

**University of Georgia
College of Education
Graduate Course Evaluation**

The Graduate Student Council of the College of Education is conducting a course evaluation of graduate level courses within the college. Its purpose is to improve course offerings, instruction, and course content. Also, the tabulated data should provide students an objective measure of courses that they are considering taking. These data will be available in Room 122, Aderhold Hall for your inspection.

Do not mark on the questionnaire. Mark all answers on the separate answer sheet provided.

Course objectives and purposes

1 How clear has the instructor made the objectives of this course? The objectives:

(a) were clearly outlined from the beginning
(b) became clear as the term progressed
(c) became somewhat clear as the term progressed
(d) were referred to only indirectly
(e) were never made clear

2 The agreement between the announced objectives of the course and what was actually taught was

(a) superior
(b) above average
(c) average
(d) below average
(e) poor

Organization

3 How well was the course organized?

(a) extremely well organized and integrated
(b) adequately organized
(c) had less organization than would seem desirable
(d) had no apparent organization
(e) too tightly organized; there was not enough flexibility to meet student needs and desires

Course content

4 How well does this course fit into your overall degree program objectives?

(a) made a very important contribution
(b) was valuable, but not essential
(c) was moderately helpful
(d) made a minor contribution
(e) made no significant contribution

5 How relevant was this course to your career plans and/or to your experience in the field?

(a) made a very important contribution
(b) was valuable, but not essential
(c) was moderately helpful
(d) made a minor contribution
(e) made no significant contribution

6 Did the instructor impartially present contrasting points of view within the field?

(a) always presented both sides fully
(b) frequently presented both sides fully
(c) sometimes presented both sides fully
(d) infrequently presented both sides fully
(e) never presented both sides fully

Texts and assignments

7 What value has the outside work (term papers, reports, individual research, projects, labs, etc.) been in your learning or understanding the course content area?

(a) a great deal
(b) some
(c) little
(d) none
(e) not applicable

8 How clearly were your responsibilities in this course defined?

(a) I always knew what was expected.
(b) I usually knew what was expected.
(c) I usually had a general idea of what was expected.
(d) I was often in doubt about what was expected.
(e) I seldom knew what was expected.

9 How valuable were the text(s) and other assigned readings?

(a) outstanding in value
(b) almost all parts were valuable
(c) generally valuable
(d) some parts were worth reading
(e) a waste of time

Teacher-student relationships

10 Considering the size of the class and the load of the instructor, do you feel that the instructor was willing to give personal help in this class?

(a) I felt *welcome* to seek personal help as often as I needed it.
(b) I felt free to seek personal help.
(c) I felt he would give personal help if asked.
(d) I felt hesitant to seek personal help.
(e) I feel that he is unsympathetic and uninterested in student problems.

11 With regard to controversial matters, how tolerant was the instructor of student viewpoints that differed from his or her own?

(a) always treated other viewpoints fairly
(b) was generally tolerant
(c) was aware of other ideas and moderately tolerant
(d) was frequently intolerant
(e) would not tolerate any opinions different from his own

12 Freedom of student participation in class. The instructor

(a) encouraged questions and comments
(b) allowed questions and comments
(c) inhibited class discussions and questions
(d) dominated the class

Course effectiveness

13 Would you recommend this course under this instructor to a good friend whose interests and background are similar to yours?

(a) recommend highly
(b) generally recommend
(c) recommend with reservations
(d) definitely not

14 How does this course compare in effectiveness with other courses you have taken and/or are taking in graduate school?

(a) upper quarter (75%–100%)
(b) second quarter (50%–74%)
(c) third quarter (25%–49%)
(d) lowest quarter (0%–24%)

Teacher effectiveness

15 How valuable were the classroom sessions?

(a) outstanding in value
(b) almost always valuable
(c) generally valuable
(d) occasionally valuable
(e) practically of no value

16 The instructor seemed

(a) always prepared
(b) almost always prepared
(c) usually prepared
(d) frequently not prepared
(e) never prepared

17 How well did he or she seem to know the subject?

(a) thorough and profound scholar
(b) knowledge broad and accurate
(c) well-rounded knowledge of the subject
(d) adequate knowledge
(e) occasional gaps in knowledge

18 How would you rate your teacher in general (all around) teaching ability?

(a) an outstanding and stimulating teacher
(b) a very good teacher
(c) a good teacher
(d) an adequate, but not stimulating teacher
(e) a poor and inadequate teacher

General

19 In comparison with other courses you have taken at the graduate level in the College of Education, how difficult was this course?

(a) much more difficult than most
(b) somewhat more difficult than most
(c) about average

(d) less difficult than most
(e) much less difficult than most

20 If I were to award a grade to this course under this instructor, it would be

(a) A (4.0)
(b) B (3.0)
(c) C (2.0)
(d) D (1.0)
(e) F (0)

If you have additional comments about the course or the instructor, write them on a separate sheet of paper.

Abstracts of Instructional and Research Materials (AIM/ARM), 314
Academic education, and career education, 90, 93
Accountability, 76
Accreditation
criteria, 439–440
evaluation, 439–441
procedures, 440
purpose, 440
Administrative Management Society, 226
Adult education, 98
Adult Education Act, 353
Advisory committees
characteristics, 384
composition, 384
functions, 385
Advisory council
career education, 52, 117, 175–176
principles, 249
purpose, 358
state, 249–250
vocational education, 12, 63, 69, 76
Affective domain
evaluation, 435–436
problems, 435
AFL-CIO, 239
Age Discrimination in Employment Act, 20
Agne, Russell M., 165, 167
Agribusiness education, 214–215
(See also vocational education objectives)
Agricultural education
changes in focus, 214, 283
classification of occupations, 283
enrollments, 284, 285
instructional areas, 283
objectives, 213–214

Agricultural education (continued)
(See also vocational education objectives)
Alberty, Harold, 273
Albuquerque, New Mexico, school system, career education project, 150
Alexander, William M., 447
American Association of Colleges for Teacher Education, 239
American Home Economics Association, 239, 245
American Industrial Arts Association, 239
American Occupational Therapy Association, 239
American Registry of Radiologic Technologists, 239
American Vocational Association, 216, 239, 245
Task Force on Career Education, 89, 109–110, 162–163
Ammons, Margaret, 403
Anderson, Ernest F., 365
Appalachian Regional Development Act, 350
Area Redevelopment Act, 350, 352
Arizona Career Education Program, grades 6–12, 152
Ash, Lane, 425
Authorizations, versus appropriations, 355

Baer, Max F., 80
Bak Amis, William A., 306
Baltimore, Maryland, placement and followup program, 195
Bankhead-Jones Act, 351
Barlow, Melvin L., 29, 65, 76
Beasley, Gary F., 146

Beattis, Glenn E., 146
Beaumont, John, 68
Beecher, Dwight, 424
Behavioral theory
    Herzburg, Frederick, 10, 11
    McGregor, Douglas, 10
Bell, Terrence H., 106, 117, 118, 172
Bernays, Edward L., 399
Berson, Minnie P., 208
Blake, Duane L., 425
Blocker, Donald H., 29
Bloom, Benjamin S., 402, 420, 431, 434
Board of Certified Laboratory Assist-
    ants, 239
Bode, Boyd H., 62
Bolton, Dale L., 422
Borow, Henry, 28
Bossing, Nelson L., 210
Bottoms, Gene, 251, 252
Brandon, George L., 310, 317, 338
Brown, Duane, 189
Bruner, Jerome S., 278
Buckingham, Lillian, 195
Budke, Wesley E., 146
Burdin, Joel L., 114
Bureau of Certified Laboratory Assist-
    ants, 239
Bureau of Occupational and Adult Edu-
    cation
    organizational structure, 240
    program funding, 325
    purposes, 324–325
    research, eligibility, 325–326
Burkett, Lowell A., 238
Burnham, Robert A., 411
Buros, Oscar K., 428
Bushnell, David S., 199, 274
Business and industry, job training,
    225–226
Business and office education
    changes, 215–226
    classification of occupations, 286
    enrollments, 284, 285
    instructional areas, 286
    objectives, 215–218
        (See also vocational education
        objectives)
    word processing, 287
Byram, Harold M., 433

Calhoun, Calfrey C., 181, 274, 400
Calkins, Hugh, 375
Campbell, Robert E., 192
Cardinal Principles of Secondary Edu-
    cation, goals, 61
Career choice, effects of occupational
    change, 6, 9, 12
Career clusters, USOE, 95–96
Career cluster approach, 151
Career development
    elementary school, 90

Career development (continued)
    general education, 89–90
    high school, 91
    middle school, 91
    vocational education
        elementary school, 89–90
        high school, 91
        middle school, 91
Career education
    academic education, 93, 94, 95
    antecedents, 106–107
    assumptions, 108–109, 133, 135
    awareness phase, 90, 147–148
    career orientation and preparation
        phase, 150–152
    changes recommended, 113–114
    characteristics, state directors of vo-
        cational education, 5
    comprehensive high school, 255–256
    concepts, 93–94, 110, 112–113, 132–133
    congressional endorsement, 117–118
    criticisms, 165–166
    curriculum renewal, 114–115
    definitions, 111, 115, 116, 118
    delivery system, 120
    dimensions, 119–120
    educational system, 93–94
    elementary school, implementation,
        96
    exploration phase, 148–150, 192–193,
        210–211
    fallacies and fantasies, 167–168
    features, 112
    federal role, 174–175
    goals, 110–112
    high school, implementation, 97–98
    implementation, 174–175
    implications of technology, 14–16
    infusion, 114, 173–174
    issues and problems, 162–164
        AVA task force, 162–163
    levels, 121–123
    middle school, 210–213
        implementation, 97
    models, 123–140
    National Advisory Council, 52, 117,
        175–176
    needs, 168–173
    organization
        college preparatory and compre-
            hensive schools, 254–256
        national level, 241
        state level, 251–253
    postsecondary school
        implementation, 98
    principles, 120–123
    purposes, 89–90
    rationale, 107
    role of counselor, 189
    secondary teacher education, 157–159
    staff development objectives, 159–160
    status, 117
    success criteria, 159–160

Career education (continued)
  total education, 93–94
  USOE generic definition, 118
Career education center, University of
    Georgia, 161–162
Career education objectives
  elementary school, 148
  elementary teacher education, 156–
    157
  four-year baccalaureate programs,
    153–154
  graduate programs, 155
  middle school, 149–150
  secondary school, 151–152
  secondary teacher education, 158
  teacher education, 156
  two-year postsecondary programs,
    153
Career Education, Office of, 52
Career exploration, middle school, 91,
    149–150, 192–193, 210–213
Career guidance
  and career education, 185–186
  changes needed, 188–189
  developmental theory, 184–185
  elementary school, 189, 192
  evaluation, 199–200
  middle school, 192–193
  objectives, 186–187
  postsecondary level, 195–198
  secondary school
    assumptions, 193–194
    followup programs, 194–195
    job placement, 194–195
    student personnel services, 196–198
    theory of vocational choice, 184–185
  trends
    postsecondary level, 199
    weaknesses, 188–189
Career preparation, 88–89
Center for Vocational Education, 314
  Comprehensive Career Education
    Model, 127–128
Chadderdon, Hester, 235
Chase, Francis, 321
CIPP Model, 413–414
Civil Rights Act, equal employment op-
    portunity, 20
Civilian Conservation Corps, 42
Clearinghouse for Federal, Scientific
    and Technical Information, 316
Cleeton, G. H., 7
Cluster-based curriculum, 273–274
Cognitive domain
  evaluation, 434–435
  modified taxonomy, 434–435
Coleman, James S., 171
Colleges and universities, vocational
    education, 224–225
Collins, Charles C., 204
Commager, Henry S., 32
Commerce Business Daily, request for
    proposals, 325

Commission on the Purposes of Sec-
    ondary Education, 60
Commissioner of Education, 45, 240
Committee of Ten, 60, 61
Committee on College Relations, 60
Communication, school and public,
    378–379
Community college, 225
  (*See also* junior college)
  multiple programs, 196
Competencies, research, 312–313
Competency-based curriculum, 276
  functions, 276
  implementation, 276
Comprehensive Employment and
    Training Act, 77, 238
  provisions, 358–359
  purpose, 358–359
Comprehensive Health Manpower
    Training Act, 353
Comprehensive high school
  facilities, 254–256
  organization, 254–256
Consumer and Homemaking Educa-
    tion, 49–50
Continuing education, 93
Cooperative Research Act, 350–351
Core curriculum design, 273
  Alberty, Harold, 273
Council of Dental Education, 239
Counselors, role in career education,
    189, 190–191
Cramer, Roscoe V., 210
Cramer, Stanley H., 199
Crawford, Lucy, 336
Curriculum
  definition, 265
  developmental vocational, kinder-
    garten-adult, 297, 298–299
  evaluation, 300, 417–419
  vocational component, 265
  vocational purposes, kindergarten-
    adult, 297, 298–299
Curriculum centers, USOE consortium,
    337–338
Curriculum construction
  principles, traditional, 268–269
  systems approach, 269–271
Curriculum design
  cluster-based curriculum, 273–274
  competency-based curriculum, 276
  core curriculum, 273
  individualized instruction, 277–278
  open-access curriculum, 278–281
  organic curriculum, 274–275
  subject-centered, 272–273
  systems-oriented, 276
Curriculum development
  approaches, 267
  components, 267–268
  criteria, selection of subject matter,
    267
  foundations, 267–268

Curriculum development (continued)
  needs assessment, 281–282
  principles of construction, 268–269
  Teske program planning model, 266
Curriculum evaluation, model, 418
Curriculum organization, 273–281
  (*See also* curriculum design)
Curriculum renewal, and career education, 114–115

Data collection, 427–432
  (*See also* evaluation instruments)
Dallas Skyline Center, 141–142
Davie, Bruce F., 365
Davis, E. Dale, 211
Davis, Rene V., 28
Decision-making
  in career development, 185–188
  model, 186–187
  skills, 186
Defense Documentation Center, *Technical Abstract Bulletin*, 316
Definitions
  career education, 111, 115, 116, 118
  curriculum, 265
  evaluation, 402–403
  industrial arts education, 223
  industrial education, 222
  issue, 433
  job, 6
  occupational education, 3
  public relations, 379–380
  technical education, 91, 294–295
  vocational education, 3–4, 44–45
Delta Pi Epsilon, 216
Denton, William T., 447
Department of Health, Education and Welfare, 238, 239
Dewey, John, 61, 62, 106
Dissemination, research, 313–317
Distributive education
  changes, 218–219
  changes in occupations, 289
  classification of occupations, 288
  DECA, 239, 288–289
  enrollments, 284, 285
  instructional areas, 288
  objectives, 218–219
Donnell, Edward S., 289
Douglas Commission, 36, 63
Drake, W. E., 338
Dressel, P. L., 419
Drier, Harry N., 146, 159, 203

Economic Opportunity Act, 51, 352
Economic structure, changes
  agrarian period, 72
  industrial period, 72–73
  technological period, 73–74

Education
  factors influencing development, 31–32
  federal legislation, 32–52
Education and earnings, 71–72
Education and labor, sub-committee report 1647, 68
Education Professions Development Act, 316, 353
Education Television Facilities Program of 1962, 51
Educational Amendments of 1972, 51–52, 196, 238
  National Institute of Education, 241–245
Educational Amendments of 1974, 52, 117
  career education policies, 174–176
Educational objectives, for economic efficiency, 209–210
Educational Policies Commission, economic efficiency, objectives, 209–210
Educational Resources Information Center, 313–314
Ehresman, Norman, 343
Elementary and Secondary Education Act, 50
  supplementary centers and services program, 150
Elementary school
  approach to career guidance, 189, 192
  career education, 208–221
    awareness phase, 90, 147–148
    objectives, 148
  objectives, 208–210
    (*See also* vocational education objectives)
  vocational education, 210
Elementary teacher education
  career education, 156–157
  career education objectives, 157
Employer-based model, career education, 128–130
Employment service, state, 250–251
Employment trends, 20–24
  goods-producing industries, 23
  growth within industries, 21–22
  outlook and education, 24
  replacement growth, 21
  service-producing industries, 22–23
  white collar versus blue collar employment, 23–24
Enrollments
  federally aided programs, 285
  postsecondary, 285
  secondary, 285
Ertel, K. H., 338
Evaluation
  accreditation, 439–441
  affective domain, 435–436
  career guidance procedures, 199–200
  classroom organization, 421–422
  cognitive domain, 434–435

Evaluation (continued)
curriculum, 300, 417–419
decision-making, 416
definition, 402–403
facilities, 425–426
formative, 417
instruments
criterion-referenced test, 428–429
informal procedures, 432
inquiry forms, 432
performance test, 429–430
rating scale, 430–431
standardized test, 427–428
issues, 433–434
model, 409–416
(*See also* model, evaluation)
components, 413–415
criteria for selection, 412
needs assessment, 426–427
Phi Delta Kappa, 415–416
personnel, 422
principles, 403–405
process, 403–404
program, 416–427
(*See also* program, evaluation)
psychomotor domain, 436–439
research proposal, 334–335
student progress, 419–420
summative, 417
teaching, 423–425
vocational education
benefits, 405–408
checklist, 406–408
criteria, 406–408
systems
characteristics, 409
steps, 411
Evans, Rupert N., 73, 102, 226
Exemplary programs, 48–49
Expenditures
vocational education
by educational level and source,
371–372
for facilities, 372, 373
by function, 368–369
by government levels, 371
by purpose, 369–370
by target group, 371, 373
for work-study, cooperative programs, 372–373

Facilities
college preparatory high school, 253–54
comprehensive high school, 254–256
evaluation instruments, sources, 425–
426
scope, 425
vocational high school, 256–259
Fair Labor Standards Act, 20
Equal Pay Amendment, 20
Fanslow, Alyce M., 235
Farmer, Geraldine M., 342

Federal Board for Vocational Education, 37, 213
Federal funding
extent of, 350–353
historical development, 350
Federal legislation
vocational appropriations
1900–1960, 34–42
since 1960, 42–52
Federal legislation and vocational education
developmental stages, 32
effects on vocational education, 67–68
method of allotting funds, 40
use of funds, 49
work-study programs, 45–46
Federal Register
request for proposals, 325
Feit, Stephen, 189
Fess-Kenyon Act, 41
(*See also* Industrial Rehabilitation
Act)
Fitzgerald Act, 350
Fitzpatrick, John C., 56
Florida State Department of Educa-
tion, kindergarten objectives, 208–
209
Followup programs, 194–195
Ford Foundation, grants in vocational
education, 316
Forestandi, Robert, 189
Formative evaluation, 417
Four-year baccalaureate programs
career education objectives, 153–154
contributions to career education,
153–154
humanism and career education, 153–
154
Fraser, John M., 8, 11
Future Business Leaders of America,
239, 287–288
Future Data Processors, 239, 287–288
Future Farmers of America, 239, 284
Future Homemakers of America, 239,
292
Future Secretaries Association, 239,
287–288
Funding
federal, 346–347, 350–365
local, 346–349
state, 346–349
Funding, vocational education research, 365–366
cost, vocational versus general, 366
federal, 366
intergovernment, 366
use of funds, 366

General education
and career education, 89–90
and vocational education, 87–89

George-Barden Act, 39–40, 290, 355
  allocation of funds, 40
  fields funded, 39–40
George-Deen Act, 39, 40, 350, 355
  allocation of funds, 39, 40
  fields funded, 39
George-Ellzey Act, 38–39, 350, 355
  allocation of funds, 39, 40
  fields funded, 39
George-Reed Act, 38, 350, 355
  allocation of funds, 38, 40
  fields funded, 38
Georgia Program of Education and Career Exploration, 193
GI Bill of Rights, 41
  (*See also* Servicemen's Readjustment Act)
Gillie, Angelo C., 224
Ginzberg, Eli, 11, 184, 185
Girthman, Carolyn, 222
Goldhammer, Keith, 7, 88, 110, 111
Graduate programs, career education objectives, 155
Guba, Egon, 403
Gust, D. D., 338
Gysbers, Norman C., 203

Haas, Kenneth B., 235
Halchin, Lilla C., 221
Handicapped Education, Bureau of, 241
Hansen, Lorraine S., 193
Harris, Wilbur, 404
Harrow, Anita J., 437
Harvey, Kenneth R., 342
Hastings, J. Thomas, 402
Hatch Act, 34, 350
Hatcher, Hazel M., 221
Health Amendments Act, 290
Health occupations education, 289–291
  classification of occupations, 290
  objectives, 219–220
    (*See also* vocational education objectives)
Health Professions Educational Assistance Act, 352
Hemp, Paul E., 336
Henderson, Lee, 366
Hendrix, I., 7
Herr, Edwin L., 106, 123, 199
Herzburg, Frederick, 10
Higher Education Act, 352
Higher Education Facilities Act, 350, 352
Hill, Alberta D., 292
Hill, Edwin K., 306
Hill, E. Joy, 220
Home-community model, career education, 132
Home economics education, 291
  changes, 221–222

Home economics education (continued)
  classification of occupations, 292
  enrollments, 284, 285
  instructional areas, 292
  objectives, 219–222
    (*See also* vocational education objectives)
Horner, James T., 234
House, E. W., 343
Hoyt, Kenneth B., 94, 112, 113, 114, 118, 175, 176, 212
Huffman, Harry, 338
Hughes, Dudley, 35
Hull, William L., 447
Hunsicker, James T., 214

Indian education, office of, 241
Individual needs, 7–8
Individualized instruction, 277–278
  components, 277
  levels, 277–278
Industrial arts education, 295–296
  definition, 223
  instructional areas, 295
  objectives, 223–224
    (*See also* vocational education objectives)
Industrial education
  definition, 222
  National Society for the Promotion of, 36
  objectives, 223
    (*See also* vocational education objectives)
Industrial Rehabilitation Act, 41
Infusion, and career education, 173–174
Inquiry forms, types of items, 432
Institute of Life Insurance, 227
International Education Act, 353
Ishee, Reese, 102
Issue
  definition, 433
  evaluation, 433–434

James, William, 61, 62
Jarvis, Oscar T., 210
Job
  definition of, 6
  motivation and satisfaction: 11–12
    Herzburg, Frederick, 11–12
  placement, 194–195
  social environment of, 6
Johnson, Lyndon B., 78
Joint Council on Economic Education, 239
Jones, James J., 380
Junior college, 196
  objectives, 225
    (*See also* community college)

Kaufman, J. J., 338
Kean, John M., 342
Kehas, Chris D., 185
Keller, Louise, 116
Kennedy, John F., 43, 78
Kentucky Vocational Education Evaluation Program Model, 412–413
Kilpatrick, William H., 62
Kindergarten objectives, 208–209
Kindred, Leslie W., 379
Kingsley, Davis, 28
Kriger, Sara F., 203
Kuhl, Robert E., 306

Labor
  market
    effects of technology, 71
    trends, 20–24
      (See also employment trends)
  supply and demand, 69–70
  unions, 226–227
    (See also vocational education objectives)
  job training, 226–227
LaFollette-Barden Act, 41
Land-grant colleges, 34
  (See also Morrill Act of 1862)
Land Ordinance of 1785, 34
Larson, Milton E., 425
Law, Gordon F., 342
Legislation, federal
  authorization versus appropriation, 37–41, 355
  and vocational education, 350–366
Lehman, H. C., 28
Leighbody, Gerald B., 70, 73, 74, 80
Lewis, M. V., 343
Local funding, school taxes, 348–349
Lofquist, Lloyd H., 28
Loreen, C. O., 338

Mackin, Edward F., 102, 234
Madaus, George F., 402
Maguire, J. O., 402
Maine Elementary Career Development Guide, 148
Maley, Donald, 336
Mangum, Garth L., 67, 85, 102, 234
Manpower Development and Training Act, 42, 77, 350, 352
Manpower Development and Training Amendments, 350
Marland, Sidney P., 106, 107, 108, 111, 114
Maslow, A. H., 8, 9
Matheny, Kenneth B., 192
McBrien, Robert J., 186, 187
McCarthy, John A., 56
McCaslin, N. L., 409

McGowan, William, 384
McGregor, Douglas, 10
McMahon, Gordon G., 294
McMillion, Martin, 343
McMinn, J. Harold, 102
McMurrin, Sterling M., 234
Meckley, Richard F., 424
Medical Library Assistance Act, 352
Middle school
  career education objectives, 149–150
  career exploration, 149–150, 192–193, 210–213
  career guidance, 192–193
  objectives, 210–212
  vocational education, 211–212
Military training, 227
  (See also vocational education objectives)
Miller, Carrol H., 28
Miller, Juliet V., 203
Miller, William C., 115, 135
Miller and Tiedeman Cubistic Model, 186–187
Minnesota Career Development Guide, 149
Mississippi State Department of Education, state plan for vocational education, 247–252
Mobility
  and education, 18
  geographic, 17–18
  occupational, 17
Models
  career versus occupational, 123–124
  curriculum, Teske program planning model, 266
  evaluation
    CIPP, 413–414
    components, 413–414
    criteria for selection, 412
    curriculum, 417–419
    Kentucky Vocational Education Evaluation Program, 412–413
    personnel, 422–423
    Phi Delta Kappa, 415–416
    Psychomotor domain, 436–439
  public relations, vocational education, 387
  subject-centered curriculum, 124
  three-C problem solving, 189
Models, career education
  local
    Dallas, Texas, 141–142
  state
    Arizona, 137–138
    Michigan, 135–136
    Wisconsin, 138–140
  U.S. Office of Education
    employer-based, 128–131
    home-community based, 132
    rural-residential based, 131–132
    school-based, 59

Moore, Earl J., 203
Morgan, Robert M., 274
Morrill, Justin S., 34
Morrill Act of 1862: 33–34, 60, 154, 350, 351
  significance, 353–354
Morrill Act of 1890, 33–34, 350, 351
Morse, Nancy, 12
Moustakas, Clark E., 208
Muirhead, Peter, 111
Mushkin, Selma J., 409
Mutual Educational and Cultural Exchange Act, 350

Nash, Robert J., 165, 167
National Advisory Council on Career Education, 52, 117, 175–176
National Advisory Council on Vocational Education, purpose, 358
National Aeronautics and Space Administration, career awareness via satellite, 152
National Association of State Directors of Vocational Education, 108–109
National Association of Manufacturers, 239
National Association for Practical Nurse Education and Service, 239
National Association of Secondary School Principals, 239
National Business Education Association, 216, 239, 246
National Center for Educational Research and Development, 321–322
National Conference for Research, 318–319
National Congress of Parents and Teachers, 239
National Council for the Accreditation of Teacher Education, 239
National Council for Educational Research, 243
National Defense Education Act, 42, 351
National Education Association, 209, 245–246
  Educational policies commission, 209
National Foundation on the Arts and the Humanities Act, 51
National Institute of Education, 241–245
  activities, 243–244
  career education, 174
  National Council for Educational Research, 243
  organization, 323–324
  purpose, 243, 324
  research funding, 320–322

National Research and Development Centers
  North Carolina State University, 323
  Ohio State University, 323
National Retail Merchants Association, 239
National Secretaries Association, 239
National Science Foundation, manpower and education studies, 42, 239, 315
National Society for Vocational Education, 63
National Vocational Guidance Association, 245
National Vocational Student Loan Insurance Act, 352
National Youth Administration, 42
Needs assessment
  in curriculum development, 281–282
  evaluative process, 426–427
  formative evaluation, 195
  procedures, 282
  purposes, 282
  sample instrument (See Appendix)
  summative evaluation, 427
Needs, individual
  and occupations, 8–10
  theories of, 7–8
    Cleeton, 7
    Fraser, 8
    Hendrix, 7
    Maslow, 8
    Vernon, 7
Needs, societal, effects of technology, 13–14
Neighborhood Youth Corps, 77
New Office and Business Education Learning System, 336–337
Nixon, Richard M., 78, 323, 358
Northwest Ordinance of 1787, 33, 351

Objectives, career education, 110–120
  elementary school, 148
  elementary teacher education, 157
  four-year baccalaureate programs, 153–154
  graduate programs, 155
  middle school, 149
  secondary school, 151–152
  secondary teacher education, 158–159
  two-year postsecondary programs, 153
Objectives, career guidance
  elementary school, 189, 192
  middle school, 193
  secondary school, 194
Occupation
  definition of, 6
  effects of technology, 13–14
  and individual needs, 11–12
  and jobs, 6

Occupation (continued)
  social environment, 6
  and societal needs, 13–14
Occupational and Adult Education Bureau, 51, 239, 241–242
Occupational clusters, 95–96, 149
  U.S. Office of Education, 95–96, 149
  (*See also* career clusters)
Occupational education
  definition, 3
  needs served, 6
Occupational needs
  versus individuals, 6–7
  versus society, 7
Occupational preparation, 90
Occupational status, 80, 81
Office of Career Education, 175
Office Education Association, 239, 288
O'Hara, Robert P., 185
Omaha Public Schools, 214
On-the-job training, 225–227
  (*See also* vocational education objectives)
Open-access curriculum, 278–281
  characteristics, 279
  role of teacher, 280
  versus subject-centered, 279
  teacher training, 280
Open school, 278–281
  (*See also* open-access curriculum *and* Valdosta Comprehensive High School)
Oregon career education program, 151
Organic curriculum
  objectives, 275
  options, 274–275
Ottina, John R., 163
Otto, Wayne, 428
Oxford-Lafayette County Business and Industrial Complex, 256–259

Parsons, Frank, 183
Patterson, Philip D., Jr., 365
Penn, Thomas L., 365
Personnel evaluation
  competency-based, 423
  methods, 422–423
  model, 423
  purposes, 422
Phi Beta Lambda, 287
Phi Delta Kappa Evaluation Model, 415–416
Philadelphia City School District, middle school career development project, 150
Philosophy of education, 61–62
  (*See also* pragmatism)
Phipps, Lloyd J., 234, 343
Plato, 87
Policies Commission for Business and Economic Education, 215–217

Pollak, William, 409
Postsecondary education, Bureau of, 241
Postsecondary career guidance, 195–198
Postsecondary school, 224–225
  (*See also* vocational education objectives)
Postsecondary schools
  colleges, vocational education, 224–225
  junior college objectives, 196, 225
  vocational-technical school objectives, 225
Practical Nurse Training Act, 351
Pragan, Otto, 85
Pragmatism, influence of, 61–62
Principles
  curriculum construction, traditional, 268–269
  evaluation, 403–405
  public relations, 385–386
Professional organizations, 245–246
Program evaluation, 416–427
  curriculum, 417–419
  curriculum model, 418
  facilities, 425–426
  formative, 417, 420–421
  and instructional process, 419
  needs assessment, 426–427
  organization, classroom, 419–420
  personnel, 422–423
  purpose, 417
  student progress, 419, 420–422
  summative, 416–417
  teaching, 423–425
  value judgment, 417–418
Proposals, research, 327–335
  evaluating, 334
  inadequacies, 335
  timing, 327–328
  writing, 328–334
Prosser, Charles A., 63, 106
Psychomotor domain
  evaluation, 437–439
  evaluation problems, 438
  models
    Harrow, 437–438
    Ragsdale, 437–438
    Simpson, 437–438
Public opinion, 378
Public relations
  assumptions, 385–386
  definition, 379–380
  evaluation, 388–397
  external publics, 380
  importance of, 380–381
  improvement, school-industry, 384
  internal publics, 380
  model, vocational education, 387
  philosophy, 379
  principles, 380–381, 385–386
  role of employer, 382
  role of student, 383

Public relations (continued)
  role of teacher educator, 382–383
  versus publicity, 380
  vocational education, need, 381–383
Public relations checklist for vocational education, 387–396
Public relations programs, characteristics, 386–387
Public Works and Economic Development Act, 350

Quigley, Thomas A., 84

Ragsdale, C. E., 437
Rating scale
  course, 431–432
  product, 430–431
  subjective evaluation, 430
  teacher performance, 431–432
Research
  analysis, 319–320
  basic types, 311
  and classroom practice, 319
  competencies, 311–313
    supervisor, 312
    teacher, 312
    teacher educator, 313
  dissemination, 313–314
  funding, 320–327
    by source, 320–322
  National Center for Educational Research and Development, 321–323
  needed, 310–311, 318–319
  preparation of proposals, 324–327
  problems, 317–319
  and problem-solving, 318
  vocational programs, 325–326
Research centers
  international centers, 315
  North Carolina State University, 314
  Ohio State University, 314
  University of Wisconsin, 314–315
Research examples
  career education, 335
  competency-based education, 336
  curriculum consortium, 337
  curriculum evaluation, 336
  curriculum modification, 336
  curriculum organization, 335–336
  curriculum revision, 336–337
  occupational analyses, 338–339
  secondary occupational programs, 338
Research, international, vocational-technical education, 317
Research priorities, 310–311
Retirement
  continuing education, 19
  planning for, 19
  societal expectations, 18–19

Reynolds, Harris W., 426
Rice, Marion J., 210
Roberts, Roy W., 102, 213, 223
Roeber, Edward C., 80
Ryan, Charles W., 180

Samson, Harland, 289
Sands, William F., 219
Sanger, George P., 56
Saylor, J. Galen, 447
Schaefer, Carl J., 43
School-based model, career education, 126–128
School population, changing nature, 60
School Systems, Bureau of, 241
School taxes, public participation, 349
Secondary career education, career-cluster approach, 151
Secondary school
  career education objectives, 151–152
  career guidance
    assumptions, 193–194
    followup programs, 194–195
    job placement, 194–195
    objectives, 194
  career orientation and preparation phase, 151–153
  social institution, 61
Secondary teacher education
  career education, 157–159
  objectives, 158
Secretary of Labor, 238
Servicemen's Readjustment Act, 41, 351
  (See also GI Bill of Rights)
Shaw, M. C., 183
Shoemaker, Byrl R., 77
Simpson, Elizabeth J., 437
Smith, Gerald R., 342
Smith, Hoke, 35
Smith, Wesley, 115
Smith-Bankhead Act, 351
Smith-Hughes Act, 35–38, 351, 354
  allocation of funds, 36–37
  provisions, 354
  significance, 354
  state plans, 37–38
  vocational fields funded, 36
Snedden, David, 106
Societal needs, effects of technology, 13–14
Staley, Eugene, 236
Stamps, B. J., 146
State advisory council, functions of, 249
  state funding
    equalization support, 348
    flat grant, 348
    sources of funds, 347
State plan, vocational education, 44, 47, 247

Stevens, D. W., 343
Stevenson, John B., 102
Student personnel services
    career guidance, 195–196
    functions, 197–198
Student progress evaluation, 419–422
    diagnostic, 420–421
    formative, 420–421
    intra- versus inter-individual, 421–422
    summative, 420–421
Study of Curriculums for Occupational
    Preparation and Education
    (SCOPE), 336
Stufflebeam, Daniel L., 411, 413
Subject-centered curriculum design,
    272–273
Summative evaluation, 416–417
Super, Donald E., 158, 184, 185
Sutherland, Janet, 180
Swanson, Gordon I., 111, 112, 119, 167
Swanson, J. Chester, 366, 405
Systems approach
    curriculum construction, 269–272
    evaluation
        characteristics, 409–411
        steps, 411

Taylor, Lee, 17
Taylor, P. A., 402
Taylor, Robert E., 88, 110, 111
Teacher education
    career education objectives, 156
    task force approach, 159
Teaching, evaluation of, 423–425
    methods, 424–425
Technical education, 91–92, 294–295
    definition, 91, 294
    postsecondary level, 92
    secondary level, 91–92
    and vocational education, 91–92
Technological changes
    and the economy, 73–74
    and vocational education, 73–74
Technology
    and career education, 14–16
    and general education, 15–16
    impact on occupations, 14–16
    and new occupations, 15
    and vocational education, 15–16
Tennyson, Wesley W., 158
Teske, Philip R., 266
Tests
    criterion-referenced
        limitations, 429
        versus standardized, 428–429
    performance
        product versus process evaluation,
            430
        and vocational education, 430

Tests (continued)
    rating scale, 430–432
        (*See also* rating scale)
    standardized, 427–428
        limitations, 428
        selection, 427–428
Theory, developmental, career guid-
    ance, 184–185
Theory X and Theory Y, McGregor, 10
Thompson, John F., 66, 212
Thorpe, Francis N., 56
Toffler, Alvin, 28
Tom, F. K., 333
Tomlinson, Robert M., 76
Trade and industrial education, 292–
    294
    classification of occupations, 293
    enrollments, 284–285
    instructional emphases, 293
Trait and factor theory, 184
Trends, career guidance
    postsecondary, 199
Tuckman, Bruce W., 343
Two-year postsecondary programs
    career education objectives, 153
    multiple career options, 153
Tyler, Ralph W., 318, 403

United States
    Chamber of Commerce, 239
    Department of Labor, 238
        Bureau of Labor Statistics, 20
        Manpower research projects, 315
    Office of Education, 239–245
        career clusters, 95–96, 149
        career education, 241
            underlying assumptions, 62–63
        career education models, 126–140
        classification of occupations, 283,
            286, 288, 290, 292, 293–294, 295
        conceptualization of career educa-
            tion, 132–133
        definition, career education, 111,
            115, 116, 118
        established, 35
        funding, by legislative program,
            366–373
        handicapped, education for, 240
        Indian education, 241
        Occupational and Adult Education,
            Bureau of, 51, 239, 241, 242
        occupational clusters, 95–96, 149
        organization, 240–241
        Postsecondary Education Bureau,
            241
        research appropriations, 320–321
        School Systems, Bureau of, 241
    University of Georgia
        career education center, 161–162

Valdosta, Georgia, comprehensive high
school, 254–255
Venn, Grant, 29
Vernon, M. D., 7
Vocational education
advisory committee, 45, 384–385
advisory council, national, 47, 52
advisory council, state, 47, 250
assumptions, 66–67
in business and industry, 225–227
and career development, 90–91
elementary school, 90
middle school, 91
secondary school, 91
in college preparatory programs,
253–254
in comprehensive high schools, 254–
256
content and method
elementary school, 96–97
middle school, 97
postsecondary school, 98
secondary school, 97–98
definition, 3–4, 44–45
economics of, 75–76
accountability, 76
matching funds, 75
reimbursement, excess-cost, 75–76
in elementary schools, 208–210
and employment trends, 20–24
evaluation, complexity, 402
expenditures, 366–373
facilities
comprehensive school, 254–256
evaluation, 425–426
Federal board, composition, 37
Federal legislation, authorization vs.
appropriation, 355
funding
federal, 350–365
local, 346–347
state, 346–348
and general education, 15–16, 87–89
high school, 213–224
implications of technology, 14–16
and lifetime earnings, 71–72
local organization, 253–259
in middle schools, 210–213
national organization, 238–246
objectives
agricultural education, 213–214
business and office education, 215,
217–218
distributive education, 218
elementary school, 209–210
health occupations education, 219–
220
home economics education, 222
industrial arts education, 223–224
industrial education, 223
kindergarten, 208–209
labor unions, 226–227
middle school, 211–212

Vocational education (continued)
military training, 227
nursery school, 208
on-the-job training, 226
postsecondary school, 225
and occupational education, 3–4
organization, 238–259
college preparatory schools, 253–
254
comprehensive schools, 254–256
local level, 253–259
Mississippi, 247–252
national, 238–246
state level, 246–251
vocational and technical schools,
256–259
panel of consultants, 43, 78
postsecondary schools, 225
principles, 65
public relations model, 387
and social class, 79–80
social forces, 78–79
socioeconomic values, 77–78
state organization, 246–251
California, 247
Colorado, 247
Mississippi, 247–251
Ohio, 247
teaching-learning method, 69
and technical education, 91–92
theories, Prosser, 63–65
Vocational Education Act of 1963, 43–
46, 67–68, 284, 322, 352, 355–357
advisory committee on vocational
education, 45
appropriation of funds, 43–44
authorization of funds, 356
distribution of funds, 356–357
provisions of, 45–46, 356
purposes, 43, 355–356
significance, 355–356
state plan, 44–45
Vocational Education Amendments of
1968, 46–50, 68–69, 77, 353, 357–358
content, 22
provisions, 47, 49, 50, 357–358
purposes, 357
research provisions, 324–327
state/local matching, 357
and Vocational Education Act of
1963, 48–49
Vocational Education Amendments of
1972, 51–52, 241, 353
antidiscrimination, Title IX, 20
Vocational high school
organization, 256–257
facilities, 259
Vocational Industrial Clubs of America, 239, 295
Vocational Rehabilitation Act, 351
Vocational Rehabilitation Amendments, 41

Vocational-technical education, historical perspective, 31–52

Waltz, Garry R., 203
Warmbrod, J. Robert, 234, 343
Washington, D.C., career education
program, 151–152
Weiss, Robert, 12
Wells, Randall L., 447
West Virginia State Department of
Education, career education pro-
gram guide, 173
Willingham, Warren W., 188

Winer, Rachel K., 219
Wirth, Arthur G., 83
Witty, Paul A., 28
Wolfle, Dael, 28
Women
antidiscrimination laws, 20
changing role, 19–20
in labor market, 19
Work, underlying concepts, 11–12
Work-study programs, 45

Young Men's Christian Association, 227